D0338563

MEMOIRS

MEMOIRS

by
Raisa Orlova

Translated from the Russian
by Samuel Cioran

RANDOM HOUSE NEW YORK

COLLEGE OF THE SEQUOIAS

LIBRARY

Translation Copyright © 1983 by Samuel Cioran
All rights reserved under International and Pan-American Copyright Conventions.
Published in the United States by Random House, Inc., New York, and
simultaneously in Canada by Random House of Canada Limited, Toronto.
Originally published in Russian as *Vospominaniia o neproshedshem vremeni*
by Ardis, Ann Arbor, Michigan, in 1983.
Copyright © 1983 by Ardis.

Grateful acknowledgment is made to the following for permission
to reprint previously published material:

Gene Sosin: Lyrics from three songs by Alexander Galich,
translated by Gene Sosin in *Dissent in the U.S.S.R.*, Rudolf L. Tökés, ed.
Copyright © by The Johns Hopkins University Press, Baltimore.

Slavic Review: Quote by Victor Erlich on Arkadii V. Belinkov,
Slavic Review, vol. 29, no. 3 (September 1970), p. 588.

Library of Congress Cataloging in Publication Data
Orlova, R. D. (Raisa Davydovna)
Memoirs.
1. Orlova, R. D. (Raisa Davydovna)—Biography.
2. Orlova, R. D. (Raisa Davydovna)—Contemporary
Soviet Union. 3. Authors, Russian—20th century—
Biography. 4. Literaturnaia gazeta, Moscow
(R.S.F.S.R.) 5. Soviet Union—Intellectual life—
1917–   . I. Title.
PG3484.2.R55Z84   1983   891.78'4409   [B]   83–42758
ISBN 0–394–52938–3

Manufactured in the United States of America
9 8 7 6 5 3 2
First Edition

*To the first readers
of the first pages of this book . . .*

Contents

Introduction

I began this manuscript in 1961.

"What did you believe in?"

"How could you have believed in THAT?"

"What do you believe in today?"

The questions echo relentlessly. They echo all around me. They echo in my soul.

I too asked myself, questioned myself.

Up until 1953 I believed in everything, including the "doctors' plot." I wept bitter tears over the death of Stalin.

It was not only shameful but strange to admit such things to myself and to others in 1961. New generations have grown up. They consider it a well-nigh indisputable truth that "it was impossible to have believed in that sort of thing."

But I did believe in it. And I was not the only one.

Naturally, the urge to understand led first of all to remorse. But confession became in itself a path into my past, my childhood, my youth. It became a path to other people, to thoughts and events that by then no longer had any relation to Stalin, to ideology, to communism.

Beliefs and convictions reach out from the past, and they cannot be altered by fervent desire alone. They possess their own logic and illogic, their own organic existence, their own rhythm of development.

I began these recollections in the year of the Twenty-second Congress of the Communist Party of the Soviet Union, which adopted the resolution (almost immediately forgotten) of erecting a monument to the victims of the "cult of personality." That was the same year that I read Solzhenitsyn's *One Day in the Life of Ivan Denisovich.*

At that time it seemed to me that my country and my Party (of which I had been a member for two decades) were also trying to come to their senses, to figure out what had happened to them, what had been done to them, and what they had done to themselves. At that time I believed in "communism with a human face," before I came to know the actual phrase.

What I was writing did not yet contradict either the way I was living or the way that people were living around me. But in time I moved further and further away from the "general" line.

The recollections that suddenly began to emerge spilled forth in a disconnected fashion, differing in form, abrupt and awkward in shape. They did not arise in an atmosphere of detachment or calm, but rather at a time when I was living in the very thick of events and was seized with the passions of the moment. The first layer of this manuscript was hastily laid down in the years 1961–1962. It continued to grow by fits and starts, without any plan and frequently in defiance of my original conceptions. Later I started to fit one piece to another, attempting to arrange the events in an approximately chronological order (but not in the sequence of their conception). Nevertheless, various strata of time kept winding their way over and over again through the heart of many chapters.

The date of writing stands at the beginning of each chapter. Today, it seems to me, I have come to understand a great deal in a much deeper sense than I did yesterday or the day before. But I do not want to alter the coloration, I do not want to rewrite previous experience by means of "hindsight" or antedating. That is why in many instances I am preserving the documentary quality of the record, the synchronous nature of time, the construction scaffolding.

As it transpired, this book recorded not only the transition from the day before yesterday to yesterday, but from yesterday to today as well.

It is difficult to look back—to the thirties as well as the sixties—but I am forcing myself to look back.

Several of the people around me do not sympathize with the fact that I cannot separate myself from my past, that it torments me, that I experience revulsion over many of its pages. They say: "If you really and sincerely believed without knowing what you were taking part in, then it means that you bear no guilt."

How tempting it would be to agree. But that is impossible. I am forced to live with my past, to come to terms with it and not forget it. It is not in my power to change it, but I am trying to see it as it was in order to overcome it.

I hesitated for a long time about whether to publish this book. Everything has been overly exposed. What I write about myself is my own affair. But what I write about others is not just my affair alone. For that reason a number of the chapters dealing with living persons have either been shortened or have had names deleted.

When I began to write, I had doubts whether it was in my power to reveal at least somewhat the workings of my former belief. Could I understand the meaning of what I had lived through? What had been the purpose of my life? Those doubts merely intensified. I began with a question and I ended with a question.

For me the past will never pass. It is not passing for others, for those who are living in a world that we created, we who believed so much and so deluded ourselves.

Perhaps in my recollections, in the experience of a single fate, the reader will find a small path leading to the understanding of a time that has passed—and even more importantly—that has not.

MEMOIRS

I

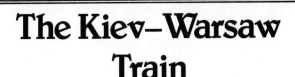

The Kiev–Warsaw
Train

I know so little. It's shocking how little I know. I know nothing about my roots, I know nothing about my genealogy. I don't even know my maternal grandmother's first name and patronymic, and she lived with us for a long time—she didn't die until after I was married. And now it is vital for me to find out. To see in my mind's eye the Kiev–Warsaw train that took my future parents on their wedding trip in March 1915. Their honeymoon.

On July 23, 1937, I turned nineteen, and I went with my boy-friend, Lyonya, to the State Marriage Bureau. We considered this a mere formality, but we followed the rules. We had been husband and wife for almost two years, but we had kept it secret and were living with our respective parents. Now we wanted to be together. Forever. So we had to register the marriage officially. Besides, one had to do this in order to get a residence permit.

We had a party and then set out on our honeymoon. We hiked along the Sukhumi Military Road, over the Klukhor Pass, wearing heavy shoes and bulky clothing and carrying knapsacks on our backs— a far cry from the elegant gear of today's mountain hikers.

Could my parents have done anything even vaguely similar? They seemed old to me. In 1937 my father was forty-nine; my mother, forty-seven. Now I'm fifty-seven myself.

The medical school that my mother applied to did not accept her: there was a quota for Jews. And it had virtually been preordained that she should become a doctor.

I have a photograph of her taken in Kiev that same year, 1915. A long dress, almost the maxi of today, high-buttoned boots, hair below the waist, hanging freely. Everything is round: the eyes, the cheeks, the chin. It is a stylized photograph, for in those days you had to look into the camera for a long time, "to hold a pose." No one wore her hair like that. Mama never had such an artificial expression on her face. But then she was not photogenic anyway. Still, even from this picture it is clear that she was a good person. Naïve. Certain that everyone around her was also good, that the world itself was disposed to goodness.

What did they talk about in their compartment? What did that young man in glasses, with the delicate face, aquiline nose, and aristocratic hands promise her?

They were on their way to Warsaw. The war was going on but had not reached this far to the rear. It was still possible to spend one's honeymoon in Warsaw.

There was no money in my mother's family. Dresses were handed down from her older sister to her, and then from her to the youngest sister. It was the same with us. My younger sister, Lyusya, got her first new dress when she was twenty. Only my father's mother was wealthy, and she probably gave him the money for the trip—so that everything would be done properly.

Mother's long hair was plaited into braids, and the braids were arranged in a crown around her head. I always see her this way in my memory. She kept this hair, her chief treasure, for a very long time. I cut it two months before she died.

Mother loved to travel, and this love might have begun with the Kiev–Warsaw train and the feeling of happiness connected with it. They had trunks and French-style *sacs de voyage*. Styles always come back, and such traveling bags are now being made again. Naturally, all of Papa's things were carefully folded and packed; everything had been seen to. He too loved to travel. It was something they had in common.

Where did they go in Warsaw? Papa would have wanted to go to concerts or the opera, but Mama had no feeling for music. Nor did she pretend that she did. They must have spent most of their time wandering around the city.

They stayed in a hotel. I saw the same kind of hotel in Kaunas in Lithuania: an old building with plush, cherry-colored curtains and a matching bedspread. To wash, one used a white marble basin, a white pitcher.

The money Lyonya and I had made was only enough for a public coach: two upper berths. It was very stuffy in the coach, so much so that it was the first time I ever had trouble falling asleep.

We got to the town of Yezhovo-Cherkessk by bus. From there we were to go on to Teberda.

I never gave a moment's thought then to that other train, the one from Kiev to Warsaw. Now I am fascinated by it. In 1937 it was hardly a stone's throw away in time—a mere twenty-two years. How many living witnesses there would have been besides Mama and Papa. Take it all in! Listen! But what kind of history could there be, either personal or general, if the world began with us, for us, and was created for our happiness?

And so one thread after another was broken, and it is a great deal more difficult to tie them together now. I don't know if it is possible . . .

In early 1945 I saw the charred ruins of what had once been Warsaw, through artillery binoculars, from the other bank of the Vistula. In 1956 I walked through the streets of a restored Warsaw, but even then I didn't recall that my parents had gone there on their honeymoon.

In 1916 a son was born to them, and they named him Misha in honor of Mama's father. He had a congenital heart defect and died at the age of eight months. A photograph remains: a small boy in a coffin. The first rough draft of my fate: were it not for him, I would not have . . . Mama almost never talked about him.

Everything became repugnant to her, even her beloved Kiev, the most beloved city in the world. My parents moved to Moscow.

I no longer remember why we decided to go to the State Marriage Bureau on my birthday. We celebrated the double anniversary for three more peaceful years . . . In 1941 Lyonya got a pass for a few hours. We had just sat down at the table when there was an alert. Bombing, the first bombing of Moscow. We went down into the subway. It was much too far and too difficult to drag the blanket and my little daughter Sveta. After that, until my family was evacuated, I carried Sveta down into a local bomb shelter near the Aragvi Restaurant.

On July 23, 1942, I left for Monino—the headquarters for the Long-Range Aviation were located there. Lyonya came back there after his flights. By 1943 I was a war widow. And I went to Monino again, this time to the cemetery. When I returned, the apartment was filled with flowers; my friends had gathered, and Mama had baked some *pirogi*.

She had probably taken *pirogi* baked by Grandmother with her on the train from Kiev to Warsaw. All of the traditions were ruptured with me, even the eternal one, the one needed by all—the tradition of baking *pirogi* for special occasions. My daughters know how to bake, thank God. It was not I who taught them.

January 1975. I drop in on Mama, and, as always, I'm in a hurry. She isn't watching television.

"Raya, sit with me for a while, read me some Pushkin."

How many times had she wanted me just to sit with her like that? But she only said these simple words once.

And I wanted to do it (probably less often than she, but I was willing). However, because I was busy, dashing around or caught up in some hullabaloo, it never worked out. Often, very often, I spent myself on other people, even those who were total strangers. There was always enough energy and opportunity to call doctors for Mama when she was ill, there was always enough money and food. But not enough time, enough free expanse of the soul, "just for Mama." Not enough of the very thing that she had so generously given us, her own children, and many other people.

I read Pushkin. She picks up the lines, the stanzas. She knows the poems from childhood, from her father. Just as she bestowed everything she possessed, she bestowed these poems, gave them as presents to others. To her nieces and nephews (she had been their nanny). Then to us. Then to her grandchildren. Perhaps she recited Pushkin to Papa even on their honeymoon?

And now I was reading to her. And I still didn't know how little time was left until those terrifying March days before her death, when the grandchildren would sing the lullaby to her, the special lullaby passed down from generation to generation in our family.

Mama was afraid to have another baby after the death of her first. All the more so since they were living in alien Moscow, where they were still without house or home. The war was under way. She gave birth to a girl on July 23, 1918, on Sadovo-Chernogryazskaya Street. And shortly afterward she took the little girl back to Kiev. Living conditions were better there, and it was her native soil.

When she learned that Papa had been unfaithful to her, she took her daughter and left the house. He begged her forgiveness for a long time. And finally she did forgive him.

My girl friends often shared their romantic secrets with Mama. And my infinitely tolerant mother, who practically refused to recognize the notions of divorce, lovers, or mistresses ("the family is the family"), could not comprehend how it was possible to have a *ménage à trois*.

Upon returning from Sukhumi and our honeymoon, Lyonya and I split up and went to our parents' homes. It was partly because we had so little money—so little that we couldn't buy food the last three days of our journey and our traveling companions had to feed us. Moreover, we had to survive for another two weeks until we got our academic stipends and various other earnings turned up.

How warm I felt in my parents' home, how tasty Mama's cutlets and *pirogi* were! For once again, it was a special day—it was my return.

Papa was out of work by this time because of the arrest of his superior, but we had not been doing that well even before this event. Still, Mama had an iron law: a holiday was a holiday.

The wheels are pounding. That coach in the Kiev–Warsaw train is moving forward, and the two happy passengers do not know what lies ahead. I never heard the pounding of the wheels on that train before—but now I hear it more clearly all the time.

II

On the Edge
of a Pond

A girl was sitting on the edge of a small pond. She had turned fifteen and had run away from the house to dream.

Words that everyone understood forty years ago now require some explanation. The girl had put on her most festive dress, called a *tatyanka*—a sun frock with small puffy sleeves. It was a light-colored flower-covered dress made of a silklike material called Liberty satin. As far as the girl was concerned, this dress did not differ in the least from the costumes worn by fairy princesses. She was walking barefoot. She was already in the eighth grade, but had not yet given up playing with dolls. Only now she hid her dolls from everyone.

Bouquets of flowers stood on the table in the morning. Later they began to put the flowers into buckets. Toward evening a child's washtub was dragged out: the girl's brother was having a bath in it. This is the way that birthday always stuck in my mind: a washtub with flowers.

The girl was sitting on the edge of the pond, gazing into the water and making three wishes (if you make a wish on your birthday, everything will come true!). She wanted to make a parachute jump; she wanted to join the Komsomol; and she wanted to travel to the Hawaiian Islands.

Mastering her fear, she would make a parachute jump; she would join the Komsomol; and she would never travel to the Hawaiian Islands.

There was nothing about love in her three wishes because she was already in love and was loved. His name was Vitya, but everyone called him Period (he frequently repeated the word "period"). He had come to the girl's school from some sanatorium. With all her naïveté, the girl felt that she could not ask why he had been in a sanatorium. Vitya had deep-blue eyes and ever such blond hair, whereas the girl was of dark complexion and there was almost nothing to be seen of her face because it was covered with a shock of dark curly hair.

At first Vitya was the boyfriend of her friend, who had brought Vitya along to the girl's dacha, but he had fallen in love with the girl.

"Don't you dare! She's my girl friend, you know."

The girl had forbidden Vitya to come to the dacha, but through the window she saw that he was strolling outside the house. And there she was in bed with a swollen cheek, all bandaged up. Looking like a rabbit, smelling of salvia. Could anyone really fall in love with someone looking like that?

The boy came in, sat down on the very edge of a chair, then moved closer and did not leave until late evening and the last train. The ugly bandage had slipped off, and she had forgotten about her tooth.

The boy told her that it was impossible to force oneself to love or not to love. It fell on us from somewhere above, like a bolt from the blue.

Afterward, Vitya would fall in love with someone else for a short while. It would be painful for the girl, but she would say nothing to him; she remembered that it was impossible to force someone to fall in or out of love. She would remember that. Vitya would return to the girl, but things would no longer be the same as during that unique summer.

In August 1933 Vitya's parents were to take him away to the area around Rostov and he would write letters to the girl every day: "I love you as far as that birch tree." That was from Aleksei Tolstoy's novel *The Road to Calvary*, where it was written that every man had his own road to travel and at the end of the road was a hill with a birch tree . . .

The girl knew nothing about graves. During that month of separation she remembered Vitya, but by no means did she think about him all the time. There were plenty of boys around her. She flirted with them and rejoiced over the attention they paid to her.

Rejoiced. That was the way it was supposed to be with people: to rejoice. Many, many years later, words about the world as a vale of tears would flash past, but she would not remember them.

In the winter of 1934 Vitya was sitting in a room with his mother and sister, reading Lermontov. He put the book down, went out into the washroom, and hanged himself.

The girl was summoned from her classroom to the principal's office. She listened but did not hear. She could not understand the words "dead" and "committed suicide." Who were they talking about? Heroes in books committed suicide, but certainly not in real life.

I never did learn why he committed suicide. Most likely a crisis, an emotional crisis. In those days I did not believe in such crises, but I would come to believe in them many, many years later.

Vitya lived at 21 Myasnitskaya Street, opposite where the Kirov subway station is now located. In those days it was a long way by streetcar from our house. He was lying on the couch—not him really, just what remained. The same kind of black leather couch stood in many studios, and eventually the leather would start to crack and the "stuffing" or cotton would come out. During the war they were all used as fuel for fire or they simply vanished somewhere all of a sudden, along with the *tatyanka* dresses and Liberty satin.

The girl felt deeply ill; her parents did not allow her to go to the funeral, and her friends kept an eye on her. At the funeral service Vitya's stepfather said that a Soviet youth should not act in such a manner. And he referred to the Party congress.

The girl was summoned to the investigator's office at 38 Petrovka. Almost everything has changed, but 38 Petrovka has remained. She was interrogated; she was terrified and ashamed that some stranger would touch upon personal and secret things. She spent more time weeping than answering questions.

She was protected from evil because she never suspected its existence. The investigator asked: "What did you talk about? Maybe he expressed some hostile views?" At that time she didn't have to repeat to herself: "Say only good things about the dead, say only good things about people to those who ask questions in places like that." After all, it was all as natural as breathing. And she was completely defenseless in the face of evil because of that very same naïveté of hers.

A few years later, people would lead her to believe, without any special difficulty, that evil was good.

She went alone to the cemetery. She kept going for several years. Then she stopped and forgot about that grave.

But I know what lies ahead of her, whereas the girl just sits on the edge of the pond and smiles. Soon she will run off to the station to meet Vitya, but she does not want to hasten that moment; she feels fine just sitting there like that, first dipping her feet into the pond and then tucking them underneath herself.

Everyone is created for joy and no one ever dies . . .

III

Youth

I was born and grew up in a house where there were always a lot of people, where someone was always spending the night, someone was having supper, someone was being nursed, people were being married, divorced, fixed up with work, sent off, or greeted. We did not lead a segregated family life.

Mama practically ignored the existence of evil, particularly in her own world, among her friends and family. For her the world was distinctly divided into the realm of her "own," where only good things were possible, and into the realm of "others," where, naturally, anything was possible.

I was president of the council for our detachment of Pioneers, received the Red Banner of our district, and was triumphantly "advanced" to the Komsomol. But within two months I learned that I had not been accepted because I was the daughter of a white-collar worker. This was called "an adjustment in advancement."

I was miserable because I had not been accepted into the Komsomol. But not only was I convinced that that was the way it should have been, I did not even ask any questions, such as why in fact should it have been like that? When my younger sister was also not accepted into the Komsomol, and for the same reason, she asked me through her tears why it should be so.

The seventeenth year of my life was a turning point, after Vitya's suicide. That was in 1935, when I was in the ninth grade and had not been accepted into the Komsomol for the second time. It was apparently then that an even earlier and typical feeling began to crystallize: namely, that there was something inferior and insufficiently firm within me. I was an "intellectual," and had to struggle against it without fail, I had to weed it out. I began to read much more than before, in the stacks of the Lenin Library, one of the most beautiful houses in Moscow and one of the most beloved to this very day. I read Dostoevsky, Sologub, Leonid Andreyev, Freud, Bergson, Schopenhauer, Nietzsche. All of this was swallowed in chunks, forming an incredible hodgepodge. It was precisely at that time that Blok came into my life, never to depart again.

I also read textbooks on psychiatry—I was seriously preparing to become a medical psychiatrist. At some moment or other I felt that I myself was beginning to lose sight of the boundary between reality and illusion. It was, strictly speaking, at that time that the first questions appeared about the meaning of life, questions that were very naïve and childish. But those seeds did not sprout for a long time.

There was an indefatigable longing for activity—above all to participate, participate in everything. Everything that related to us I felt to be the most vital part of myself. What doubts could have arisen over that? I studied voraciously, I read everything that was required in the curriculum, I became involved in social work at the Institute of Philosophy, Literature, and History and practically in all sports. My friends and I were all set to write a history of the Soviet school system. We paid visits to the People's Commissar of Education, Andrei Bubnov (subsequently shot); to the secretary of the Central Committee of the Komsomol, Aleksandr Kosarev (also shot); and to the newspapers *Komsomolskaya pravda* (Komsomol Truth) and *Literaturnaya gazeta* (Literary Gazette). We wrote about the relationships between professors and students. We made trips to our assigned kolkhoz.

We had to earn money and so we compiled a collection of pronouncements by Marat, we selected quotations from a book entitled *Lenin and Stalin on Technology*, we wrote detailed reviews on the verses of hack writers.

As a third-year university student, I began to teach ninth-grade students in a school.

Yet all of that seemed insufficient; I had to do more, I had to leave Moscow—life was too ordinary there. The extraordinary was what was required: a soaring flight, the north pole, far-away cities. Run, hurry, don't get left behind! So where was there time to think, to ponder, to doubt, to pose questions? There was neither the time nor the know-how for any personal life. And was it really necessary?

And my soul, barely, barely aroused, fell soundly asleep for a long time.

Incidentally, the absence of questions in no way meant the absence of answers. There were answers: categorical, decisive, and unambiguous. Not ones that I had worked out or had arrived at after much anguish. They were secondhand answers, like ready-made formulas, conclusions, laws, and incantations.

By my character, by my upbringing, and by the very atmosphere at home, I was not at all prepared for protracted and solitary meditation, or even for a solitary existence. Many years were to pass before I comprehended that this was essential for every person.

I am not turning my back on my youth. A belief in the world emerged in those days, a feeling for clear-cut and good human relations, that sense of fellowship without which it is impossible for me to exist.

Probably it was at that time that my belief in the infiniteness of human possibilities was born. If only the belief had not been born with me that a person could do *everything*!

I was very happy in my youth. I graduated from the university of happiness without passing through the school of unhappiness. My first genuine love was a happy one, our marriage was a happy one. Over and over again the feeling was reinforced in me that this was the way it was supposed to be, that this was the normal way, that man was born for happiness. Whereas unhappiness and grief were deviations, anomalies. In my youth I could neither comprehend nor accept the wisdom of Chekhov's story "Gooseberries": "Behind the door of every contented, happy man there ought to be someone standing with a little hammer, continuously reminding him with a knock that there are unhappy people . . ." *My* very own heroine was Tolstoy's Natasha Rostova, overflowing with the joy of life. And everything bad, everything horrible that subsequently occurred in my life seemed to be a deviation, a haphazard incident. Over and over again I expected happiness and was unwaveringly certain that everything still lay ahead.

My youth was not stormy. There was no need to protest. The norm was when everyone loved you. A person, so it seemed to me, must live at peace with himself and with everything around him. I never prepared myself for Luther's dictum "Here I stand, I cannot do otherwise." I stood where everyone else stood. Where truth was, according to my convictions . . .

The need to succeed. From earliest childhood I had fantasies of becoming a ballerina, applauded by the audience. And so on and on throughout all of life, through my teaching and lectures, so that people would like me, so that everyone would treat me well.

At seventeen I read all of Marx's *Das Kapital,* but I did not understand his quotation from Dante: *"Segui il tuo corso, e lascia dir le genti"* ("Follow your own path, and let people say what they will").

IV

Father

I can no longer remember him when he was young and strong. I remember him when he was old, rejected, soft, tender. After 1937, after the arrest of Artemii Khalatov, with whom my father had worked from the first years of the Revolution, he survived for another twenty-three years. He was not arrested or exiled. However, his first and his most important life came to an end in 1937.

My father, David Grigorievich Liebersohn, studied at the Kiev Institute of Commerce. He was one of the progressive students in the 1910s. He read Ibsen, Plekhanov, Nietzsche, and the *Communist Manifesto*. I later found the books with his notes in the margins. He read Gorky and participated in student demonstrations.

His greatest love was music and opera. Here is an old photograph of him wearing the costume of Mephistopheles. He was constantly striking up operatic arias, and he knew entire operas by heart. He himself had a desire for the stage, even more so for the conductor's baton.

During his final years he relished his phonograph. Tchaikovsky's First Piano Concerto is forever inextricably linked with Father. He dreamt of cultivating a love for music in us as well, but was unsuccessful.

A family anecdote has stuck in my memory from childhood about how Father's young brother Michel made a trip abroad and brought back two top hats: one for himself and the other for the usher at the Kiev Opera House.

Michel exists for me only in an old photo album: a handsome man in a theatrical costume, a wide ribbon across his shoulder. On closer examination it is possible with some difficulty to discern a famly resemblance. He was one of Anna Pavlova's partners. He danced in Diaghilev's ballet company in Paris. Before World War I he emigrated to America. When he grew old, he gave lessons to dancers and organized revues.

I found everything about him disturbing: especially the fact that he had gone abroad. True, it had still been 1913. He did not want to serve in the tsarist army; but, after all, he had not joined the Bolshevik underground, he had not become a warrior against the imperialistic war. He had simply taken to his heels! I also found it disturbing that he had chosen such a bizarre, unmasculine profession for himself. And despite the fact that he was an utterly unreal person for us, he spoiled our lives and promoted strife. In some year or other, Papa had ceased to write on the official forms that he had a brother living abroad, but I wrote it everywhere (how could I write a falsehood on an official form?). And I could not be persuaded otherwise by whatever arguments.

In 1937 a number of students in the Institute of Philosophy, Literature and History were selected who knew French better than the rest, and they underwent preparation for the trip to the international exposition in Paris. They were to work as guides in the Soviet pavilion. Our instructor told us repeatedly: "*La première phrase doit être brillante!*"

In French we learned Stalin's speech about the Constitution. I never had the opportunity to pronounce this first brilliant phrase. I was not sent to Paris for the exposition. Perhaps for the reason that in reply to the question of whether I had relatives abroad I answered: "There is an uncle in Paris."

In 1959 Michel arrived in Moscow with an ice ballet company. Father and he had a very tender reunion after forty-five years of separation. Michel embodied a part of Father's soul: the dream about music, applause, the smell of backstage.

But Papa's ambition reached even beyond the conductor's baton: he wanted to be in charge.

In the 1920s he moved swiftly through the ranks. At times it seems to me that the ambition that helped him so much, at the same time prevented him from finding a clearly defined position in life, from selecting not a post but a pursuit that one could devote one's life to.

At first he was ambitious on his own behalf, then subsequently on ours. There was the insistent way he used to beg or demand that his son enroll in postgraduate studies.

Father was a very capable person, imbued with a genuine gift for work. As an eight-year-old boy he began to work in a flour mill. And on the very day that was to be his final day on earth, he left the house and made his way to the carpenter's to order new bookshelves for us. He was almost seventy-three. After he retired, he languished without any work; he grew irritable, started to nag, and became intolerant. Incidentally, he was never entirely without work of some sort. Only after his death did I understand how many of the insignificant household chores he had taken upon himself. He always worked so beautifully and would organize everything around himself with such intelligence and care. Witness his room, his desk, his handwriting, which was graceful and legible, a handwriting that displayed a respect for the person who was to read it.

Now I can understand (albeit not completely) how repellent he found our slovenliness. It was something that he unconsciously provoked in us with our sense of opposition that was so typical of youth.

He would walk into my sister Lyusya's room when she had friends visiting and would say with disgust and without addressing anyone in particular: "Watch your feet!" In other words, you are sitting on the bed with your shoes on! She, like me, would take offense, get angry, and, unlike me, be rude. I wept silently.

When Lyusya got married, she left the house to go and live with her mother-in-law even though her husband was still serving in the army in the Far East. She left because she wanted to be independent, but also because she was tired of father's moralizing.

But he did pass on a love and respect for work to all of us. And he did so not with his preaching, which was an obstacle, but by his own example.

He himself had grown up in a strange family, under the cross fire of two directly opposing influences. I never saw my grandparents on my father's side, but I often heard about them, particularly a lot about my grandmother. She had been an imperious woman, good-looking, although somewhat masculine; a mother-tigress. Predatory, industrious, and energetic, she bore fourteen children. She once sent them for a vacation by the sea and became frightened: what if suddenly her children grew hungry? She departed in their footsteps, brought a hundred eggs, and set the samovar up directly on the beach.

Only her children existed for her. She had no interest in anyone else. I remember this kind of story about her.

"Who's coughing there?" Grandmother asked.

"Don't worry, Madame Liebersohn, it's only me," replied Father's playmate, who was to remain a life-long friend.

Grandmother ran a linen-drapery store, ran the house, toiled from dawn to dusk. Her husband was a small, retiring, truly religious person (he prayed for the sins of his sacrilegious wife). And he drank.

My father did not love his family or his relatives. He was embarrassed by his relatives even though he fixed them up with work. They came to us with all their woes. By turns, everyone lived, ate, and drank in our home.

But for all that there was not a single drop of warmth in his relations with them as far as I can recall. He was miserly with his affection, particularly where his brothers and sisters were concerned. He would heap abuse on them, both to their faces and behind their backs. He would greet them so badly that I always felt awkward. On her own behalf, as well as Papa's, Mama was the one who was supposed to mourn, rejoice, congratulate, and express condolences.

When guests gathered in our house I invariably heard arguments: Mama was always attempting to invite yet another one of the relatives, but Father would be opposed. He respected only his older brother Yakov, one of the first radiologists in Russia.

Who was the person who invented the idea that an only child grows up to be an egotist? In Father's family there were fourteen children. And all of them displayed the most varied shades and nuances of egotism.

Abrasha was the youngest, the most sickly, the most spoiled, the most ill-starred. When he was still a child, they discovered he had tuberculosis (a disease that ran in the family), and insofar as I remember him, his principal concern was to protect himself. A rowdy scene sticks in my mind: Abrasha is dashing about our enormous apartment, chasing after his wife; he wants to beat her, she cowers in a corner. My parents are shouting, I am shouting, they take me away. It turns out that he was jealous of his wife and someone else. Falling asleep, I whisper to my nanny that I'll never ever get married . . .

When I returned from the evacuation on April 30, 1942, Lyonya and I saw each other for the first time after the first and only protracted separation in our lives. We were together in our room in

Moscow. The war was forgotten; we did not know that Lyonya only had four more months to live. But we did know for certain that we only had all of three hours together before he had to return to his unit.

There was a ring at the door and Uncle Abrasha appeared. And, as always, he was demanding my attention and precisely at that instant. At first I objected calmly, but then I grew more and more heated. "I'll talk to you about everything later; my husband and I only have a short time together."

He would not listen to any arguments. His concerns, his desires were always the most important things in the world. Though he cursed him, Father would go on bearing him as a burden all his life.

The way things looked were very important to Papa: the house, the room, the family, work, he himself. He even frequently took pains not over the essence of things but over their appearance, over their external expression, over the result, over what he could show others.

By profession an economist, Papa spent the first and major portion of his life as the assistant to the director—in the Commissariat for Food Supply (Narkomprod), in the Commissariat for Transportation, in the State Publishing House (Gosizdat), back in Food Supply—transferring wherever his chief, Khalatov, was.

His posts did not correspond in the least to his aspirations: he wrote articles, and they were signed by Khalatov. But father's ambition grew all the more. At times this ambition was satisfied. During the years of work at Gosizdat, he became acquainted with famous writers, had pictures taken with them (he very much liked to be photographed and he photographed well), participated in the most diverse congresses, conferences, and consultations. He loved to go on business trips. He traveled abroad several times. His trip to see Maxim Gorky in Sorrento in 1931 was the pinnacle of his success. Gorky knew my father back in 1920, when the Central Committee for the Improvement of the Living Conditions of Scholars (Tsekubu), which Gorky had founded, was in operation. At that time, Father was working in Narkomprod and was assisting Gorky and carrying out his innumerable instructions. Then in the thirties he worked with Gorky on the magazine *Nashi dostizheniya* (Our Achievements). Preserved among Papa's things were books with Gorky's signature. I had no appreciation of such things in my youth. In one of Gorky's letters from Italy to Khalatov there is the following line: ". . . send my regards to comrade Stalin and Liebersohn and Proskuryakov."

How overjoyed Papa was when after Khalatov's posthumous rehabilitation Papa was able once more to pull out this letter and show it around.

It was quite late before I began to get to know my father and grow closer to him. I'm not referring to filial love, but rather to the beginning of friendship. For instance, it was only when I was already married that father told Lyonya and me about his trip to see Gorky.

Papa was rarely at home. I cannot remember any serious discussions with him during my teens. But when he did wish to talk with me, I was in no hurry to be forthcoming. Papa had no idea of how to establish any relationship with me as an adult. And if you were to ask me at that time who was closer to me, my girl friends or my father, then I would have replied: my friends, naturally.

Papa believed that the person had not yet been born who was worthy of his daughter. He was jealous of Lyonya and did not conceal it. Moreover, my marriage coincided with the most difficult period of his life. Yet I proved to be both deaf and dumb and did not understand his anxieties, did not share his grief.

Our friendship began during the war. Father was very proud of my responsible work in the All-Union Society for Cultural Relations with Foreign Countries (VOKS). He was impressed by everything: the foreigners, the receptions, the meetings with important people. Perhaps it seemed to him that at least in part I was the embodiment of his dreams of success that had not been fully realized.

He and Mama took my little daughter Sveta away with them during the evacuation, and they wrote me beautiful and detailed letters that cheered me up (wherever Father happened to travel, he would always write us daily letters). My parents stood beside me in my grief when Lyonya died. My widowhood brought Father and me closer together. Until my second marriage sharply divided us once more.

Father's advancement had come to an end, but he refused to acknowledge it. His nature demanded unceasing activity.

He looked for some other work so that his abilities and experience would be used. Everywhere he worked he was appreciated and liked. Even though he was very severe, he was always fair. He demanded the same from others as he demanded from himself. The final years before retirement he spent in charge of the proofreading section of a large printing firm. He was descending the ladder of posts, and everything was being repeated: earlier he had written Khalatov's speeches, now he was writing all the formal speeches for the director of the printing firm, not a bad man but an uneducated one. Yet even in this,

Father managed to find some crumbs of satisfaction. His coffin was borne from the hospital to the printers. The remains of a soul that was utterly devoted to work rested there, and from there he was accompanied on his final journey.

Not only did he seek a new position, he even attempted to change his profession. He wrote and stubbornly sought to get into print. Papa would have been a marvelous archivist, bibliographer, or coworker on an encyclopedia.

I had little sympathy for his attempts to get into print, and he was very hurt. But I did not like the *way* he wrote and *what* he wrote.

At that time I still did not understand the importance of recollections, documents, and any form of codified memory. Incidentally, Papa "selected" and "edited" his recollections to such a degree that very little remained of the facts. If only he had really written about everything that he had seen in Gorky's home! But subconsciously he either understood or perhaps sensed that it was impossible to write about such things. And so he wrote the way he was supposed to. The manuscript of his recollections of Gorky is preserved in the archives, and it is used by those who conduct research on the history of the magazine *Nashi dostizheniya*. The other manuscript of his recollections is about Vyshinsky,* with whom he had worked in Narkomprod, and it is full of praise. I was able to comprehend his infatuation with Gorky then and even more so now. But Vyshinsky . . . Was it possible that he did not know what a horrible and bloody role Vyshinsky had played?

The November celebrations in 1941. The city of Kuibyshev. We are at a festive gathering together with the staff from the People's Commissariat for Foreign Affairs. Vyshinsky is delivering a speech. He was the deputy minister to Molotov at that time. He casually mentions his Menshevik past (in a negative fashion, of course). He too expresses the hope that soon, very soon, all of us will see Moscow again. And together with the rest of the hall I applauded as well— for what I thought was his courage and his self-criticism. And I applauded because of our hopes, for we all were living on hope. But this was after the bloody purge of 1937 . . . So it is not for me to judge my father.

In 1944 Father joined the Party. He was fifty-six. I cannot under-

---

* Andrei Yanuarievich Vyshinsky (1883–1954), prosecutor-general for the show trials of the thirties.

stand at all why he didn't do it before, in his youth. Perhaps his social origins prevented him? Was he afraid of questions about his mother's store?

Perhaps Father joined the Party because it seemed to him that his misfortunes might come to an end and he would once more occupy a position in society. He did not look upon a position as an advantage (he did not think about advantage in wartime), but he saw a position as a means to work, to be with the others. Perhaps one of the reasons he joined was that I had joined the Party two years before.

As far as I could remember him, he was always afraid. But then a person of his era had plenty of reasons for fear.

There was a pistol in his wardrobe. At some point much earlier, during the period of grain requisitions (a task to which he had been constantly dispatched), he had been given the right to own a weapon. But subsequently that same pistol became a source of constant fear. He was afraid that the pistol would be taken away. He was afraid that he would be asked who gave him permission to have it.

All those people whose letters, photos, and autographs he preserved, whose friendship had been a source of pride to him, were gradually arrested and destroyed. He held out for some time, but then he began to destroy the letters and photographs. He was afraid.

He did not believe that the doctors who were treating Gorky had allegedly wanted to kill him. He knew these people personally. He knew Pyotr Kryuchkov, Gorky's secretary. It was unlikely that he believed in Khalatov's guilt. But he forbade himself not only to talk about it but probably even to think about it.

He was always attracted to power and authority. Power was in the hands of Stalin. And he wanted to be a part of that power. Stalin's power and authority had attracted people like Gorky (and Papa worshiped Gorky) and Sergei Eisenstein. At that time there were a great many people in our country and abroad who experienced that magnetism.

Moreover, by his very nature Papa was not a rebel but a con-formist—and I inherited that from him. Naturally he had doubts that by turns would wax and wane. But he attempted to suppress them. He probably did so unconsciously and I must have aided him in that. Subsequently, without realizing it, I was to repeat his course to a significant degree.

Father knew not only how to work well and smoothly, but to rest as well. He took his recreation tastefully, cheerfully, emptying his mind of all annoying thoughts about the family and about work. He always brought home new acquaintances from the health spas and holiday villas. Groups of people were always forming around him—he was the "heart of the crowd."

He courted the ladies. To the very end he never lost his taste for that. He did not turn into an "old man." He could drink and have a good time. He knew how to welcome guests and loved to do so. He would be transformed in people's company; he was witty, laughed, sang, and danced.

The relationship between my second husband, Kolya, and my father took a horrible turn. For five years they did not even talk to each other. Everything was repulsive in their conflict, both the content and the form, as well as the behavior. Kolya's drunkenness, his attitude toward Sveta, and toward me as well, made my parents indignant. Each of them, my husband and Papa, considered himself to be utterly and entirely right.

On October 2, 1960, we decided to celebrate the publication of Lev's* first book, *The Heart Is Always on the Left*. The table was laid out, the guests invited. Papa fell ill during the day, but he was firm in his demand that the celebration not be postponed. The friends who had gathered sat in the dining room, while I spent almost the entire time in Papa's room, calling doctors and the ambulance.

Father was moaning on the bed. But then we had grown accustomed to his moans, to the fact that he was unbelievably anxious about his health and could not bear any pain. He would barely fall ill when suddenly he would cry: "I'm dying!" This time there was no cry from him of "I'm dying!" He was simply moaning. We grew more and more frightened. My brother carried him in his arms into the bathroom. Suddenly he had become quite small, a withered little old man. And then the onslaught of a collapse, and they ordered him to be taken immediately to the hospital. I took him there at dawn. Papa's face was all gray. I sat in the corridor with his things, rolled up in a brown bathrobe. The doctors told me not to wait and so I returned home, dozed awhile, and then had barely reached the office when they phoned there: "Your father died." And I returned home. All my thoughts came in a rapid, haphazard fashion. The main thing

* Lev Kopelev, literary critic, author, Germanist, and my third husband, whom I married in 1956.

was Mama. She was in Rostov on vacation. My brother flew to fetch her back.

Two days later, after Papa's burial, we made a trip to the country, simply to relax, to gain a respite. Our friend drove us in his car. He said: "What good fortune that your father's final years were good ones." Yes, the final years were good. My friends treated him well, and my parents participated in our celebrations.

Time passed and I began to feel sorry for myself. Who else had loved me so wholeheartedly, had wished me well in such a peremptory, impatient, and jealous fashion? Who else had shared my joys and shared my sorrows? My childhood departed with him.

I have been thinking about him more and more frequently since his death. Because I am guilty before him, and now he will never, never know that I cannot forgive myself for those long months when I used to pass him by like a stranger. My turn will come as well, and I too will stand before that door where my sins will be inquired into: I am guilty, Lord, I turned my back on my own father . . . I know not whether I will be forgiven this sin There. Here I have never forgiven myself and shall never do so.

Then came the necessity to think not about myself, but about him. Now I can more profoundly understand his worries, his actions, even his fits of temper. I understand his sense of responsibility for the family, and a great, great deal of what the burden of responsibility involves, what it means "to be the eldest."

I think about him not only there on the bench in the cemetery, beside the grave, where the green grass is spread so smoothly, but also in those rare moments when I find myself alone, on sleepless nights, when the engulfing clamor of everyday life is reluctant to disperse or retreat.

How I loved him, how impossibly mutual had been the force of that love, and how it would never again be repeated.

V

Home

(After Seeing Fellini's *8½*)

1967

The address of the house in which I was born and spent half a century was formerly 24 Tverskaya Street, apartment 12. Now it has been changed to 6 Gorky Street, apartment 201. Twelve buildings used to stand along Tverskaya Street from our home up to Okhotny Row. Now there are three. The streetcars were removed, asphalt appeared in place of the paving stones, and lindens were planted along the sidewalk. The physical appearance of the street has altered, but our apartment has remained.

It's a large apartment of 100 square meters. According to official estimates, there are 75 square meters of "usable space," but in actual fact there is less. There are a lot of corridors. The right-hand portion of the apartment was originally taken up with a room that was 40 square meters in size. One of my first recollections is that of our table. A rectangular table that has been opened wide, with thick carved legs. The same table we used to crawl under when we were children.

The table is set, there are a lot of guests, it's noisy, and probably for the first time in my life I have been allowed to stay with the adults. People seat me on their knees, give me an orange—not an ordinary orange-colored orange like all the other oranges of the succeeding years, but a red one, called a blood orange.

We are celebrating the return of my aunt's husband from the concentration camp at Solovki. No, he was neither an enemy of the Soviet state nor one of its innocent victims. He operated somewhere on the fringes of the criminal code and from time to time got caught. But I only discovered that much later. A congenial feeling remains from that evening: a "celebration" is a laid-out table, many people dressed up, noise, a red orange. Something unusual.

I lived with my nanny in the most distant room, in the nursery. Today my grandson Lyonya lives there. When the younger ones appeared (my sister and brother), I gradually moved closer and closer to the front of the apartment. The portion that was screened off from the large room and separated by a wardrobe, which is now called "Masha's nook" (after its last inhabitant, my youngest daughter), was highly prized by us in our childhood because it was possible to come and go without the parents noticing. I have several times made a complete circuit of our apartment: I returned with my first husband to the nursery; then, many years later, Lev and I also began our life together there.

Papa used to shout "You lodger!" to me much less frequently than to my sister, Lyusya, but I too, of course, was a lodger. I slept here, ate, changed my clothing, prepared my lessons, read books, but lived outside the house, at school, in the Pioneer detachment, at the institute, at work.

Outside the house and outside my own soul.

I had an unshakable faith that my existence between these old walls was merely a preparation for life. Life, properly speaking, would begin in a new and sparkling white house. There I would do exercises in the morning, there the ideal order would exist, there all my heroic achievements would commence.

The majority of my contemporaries, whether they lived in tents, mud huts, communal apartments, or what in those days were considered to be good apartments, all shared the same kind of rough, provisional, slapdash way of life. Faster, faster toward the great goal, and there everything would begin in a genuine sense.

It was both possible and necessary to alter everything: the streets, the houses, the cities, the social order, human souls. And it was not all that difficult: first the unselfish enthusiasts would outline the plan on paper; then they would tear down the old (saying all the while, "You can't make an omelette without breaking eggs!"); then the ground would be cleared of the rubble and the edifice of the socialist phalanx would be erected in the space that had been cleared. That was precisely the way that people attempted to proceed with mighty Russia. That was the way it had to be done with individual lives and with individual homes as well.

Plans for a new Moscow were exhibited every holiday in the windows along Gorky Street. We saw with our own eyes how these plans were being transformed into new homes.

Before the Revolution, our house had been the Savvinskoe Hostel, a lodging house for visiting monks. Hence the strange shapes of the windows, which were small and vaulted and thanks to which the rooms resembled cells.

According to the 1935 plan for Moscow's general reconstruction, it was decided to tear down our variegated gingerbread house with its turrets. But the house rose up in opposition. And resisted. Several of its engineering inhabitants made calculations, went to the Moscow city council and proved that the house was still solid and that it would be cheaper to shift it rather than tear it down.

In those years, when houses were torn down each tenant was given 2,500 rubles. And afterward no one took any interest in what would become of the evicted people. There wasn't anywhere to move to (co-op construction had not yet come into existence). If there was anyone who had been deprived of the roof over his head, well, he just could go ahead and leave Moscow. Workers' hands were needed everywhere. And anyway, what did it matter where one lived?

This was in the midst of 1937. However strange it might seem against the background of the insanity of those years, our group of engineers was neither charged with sabotage nor with foreign espionage. What was more, they were actually listened to. Over the course of two years, the house was shifted into the depths of the inner courtyard, a millimeter a day. A small island of rational changes in the midst of thousands of senseless ones.

Everything was excavated all around; for two years it was as though we were living on a construction site. But the heating and sewage were functioning (gas was brought into the building only in 1947).

People remained in their apartments. According to the standards of those times, they were handsome apartments. Perhaps they wouldn't tear it down after all. Naturally, the moving of our house was talked about on the radio and written up in the newspapers.

It wasn't that I didn't love that house, I simply always wanted to leave it. To leave it for where my real house would arise of its own accord. Why bother with organizing, decorating, and simply upkeeping something that was not the real thing? Besides, I did not even know how to set up house. In those days there was no course on home economics in our schools. In practical work classes we learned to saw and to plane. We learned the difference between coarse and smooth files. How could one imagine a course on home economics in an era of wars and proletarian revolutions, when women had become the equal of men in everything? Yet all the while people continued to eat, drink, dress, and bear children. And someone had to prepare the food, clean the house, and raise the children. Someone. But not me.

My childhood was spent outdoors. On the left, at 22 Tverskaya, was the studio of the Moscow Art Theater. In the summertime, stage sets stood in the street, and we played among them. There was a fountain in the courtyard. In fact, there were several courtyards, which offered unlimited possibilities for playing "cossacks and robbers" and other games.

Our elaborate main entrance, with its gigantic staircase, played a very important role. I used to stop in the entrance on the way to school, remove my hat, and roll up my heavy stockings. It was considered a sign of utmost courage to go the whole winter with bare knees.

Then boys started to accompany me as far as the entrance. Our staircase seemed to be specially equipped for working out relationships. First of all while standing outside. Then, "Well, I have to go," but he would follow me and we would seat ourselves in the alcove on the first landing. Apparently, at one time there used to be a statue in this alcove. However, it was dangerous to sit there for long; our neighbors might see us, or even my parents. We would move higher up and install ourselves on the large landing on the first floor, on the windowsill. Passions would rise and here we would throw caution to the winds. Then higher still, on the landing of the second floor, and once more on the windowsill. And finally, our own landing. It was cramped here, but at one time, before our building superintendent at that time had built himself an apartment, it had been quite spacious. During the construction of that apartment, homeless children used to live on the landing.

The principal residence was the window to the right of our apartment door. How many hours I had spent sitting in it!

My sister and my daughters subsequently traveled the same path.

Here lovers and girl friends worked out their relationships. Here, on these stairs, all the great problems were debated: revolution, love, friendship, books, choice of profession. Pronouncements were made on everything, and everything was resolved many times once and for all.

The first ice-cream café in Moscow was opened in our main entryway, and it was the ancestor of today's innumerable ice-cream parlors called Arctic and Cosmos. Strangely enough, there were none of today's lines, although for a long time it was the sole ice-cream café in all of Moscow. When now I look with amazement at the long lines and think who could be standing there both day and night, in the heat and the cold, and in the mire, just to enter an ice-cream paradise, I am told that they are people who have no roof over their heads, people who have no other place to meet. But in those earlier days, in my youth, although there were a great many more homeless people, there were no lines on the streets. Perhaps because Muscovites did not know how to go to cafés, or did not want to. There was no money even for ice cream. And for many people the word "café" was linked with bourgeois notions.

I made efforts to get away from this house, this apartment, and this entryway. It was impossible to even call it a dream. It was simply a plan, just as concrete as the plans that were exhibited in the windows along Gorky Street.

But we didn't go anywhere. Life in the apartment went on—not a preparation for life, but life itself.

The apartment gradually changed. In the right corner of the kitchen, where the gas meter now stands, there once stood a tall chimney pipe; wood crackled, and a prehistoric iron tub was heated up. We used to take our baths in it, and later I bathed my daughters in it.

There was a wooden stove in the kitchen, and Mama used to bake *pirogi* in the oven. The smell of freshly baked dough was one of the first smells of my childhood. *Pirogi* were baked for November 7 (the anniversary of the October Revolution) and May 1, for New Year's, for Christmas, for all our family celebrations. And at Easter they would bake Easter bread for us children, a small one for each child. At Grandmother's there was matzoh for Jewish Passover. Later Mama bought the matzoh. After Mama's death both the Easter breads and the matzoh disappeared.

The apartment was often remodeled, partitions were erected—first the length of the large room, then crosswise. Heavy plush drapes were hung. They seemed the height of luxury to me, a symbol of that same opulence that embarrassed me very much during the years of my ascetic youth. Many years later the remnants of this "luxury" were used to patch up the holes in all the chairs and couches.

As in any house, a number of old things that no one needs but for some reason are impossible to get rid of settled in our apartment. The past can materialize out of that same rubbish. For instance, here is a red trunk. When in 1931 Father brought it in youthful shape from Italy, it was honored with the title of "coffer." There were wild and improbable things in it, such as crepe-soled shoes for me. Could a poorly dressed and unshod Moscow in the year 1931 possibly conceive of crepe-soled shoes?

We used to transport things from the city to the dacha in the "coffer." In 1941 on the side of the trunk appeared the inscription "Liebersohn, Bagaryak" (the place in the Urals to which my parents were evacuated). The onetime foreign "coffer" became a Russian trunk and remained solid for a long time. Now it has become a wreck and no longer deserves the honor of making the trip with us to the new apartment on Aeroportovskaya Street.

Once my girl friend and I decided to inhabit the attic over the kitchen. For three days we washed, cleaned, scrubbed, and somehow managed to throw out some of the old things. We set up a room for our dolls there.

It was there in the attic that we read an epistle written in invisible ink. Incidentally, everything was already clear even without any epistles. But a ritual existed whereby it was necessary to explain things. A boy from our class had whispered to me: "Hold it up to a flame, then you'll be able to read it." We lit a candle in the attic and started off by holding the candle *above* the letter. The wax dripped and we almost burned the letter. Finally, the words somehow managed to appear: "I love you." But what language was it in? I was learning French at that time. We got hold of an English dictionary and with no small difficulty translated the text.

We forgot about the attic just as quickly as we did about our other diversions.

The apartment was inhabited by dreams, feverish apparitions (I was frequently sick), and the legends of my childhood. At night my imagination would soar. It was here that we played at fairy kingdoms; it was here that we waited for our prince charmings, who immediately after a declaration of love on bended knee were supposed to throw their princess into the saddle and dash off to the ends of the earth. Far away from this house.

My prince did appear. But there was no journey to the ends of the earth. My daughter was born. And so up and down that same staircase

I dragged the baby carriage (closer to our modern-day refrigerators than present-day baby carriages). The prince was serving in the army.

In October 1941 I left our apartment for the first time with the evacuation to Kuibyshev. For five months. In those times a great many of the houses were ruined, many were destroyed. Mine as well as others. Cold, stately, wartime Kuibyshev did not in the least resemble the dreams of fairy kingdoms from our childhood fantasies.

I returned in April 1942. Father was already in Moscow with my sister. Mama came a short while later with my brother and my daughter.

We started to live in the two smallest rooms, while the big room, the former reception room, came to be known as the "refrigerator"— here the winds whistled. The heating did not work, like everywhere else, and so we set up two smoky and sooty potbellied stoves. On top of them, directly on the iron tops, Mama would bake her flat cakes, which bore no resemblance to the prewar *pirogi* but were just as tasty given the hungry times. Mama fed us yeast, which was loathsome but beneficial.

My husband died in the war. Once again I was yearning to get out of this house. I wrote one application after another. I was not accepted for the front lines, nor did I run off of my own accord.

My attempts to leave did not cease. After my second marriage we spent a year in Bucharest, which was certainly the ends of the earth. Only there was no home. We lived in a hotel and returned to the same walls in Moscow.

We began to search for another home. But what is a home? A castle, so say the English. But in our country there was not a single home that was a castle. No one was taken away in a Black Maria from apartment 12, but that was not because of the thickness of its walls. We were simply lucky.

Of course, a home is a definite arrangement of doors and windows. Things. For example, Mama's dentist's chair in the hallway. At first patients used to sit in it, then friends and relatives whose teeth Mama fixed. Later, during parties, people would smoke standing around it, exchange secrets, work out their relationships. Or there was the carved buffet, which would probably collapse now at the slightest movement.*

But to a greater degree a home is made up of people, the ones who

---

* It was moved to Sveta's new apartment. It seems all right and is still standing (1977).

have settled in it, the people who come and go, those who can say: "It's just like being in my own home." Several generations have come and gone. Take Sveta's girl friend, who has been coming here for twenty years now.

During the years of my second marriage the apartment was divided into two warring factions that were joined by common corridors. At that time I genuinely hated these walls. I maintained that an evil force emanated from them, and I believed that it would be enough to leave and then everything would straighten itself out. Kolya, whom I married in 1945, would give up drinking, and a family would become a family once more.

But this was an illusion. And everything that was good in me shrank, disappeared, and perhaps pulled up short, together with my childhood fantasies, before these walls. Who can say?

The atmosphere in our apartment became poisoned. Frequently in those years I used to climb the stairs unwillingly, with difficulty (though at that time I still didn't puff the way I do now). It was simply that I was fearful that some new quarrel was awaiting me there.

There was a final attempt to run off to the "real" life: in 1951 we left for Tallinn in Estonia. There we settled into a bright new apartment. At first I decorated our new home and did so with a certain amount of enthusiasm. Only it was all far too late. The home that had existed outside the walls, our real home, had long since collapsed in ruins. It was hardly a coincidence that when I went to Tallinn again, in 1958, not only could I not find the apartment in which I had lived for two and a half years, but I did not even recall whether it was to the left or to the right of the entry.

In 1953 I again returned to my parents' home and lived there for another fourteen years.

From that first festive occasion that I recalled as a small girl, there was an endless stream of parties in our home. Birthdays and name days for us, our relatives, and friends. Baptisms, weddings, graduations from schools and institutes, dissertation defenses, publications of books. Celebrations that were noisy, crowded, and cheerful.

There were two exits to the big room, and sometimes the following scene was conjured up: people would enter by one door and suddenly disappear out of the other. Lots of people used to insist that we ourselves did not know who came and went.

Here we experienced our own grief, as well as that of others. At the weddings there would be toasts to "happiness at the first try," and later divorces would be toasted. When abortions were prohibited, the old doctor "rescued" me and my girl friends right here, in that former reception room. For large sums of money. And under fear of criminal prosecution.

Papa was taken away from here in 1960 to die. At some point he had received the apartment, had loved it and cherished it.

To that very same large table on which bawling little Sveta, softly whimpering little Masha, and my foot-kicking little niece Marishka had their clothing changed, a new bundle, my grandson Lyonya, was brought in December 1963. The fifth generation had appeared in the apartment.

And now, in 1967, I've gone and left. All of four stops on the subway. It's nice in the new apartment, quiet, calm, easier to work and rest. Even somewhat easier to be ill. I can do my exercises and shower. We feel a little better here.

But I no longer believe that it is possible to change everything by moving to another abode. It is nice in a new place. But how much of life remains that might be lived in a new fashion?

VI

Lyonya

My grandson was named Leonid—in memory of his grandfather and the father of my oldest daughter, Leonid Shersher, who had perished at the front. There's truth in the old words: "The dead stay young." That's why it is hard to imagine Leonid as a grandfather when he was a father for such a short while: two and a half years in all.

He was killed in action on August 30, 1942. On September 2, he was buried, together with those who had died with him, in the cemetery for pilots at Monino. We were forewarned that only relatives would be admitted to the military area. Welded steel boxes (that was how they were brought back from the border) were lowered into large pits. A clump of earth, a piece of your heart; another clump of earth, another piece of your heart. A rhythmic tempo that would never seem to end.

A few days later we found out that one could visit the graves on special passes, and we set off for Monino, I and my close friends who were in Moscow in September 1942.

We were laughing as we returned from the cemetery. It was a laughter through tears, and all the same we were laughing. It was almost unbelievable, but recalling Lyonya's innumerable witticisms, his favorite expressions, the entertaining anecdotes, we were laughing even then.

Private humor is very difficult to communicate to someone else. But our youth is inconceivable without this atmosphere of humor. I was simply a consumer: I did the laughing.

Lyonya laughed more rarely than I did, but he was always prompt-
ing laughter.

We studied in the same school, and in the same grade, but seemingly
I first took notice of him in 1930, at a Pioneer rally in the Radio
Theater of the Central Telegraph Building. An announcement:
"Leonid Shersher, a pupil from the Twenty-seventh School, will now
speak." He read a poem with an epigraph from Stalin: "We must
cover this distance rapidly within ten years, otherwise we will be
crushed."

> *We won't be crushed if hundreds of blast furnaces*
> *Can find for themselves a leader.*
> *We won't be crushed if to the aid of steel*
> *Comes our shock labor.*

I had no idea that he wrote poetry. It was difficult for me to
imagine anyone writing poems, much less a boy that I was acquainted
with from my class. Poetry seemed like a miracle to me—it had to
be born spontaneously. Even now, many years later, when I know
that contracts must also be signed for poetry collections, that these
kinds of books must be edited, that they too must go through galley
proofs, nevertheless, I remain firmly attached to my childish belief
that the creation of genuine poetry is a miracle.

Lyonya did not read his poems the way he usually talked. He read
them by drawing out the words, lengthening the vowels, in a strange
kind of voice.

He was tall, somewhat stooped, and very thin. He had upturned
eyebrows, intelligent gray eyes, a large nose, and his face seemed to
end suddenly toward the bottom sooner than one would normally
expect. He reminded one either of a bird of prey or a ruffled hen.

I listened to these mediocre lines in the Radio Theater. There were
many who wrote in that style and there was no sign of any poetic
gift in them. But I do recall precisely those verses because they
contained a part of a life we shared in common.

In the summer of 1935 I was living outside Moscow, on the
Klyazma River.

That same summer we saw the German film *Peter*, one of the first
foreign films to be shown. *"Heute fühl' ich mich so wunderbar!"*
"How happy I am today!" we sang in imitation of Franziska Gaal.

By chance I met Lyonya on the Klyazma, and together we decided not to continue our studies into the tenth grade but to attempt to pass the entrance examinations for the university.

Lyonya's father reminded me of the caricatures of the bourgeois that were being printed in our magazines in those days: fat, evil, and gluttonous. From that time, I disliked my future father-in-law. Moreover, this personal dislike became combined with a "class" dislike. Even after Lyonya died, when it would have been possible to share our grief together at the funeral in Monino, his father stood sobbing in one corner, while I stood in another, stonelike and without a single tear. But an entire era in life was to elapse before that.

We went to the Institute of Philosophy, Literature, and History to hand in our documents. All the young fellows and girls passing by seemed to me to be geniuses. I hardly would have resolved on such a courageous step as this without Lyonya.

The examinations ended and then, on August 18, Lyonya came to visit us at the dacha in an unusually gloomy mood.

"Do you want me to read you some poems?" he asked.

"Of course."

They were love poems.

"Who are they dedicated to?"

"To you."

To me? From you? But that's impossible. The Lyonya with whom I had sat at the same desk? That awkward and unathletic Lyonya? And I had firmly believed that I would love only a fine volleyball player. And this Lyonya, a native of Odessa on the Black Sea coast, I even had to teach how to swim. How many times he described the way his wife should be: she would be blond, she wouldn't work (unless she were a ballerina), and she would totally devote herself to the home, her husband, and the children. No resemblance to me.

Soon we would kiss beneath the birch tree opposite our dacha and be amazed at how all of this had come to pass.

We spent our honeymoon in Yasnaya Polyana, where our former schoolteacher was working.

At the institute they called me little Rayka—I was the youngest and the shortest in my year. It seemed to me that my waist was not sufficiently tightly drawn in. "Do you want to burst?" our seamstress grumbled as yet again she made something for me out of one of Mama's old dresses.

Lyonya's wife had to be well dressed. Later, when he was stubbornly breaking into print and earning some money, he really began to buy me dresses and shoes. But in that summer of 1935, like the majority of the girls in Moscow, I too was going around in canvas pumps that were white with blue trim.

When, in my presleep reveries, I was not ascending the stages of all the world's forums or riding astride a white steed into cities that had just been liberated by the whirlwind of world revolution, I was robing myself in dresses of incredible beauty. I didn't know of a single contemporary of mine who didn't dream about a long, black velvet dress. And I didn't know of a single one who had such a dress. Instead of this fantasy velvet (after the war a prefix was added to the word to get "panne velvet"), the height of luxury for us was a white blouse with black polka dots.

I would spring up in the mornings, and a fresh day would cheerfully begin. Were there misfortunes in the world? There probably were. I read about them in books, in newspapers (incidentally, I rarely looked at newspapers). Things like that were happening elsewhere but not here. Here, only friendship, happiness, and love existed.

Mama was ill from time to time, but it was expected of mothers to be ill. Would I someday be a mother? I didn't think about it. When my fellow students talked about being pregnant, about abortions, I was amazed, supposing that such things happened only with adults and that I was separated from all of that by some impassable abyss.

Heute fühl' ich mich so wunderbar.

Today and tomorrow. And forever.

At times Mama complained of my lack of attention.

"Mama, you tell me what to do and I'll do it."

"No, I'm not going to tell you, you're an adult now and you should know yourself."

I was grown up only in one respect: I wanted to start earning my living as soon as possible. In Yasnaya Polyana, Lyonya and I recorded the reminiscences of the peasants who had known Leo Tolstoy. Only twenty-five years had passed since the day of his death.

We shared our experiences. It seemed to us that we had lived long lives separately and we had to share every single day and every single hour. How did we manage to accumulate enough stories to tell sixteen hours a day? But we did.

On September 1, 1935, we crossed the threshold of the institute in complete awe. Professor Sergei Radtsig appeared at the lectern. He was a little old man (probably he was all of fifty), and in an unexpectedly high falsetto he began to give an account of the Trojan War. For us it seemed as though he had come from there, from antiquity.

The past. Troy. Including Achilles and the Russian tsars and Radtsig and our own parents. We had nothing in common with the past, nor could we possibly have had. In 1917 a line had been drawn. This past was of interest to a few, to historians, for example. But it was of no interest at all to me. Everything that was important was in the present; the measure of everything would begin with us. I wasn't the only one to feel that way.

In her book, *Close Approaches*, Yelena Rzhevskaya writes:

> However much I can remember of myself, it was always the *general cause*. Now it was the war. Before the war everything that was called "our time" was the general cause. Everyone loved it and romanticized it. It was a time "when everything is coming to pass." A time "when all things are starting with us." Whereas everything before was the flood that had wrenched free and carried off the cultural stratum of our forerunners and our ancestral roots and the very conception of them.*

I am trying to immerse myself in that summer, but I keep being forced to the surface, to the present, and not simply because I have forgotten a great deal. But because I cannot find the words, and after all, I wanted to reach out for the origins of happiness, but they elude me.

In 1939 I finished my class with great difficulty, hurried out onto the street, and almost fainted. Those were the first tidings of Sveta, of the extension of Lyonya and myself.

Heute fühl' ich mich so wunderbar.

Today and forever.

"Nothing in the world so purifies, so ennobles youth, so preserves it, as a strongly aroused interest in common humanity." So wrote Herzen.† Whatever else might have been the case, our childhood,

---

* *Novy mir* (The New World), No. 5, 1980.

† Aleksandr Ivanovich Herzen (1812–1870), leading Russian revolutionary, writer, and philosopher.

our adolescence and our youth did not imbue us with a strongly aroused interest in common humanity. Years passed before I understood that those ideological class interests on which our youth had been nurtured contradicted in many ways the idea of a common humanity and led to inhumane practices. As for Lyonya, whether or not we were to be crushed concerned him from the time of his adolescence, but then he was among those who did not allow the Nazis to crush us.

In those days we all knew by heart the figures 518 and 1,040: 518 new enterprises and 1,040 tractor and machine stations. Those were the holy figures of the first five-year plan.

The war confirmed the fact that our personal fates were inextricably linked with our common fate. "I have lots of news," Lyonya wrote me, "but it will reach you in one way or another because it's connected with the general news" (November 10, 1941). "What I find most cheering are the details and facts from the newspapers that I've been able to learn here. This truly brings cheer and atones for all the grief that envelops one in all manner of thoughts of a personal nature" (December 28, 1941). "My mood has been buoyed up by the gifts of the New Year: the Crimea the day before and then Kaluga on the eve itself" (January 2, 1942).

For Lyonya this feeling of indissoluble and important ties with the world was embodied above all in the printed word. He used to buy all the newspapers and journals whenever he was traveling and would get very excited. It always seemed to him that it would be precisely at such a time that something important would happen and he would miss it.

He was a born journalist, and journalism was a calling and the incarnation of what was typical for his generation: knowing everything, being connected with everyone, and participating, participating personally and without fail.

His professional journalism began with the bulletin-board newspaper *Komsomoliya*. The year was 1936. In the corridor of the institute's building an unusually large student crowd had gathered. The headline stands out in enormous letters: "LOVE, FRIENDSHIP, HATRED." A rose and a rifle. Ivan Khmarsky prepared this edition. And there is a questionnaire: "What qualities should the person possess whom you could love?" Students came from all over Moscow to read this issue of *Komsomoliya*.

Even before the institute, Lyonya had been a child correspondent for *Pionerskaya pravda* (Pioneer Pravda). Later he worked on *Illyustrirovannaya gazeta* (Illustrated Gazette). The newspaper was the greatest love of his life; everything was important to him—the topics, the language, the headings, the type, the drawings.

He was not in the least intimidated by people, he wasn't afraid of people. Together with his friends he had interviews on behalf of *Komsomoliya* with well-known writers (Ilya Ehrenburg and others).

When by a special resolution of the Party committee in the institute the subsequent editorial staff converted *Komsomoliya* into an all-institute newspaper with a clichéd Party title, Lyonya reacted bitterly, as though it were an insult leveled at him.

During his student years he became acquainted with the older journalist Vasilii Reginin and would return from visits to him in ecstasy. Retelling episodes (both actual and fabricated) from the history of the Russian press, Lyonya would be overjoyed. He was a voracious reader of the stormy reporter Egon Erwin Kish. And his ideal was Mikhail Koltsov's *Spanish Diary*.

Probably of our five years as students, the pages of life connected with the Civil War in Spain are the loftiest, most radiant. They were, to the greatest degree, suffused with an interest in common humanity.

Even that conception proved to be partly an illusion. Partly, because the maps of Spain in our city squares, the sense of the Spanish tragedy as our own personal tragedy, these were the reality. And the ships arriving with Spanish children. But the dirty politics of our leadership, for whom the Spaniards had become merely pawns, and the schism within Spain itself were also reality.

However, even today the Spanish Civil War represents the possibility, if only for a moment, of human brotherhood. The International Brigades.

What a terrible dream it would have seemed at that time to know that three or four decades later the question would be asked of practically everyone: Who is he? Russian? Hungarian? What percentage of blood by nationality? Ukrainian? Jewish? French?

Our attitude toward Spain at that time coincided with the attitude of people who were infinitely removed from us. I won't make reference to Hemingway or Malraux, I shall cite Orwell's book *Homage to Catalonia*.

It sounds like lunacy, but the thing that both of us wanted was to be back in Spain . . . This war, in which I played so ineffectual a part, has left me with memories that are mostly evil, and yet I do not wish that I had missed it . . . the result is not necessarily disillusionment and cynicism. Curiously enough the whole experience has left me with not less but more belief in the decency of human beings.

In September 1936 there was an evening reception for the newly admitted students. We, the second-year students, considered ourselves hoary-headed with experience. But the evening developed of its own accord and was devoted to Spain. Lyonya and another student wrote a salutation on the occasion of that reception that was excited and romantic. At the conclusion of the address, which touched on the topic "If War Should Come Tomorrow," came the words: "Then the people's commissar for defense will become the people's commissar for offense." It seems to me that this never entered the head of a single writer in such a fashion during the course of the entire war.

We hated clichés in our faculty, we feared clichés, and we tried to exterminate clichés. After all those speeches and resolutions of ours that had been written like verse, with words subjected to severe scrutiny in order to create rhythm and, above all, to create a fresh thought, for years and years afterward we had to listen to, read, and support yesterday's worn-out, monotonous resolutions replete with standardized zeal.

Our friend Vitya Perov was also attracted to newspaper work, he too dreamt about journalism. He married Khanka Ganetskaya, one of our students. Young, handsome, and happy, they departed on their first journey. But in the summer of 1937 Vitya's acute appendicitis was not diagnosed in time and he was given castor oil. Peritonitis and death followed. We stood in the honor guard in the club of that building on Serafimovich Street, which at that time was still called Government House. Already at that time the doors were being barred and sealed off, one after the other. A month later the door through which Vitya's coffin had been carried was sealed off as well. After the arrest of his father-in-law, the old Bolshevik Yakub Ganetsky, someone even claimed that Vitya had been killed by the "enemies of the people." We didn't reject it indignantly or call it absurd. We believed it, I to a greater extent than Lyonya, but all the same we believed it, just as we believed things that were foolish and much more horrible.

A struggle was raging in our hearts and minds between trust and suspicion. Most of us, even considering the differences in our natures, were much more disposed to believing in people. But we were educated differently.

Lyonya possessed a strong and skeptical mind. He had neither the desire nor the ability to be worshipful. He was precisely the kind of person who seemingly should have declared: "This is a hoax and I do not believe that enemies of the people have turned up in every area of the country's leadership. Such a thing simply could not be."

But Lyonya did not speak out in this manner, and so, conclusively and irreversibly, he did not let it enter his mind. Probably for the additional reason that new and threatening questions would have unavoidably arisen: Who is doing all this and for what reason? Who stands to gain by all this? He was not in the least prepared for those kinds of questions. In order to pose questions one probably would have to have been an outsider, with a rather detached view. But Lyonya was on the inside. He had not been admitted inside immediately. At school he had been turned down once by the Komsomol because his father was an independent small businessman. But when he felt that he was on the inside, he was inordinately proud of this fact, he was happy about it. Happy not only because he was conscious of his participation, but also because he received recognition for that participation.

The mind was able to find various ways out.

He very much liked to play an absorbing game. Wasn't he the one who had devised it? "Uncover the enemy." Plays were being printed in all the magazines of those days about the "enemies of the people." The object of the game was to determine who the enemy was from the list of characters, without reading the play. And one could be successful most of the time. The hack playwrights used to array their negative characters in appropriate names.

Lyonya found fanatics repulsive. He did not share my worship of Joan of Arc. He loved that part in the foreword to Ilf and Petrov's *The Little Golden Calf* where the authors make fun of the gloomy gentleman who proclaims that "when socialism is being built, it makes you want to pray." He was merciless in his mockery of stupidity, baseness, and opportunism.

Often I felt sorry for the people he made fun of.

Like many of our contemporaries, he gave a sigh of relief when the war began. The line between friends and enemies became the line at the front.

.   .   .

Lyonya had thousands of plans for works, books, and trips. Not all were realized in his life, but he did accomplish a great deal, a very great number of them.

We—I find myself forced to say "we" almost all the time. Because we did everything together. We ate from the same bread roll, lived our lives with people, shared everything with our friends. The very thought of being alone would have seemed in any event abnormal, strange, and suspicious. It seems somehow completely natural that Lyonya should rest in a common grave together with those who perished in the same airplane. Creative work was always conceived of as something collective, although he was always the heart, the beginning, the moving force of all these creative plans.

We planned on writing a scenario about Mayakovsky. We did write a vaudeville, about bartering over an exchange of apartments. We thought up a drama somewhat in the vein of Priestley's *Time and the Conways.* Along with a friend, we worked on a satirical novel about a certain citizen Evanov.

Lyonya was frequently dissatisfied with himself. In his diary he wrote: "How little I've succeeded in, how little I've done. And there was no end to the number of opportunities, only I should have had more patience, more industriousness, and more self-confidence. Of course, it's very difficult to admit such things even to oneself. All the time I keep thinking that now I'll make up for it, but time passes by once more, the years of consequence keep piling up [he was twenty-four!], and yet hardly much more has been accomplished. Frustrating!"

In 1939 we conceived the idea of creating an anthology about remarkable people. Four of us went to the Young Guard Publishing House to see the editor Olga Ziv. She drew up a contract with us, inexperienced unknowns that we were, and sent us off on our research.

How essential it is that the first important person in your life should believe in you. Whether it be your first friend, your first lover, your first commander, your first editor. We were lucky—we met that kind of editor. I regret that I am writing this only now, after the death of Olga Maksimovna Ziv.

Are there many editors today, including former students of our institute, who would believe in young people?

Lyonya and I traveled to Kiev, where I stayed, while Lyonya continued on to Odessa (he was writing about Eisenstein and the film *The Battleship Potemkin*). He flew for the first time in his life. In an ordinary passenger aircraft, the flight probably lasted for an hour and a half in those days, but to me it seemed to last an eternity. And Lyonya made the honest confession to me that he was very much afraid of flying, but that evening he telephoned me in Kiev and triumphantly informed me that everything was all right. A year later, as though it were something completely matter of fact, he wrote in his diary: "I spent a lot of time with the units, worked a great deal, and on top of it all, flew on a combat mission as a full-fledged member of the crew for two days in a row."

He was entirely aware of the dangers. "At headquarters I watched them signing the letters that began with the words 'Dear Mrs. . . .' The content is familiar. Wartime. I have estimated that one person dies every second. Every second!"

He used to read books almost in a drunken stupor. While still a schoolboy, he fell in love with O. Henry, he knew by heart Ilf and Petrov's *The Twelve Chairs* and *The Little Golden Calf*. He read and reread Chekhov, Mark Twain, Anatole France, discovered Sherwood Anderson, Ambrose Bierce, John Dos Passos, and Ernest Hemingway.

In the summer of 1936, after the end of our first year at the institute, we were in military camps near Moscow. There, one evening, after our military exercises, we learned that Gorky had died. We gathered in a single tent. One student recited Gorky's *Italian Tales*. I don't recall that Gorky loomed large in our thoughts before, but at that moment we felt like orphans. The authorities would not give us permission to attend the funeral. So we organized our own impromptu procession without their permission, made our way on foot, and formed part of the over-all procession.

Lyonya was familiar with Mayakovsky's work and loved him a great deal. Mayakovsky was not simply a poet. He was everything: a legislator, a judge, a mentor. Lyonya loved him at a time when he was not being published extensively. We were far from understanding everything in Mayakovsky's verses, but we tried very hard to understand, to study, to interpret every line. We tried to grow and raise ourselves to his level. We measured everything around us by his standards. We hated his enemies and all of those with whom Mayakovsky fought.

At times we used to take it into our heads: "Maybe Mayakovsky was even murdered? And it was staged as a suicide?" At that time we could not believe that such a man as Mayakovsky could have committed suicide.

Stalin's words in 1935 to the effect that Mayakovsky was "the best, the most talented poet" and that "disrespect for his memory is a crime" were reason for personal rejoicing. Our poet, our very own poet had been recognized.

Lyonya wrote his term paper on the topic "Heine and Mayakovsky."

Vladimir Yakhontov* played a large part in our attitude toward Mayakovsky, and he was the one who taught us how to hear, understand, and distinguish not the cry but the moan of the poet. Yakhontov could be sitting in an armchair, playing with a rose, and Nastasya Filippovna from Dostoevsky's *The Idiot* would come alive before your eyes. Or there he was creeping stealthily about the stage like a cat, reciting Pushkin's narrative poem *Count Nulin*. His performances were a part of our education, more important than the lectures themselves when in the hall of the students' club at Moscow State University the crowd of ecstatic youth would scream out as they clapped their hands in time: "Ya-khan-tav!!!"

Dimitrov,† a person who was transformed from an accused into a judge, spoke with the voice of Yakhontov. What we read about in the newspapers became art in his compositions.

Lyonya loved the theater a great deal, especially the Moscow Art Theater. He knew all the actors. We saw Bulgakov's *The Days of the Turbins* about fifteen times, no less. For long and desperately happy nights we would stand in lines in order to get tickets for *Anna Karenina*.

Together we saw current Soviet films and Chaplin's *Modern Times* and *City Lights*. He loved those films. And the newsreels. The newsreels were similar to the newspaper.

It was from Lyonya that I first heard the verses of Eduard Bagritsky, Nikolai Aseev, Ilya Selvinsky, Yaroslav Smelyakov, and Rudyard Kipling. It was with particular enthusiasm that he recited Bagritsky's *The Man from the Suburbs* and poems from *The Last Night*.

We had a poor knowledge of Pasternak, although we did try to

---

* Vladimir Nikolaevich Yakhontov (1899–1945), Russian actor, one of the best interpreters of classical and modern Russian poetry.

† Georgii Dimitrov (1882–1949), a Bulgarian Communist who had been accused of helping to plan the Reichstag fire of February 27, 1933; later, president of the Communist International (Comintern).

understand him. We knew almost nothing of the poetry of Akhmatova and did not know about the existence of either Tsvetaeva or Mandelstam.

Lyonya was constantly writing. He was not at all intimidated by a blank sheet of paper. But he was too shy to read his verses aloud, even to friends. "It's already the fifth month of the war, and I keep trying to record what I see, hear, and think . . . But the days go by, everything takes wing from my memory, and later you'll never forgive yourself for that, if, of course, you do stay alive" (October 24, 1941).

"*Izvestia* keeps after me all the time and they've sent me an official commission, but I simply don't have the time to write. We literally have no time to sit down at a table. Our paper is now four pages long and soon we want to make it a daily. The material I have now (judging from my own impressions) is particularly interesting. But I just can't sit down to it. If I can visit you, if only to have a brief rest (to have more than four and a half hours of sleep in a row, which is the norm that I have now established), then perhaps I will write."

He did not like to whine, he did not like people who whined, and he did not like failure or people who failed. With relish he frequently repeated the words from Ilf's notebooks: "Let us drink to those who succeed." He strove to avoid unpleasantness, trials and tribulations, and ugliness. Naturally, no one strives for what is unpleasant. But there are people who meet misfortune head-on, who wallow in misfortune whenever possible. Lyonya was one of those who wished to avoid it.

He seemed predestined for an easy and pleasant life. He liked to eat well, to linger with friends in a restaurant. Sitting at home over tea with the invariable ring-shaped crackers, Lyonya and our friend Marina could spend hours composing a menu of extraordinary luncheons and suppers.

Once, a talented artist and student (who subsequently perished at the front) was a guest at Lyonya's birthday. Taking part in a conversation about food, he noted that personally he could eat an entire goose. And, in fact, we did have a goose—for about twenty people. But a sporting interest transcended all. We made a wager, and Edik ate the entire goose, depriving the guests of supper.

Lyonya was a confirmed city dweller; he did not in the least share my leanings toward a rural life. He could not bear to go on hikes (so

I never succeeded in making a sportsman out of him). He needed Moscow, the noise of Moscow, the streets of Moscow.

He placed what was for those years a considerable importance on dress, and he loved to buy things. He loved to go to bed late and get up late, to go visiting and invite guests.

After the institute, all of our young men were called up by the army in 1940. Like the majority of his friends, he felt absolutely no enthusiasm over this. But he went because one had to. "I am so physically exhausted. After all, a sixteen-hour day of physical work (now we're doing ground work, loading stones, and so forth) over a period of a month and a half without a single day off, that is a serious burden even for a person who is physically better prepared than I am. But I must admit that I'm already beginning to get used to physical work. I can get through a day now without pain. And our day goes something like this. In keeping with the winter routine we get up at 6:00 A.M. and we head straight for the stable. We take the horses to water them and groom them until 8:00. We feed them and then return to have our breakfast. At 9:00 we draw up our formations and go to work. Until 3:00 (that is, a full eight hours) we work without straightening our backs. At 3:00 we clean up the horses once more. At 3:30 we have dinner and immediately (the rest hour has been cancelled) return to work. At 7:30 we return to the horses to feed them and give them water, and then at 9:30 we eat ourselves. After this we have an hour to an hour and a half of free time (we go to bed at 11:00). During this time there are sometimes get-togethers, but every minute you catch yourself on the verge of falling asleep."

He further wrote about the former students around him: "In less than a few months they have managed to lose any signs, internal and external, of culture." But that was one thing that Lyonya never lost.

When the war began, he was a soldier in the theatrical unit of the Red Army. He worked in the literary section, but lived at home. From the first day of the war Lyonya was anxious to get to the front.

He bombarded all the military departments with his applications. It was more difficult in the army to get oneself transferred than to simply leave civilian life and turn up at the front. But by August 1941 he got his wish and ended up on the divisional newspaper *Za pravoye delo* (For the Right Cause), in the Long-Range Aviation. Even then he did not rest until he started to fly as a regular crew member.

The war began for us even before June 22. We were living the whole while beneath the advancing shadow of war.

When our daughter, Sveta, was born in January 1940, the ski battalion from the Institute of Philosophy, Literature, and History was departing for the Finnish front. Lyonya telephoned the maternity hospital and informed me in a dispirited voice that he had not been taken because they had only taken the good skiers. He was in a hurry, he was afraid that he would not make it in time. He did make it. On September 12, 1941, he wrote in his diary: "And none of us can say whether we shall all meet together once more. Marina and I were talking today about how we would celebrate our victory. She said that we would probably be sad. There would be many missing from our midst. But I believe that all the same it will be very cheerful. And if I won't be there, then let someone remind Marina about this."

He believed in the future. In verses that were dedicated to our as yet unborn daughter (we both firmly believed that it would be a daughter), he wrote:

> *We shall name you Svetlana*
> *And lead you forth into the world.*
> *Take this world*
> *As a present from us.*
> *And as children always do,*
> *Look to see what's inside,*
> *Open wide*
> *And see.*

VII

Faith

I'm attending evening mass in Kaunas, in the basilica. It's July 1966. For the first time in my life I am *sitting* in a church. The pews are high and my feet do not reach the floor. I can put my feet on the wide ledge below. This ledge is for kneeling.

An ordinary Roman Catholic church doesn't belong to the outstanding creations of world architecture. And for that reason the ritual that has been carefully considered and hallowed by the centuries stands out all the more clearly: the sounds, the colors, the words, and the effusion of light have their effect on you.

The cathedral is large. There are a lot of people, but empty spaces exist. For the most part there are old women. A young couple is behind me. He's wearing a blue jacket with a light-blue shirt buttoned almost to the top. No tie. This style is semiformal. Other men are formally dressed in black. The girl is obviously bored—she keeps turning her head, she's not listening, she's tugging her companion by the sleeve. He's trying to resist feebly, but soon he gives in and they leave.

Quiet but unceasing movement. An old woman comes in with a small boy and kneels down. She pushes the boy down on his knees, forcefully, as though she wants to prove something to someone. Perhaps to her daughter or her son-in-law?

My presence angers my neighbor, with her amber rosary beads. I barely turn in her direction, but I sense that she bears me malice. And she's probably right; she senses that I'm an outsider.

In 1956, ten years ago, I was riding around Warsaw on a bus on the first day of my arrival in Poland. Suddenly it was as though the hats were blown off all the men. At first I didn't understand what was happening, but then I was shown that we were riding past a Roman Catholic church. "The influence of Catholicism is still strong in Poland" was all that I thought at the time. But today it moves me in an earnest way.

God entered my life early. My nurse introduced him. I remember how she appeared for the first time, closed the door, and we found ourselves alone. I started to cry. She sat me on her knees in front of the window (the very same window from which my grandson now looks out onto the world) and began to tell stories. At that time the four sharp spires of a Protestant church on Stankevich Street were visible through the window. Nanny said that when I got bigger, she and I would visit all the churches.

She was impassive and ascetic, a round face with fine wrinkles, and a minuscule bun tied up in a white kerchief in the back of her head. She lived for twenty years with us. I can only recall her as an old woman. She was not about to wait until I got bigger, and she took me to church. I kissed the Iverskaya Icon* with fervor, I imitated everything my nanny did. Nanny's God was kind. It was easy to talk to him. He readily forgave you and absolved you of your sins.

Nanny loved to drink. On Saturday and Sunday she would drink a little and offer some to me, but I didn't like vodka. On holidays she would go to visit her sisters, somewhere in the Tverskaya-Yamskaya District (in those days it seemed to be a real journey), and she often took me with her. There was a lot of drinking, noise, swearing, and fighting there. We would return home and drop in at our church on Bryusovsky Lane. "Oh, Lord, I, your servant, have made you angry, I am leading a sinful life," Nanny would begin noisily. And I too would imitate her and repent before God the Almighty. I didn't know why I was being repentant, but God loomed over all of my childhood actions, games, and fantasies.

In fact, there was not one but two gods in my childhood. Grand-mother—my mother's mother—lived with us; she was very old. She slept in the middle room, and I can only recall her lying in bed. It was stuffy in there and smelled bad and was somehow frightening. Grandmother told me stories about her God, about the Bible. Grand-

---

* A well-known icon on the Voskresenskie Vorota (Gate) at the entrance to Red Square. It was destroyed in the early thirties.

COLLEGE OF THE SEQUOIAS

LIBRARY

mother's God (in contrast to Nanny's) was malicious, hurled stones, and was forever doing battle. For a long time stones remained for me the sole image of the Bible. Perhaps it was also because Nanny and Grandmother were ever at odds, and I was always on Nanny's side.

My parents were not believers—I cannot recall a single conversation about religion in my childhood. I cannot say precisely how and by whom my childhood faith was undermined. And thus that spring day came in my life. I was returning home from school. As was usually the case, I would frequently pause along the way. In that spot where now stands the lofty bronze horseman Yury Dolgoruky* (but in those days stood the Obelisk of Freedom), it suddenly dawned on me: there is no God. For the first instant I felt bathed in a cold sweat, so terrified was I. Right then, right at that very moment I should have been swallowed up by the earth. Or the Lord should have sent a thunderbolt down upon me. I stood there; everything was calm around me, people were walking, laughing, and chatting.

There is no God. I felt like shouting, like tempting fate. I wanted to shout loudly: "There is no God!" Everything was calm as before.

What should I do now? How was I supposed to live? What would I say to Nanny? I still continued to go to church with her for some time, but it grew more and more awkward.

Meanwhile, another religion was entering my life.

Much later, after this chapter was written, I read the following in *Self-Knowledge* by Nikolai Berdiaev:† "Totalitarian communism is a pseudoreligion. And it is precisely as a pseudoreligion that communism persecutes all religions, persecutes them as a rival."

In a letter from exile (May 1980), Andrei Sakharov states: "The communist ideology in the Soviet Union, its ideological epicenter, emerged from a striving for truth and justice, just as did other religious, ethical, and philosophical systems."

My earliest recollection of this religion dates from January 1924. I am five years old. I'm looking out the window. Crowds and crowds

---

* Grand Prince of Kiev and the founder of Moscow (1147). The monument was erected in 1954.

† Nikolai Aleksandrovich Berdiaev (1874–1948), a leading Russian religious philosopher and mystic; associated with existentialism. He was exiled in 1922.

of people are walking along Tverskaya Street, going to bury Lenin. All the grown-ups are there on the street. I start to cry and beg them to take me. We children (I and my month-and-a-half-old sister) have been left at home with Nanny. It's cold. I'm looking out the window and more than anything else in the world I want to be there, with everyone else, in those stern and solemn processions.

In 1928 I was accepted into the Pioneers. "I, a young Pioneer of the USSR, solemnly swear before my comrades that I shall firmly support the cause of the working class in its struggle to liberate the workers and peasants of the entire world . . ." I remember the words from those times by heart.

I was certain that I had ceased to believe in God. A childhood in the Pioneers, a youth in the Komsomol.

In fact, I became a communicant, I entered a new church for a long time to come . . .

The movement continues in the Catholic cathedral. My neighbor keeps turning around sharply and with disapproval: tourists have come in, all tanned and carrying knapsacks, and the girls are in slacks. They gaze around, exchange whispers, peer into their guide-books, and quickly leave.

Sitting on a pew in front of me is a woman whom I would have taken for a trade-union activist on the street: closely cropped hair, worn briefcase. She is fingering rosary beads that look like pearls. She is fingering them in time to the organ. She is sitting on the pew, but from time to time she kneels down and then just as unexpectedly straightens up. As though she were hearkening to a bell that I can't hear. On the bell's cue people enter the church, on cue they complain to God, on cue they confide all their secrets to him and confess.

A family has come in: a father, a mother, and two children. They are dressed up as if for a holiday. Isn't that the family that was dining beside us in the Tulip Restaurant? An extended holiday program: first the restaurant, then church.

A woman had just entered, put down her two heavy baskets, and sighed. Apparently she has come a long way—for Sunday market tomorrow, and for God today.

When the mass ends, I leave the church behind three older men. In front of the altar they are performing the habitual action of something resembling a bow and then the action of crossing themselves, but once out on the street they start a businesslike negotiation about sharing a bottle of vodka. Render unto God what is God's, but life goes on in its own fashion.

When Father started to take me to the conservatory, I couldn't listen to the music and out of boredom I counted the pipes in the organ. Every time it would come out a different number. Consequently, to this very day I don't know how many pipes there are in the organ at the Moscow Conservatory.

But in the Catholic cathedral in Kaunas I was no longer counting the organ pipes during the mass. The solemn music permeates you like air, and when the organ falls silent, the walls, the cupola, the altar, the sculpture all reverberate in a soft echo. The church is alive with sound.

How strange to sit in a church! How many times I read about this in English and American novels and saw it in films. People are constantly coming to God, it is a part of everyday life, they want to be in God's company with all the comforts.

In our student years we used to read aloud the journal *Ateist* (The Atheist) in the workers' dormitories. For every reading, the publishers for some reason or other used to pay the fabulous sum of 25 rubles. I don't recall a single question or a single argument; there simply wasn't any. Either the workers listened to us or pretended that they were listening. My atheism was subjected to no tests.

In September 1942, after a long interval, I once again went to the church on Bryusovsky Lane. Grief had come crashing down on me. My husband had perished.

I wanted to be alone, but I was not allowed to be. For three days someone was always sitting beside me and walking around me. On the fourth day I simply ran off and hid in the church.

Women were praying in the cool semidarkness, and they were dressed in black. I too was in black. No one looked at me, no one asked about anything. There was no service that day. At long last I had found a refuge and silence, something I had been striving for all of those seventy-two hours that had stretched out into an entire lifetime. Here I was able to weep quietly, to reminisce, to dream about a miracle, to return to our love.

Each day I would leave an hour or hour and a half early and on the way to work cross the threshold into the church. I gazed at the icons, but my mind was elsewhere. People were dying, my friends, people who were quite young. They were dying in the trenches, in the field hospitals, behind the barbed-wire fences of German prison camps.

How did Lyonya die? What was he thinking about during those final moments when the plane went down in flames?

He wanted to live very much. Yet on one of the first nights of war, when he was still at home, he said to me simply and calmly: "I won't return from this war." And he, predestined for life, didn't.

From the age of seventeen to twenty-four, I had lived encircled by the ring of his love, I had spent a life that was magically protected from all misfortunes, in the best of all worlds. The ring had disintegrated and I found myself facing life alone, defenseless.

But then I was just like everyone else. My grief was only a small portion of the common grief. "Don't you dare feel sorry for yourself," I ordered myself, but I could not always or immediately carry out that order. In church and only in church I was not ashamed of feeling sorry for myself. "Don't you dare feel sorry for yourself, you're better off than others."

True, I was better off. I had work that seemed necessary. My friends respected and liked me. My husband's death was not followed by poverty—I was earning enough money to look after my family. I was able to allow myself to visit the church before or after work. I didn't have to dash to join a line to get rationed potatoes to boil, because Mama could prepare the soup. And if necessary, one of my relatives could bring my daughter home from the day-care nursery.

At that time I had as yet no knowledge of that other kind of grief, when you lose those close to you but you dare not weep over them except in secret.

I was better off than many widows. But that realization did not console me. Love, that kind of love, would never come again. Lyonya perished, he will never be again. And there was nothing to compare with that kind of grief. The fact that only my happiness, and not my life as well, had been shattered did not make it any easier for me.

The faces in the church grew familiar. I came to recognize people and they recognized me. After about two weeks a woman (we often stood side by side) said to me: "It sort of helps having a cry here, doesn't it?" The words were kind ones, but I didn't want to share my solitude, or my refuge.

Then on the same kind of sunny, clear, and serene day as had once happened in my childhood, I left the church.

As a war widow, I had come into God's house to be healed, by darkness, by silence, and by solitude. I had come to lick my wounds. If I had had a separate room where I could have locked myself in and where I could have avoided the question "Well, how are you today?" it never would have entered my head to go to the church. Moreover, I had been experiencing a vague anxiety: here I was, a member of the Party, and I was attending church.

For many years I had not come across any believers. But now I encounter God more and more in books and people. At times among people close to me.

Before my eyes stands a flooded church in Kalyazin in Kalinin Oblast, a lofty bell tower emerging out of the whitish mist. Run-down churches, with missing crosses, half-ruined and renovated ones on the Volga, in the north, and here in Lithuania.

One of the tourists on the Volga steamer has made the sarcastic remark: "Nothing but churches and more churches, what do they want to do, make saints out of us?" A man of high-ranking appearance said sternly: "Not a single factory on the itinerary, not a single new construction site, nothing but churches and more churches. This should be investigated."

Even a long time ago I would not have thought something similar. But I began to sense and understand the peculiar beauty of churches very late.

How much easier it would be for me today if I could once again believe in God, in the Godman, the crucified Godman in agony of millions of canvases and sculptures! I envy those who can. I envy those who have a church, regardless of which one—Christ's, Buddha's, Mohammed's, or Marx's. I envy the naïve faith of children and peasants, as well as the wise faith of an Einstein or Akhmatova.

I saw Pasolini's film *The Gospel According to St. Matthew.* I saw it and irritation welled up in me. That wasn't my Christ, nor my Nanny's. He didn't resemble Prince Myshkin* either. When he says, "Turn the other cheek," these words contradict his character. And he spews out the Sermon on the Mount with machine-gun rapidity, businesslike and angry. Whereas when he says "It is not peace that I bring but the sword," when he disavows his mother—that is in keeping with him, with his nature. If he is to save the world (and that

* The Christlike hero of Dostoevsky's *The Idiot.*

is how he senses his mission), then it is probably impossible to do so without the sword, without cruelty.

In Pasolini's view, Christ is the leader of a peasant revolution, an obsessed and intolerant fanatic. People probably would not have followed any other kind. But it was that kind of Christ who was for me fully replaced by the standard-bearers and martyrs of my second religion: Robespierre (until he started to spill blood) and Aleksandr Ulyanov.*

One single time, a human smile—for the children. Only when his calvary commences does he become my Christ, the Christ of Dostoevsky, the Christ of Pasternak.

I parted, or rather I am in the process of parting, with my second religion in a way that is different from my first. There was no instantaneous illumination. There were, and still are, difficult years of soul-searching. And how many times during those years I had the wish to return. To return from this wasteland, where there are only questions without answers, where idols have crumbled, and where even though you were not completely crushed beneath the rubble, it was still cold and deserted. To return to that romantic world where old revolutionary songs were sung, to a world where the world revolution still marches triumphantly for someone.

But it is impossible to return. There is no turning back in thought, there is no turning back in knowledge, in perception. Just as there is no turning back to childhood.

Herzen speaks about how seductive the thought of meeting beyond the grave is, but in bidding farewell to his beloved wife, Natalya Aleksandrovna, he does not permit himself that kind of consolation.

As a seven-year-old I could understand little in the sermons. But it was precisely in the church that I heard for the first time that people were equal. That poor people were even better than the rich.

Later I was to be taught the very same thing in school and in my Pioneer detachment.

That little girl heard in church that the kingdom of God, the best world, lay before her. And one had to proceed to that better world not by oneself but as a community, together. I learned only much later that the very word "religion" signified a "binding together,"

* Aleksandr Ilyich Ulyanov (1866–1887), Lenin's older brother. He was hanged because of his involvement in a conspiracy to assassinate Tsar Alexander III.

from *religare*. "The basic religious feeling," according to Tolstoy, "is the consciousness of the equality and brotherhood of people" (*Resurrection*). One had to live by goodness and justice so that this better world might come sooner for everyone.

Both at school and in my Pioneer detachment I was taught that the better world that awaited us lay on earth and not in heaven and that it had to be built together with other people.

Of the three sacred concepts from my youth (Liberty, Equality, and Fraternity), the first two were mutilated. Fraternity depended solely on you, whether to be a brother to others, and that ideal remained pure.

Why was I fascinated by the idea of equality in my childhood?

It was in our separate apartment that we played tag, hide-and-seek, and the three musketeers. My friends all lived in communal apartments. It was unjust, it was shameful that I was better off than others.

Later I learned that Mama never managed on a regular wage and looked for extra work; she took our heavy winter coats to the pawnshops because we had no other valuables. When I found that out, I had a feeling of relief: it meant that we weren't so rich after all.

The first year at the institute I was a Komsomol organizer and I went to the dean on behalf of our honor student: she had been refused a stipend.

"It was right for her to be refused a stipend. So what if she's an honor student? She attends lectures in silk dresses."

He was a fool, that official who had been assigned to the dean's office from some tractor and machine station. But after all, she did dress quite smartly.

The beginning of the 1970s. Lidiya Chukovskaya asked a well-known poet to speak before pupils from surrounding villages at a children's library that had been built by her father, Kornei Ivanovich Chukovsky, a distinguished writer and critic.

"Lidiya Korneevna, I'll do it for you. But in my opinion, no one needs it, neither I nor they."

Lidiya Korneevna was full of wrath: she recalled that Kornei Ivanovich Chukovsky had been expelled from Gymnasium because of the famous law about "the children of kitchen help." And here once again a poet was reckoning that it was superfluous to read his verses to today's children of the kitchen help, half a century after the Revolution.

In my youth I dreamt about equality. Today we have the most monstrous inequality. A kingdom of privileges: in power, in rank, in riches, in connections, and in whatever else you like.

What led to this? Could it really have been the dream of equality? But after all, that dream had been suppressed almost immediately, at the dawn of the Revolution.

Some of those who lived in huts began to move into palaces, and later new palaces were built that were more luxurious than all the former ones. Those who survived from among the former inhabitants of the palaces were, in the best of circumstances, tossed out into the huts, or else into prison barracks.

Later a caste was formed. One inequality was exchanged for a greater one, immeasurably more hypocritical.

The enforced equality of the prison, the barracks, and the kolkhoz is terrible. That doesn't have to be proved to anyone today. Whereas the fact that there was and can be something attractive in the absence of privileges and the refusal of privileges is a difficult thing to convince people in Russia today, and in many cases it meets with resistance.

Even today I feel awkward before those who have less than I do, be it money, the number of square meters in an apartment, freedom, books, or dresses. I am alienated by today's widespread veneration of the gentry. Yet there are more and more supporters of this attitude, and not merely among the ruling people, but among the opposition as well.

I can understand that in different circumstances one is capable of desiring and should desire privileges for other people ("He is so talented"; "He is so sick"; "He is so defenseless"). But one should not desire them for oneself.

We are sitting in the Sakharovs' kitchen. A tense conversation is in progress. The hands of Yelena Bonner-Sakharova are darting over my head: she is taking sausage and canned goods out of the refrigerator and sharing their extra academic rations. Relatives are going to visit exiled members of the family and they have to take them food.

I deeply sympathize with and understand this longing to *share*.

· · ·

I do not belong to the church. But more and more frequently, I enter the empty churches, light a candle, look at the crucified Christ, think, remember, dream about my loved ones, who are so far. I feel more and more deeply how important, how necessary is religious support in order to endure life, in order to endure the horror of disappearance. I ask myself whether religion helps people to become kinder to others, both near and far.

And I cannot take my eyes off the glimmering candle, fading, fading away . . .

VIII

1937

1937—the apogee of the Great Terror, when millons were imprisoned and killed—is a password, an incantation. And the endless searchings for an explanation: how and why did it happen? Like the second part of *Ivan the Terrible*—the red dances of Eisenstein's *oprichniki*. As Maksimilian Voloshin* predicted: ". . . the entire scroll is not yet unrolled."

I was nineteen years old, a second-year student of the philology faculty. From those close to us only Artemii Khalatov, my father's superior, was arrested. Father lost his position and went around crushed. My world had not as yet been touched. True, all that winter I used to wake up around three or four in the morning and lie sleeplessly listening for the knocking and doorbells. I was afraid. Now I understand how many people did not sleep then. And how many were taken away . . .

Meanwhile, the Komsomol meetings proceeded at the institute. People were expelled from the Komsomol "for loss of vigilance." There were almost no protests. I recall that Nina Vitman, a girl with long braids, was expelled, and she said softly but very firmly: "My father is not guilty."

"But how do you know for sure?"

Agnessa Kun said that her husband, the arrested poet Antal Hidas, was not guilty of anything.

Our turn came as well. I was a member of our faculty bureau. We

---

* Maksimilian Aleksandrovich Voloshin (1877–1932), Russian poet who wrote a great deal about terror, Red as well as White, in the first years of the Revolution.

were summoned to Volgin, the secretary of the institute's Party committee. He told us that we were obliged to expel Yelka Muralova and Khanka Ganetskaya from the Komsomol.

How many Volgins I have seen since those distant times, but he was the first.

Yelka Muralova was the niece of Nikolai Muralov, who was then on trial. Her father was the deputy director of the People's Committee for Agriculture. He too was arrested.

Khanka Ganetskaya's father was one of the founders of the Polish Communist Party, a friend of Lenin's. During the final years he was director of the Museum of the Revolution. He too was arrested.

We told Volgin firmly that we would vouch for Yelka.

"It is impossible to vouch for anyone."

We were taught not to believe our eyes, our ears, our feelings, our minds.

We didn't bother to defend Khanka, we didn't care for her much—she seemed to be too much the fine lady. But what did that have to do with political charges?

In the beginning we had the will to defend our conception of justice. At the meeting of the Komsomol a few of us voted against the majority. Then an instructor came from the Moscow committee of the Komsomol and I wrote a good recommendation for Yelka.

Yelka was rehabilitated and once again became a member of the Komsomol. We embraced on the street, in view of the entire institute. Justice had triumphed! Volgin was humiliated! At that time we didn't comprehend that we were only infuriating *them* with this fervent and childish joy.

Our institute marked the May celebration in the grand hall of the conservatory. During the lecture (they were talking about the Constitution, about our fortunate Soviet youth—and those words represented the truth for me), Yakov Dodzin, the chief of the Special Department, that is, the secret police section, quietly called Khanka out of the hall. Yelka had been arrested the night before. Seventeen years later I found out what happened afterward.

The word "imprisoned" was meaningless to me—just a black void, an abyss from which there was no return. It was terrifying to peer into it.

The following day a few of Yelka's girl friends, including me, went to see Dodzin at the institute. We took a long walk, everyone trying to comprehend what had happened and rehearsing what we would say to him. "It can't possibly be that Yelka is guilty."

Slowly, diligently, and patiently, like a schoolteacher, he explained to us: "Children of arrested parents have stuck together, united by their embittered feelings. They have formed a terrorist organization. It's a very serious matter. They'll figure it out there, namely, what Yelka is mixed up in." He begged us and implored us not to go anywhere else, not to ask questions, and not to speak to anyone about this.

Dodzin had kind eyes. Nearsighted ones. How many of us did he save in those years? He was protecting us. And we allowed ourselves to be protected.

The retribution began soon. I was expelled from the bureau. Another was expelled from the Komsomol. The reprimand that I and two others received was "for the loss of political vigilance as expressed in the defense of the enemies of the people."

Our doubts and timid attempts at protest were quickly cut off. You really can't make an omelette without breaking eggs.

Papa and I were standing in the living room listening to the radio. Again they were broadcasting something about vigilance, and he asked me: "What if I'm arrested?" And without stopping to think for a moment I said: "I'll reckon that you have been arrested for a reason." I said that and the floor did not heave under my feet, and there was no fire or brimstone—nothing. God was merciful to me, and Father was not arrested.

Did he accept my monstrous words as his proper due? He himself said it was the only way to look at it.

But perhaps that wasn't the answer he was hoping for? Otherwise he wouldn't have asked me.

I don't want to try to justify myself; indeed, that would be impossible. But in those years I was constantly arguing with Father, and I was always defending something that was directly opposite to what he was saying. It was that kind of youthful bravado.

Today it seems fruitless to ask oneself the question: did I really believe that? Perhaps, in fact, automatic words had outstripped automatic actions? After all, I did know my own father better than Yelka.

In those years there wasn't a person near me who would have thought otherwise. That is, such people did exist and somewhere quite close by, but I did not see them, I did not hear them. And, naturally, they had no desire to be close to me, they didn't trust me. I had a loving husband whom I loved, I had loving friends and a family that I loved. But there was no one who might have attempted to change my mind, no one who might have taken me away from the meeting: "Don't vote. At least don't add your voice to the others." But no, I added my voice to everything. A deathly silence, a deathly cry, everyone votes yes.

In 1956 I was at the home of a literary critic on some editorial business. She said to me: "Nothing has changed around us. But if I'm arrested tomorrow, no one will believe that Yelena Usievich is an enemy of the people." That was truly a substantial change for my generation and the older generation, for those who had lived through it all. But what about the young people?

A December evening in 1960. I had arrived from Peredelkino* for the twentieth-anniversary reunion of our graduating class. I was supposed to deliver the opening address. I didn't recognize many of the people in the lobby of the Hotel Prague. Being very nervous, I uttered the sacramental phrase: "I am happy that those who have been wrested from our ranks by cruel and unjust circumstances are here with us." Sitting there were Yelka, Khanka, Dima Yasny, Leonid Pinsky, and other people who had been arrested after we graduated from the institute.

Only in 1956 did I begin to understand what had happened to them and to us. Yelka's shattered life, her beautiful and haunted eyes.

At the reception in the Hotel Prague we drank wine, delivered toasts, and reminisced: only the memories united us.

As I walked home, I kept thinking that, in fact, I too had had a hand in the crime. In the silence. In the cowardice. Even in the cover-up.

In *Within the Whirlwind* Evgenia Ginzburg writes:

When you can't sleep, the knowledge that you did not directly take part in the murders and betrayals is no consolation. After all, the assassin is not only he who struck the blow, but whoever supported the evil, no matter how: by thoughtless repetition of dangerous political theories; by silently raising his right hand; by faint-heartedly writing

* Writers' colony 25 kilometers from Moscow.

half-truths. *Mea culpa* . . . and it occurs to me more and more frequently that even eighteen years of hell on earth is insufficient expiation for the guilt.

How can I make a judgment of myself when I never went through even a year of hell on earth? *Mea culpa, mea maxima culpa* . . .

We had been persuaded and we had persuaded ourselves, and it really had seemed to us that we had been protecting sacred principles. Yet these same principles were the very ones that were being trampled underfoot by the prosecutors, the investigators, and the jailers.

One day Agnessa and I were walking toward my house and she read me some lines written by Hidas, which he had sent from his prison camp:

> *Through what barbaric sufferings*
> *Do we drag humankind out of barbarity.*

For a long time I lived on those verses. The main thing, after all, was that we were indeed dragging humankind out of barbarity.

All of this did not seem very real (the verses, the letters, and the telegram that came from there or from Agnessa's mother), particularly on the evening of November 7, 1939, when we were reading Blok and Tiutchev and kept thinking that something had to happen.

The enormous line in the prosecutor's office, where I used to go with Agnessa, did seem real. However, once I left, I would try to forget as quickly as possible. The sealed doors in the former Government House on Serafimovich Street were real.

But at that very same time, we were reading Marx, Lenin, Stalin and it seemed that the world was expanding and that we had to learn to think and to absorb Marxism in a creative fashion. I marveled at the clarity of *The Short Course**—that falsified history of the country and the Party. The book contained philosophical and moral (immoral!) conceptions, everything that every citizen of the country should have known. The book fulfilled the function of a standard reference bible for that time. I understood that the ideas of Marx and Lenin were more significant, complicated, and profound, but I reckoned that on the other hand this book had been meant for the masses.

I am writing this on a summer day in 1961, at the dacha. I am

* *Short Course of the History of the CPSU*, the official Stalinist text of Party history, introduced in schools in 1938.

healthy. I have not been beaten, I have not been locked up behind bars, I have not been driven in convict convoys. All that has happened to other people.

I can do the only thing that is available to me today. It's not much and certainly not comparable to the sufferings of other people. I can tell how the rest of us lived at liberty in those times.

IX

André Gide Returns from the USSR

1970–1975

I am still trying to comprehend that elusive phenomenon: how was it possible to believe?

From the time when I started to remember, it became even more difficult to comprehend. I am summoning the experience of others to my aid.

In 1936 André Gide, who was a famous writer by then, published the book *Return from the U.S.S.R.* Like my compatriots, I found out about it from a special article in *Pravda*, "The Laughter and Tears of André Gide." Mikhail Koltsov, the author of the stern excommunication, had two years left before his own Black Maria arrived.

In 1970 I read Gide's book, which had not become outdated in the least. He wrote: ". . . too often what is true about the U.S.S.R. is said with enmity, and what is false with love." He attempted to tell the truth with love. He accepted a great deal and praised a great deal. Although not a young person, he felt good in our country. He laughed more than he ever had in his life. He felt cheerful: ". . . immense crowds [in the park of culture] behave with perfect propriety and are manifestly inspired with good feeling, dignity, and decorum . . ."

After thirty-five years I can vaguely distinguish myself and my friends in that crowd. In those days we still didn't embrace one another and exchange kisses in front of other people. The height of intimacy was for a man to throw his jacket over a girl's shoulders and take her by the arm. We were a young secretly married couple and we walked along the paths in the park, and the garlands of light bulbs seemed to us to be of an incredible beauty, our own special beauty. We made parachute jumps, conquering our fear. We made boating trips along the Moscow River.

My husband Lyonya wrote verses that were dedicated to Nina Kamneva, one of the first women parachutists. André Gide also made the acquaintance of women parachutists and he liked those brave, sweet, beautiful girls a great deal.

In that summer of 1936 we were at a student military camp outside Moscow. "Sixth Company, rise and shine!"—at five o'clock in the morning. We stomped out in heavy boots, and at times stripped down machine guns. We weren't taught either how to shoot or to dress wounds.

When we learned that Gorky had died, we went off to the funeral on our own, proud of our courage, confident that we were acting the right way, that we were the genuine children of Soviet power.

We didn't make it as far as Red Square, where André Gide was speaking. Nor did we see anything of what Louis Aragon was to depict thirty years later in his novel La Mise à mort, namely, the guards who were shoving the people aside.

We marched in columns, experiencing but one thing: the ecstasy of being part of it. Together with everyone else.

No one had told us yet that Gorky had been killed by the doctors (I was to believe in this lie two years later, when it was found suitable for explaining the extermination of all those around Gorky: Levin, Boris Holtzman, Pyotr Kryuchkov,* and others).

We weren't told that it was all an unscrupulous pack of lies (I only found out about that twenty years later).

Gorky himself was, after all, essentially a prisoner in his own house. Armed agents of the People's Commissariat for Internal Affairs (NKVD) sat in the bushes around his dacha. Even now I don't know whether Gorky was killed on Stalin's orders (which is the most widespread version) or died of natural causes.

Gide was able to capture the soul of a crowd that was united even in its sorrow: "Their happiness is made up of hope, confidence, and ignorance." The only thing he couldn't appreciate (coming, as he did, from the outside world, as well as being the son of the French tradition of skeptical reason) was the degree of our ignorance, or to what extent we had been brainwashed.

---

* Levin and Holtzman, Gorky's personal physicians; Kryuchkov, Gorky's personal secretary.

Yes, I think that nowhere is the feeling of common humanity so profoundly, so strongly felt as in the U.S.S.R. In spite of the difference of language, I had never anywhere felt myself so fully a comrade, a brother; and that is worth more to me than the finest scenery in the world.

My husband, a nineteen-year-old student, wanted to be part of humanity, just as André Gide did. And he expressed it in helpless but entirely sincere verses. Is it so amazing that he adopted a foreign vocabulary when even Gide adopted a language that was alien to him? The famous French stylist said to the Leningrad writers: "So that it is not only in my own name that I am speaking, but when I reiterate my love for the U.S.S.R., I am also expressing the feelings of the vast toiling masses in France."

Gide was so attracted to us because he was looking for something that he lacked himself. Today's French, English, German, and American writers look for that fulfillment in the countries of the Third World. That is how, in my opinion, one can explain the ecstatic articles of Jean-Paul Sartre and Simone de Beauvoir about Cuba, the books about the countries of Africa, the books about China and Vietnam. Even Graham Greene's vegetarian, Smith, one of the heroes of the novel *The Comedians*, full of bitter and charming irony, even he seeks in the bloody night of Haiti what he lacks in his own country, in prosperous America.

Once Gide saw, sensed, and communicated a great deal of what was good, he also saw, sensed, and communicated the anxiety, an anxiety that was all the more poignant and bitter inasmuch as it was inseparable from that very sacrament in the name of humanity. His anxieties and his doubts reached out like feelers in various directions. They reached, as I can clearly see now, into the most vulnerable areas of the system. His anxieties were dictated by a fear: hadn't an error been committed in the original calculation? By a fear from the point of view of the Revolution. Gide himself had never been a revolutionary, but even he had believed for an instant that the Revolution would drag humanity out of its misfortune.

However, he had seen too many poor people, whereas "I had hoped not to see any [poor]—or to speak more accurately, it was in order *not* to see any that I had come to the U.S.S.R." Yet I know that he had seen insignificantly little, that everything had been hidden from him.

The Stakhanovite movement arose. We put together a display about the Stakhanovites and I made an intoxicated speech in the grand hall of our institute: "The miner Aleksei Stakhanov from the Central Irmino Mines, instead of the standard norm of seven tons, has hacked out one hundred and two tons of coal with an air hammer in a single shift."

André Gide asked whether that meant that Stakhanov and others worked seven times worse before than they might have. The reply he received was a bewildered expression and stony silence.

Gide was upset by the inequality: "I fear that a new sort of workers' bourgeoisie may soon come into being. Satisfied (and for that very reason conservative, of course!), it will come to resemble all too closely our own petty bourgeoisie."

Incidentally, he expressed his anxieties cautiously, excusing himself by the fact that he was not an economist, not a sociologist, not a politician.

But there was one area where he felt confident of himself: the realm of art. He was terrified by the unanimity in thought and the government control. On this point he was able to speak out loudly about the threat of cultural ruin. He asked how a poet like Rimbaud, Baudelaire, or Keats was supposed to feel in the USSR.

Life provided the answers to his questions.

Yesenin had already hanged himself. Mayakovsky had already shot himself. At that time Gide didn't know, and we did not know, that Osip Mandelstam had already been under arrest for two years, in a fit of madness had hurled himself out of a window in a hospital in Cherdyn, and had received, thanks to the efforts of Pasternak, who had appealed to Bukharin,* a "merciful" exile to Voronezh.

The state of art was inextricably linked with how a single and unique person felt in society (Gide had no doubt about that). And Gide immediately identified our "captive spirit" with the captive spirit in Nazi Germany.

At that time, if I had been told that someone, even though he were famous a hundred times over, was comparing us with Nazi Germany, I would simply have answered that "he is a Nazi himself."

Gide was also an heir to the ideal of the enlightenment. He believed that it was possible to explain. After all, he had been surrounded in the USSR by people who were educated and who knew and loved the

---

* Nikolai Ivanovich Bukharin (1888–1938), Russian revolutionary, Party official, and Marxist theorist; beginning in 1934, editor of Izvestia. Bukharin was executed in 1938 after a show trial.

French language and literature, people, so it seemed to him, who were of similar mind: Arosev, Luppol, Stenich, and Koltsov himself, all of them translators, critics, and literary scholars (within a short while they all became victims of the Great Terror). They belonged to the first generation of intellectuals. The organic and ongoing connections with prerevolutionary culture had not been entirely broken.

Gide tried to explain to them, and through them to the authorities, that man needs freedom like he needs bread. He tried to explain that it was not a question of him, or even of the Soviet Union, it was a question of humanity, its fate and its culture.

Gide's book was truly dangerous to those in power.

It's understandable why Koltsov was ordered to write a prosecutor's indictment and it's understandable why he couldn't do otherwise than fulfill the order. (He himself knew a great deal. Hemingway gave a sensitive depiction of Kolstov/Karkov's intellectual cynicism in his novel *For Whom the Bell Tolls*.)

Gide's book was very dangerous because it was written with the genuine desire not only to understand but to approve as well. It was dangerous because it contained a sensitive and talented record of those doubts that some people tried to hide (among the Soviet people surrounding Gide, there were probably more than a few like that), while others tried to eliminate the seeds of doubt (and there were some that should have been eliminated). Gide was counting up both the good and the bad from a world revolution—a world revolution such as he and many other intellectuals from the West imagined it to be.

In his autobiographical book *Conclusive Evidence* Vladimir Nabokov writes:

With a very few exceptions, all liberal-minded creative forces—poets, novelists, critics, historians, philosophers and so on—had left Lenin's Russia. Those who had not were either withering away there or adulterating their gifts by complying with the political demands of the state. What the Czars had never been able to achieve, namely the complete curbing of minds to the government's will, was achieved by the Bolsheviks in no time after the main contingency of the intellectuals had escaped abroad or had been destroyed.

That was the historical tendency, but the phrase "in no time" is not correct here. It didn't happen immediately and completely. This tendency was opposed by another stubborn outgrowth of culture within Russia, despite all the old and new persecutions of whatever type.

Nabokov's charge issues from the outside; Gide's, from within.

Gide's book remained dangerous. In 1949 a student of Riga University, Maya Silmalaa, translated *Return from the U.S.S.R.* into Latvian and gave the translation to her friends to read. She and her comrades, members of the French Circle, were arrested. Maya was rehabilitated in 1956. In 1970 she was involved again in a case dealing with *samizdat*.* In 1973 she died. Young writers "were not advised" to go to her funeral.

There is more "positive" than "negative" in Gide, but it was impossible to use his book as support for Stalinism. Yet they were able to make use of Lion Feuchtwanger, with a great deal of success. Within three days, his book *Moscow, 1937* was typeset and issued in a large printing.

I don't know how Feuchtwanger felt rereading his book. In 1949, during the time of yet another campaign, he too was excommunicated for cosmopolitanism. I felt ashamed rereading him. Ashamed for him and for us, and for those who wanted to believe, and for those whom he helped to believe or whose belief he strengthened.

Gide's doubts, Romain Rolland's doubts (they are all still locked up in his diaries under seven seals in our restricted archives), the doubts of Bertolt Brecht ("And what if the tribunal is wrong?" Brecht asks in his poem on the execution of Sergei Tretyakov†)—they represent all our doubts as well.

But perhaps part of our self-justification comes from the fact that if people like that were able to believe, what do we have to be ashamed of in those days?

We do have to be ashamed. They were here only for a while, they were cut off from reality in all manner of ways. One would have had to possess an enormous perceptiveness, intelligence, and sensitivity in order to penetrate through the veil. Each of them, including Gide, was shown how he was translated, published, known, and loved. They truly were translated, known, published, and loved. The incense was part of the veil. It's difficult for a writer to resist that.

---

* Literally "self-publisher"; a term coined after Stalin's death for the practice of passing around uncensored works, generally in manuscript form, among private individuals.

† Sergei Mikhailovich Tretyakov (1892–1939), Russian writer; one of the theorists of the Left Front of the Arts (see p. 76).

But we were living here. This was our country and not theirs, it was our people and not their people who were subjected to incredible persecutions. These were our compatriots and not theirs who disappeared by the hundreds, the thousands, and the millions.

The experience of André Gide makes it easier to understand our own delusions as well as those of others. To understand but in no way to justify them.

X

The Institute of Philosophy, Literature, and History

1961–1970

The heroine of the stage version of *The Member of the Wedding* by the American writer Carson McCullers says "The trouble with me is that I have been just an 'I' person. All other people can say 'we.' "

Many people have their own village. That community of people where they were known as children, where their childhood escapades are remembered, where judgment and forgiveness operate according to particular local laws, where exist one's own language and one's own jargon that are incomprehensible to others . . . One's own household, one's clan, one's commune, one's own army company.

But where is my village? Who, besides my family, will be proud of my accomplishments and grieve over my failures?

Looking back, I think that for me and many of my friends the Institute of Philosophy, Literature, and History became this kind of village. Not simply for the reason that we, its graduates, were people who belonged to the same profession and I was obliged to meet and confront my former fellow students later on in work situations. But also for the reason that we were bound by a youth that was happy, carefree, and unique.

It was called a "communist lycée" and prepared people for a government career, for service to the fatherland. Undergraduate and graduate students attended lectures, individuals who subsequently became well-known literary figures: Aleksandr Tvardovsky, Konstantin Simonov, Aleksandr Chakovsky, David Samoilov, Zinovii Paperny, Semyon Gudzenko, Lev Kopelev, and others. Aleksandr Solzhenitsyn, an external student, came from Rostov to take the examinations.

Aleksandr Shelepin, the future Minister of State Security, studied there, as did Vitalii Ozerov, the future editor in chief of *Voprosy literatury* (Problems of Literature); Fedor Vidyasov, Molotov's future assistant; Oleg Troyanovsky, Stalin's future personal interpreter and later ambassador to Japan and the United States and the Soviet representative to the United Nations; Sergei Narovchatov, the poet and future editor in chief of *Novy mir*, after Tvardovsky; Aleksandr Karaganov, the future secretary of the Cinematographers' Union; and many others. The graduates of the Institute of Philosophy, Literature, and History graduated into state functionaries. But in those days they were just students called Shurik, Vitka, Seryozhka, Alyoshka . . .

Others became scholars, university instructors, schoolteachers, librarians.

There were also those who "never made it . . . who simply became overgrown with grass," as the poet Boris Slutsky put it. Their names are on the marble plaque in front of the Moscow State University in the Lenin Hills.

There, beyond the pale, all our fun evenings, witticisms, good-natured and malicious jokes and epigrams, have been left behind. "Brigantine," the song that spread far beyond the precincts of our institute, was born out of all of that.

On Victory Day, when Pavel Kogan, the author of "Brigantine," was already buried in a soldier's grave near Novorossiisk, people were singing "The brigantine is hoisting its sails . . ." on the streets of Moscow and other cities.

There's nothing in the song about war, revolution, or student life. A vague dream about the sea, stern captains, languid female eyes, a tart golden wine . . . There's no explaining the attraction of words like "filibusters," "the Jolly Roger," "Flint's people." They echoed romantic poetry, both Russian and foreign, but it all had to do with us.

The sail being hoisted on the brigantine was our youthful reverie of liberty: "Just narrow your eyes ever so slightly" and that reverie would arise, an incorporeal and silver reverie to which we were bidding farewell, and to which the people of the new generations are still bidding farewell.

The fate of a song that has become part of folklore is inscrutable. For forty years people sang it, played it, and vulgarized it. It's still being sung at holiday concerts, on tourist outings, at house parties. Like their fathers and grandfathers, the students and pupils of today want to be "rebellious and indomitable," they too want "to scorn penny-cheap cosiness." Even my granddaughter, with her thin little voice, comes out with: "The brigantine is hoisting its sails . . ."

The graduates of the institute who became *zeks** would remember it even in their jail cells.

Meanwhile, it turned out that the graduates of the institute were required to serve not on romantic brigantines but in the real world. After the destruction of 1937, vacancies appeared in the state, Party, and ideological sectors. Vacancies that required filling.

The graduates of 1939, 1940, and 1941 did not go looking for work—the work came looking for them. I filled out applications in dozens of departments, including the Party Central Committee, the People's Commissariat for Foreign Affairs, and the Council of People's Commissars. Like the majority, I had the opportunity of choosing.

A cult of friendship reigned among us. We had our own peculiar language, Masonic signs, and a keen sense of "our own." We came together in a flash and our ties spanned a long period of time. Even now, regardless of the moats, regardless of the abysses that divided some of us, I still repeat from time to time: "May God help you, my friends . . ." (Pushkin).

The Institute of Philosophy, Literature, and History stood out among the other institutes of higher learning in Moscow in those days. The best surviving professors in the humanities, who had avoided the prisons or exile, or who had succeeded in returning from there, were Nikolai Gudzy, Aleksei Dzhivilegov, and Selishchev. The long absence of a philological faculty had its effect. The era of the Proletarian Cultural and Educational Organization (Proletkult) and Left Front of the Arts (LEF) had come to an end.† A different era had arrived, when the "ship of modernity"‡ could be, and had to be remanned and not depleted. The interval was a very brief one: by 1936, the crusade against formalism had begun with an article about Shostakovich, "Muddleheadedness Instead of Music," in *Pravda*. At the institute, in contrast to Leningrad University, no school of philology emerged as such. The institute hadn't existed long enough for

---

* An acronym for the Russian *zakliuchennyi*, "prisoner," or "convict."

† The period immediately after the 1917 Revolution was characterized by experimentation in the arts. Thus, Proletkult sought the formation of a proletarian culture by developing the proletariat's creative abilities, while LEF propounded futurist ideas.

‡ Slogan of the futurists: "Let us throw Pushkin off the ship of modernity" (1916).

the creation of a philological school, even though the scholarly level of some of the young instructors was extremely high. The unique qualities of our institute were not simply and exclusively a question of our teachers. I belonged to that majority of students who were not at all connected with the teachers.

Enumerating the separate elements could not give any idea of the special overall makeup. To some degree it was illogical. The institute was not simply a pedagogical institution; rather, it reminded one of a creative organism, a theater: it appeared and then during the war disappeared. People did notice after it had disappeared.

Perhaps back in 1935 the laws of a selectivity that is so all-enveloping and all-prevailing today had already begun to operate, or perhaps it came about quite by chance, but the sons and daughters of highly placed and important fathers in those days entered the institute.

Lyonya and I simply read the announcement for applications in the newspaper. I don't recall that we felt the least degree of class distinction. Any such feeling was eliminated the following year, incidentally, when almost all of the inhabitants of the Government House became "children of the enemies of the people."

In Spanish there exists the concept of *patria chica*, or second homeland. It is not the place where you were born but the place where you were born into your profession, where you see the birth of your relationships with other people. That is the place on earth that is closer, dearer, and more beloved to you. That is the second homeland.

The place of birth is aptly called our motherland: like our mother, it cannot be chosen. Our second native land—*patria chica*—is the result of free choice and is more like a loved one or a wife: you can fall out of love with it, and abandon it, or you can go on loving it all your life.

For many of us the institute became the second homeland. Not only a counterweight to our first homeland, but bound by thousands of threads to it. At the same time it was an independent and relatively stable community, with its own mores, even with its own language, and without a doubt with its own personal makeup.

Others were subsequently to find other "second homelands" as well: their military units, publishing houses, or schools. And for a long time the gray-headed and graying, the bald-headed and balding, the men and women simply go to pay their respects to these native places, concealing these trips from their frequently unsentimental children.

We used to hang around the institute from morning to night, whether we were busy or not, and we were always waiting for someone. It was embarrassing and awkward to go home alone; besides, no one wanted to go. Naturally, all of this could be explained as being typical of youth. But youth does not create its special voluntary attachment just any time or any place.

My second homeland was densely populated; it strengthened a sense of attachment to people and a responsibility toward others. This jealous sentiment remained for a long time, perhaps even to this day. Who is behaving how? How is he or she performing? What books are they writing? Maybe their important positions have turned their heads? Maybe failure and misfortune have bowed their heads?

There were a great number of gifted boys and girls at the Institute of Philosophy, Literature, and History. It was difficult for untalented teachers to teach talented students.

I recall one meeting. The assistant dean, Naumova, was addressing us. She angrily enumerated the sins of our poets, and, indeed, they did have their sins: our poetically gifted fellows truly "did not attend lectures, did not come to classes, and did poorly on the exams." But Naumova spoke about those people with an obvious expression of personal mistrust and personal hostility. "They are looking for places where monuments can be erected in their honor, but don't count on it, we won't be putting any up," she concluded to the applause of the hall.

The people of whom Naumova was speaking at that time are almost all laid to rest in the ground. Monuments that they have earned with their own blood have been erected in their honor. They still managed to leave something of themselves in the most enduring material: in the word. Many of those who survived entered literature.

So the heart of the matter was not in the rehabilitation of justice in regard to the poets. The heart of the matter was in the applause. The fellows were clapping, base feelings had been aroused in them, feelings of envy for everything outstanding, brilliant, and talented. Lyonya was not mentioned in the "black list," although he might well have been. He was upset both with Naumova and the behavior in the hall.

At that time we were having a rather significant negative experience of collective behavior: there were few who understood the experience of Komsomol meetings in 1937–1938, where one student after another renounced their arrested fathers and mothers.

I strove to find some kind of justification for those who were clapping their hands: why should one place oneself higher than the rest? Let others say you are a genius. Lyonya disagreed very sharply with me. He too did not yet know what all this could lead to. But as is frequently the case with gifted people, he was inexorably attracted to the talent of others and was repulsed by stupidity, meanness, and gray mediocrity.

I belonged to my institute, as I belonged to my youth.

XI

Side by Side

1

1963–1965

In June 1935 the first celebration of the graduation of the tenth grade took place in the Hall of Columns of the House of Unions.

I had finished ninth grade. We were hanging out on Gorky Street,* which we more often than not called Tverskaya and which was not yet referred to as "Broadway."

Our lads were just beginning to drink. The young girls were just getting interested in dressing up. Tamara Zeifert, from the Bolshoi Theater ballet school, made her appearance in our group. I can recall her feet from those days. Later, people were to grow ecstatic over them in various countries of the world when she became the leading dancer in the Igor Moiseyev Ensemble.

Tamara was wearing something incredibly beautiful on her feet. In those days all of us wore the standard rubber-soled shoes. But delicate straps rose directly from the fine soles of her shoes and wound around her legs. We had seen things like that only in the drawings in anthologies of Greek and Roman literature. Later such shoes became the ubiquitous open sandals. But at that time I couldn't tear my eyes away from them.

In June 1935 I found myself for the first time in my life at a "real party," with a gramophone, the songs of émigré singers, dancing, and kissing.

But in the midst of the general gaiety I suddenly ran out of the

* After Gorky's death in 1936, the street was renamed in his honor.

apartment and burst into tears on the street. Why was I crying, what about? I was sober. I wasn't getting any pleasure at all out of what was going on. Suddenly it had all turned sour, everything seemed repulsive around me, all my comrades and girl friends, I myself. I was a traitor! I had betrayed my lofty dreams.

The following morning, in a mood of the most profound dissatisfaction with myself, I opened up the newspaper and read about the festivities at the graduation of the tenth-grade students in the Hall of Columns. I read the speech of one of the graduates.

While I had been indulging myself in the "sweet life," over there in the Hall of Columns a girl my own age was delivering real words about real life from the stage.

People my own age recall that speech to this very day. Apparently that girl, Anya M., succeeded in expressing something of common significance, something that affected all of us.

"Our generation," she said, "has come of age together with the country. The highest mountain is the Stalin Peak, which has been conquered by our country. The best subway in the world is our subway. The highest heaven is above our country: our aeronauts have raised it so high. The deepest sea is our sea: our deep-sea divers have made it so profound. And we want to work, to study, to run, to draw, to play better than everyone else, faster than everyone else, more beautifully than everyone else."

If one were to do a statistical analysis of the newspaper language of those years, phrases like "the very best [whatever] in the world," for the first time in the history of mankind," and "only in our country" would prove to be among the most frequent. But even today, when I reread this speech, I see that she was speaking in a way that was fresh and without clichés. This was a product of both her personal giftedness and an unconditional sincerity. At the age of eighteen, who would think the urge foreign "to run, to draw, to play better than everyone else, faster than everyone else, more beautifully than everyone else"!

Besides, was it only a matter of youth? After all, by 1935 we had attained first place in many areas of human knowledge. The universe was expanding. Discoveries of worldwide significance were being achieved one after the other.

Anya's speech exuded not simply a subjective sincerity. She succeeded in expressing the pulse of the time as well.

In a very short while, many of the original discoverers, like Nikolai

Vavilov,* were arrested; many were killed, their associates were broken, and the discoveries themselves were trampled underfoot. With the result that ten years later the discoveries had to be made anew or foreign experimentation utilized.

When I reread Anya's speech in an old newspaper and set about writing this part of the chapter in 1963, I had an urge at first to strike out her zeal. To deny it for myself and within myself, for she had been an integral part of my former self.

But then, after living through the years, I have the feeling that, no, it is not enough to simply strike it out. I am trying to penetrate at least another layer deeper—to a perception that was infinitely difficult to arrive at or even unreachable: the times were not simply pernicious; they bore fruit as well.

In the speech of Anya M., as in the times themselves, there was a reflection of a resplendence, a reflection of faith: people could achieve a great deal, they could be the first. "Could" meant they had to be.

In the Hall of Columns our common certainty was being voiced from the stage: we would be that first generation of happy people.

Greetings to our leaders (Bubnov, Kaganovich, Khrushchev, Bulganin) came at the conclusion of her speech: ". . . and greetings as well to the one who is the most beloved, whose name is synonymous with mighty victories, to our very own Joseph Vissarionovich. A friendly, youthful, sunny, and joyful three cheers to him from the tenth-grade students!" At this point, of course, there was an ovation.

Her speech was constructed according to the rhetorical laws of those years. Her character, her abilities, her education in school, in her Pioneer detachment, in the Komsomol, had all been determined by this rhetoric, which had been nourished by the myths and legends of the revolutionary struggle, the Civil War, and the new legends about the first five-year plan.

As far as the price that was being paid for our glorious victories ("for the first time in history . . . only in our country"), we knew nothing of that. If someone had told us, we would not have believed it.

In its editorial commentary on this speech, *Pravda* said: "And when the eighteen-year-old Anya M. waxes eloquent over our life and our

---

* Nikolai Ivanovich Vavilov (1887–1942), brilliant biologist and botanist who starved to death in prison.

homeland, the entire hall feels together with her the quickened pulse of its heart and showers exclamations of approbation over her words."

On this occasion, *Pravda*, which means "the truth," had lived up to its name. In the hall there may perhaps have been ten, fifteen, or say even fifty people who would have been thinking otherwise, who would have permitted themselves to think differently, to say things to their closest friends or their parents, who would have been reading an alien literature that was still preserved in a number of homes before the great bonfires of 1937–1938. But the mood of the overwhelming majority in that hall, and in many places beyond its confines, was being expressed by Anya.

If in 1935 a person had appeared on the stage of the Hall of Columns who was courageous enough to talk about the peasants who were starving and who had been driven from their land, about the workers in freezing barracks who were dying from epidemics and backbreaking labor, about the concentration camps, if that person were to speak about the show trials of saboteurs, the arrest of agronomists, microbiologists, Christians, and philologists, about the collapse of our genetics and science, about the falsehoods of propaganda, no one would have believed him, he would have been jeered and cursed. No one would have believed his words even in the unlikely event that he might have managed to utter such words.

The fellows themselves would have trampled that sort of truthlover underfoot right on the spot. No intervention from "official quarters" would have been required.

In the admissions committee of the institute I learned that Anya M. was taking the entrance examinations to the same faculty as I. Then I saw her. She had high cheekbones and round, shining eyes, and reminded me of a Kalmyk or a Bashkir. Straight, close-cropped black hair. I was afraid of her, but she was the first to talk and proved to be friendly and unassuming. We didn't become friends, but our relations were good throughout all of our student years.

To this very day I recall the speeches that she frequently made. A deep voice. Her chest would heave. She didn't speak with just her voice, she was all charged up, she spoke with her hands, her feet, with her entire body. She put her whole being into her words. Every speech of hers had the ring of being her last. She would speak on the most elevated level. Some would be influenced and aroused by her speeches, while others found them affected and artificial. Declamation was one of the maladies of the time. Later, I learned that Anya irritated a lot of people, that many found her insincere. But I was among those who accepted her every word practically with reverence. Whenever I made speeches, I always tried to imitate Anya.

She knew how to seize on what another would drop in passing. Those who spoke to her were stimulated by this to demand more from themselves and to give more. A kind of energy field would be created around her, and everyone who fell under its sway would be transformed. She was talented, although I cannot name the fruits of her talent. Seemingly, there is no name for that kind of talent.

Her best girl friend during her student years was Agnessa Kun.

After the arrest of Agnessa's father, Béla Kun,* Anya and another female student came to Agnessa's husband, Hidas: "You're a member of the Party, you understand everything, you must explain to Agnessa that we cannot see her anymore after what has happened." Hidas was sullenly silent and promised to "explain."

A short while later he too was arrested. Anya reckoned that as a member of the Komsomol, she shouldn't see the daughter and the wife of an enemy of the people. But she didn't act according to reason but according to instinct. She acted according to the dictates of her kind heart.

She began to make the rounds of all the government offices with Agnessa and sent parcels to Agnessa's mother and husband, who were in a prison camp. Hidas came directly to Anya's apartment from the prison camp in 1944 (Agnessa was still in Frunze and hadn't yet received permission to return to Moscow). I was overjoyed to read an article by Hidas in which he spoke of this with gratitude and mentioned Anya and her mother.

Anya was prepared to sacrifice herself. But even in those terrible times, when Anya was helping Agnessa (and not just her alone), she (like me) did not comprehend and did not strive to comprehend what was happening around her.

Anya was a generous person: she did not fuss over money and paid no attention to it. Her father had died early and her mother was in charge of a department at Mostorg.† They lived better than many others. When her mother would inform her friends that such and

* The founder of the Hungarian Communist Party, then of the short-lived Hungarian Commune.

† The biggest department store in Moscow.

such an item would be on sale the following day in Mostorg, people would "thank" her. (Nowadays this is a regular custom, but in those days, at least around me, it was the exception.)

Anya's passionate revolutionary zeal may well have been a conscious effort to counterbalance or atone for the bourgeois sins of her mother.

During the war Anya was working in the Central Committee of the Komsomol. There she met M. O., who became her great love. And, in my opinion, her cross and misfortune.

M. O. was a handsome cossack, the way I imagined Sholokhov's hero Grigorii Melekhov to be. In those days people used to say: "M. is working on a novel." Twenty years have since passed and once more I've heard: "M. is working on a novel."

One of his innumerable ladies, Olga Mishakova (the same one who in 1937 had Kosarev, the secretary of the Komsomol Central Committee, arrested and then took his place), when she found out that she wasn't M.'s one and only, drove him out of the Komsomol Central Committee. He was sent to the front. He was a brave man and acquitted himself well there.

Anya married him and had a daughter.

In 1947 M. was arrested in a scandalous criminal affair (at that time he was assistant editor at a major journal). Anya forgave him everything, sent him parcels, submitted petitions on his behalf, and once more made the rounds of the offices at the prosecutor's. She made trips to visit him in the prison camp at the work site of the Volga-Don Canal. He rejoined her after the amnesty.

Anya squandered her gifts in a suicidal fashion. If only she hadn't had that complete atrophy of will. If only she had not suffered from that mindlessly sacrificial loyalty to a false ideology. It was the same kind of blind and destructive loyalty as the unreserved faithfulness she maintained for her husband.

I cannot call her a hypocrite. Rather, she was a one-dimensional and blindly faithful person. In each instance she convinced herself of the correctness of this sort of perception. The circumstances of our life, of our upbringing from childhood and from our Komsomol youth, facilitated this contradictory thinking.

In December 1962, after a long interval, we met at the Writers' House, where a discussion was being held on Aleksandr Solzhenitsyn's *One Day in the Life of Ivan Denisovich.* She and her husband were sitting in the first row. When the opponents of the novella spoke, the two of them would nod in agreement. When there was praise (there were far more of those who gave their enthusiastic praise), Anya and her husband would exchange angry and rather loud whispers.

Later, in the vestibule of the club, Anya came up to me just as if we were back once again in the corridors of the institute. She was breathing heavily, excitedly, and she declared solemnly: "If one is to believe what you just said [I had spoken strongly in favor of Solzhenitsyn], then our lives, mine and yours, have been lived in vain."

2

1966–1979

The year is 1936. I am completing the first year of the institute. The elections for the Komsomol Bureau are under way. My name is brought forward as well.

"Any objections?"

"No . . . No . . . No . . ."

"I have an objection."

Agnessa Kun. A beautiful girl. In a leather jacket. A red triangular scarf on her straight black hair. Burning eyes. A girl directly out of a poster.

"I am against. Raya is still quite a young member of the Komsomol. Let her prove herself as a rank-and-file member."

The fact that I turned crimson was not important; if only I could hold back the tears. What a disgrace crying would be. I'm wearing a beige crepe de chine blouse. How can I explain to the Komsomol meeting that it has been made over from the lining of Mama's old coat. It would be nice to wear a leather jacket rather than bourgeois blouses. (But in those days a jacket was just as difficult to obtain as jeans are today.)

What kind of nonsense is creeping into my head at such an important moment? The disdainful girl of course is correct. Although it would have been better not to propose me in the first place, rather than . . .

Her name is Agnessa Kun.

The world revolution. Rosa Luxemburg and Karl Liebknecht. The Austrian Schutzbund. The "Marseillaise" in French, the Brechtian

"Song of the United Front," the "*Avanti popolo, bandiera rossa.*" And the leader of the Hungarian Commune, Béla Kun. World revolution is a universal brotherhood. Agnessa belongs to this brotherhood. I dream of belonging.

Agnessa was a special case from all of this. Both in prosperity and grief she was always special.

We became friends. But she would always be instructing me because she was older, more experienced, and more intelligent.

In 1938 a few of us students decided to go to the district committee in order to intercede on behalf of a daughter of an "enemy of the people," Yelka Muralova, who had been expelled from the Komsomol. Agnessa whispered a warning to me: "Don't do anything stupid. You won't help her, you're more apt to do her harm. You don't understand the times you're living in. But if you're going to go, then do it singly, and not in a crowd."

We went in a crowd. We really didn't help Yelka. She was arrested shortly afterward. At least we proved to ourselves that we didn't always fail these horrible tests.

My friendship with Agnessa began after her father had already been shot, her mother and her husband were in prison camps, their apartments had been taken away, and she was living with her aunt and younger brother in a single room on Comintern Street. The past still lingered on in the names of streets. Her leather jacket still survived as well.

Agnessa read Blok in a voice that was hoarse, distant, and beautiful. Blok was her present to me for the whole of my life. And not only Blok.

A regular Komsomol meeting is under way. Agnessa is summoned to the podium. "I am speaking here for the final time. You are about to expel me. But first hear me out. I did not know about the activities of my father. All of that, as you yourselves understand, was secret. Moreover, I have been living for the past years apart from him. I cannot judge what I have no knowledge of. Probably now that he is arrested . . . that will be more obvious . . . Perhaps he had been involved in something . . .

"As for Hidas, I saw him for the first time when I was ten years old. And I fell in love with him. I married him when I had barely turned sixteen. I do know him, I do know everything about him, his every thought, every movement of his soul. I am convinced that his arrest is an error and his longtime friends think likewise, and this error will be corrected. He is not guilty of anything." (I reproduce her words from memory, confirmed by several eyewitnesses.)

She walked down the corridor to the exit, her eyes lowered but without bowing her head. She turned around to face us all for an instant.

Dozens of people went through those meetings. Only two of them refused to condemn the arrested members of their family.

At the institute, as everywhere else during those years, songs were sung and verses composed about courage, albeit of a different kind. But the kind of courage that was demanded in those days at the meetings (and the kind that is vitally necessary today)—there was nothing of that in the "Brigantine."

Each of us had close friends. Agnessa frequently spoke ill of mine, but it was hopeless trying to argue with her. Here, for example, is what she wrote to me during the war about one of my friends of that time: "Do you understand, Rayka, what it means to live inorganically? It means that whatever is subject to sensation, what is natural in life, gropes along by means of intelligence and logic . . . There are people born with their heart on the right side, or with six fingers, but there are also those who are born without a leg as well. So what should be surprising in the fact that a person has no soul? The only thing for that person to do then is to make one up. And as you know, an imitation is a flimsy, worthless thing and there's no mistaking it even in clever people."

When after each argument we parted, her arguments would seem to me to be convincing and irresistible, and I would shrink under her gaze.

An evening at her place. We are reading poetry. Among the guests is a small youth with a thick head of hair: Grigorii Pomerants. An argument starts up over Dostoevsky. Grigorii has just given a lecture that teachers, undergraduates, and graduate students are discussing.

People said that Grigorii was in love with Agnessa. Yakov Dodzin, the head of the institute's Special Department, treated her with great affection as well. Carrying out the inhuman orders, he could not help but participate in the secret investigations, in the gathering of "materials" that subsequently became "cases" and doomed people to prison. But there were many, a great many, that he protected. We reckoned that he was the one who saved Agnessa in those days.

If I had been a man, I would have fallen in love with her without fail. Lyonya objected. "Far too imperious for a woman."

Yes, she was imperious. Particularly during arguments. In those days we were confirmed debaters. No one listened to anyone (we weren't taught how to, and we hardly would have mastered the art of dialogue in those times). Everyone would loudly voice his or her own opinion. Sometimes it turned out that everyone was in agreement, but it was impossible to clarify that fact in the general din.

But if Agnessa's quiet voice was heard, the rest would fall silent.

What didn't we argue about!

"Did Annette Rivière, the heroine of Romain Rolland's *The Soul Enchanted*, act properly, having a child without a husband?"

"Who was greater, Blok or Mayakovsky?"

"Is *How the Steel Was Tempered* by Nikolai Ostrovsky a document or an artistic work?"

"Should you marry a person who is much older than you?"

"Is the law prohibiting abortions right?" (This was practically the only law the justice of which I allowed myself to doubt.)

In 1939 and 1940 a discussion was under way in the literary journals and newspapers. One group of critics stated that a reactionary world view is always harmful to the writer. The great artists of the past (for example, Balzac and Dostoevsky) rose above their views and became great *despite* their mistaken world view. In the jargon of those times these critics were called "despitarians."

Another group was opposed, stating that the relationship between the world view and the creative work was more complicated. Artistic truth often emerged not only despite but also *thanks to* conservative views. They were called "thankstorians." The "thankstorians" were grouped around the journal *Literaturnyi kritik* (Literary Critic), while the "despitarians" were centered around the journal *Internatsionalnaya literatura* (International Literature).

In 1956 Georg Lukács, the head of the "thankstorians," would become the heart of the dissenting group of Hungarian intellectuals known as the Petöfi Circle and would still manage to be Minister of Enlightenment in the short-lived government of Imre Nagy, who was shortly to be condemned to death. Lukács was eventually to write the work *The Prose of Aleksandr Solzhenitsyn*, where he would prove that Solzhenitsyn's works were the apogee of socialist realism. But all of that was in the future, beyond our knowledge and imagination. I'm not talking about Lukács, I'm talking about Agnessa. For the moment she and I are still in the "prewar" era.

Agnessa despised Lukács. One of her closest girl friends, Evgenia Knipovich, was a rabid anti-Lukácsist.

During my student days I felt closer to the Lukács adherents, perhaps because my favorite teacher, Vladimir Romanovich Grib, was one of them. In fact, it was from Lukács's works on Flaubert, on *Anna Karenina*, and generally from the articles in the journal *Literaturnyi kritik* that we studied.

After a regular set-to on world view and creative work, Agnessa said to me, waving her hand: "Why bother arguing with you? You don't know in the least how to think in abstractions."

That was true. Agnessa's hatred for Lukács was also a personal hatred, however. Back in the 1920s, Béla Kun and Lukács had quarreled publicly. They became enemies. Moreover, Hidas was drawn to modernism, which Lukács rejected.

All of Hidas's friends, as well as he himself, were former members of RAPP,* and in Lukács's theories they discerned, not without cause, a lack of regard for their literary work. Lukács did not consider revolutionary spirit to be a literary value.

"So much for them, the Lukácsists. Read some verses." And she would read. We would listen for hours.

Agnessa knew poetry better than all of us. Lyonya always wanted to read his work to her. Agnessa praised some of his verses, but as was always the case, she also added her comments. She and Lyonya would talk about rhythms and meters. Over and over again we would vie with one another in reading poetry. "I remember that evening when I was at your place and we were analyzing Lyonya's poem. The best thing, the best thing by far, was how I made the mulled wine then, do you remember?" she wrote me during the war (October 4, 1942).

In October 1941 I left Moscow together with VOKS for Kuibyshev. It was there that I learned that Agnessa had been arrested.

In those days the rear lines were "purged": people who were born in countries that were at war with the USSR were imprisoned— Rumanians, Hungarians, Italians, Bulgarians. And most of all, Ger-

* Russian Association of Proletarian Writers (dissolved in 1932).

mans. It was at that time as well that all the inhabitants from the German republic in the Volga Region were exiled (and still haven't returned to this day). The Hungarian Georg Lukács was arrested on the same day as Agnessa. He was released shortly afterward, as was she.

From wartime letters:

From me to Lyonya, November 22, 1941. His unit occupied positions near Moscow:

"Where is Anya M., any word from Agnessa?"

From Marina Ivanova to Lyonya, January 25, 1942:

"Lyonichka, if you'll be in the city, I beg you to telephone or drop in on the Kuns (Tel. K 4 57 59) to find out any news at all about Anya . . . Does anybody know anything about Agnessa?"

From Marina Ivanova to me, March 11, 1942:

"Rayek! Did you get my postcard about Agnessa? I was so happy that I wanted to share it with you immediately . . . Yesterday I received a letter from Agnessa. She's absolutely all right. They were evacuated to Frunze, and as fate would have it, Kolya, the aunt, and Eva* had been evacuated to the very same place. It was completely by chance that they met there. There's good luck! Now they are all living together. Write her c/o *poste restante*: Post Office, Frunze, Kirghiz SSR. Obviously her recuperation was very hard on her. I ascribe all of that to her remarkable mind, in which I always had faith. I had faith in another, in a greater happiness, when despite everything a faith in one's friends overrules all else. I'm very happy with all of these events."

To Lyonya from me, March 14, 1942:

"Very good news: Agnessa is in Frunze with her aunt and Kolya. I wrote her and sent her 150 rubles."

A quarter of a century later. November 1966. A new era. In the hall of the Writers' House the first part of *Cancer Ward* is being discussed. Aleksandr Solzhenitsyn is in the presidium. One of the speakers tells how his father was shot in 1937 and continues: "I was a soldier in the NKVD forces. In September 1941 we were ordered

* Hidas's daughter from his first marriage. She subsequently committed suicide.

to arrest and remove from Moscow those who were, so we were told, Nazis and fifth columnists. Only after reading *Cancer Ward* did I learn who those people were and what later became of them."

Perhaps he was the one who took Agnessa or Lukács from their homes on that September night.

One past overtakes the next and is crossed out by the other. Today all of this seems unreal: Solzhenitsyn diligently recording all the speeches in the Writers' House, everybody urging the publication of *Cancer Ward* . . .

Agnessa repeated a great number of times that the most important thing in the world is love: "The kind of love that Hidas and I have does not exist, it never has and never will." I accept that as an absolute truth. Our love has not experienced trials and tribulations.

She obviously patronized Lyonya and me. She liked me as well because I was loved. I don't recall a single instance of jealousy or even of bitterness: we were together whereas she was alone. Bitterness would have been quite understandable.

When I gave birth to my daughter Sveta, she was among those few of our closest friends who together with Lyonya drank champagne in some gateway near the maternity home.

Learning of Lyonya's death (August 30, 1942), she sent me a letter (September 16, 1942): "You know yourself that you can never believe in such utterly horrible things, they seem not to have happened, they seem unreal. That is the atavistic structure of our human brain.

"I know and understand everything that is happening to you: to express it in medical terms, it's necrosis, a deadening of a part of your soul and your heart . . .

"Despite all the sundry things that have happened to me in my life till now, I have always possessed a childish faith in its justness, as long as justice triumphed in the end. What has happened to Lyonya flouts that conviction with a ruthless cruelty. It is very unjust, inexcusably unjust . . ."

A little later she wrote to me: "I receive good and cheerful letters from Hidas and Mama. They are real people and of course they possess amazingly vital powers. However paradoxical it may seem, the following words by Blok suit Hidas: 'And I am young and fresh and in love.' Physically he also feels better and he's working as a medical orderly in a hospital. I have been writing constantly on his behalf, but there is no response. I fear that right now the time is not very suitable."

On every letter there is a stamp: "Passed by the military censor." It never occurred to me that we could be doing something prohibited. We were simply talking about the fate of Agnessa's husband.

The fact that she had been arrested, that she had spent four months in jail and in transit camps, she only told me once many years later.

On one occasion Lev started to reminisce about his prison camp episode in humorous terms. Agnessa furiously interrupted him. "Silence! Hidas and I never talk about THAT!"

Immediately after Hidas's arrest, Aleksandr Fadeyev* and some more of his comrades from RAPP interceded on his behalf. Perhaps this intercession did in fact help to free him in 1944, when few people were being set free.

For the first time I saw Hidas in their new room on Banny Lane, and he was still very handsome. It was then for the first time that I heard the name of Sándor Petöfi, the nineteenth-century Hungarian poet: their translations of the Hungarian poets had begun, and this would become a labor occupying many years of their lives.

Agnessa's long friendship with Anya M. was terminated at that time. It ended partly because of M. O., Anya's husband.

"I despise idleness. After all, they get up after midday, when the workers are finishing their noon break. There's a mountain of yesterday's dirty dishes, herring heads on newspaper, and cognac bottles on the table. That is, if they hadn't spent the evening before sitting in the Aragvi Restaurant. Hidas had been asking me for a long time to end it, and I can't put up with it any longer."

Yes, Agnessa isn't making any of it up. And still . . . After that kind of friendship, when Anya had so selfishlessly and devotedly shared Agnessa's grief. How could it be?

Agnessa continued to denounce my friends. Where did N. get her money from? Why isn't K. working anywhere? How could R. live on the support of her husband's parents, whom she still curses constantly?

Agnessa frequently proved to be right in her vicious judgment of people and events. But I never extracted any lessons from this rectitude of hers. I was repelled by it in the same way as I was repelled

---

* Aleksandr Aleksandrovich Fadeyev (1901–1956), at that time, head of the Writers' Union. He had to sign orders approving the arrest of all writers. Fadeyev committed suicide.

in my early youth by suspiciousness and vicious gossip. That never changed.

Shortly after our acquaintance, the Hidases came to visit us at Serebryany Bor [Silver Pines]. Hidas was playing with my small second daughter, Masha. I asked Agnessa why they didn't have any children. ("They are both so handsome," I involuntarily thought as I asked.)

"I didn't want to before and I don't want to now. I never wanted to in those days when I couldn't imagine what lay before us. A third person would have interfered with our love. It interferes with the love of others, only they never admit it to themselves."

Talking about a child as a "third" person. That frightened me. That fear didn't pass for a long time.

March 1949. Morning. The Hidases arrived all of a sudden. Usually they sat at their writing desks from morning on. In a whisper, they said: "Startsev has been arrested."

At the time, I was a graduate student at the Institute of World Literature, in the very same department where Startsev, a scholar of American literature, used to work before I had been admitted to the institute.

"Be very careful, don't talk to anyone and don't trust anyone. It's a serious time, and danger threatens you. It would be best to go away somewhere or hole up somewhere."

Where was I supposed to go? Moreover, I didn't feel any immediate danger. But to this day I am grateful to them for that early visit. After all, Hidas himself, like all former prisoners, was under the threat of a second arrest, yet they had thought about me.

When I returned to Moscow in 1953 (after my graduate studies I had taught for two years in Tallinn), they were already living in the older Writers' House on Furmanov Street. The two-room apartment seemed very cosy. In one corner stood an enormous ottoman, and we used to curl up on it and chat for hours. Agnessa would wrap herself up in a shawl. We read Blok.

By my standards, the table was set in a luxurious fashion: three plates each—for the *hors d'oeuvres*, the first course, and the second course. Their prewar maid, Marusya, had returned.

The leather jacket and red scarf had been replaced with fashionable clothing. A purse, gloves, high-heeled shoes, everything in style.

A black dress, a tight black sweater (dark colors suited her). The short hairstyle was gone, and her hair was drawn back in a heavy bun at the back of her head, with the most even part down the middle. Not a single one of my girl friends had such meticulously manicured nails. This was only possible if one didn't have to peel potatoes and wash pots.

I saw her by the big mirror trying on a new dress. A queen gazed at me from out of the mirror. Here we were, wives and mothers, and we were still calling each other "girls"—that was the kind of vocabulary we used then. Agnessa had turned into a lady.

She said to me very sternly: "Look after yourself, don't you dare let yourself go."

All evening long we sang old revolutionary songs. Hidas sang beautifully in Hungarian, German, and Russian. I can't recall Agnessa singing. Choral work doesn't suit her; she's a soloist. But even she would join in our singing after a fashion, she too would open up in the songs. In them that bygone dream of universal brotherhood virtually became real for a fleeting instant. "With the 'Internationale' the human race will awaken." We sang the words with such passion that they no longer seemed dead, cursed, spoiled by falsehood, or stained by blood.

The fifties were under way. Through song we were attempting to resurrect the mythology of the twenties.

I asked Angessa on the telephone to come out and meet me.

"I can't. Hidas isn't here and you know anyway that I never go out alone."

"Why?!"

"I'm afraid of crossing the street. And Hidas is afraid for me. If it's impossible for us to go together, he always takes me there and then meets me."

At that time I thought: she's just spoiled. She's convinced herself and him. They both believe she can't do it alone.

But after all, Lev and I don't like to be apart from each other either. The further time advances, the more meaningful become the lines of Tiutchev:

> O in the evening of our declining years
> How more tenderly and superstitiously we love.

More superstitiously. And after all, they had already been forced to part once and under terrible circumstances as well. Perhaps the hope arises from the belief that if your hands do not let go, then the evil cup will pass.

It's still a long way to the declining years: a quarter of a century has passed since those days.

In 1954 the first *samizdat* (the word became current a little later) manuscript found its way into my hands: Tvardovsky's poem *Tyorkin in Hell*. I memorized a great deal of it at once and I read it everywhere, at the Hidases as well.

Instead of the joy with which my earlier listeners had greeted these verses, they expressed their cool indifference. With Olympian calm and Olympian infallibility Agnessa said: "What appeals to you here? He's just thumbing his nose behind their backs. Nothing but petty intellectual opposition."

"Petty intellectual opposition," that is what we would hear over the course of two decades. On various pretexts. From various people.

"Agnessa, are you doing anything about the rehabilitation of your father?"

"No one asked me anything when he was arrested and shot, so what's the point now. Let them do what they want."

Later, on one occasion, I reminded her of these words that had so shocked me, especially since a significant part of her life had been taken up with Béla Kun. Hidas had written about him in verse and prose, her mother had written his biography. Agnessa had translated all of this, organized the publication, and she had even translated the works of Kun himself.

"I never could have said that. You're mixing me up with someone else."

No, it was impossible to mix her up with anyone else.

She frequently repeated: "No one has the kind of husband, the kind of mother, and the kind of brother that I have. No one knows how to work like them. Mama loves Hidas as no other mother-in-law can love her son-in-law. Hidas loves Mama as other mothers-in-law are never loved."

She assured me, and I believed. For me she became the very embodiment of beauty, intelligence, and talent.

November 8, 1956. Soviet tanks on the streets of Budapest. I'm sitting at Agnessa's. Over and over again we come back to what is happening there. The Hidases are far away from their homeland; they have few ties and they know little. They are distracted and frightened. But their world, erected with such effort and with such suffering, cannot, must not falter. They quickly devise their own "protective" version. "Provocation. Lukács has been lording it up there, it has to be provocation. You yourself know that Communists are being hanged there."

Lev translated for me Wiktor Woroszylski's "Hungarian Diary" and other articles out of the Polish newspapers about the events that were taking place. I was hardly acquainted with Woroszylski, but I believed the Polish poet, who was an eyewitness, and not our friends the Hidases. All one had to do was read our own newspapers attentively and one could realize that this was no provocation, but rather a national uprising.

It was strange that I was forced to defend the Hungarian workers in front of Agnessa.

At the end of 1956 and the beginning of 1957, I read for them the lines of Boris Slutsky: "We all lived beneath God"; "But my Master did not love me"; "On that morning Stalin was buried in the mausoleum."

Agnessa frowns and shrugs her shoulders. "Bad verse and just nose-thumbing."

"You're not right. We did live under a god. Even if it isn't the whole truth, at least it tells part of it."

"You can't do that, give just a 'part.' If you can't give the whole truth, don't bother."

But who has succeeded in telling the whole truth about those times?

Slutsky wasn't *my* poet. But in his verses, for the first time, things were expressed aloud that I and many around me were thinking in those days.

The winter of 1957–1958 was spent by the Hidases at a dacha in Peredelkino.

A dacha (based on my previous experience) meant flimsy partitions, outdoor toilets, kerosene lamps, and wood-burning stoves. To be sure, I never took all of that to mean a lack of comfort; it was a cheap price to pay for the grass, the trees, the singing of birds, the crackle of the pinecones in the samovar.

We came to visit the Hidases and found ourselves in a suburban house. I had read about such things only in novels.

We were talking about Erich Maria Remarque (Lev had translated

Three Comrades and had written an introduction). The Hidases were also fond of Remarque. Lev was telling us about Heinrich Böll, whom we didn't know as yet. China was our new passion. "May a hundred flowers blossom!" was the Chinese call for renewal. We grabbed every issue of the Chinese newspaper in Russian. Agnessa and Hidas (the first in our circle of friends) were indignant. "Can you really believe in that? Don't you realize that it's a grandiose provocation!"

In China (as distinct from Hungary) it really was a provocation: it ended in the so-called Cultural Revolution, in mass deportations, arrests, all kinds of humiliation of intellectuals. The Hidases turned out to be right.

There was another girl at the Institute of Philosophy, Literature, and History in a leather jacket and a red kerchief who also came from an earlier higher echelon: Irina Grinko, the daughter of a people's commissar. She was about to marry the secretary of the Komsomol committee at the institute, Valentin Neupokoyev, a straightforward, handsome, and cheerful fellow. No one had urged us specifically to elect him. Everyone really did like him.

The former People's Commissar for Finances, Grigorii Grinko, was among those charged at the 1937 trial of the Right-wing Trotskyite faction. There was a meeting at the institute, like everywhere else. I couldn't bring myself to look in the direction of where Irina was standing, and yet I could not help looking. That is how her somber face had stuck in my memory.

The students and teachers of the institute, like all the workers of our country, demanded in a single voice the execution by firing squad of these traitorous scoundrels. I voted with all of them. For a very long time I voted with all of them.

She too raised her hand, she too was in favor of having her father shot.

Valentin was summoned to the district committee and coaxed: "Why are you ruining yourself? You have everything before you. We're about to nominate you and you'll get a promotion. Forget about that girl. If you don't, you'll only have yourself to blame. You know yourself how it might end up."

He submitted neither to terror nor to bribes; he took her to be married at the State Marriage Bureau.

Two years later I met Irina.

"How are you getting on?"

"I've transferred to external degree studies. I'm taking the state examinations. Valentin is teaching in a school. I have to earn money: I'm washing floors and cleaning apartments for people. The only thing is that I'm going to have a child soon. It'll be almost at the same time for both of us, won't it?"

We were both in the eighth month.

What heroic people they were: his devotion, her courage, to go through such things.

"And how are *you* getting on?"

"I have to work for a living too. I was a teacher but I had to leave because of my pregnancy. I'm taking the state exams." I'm too embarrassed to say that I go regularly to the Museum of Fine Arts so that my child will be born a beautiful child. I walk miles around Moscow; they say it will make for an easier delivery. I'm being fed on mandarins. But could there possibly be even a comparison? My prosperity weighs on my conscience.

The Neupokoyevs both worked at a Siberian university. Both defended their candidate's dissertations. Irina's was on the literary work of Shelley.

For a long time I had known nothing about her. Then we met at the Institute of World Literature and chattered through some endless session on Gorky.

She was preparing her doctoral dissertation and was satisfied with everything. They had spent several years in Vilnius, and Valentin had waged a war against Catholicism. "A very great power in Lithuania." Their son, Artem, was studying well. She had given birth to a daughter. They no longer suffered any wants, and they had mandarins and everything that they needed. If she was washing floors, it was in her own apartment.

Later I met Irina several times in passing and I would come across her tedious articles.

She climbed confidently upward along a new career ladder. She became an indispensable specialist on literary interrelationships and presided over international symposia, at conferences both here and abroad. She was in charge of the preparation of the multivolume *History of World Literature*. Valentin defended his dissertation somewhat later than she. Their son graduated from a university.

In the summer of 1977 Irina died. Sixty years old. A year later, Artem, who had been born in that horrible time for his parents, murdered his father's mistress. Valentin demanded capital punishment for his son.

Nobody knows the relationship between cause and effect, and unmotivated tragedies occur even in families that do not have the accursed year of 1937 in their prehistory. Still it seems to me that it is those distant mines of a bygone era that continue to explode.

Although Irina, unlike Agnessa, was not very clever, not very deep, and not at all artistic, still, these two powerful and willful natures seem to me to be kindred spirits.

Irina passed by on the distant periphery of my life. Agnessa stood alongside me for many long years.

I'm working in the editorial offices of *Inostrannaya literatura,* and I attend the editorial consultations at the Progress and Fiction Literature Publishing Houses. Sometimes the editors know things that readers don't see. More and more frequently I hear: "The Hidases have got an iron grip. They always grab the largest editions and the highest honoraria."

I block all of that out: Agnessa comes from an unselfish youth that we shared together: Blok, the proud beauty, tragedy. Surely money doesn't matter?

I ask her. She replies unperturbedly: "How is it that you haven't realized until now that money is freedom, money is independence? Sure, we want to have lots of money. We don't steal it, we earn it, we labor from morning till night, with no days off, no vacations. And we don't drink it away like that editorial mob. Who is the scoundrel who gave you that tune? We have earned our money. We've both had our full share of ups and downs. There's been enough of both grief and poverty. Who would dare to condemn us?!"

I didn't dare. But I still preserved from my youth the thought that to strive for riches was unseemly. And it's shameful to say of oneself: "I have earned it."

"I'm not going back to any Hungary."

"But what about Hidas? His homeland is there. He's been living here for thirty years and he still speaks Russian badly. You yourself know how important language is for a poet."

They went for a short while the first time. They returned very excited. Agnessa had not expected that it would prove to be so essential for Hidas. She had loved her father and she often reminisced about him. But in those days, only in Hungary could she once more become the daughter of Béla Kun.

Whether they should go or stay was not simply a personal matter, it was a matter of state. The government of Hungary was insisting that the family of a national hero should live in their homeland. Her mother and Hidas wanted to go to Budapest. Several months of vacillating. Finally they made up their minds.

Their return reinstated them in that lofty echelon (Hungarian now) from which they had been suddenly thrown out of in the USSR in 1937.

An apartment was maintained for them in Moscow. They organized their life in two houses, in two countries. In Moscow there was a multitude of contracts for one-volume editions, two-volume editions, and the collected works of Hungarian poets of the past and present. They came to Moscow not less than twice a year. They could go wherever they wished (they've never been anywhere, they always come here).

First impressions of Hungary: "Everyone lives wonderfully. Plenty of everything. If only it was the same for our people here! [For Agnessa the Hungarians were 'they.'] But they're narrow-minded people, bourgeois, really bourgeois. No soul. At times you wake up and you wish you would suddenly find yourself in Moscow, together with all of you, and you could take a deep breath of fresh air. They don't read poetry to each other there. They invite you to show off their new apartment, a new set of dinnerware and to treat you to a special torte."

As usual, Agnessa was more fierce, more outspoken, but Hidas didn't correct her. They do not see a lot of things. In Budapest they have a private government residence. But a home, the kind that they had on Comintern Street, on Banny Lane, and on Furmanov Street, they don't have that kind of a home. "Here it's springtime and lilacs and chestnuts and the sun, and the birds are singing. But there's nothing to talk about with all the creatures of an animate and inanimate nature," Agnessa wrote to us (May 3, 1965).

As far as the other Hungarian poets were concerned, we heard mostly unpleasant things about them from the Hidases. Our friends who visited them in Hungary told us about their loneliness. People didn't consider Hidas to be the number one poet there, the way we had grown accustomed to doing so here. There were those who obviously wished them ill and who called them "agents of Moscow."

Meanwhile, we were beginning to find out about Kun. It wasn't at all what we had heard in our youth. Instead, we heard about the merciless member of the Revolutionary War Council who, with others like him, had flooded the Crimea with blood, who had given the orders to shoot the White officers who had voluntarily laid down their arms after a promise had been given to spare their lives. I was often told about how he had continued his vicious reprisals even later, when he returned to the Crimea.

But we weren't about to question Agnessa about that: a daughter shouldn't have to be responsible for her father.

Lev was writing about Brecht. The Hidases, like several of our friends, read the manuscript and gave it a great deal of praise (the book *Brecht* came out in the series Lives of Remarkable People in 1966).

At that time the idea also arose for Lev to write about Hidas. They had an outstanding affinity for each other; it was a natural theme for Lev, and no one would write it better than he.

A contract was drawn up with amazing speed in the publishing house. Lev studied Hungarian in order to appreciate the sound of the original. Hidas would tell him the story of his life for hours (he subsequently published a few things from those stories himself). Whenever they came, Lev would read them the chapters he had written. Agnessa and the hero liked it. It was less liked in the publishing house. There they wanted to "streamline" the biography and pretend there never had been any arrest.

In 1968, when Lev was expelled from the Party and fired from the institute because of his letters defending those who had been arrested, all of his works, including the manuscript on Hidas, were banned, and the typeset copies destroyed.

There were some good parts in it: the poet's early biography, the early origins of his poetry as such, and several meditations on verse. As frequently happens with the authors of such monographs, Lev fell in love with his hero. He "read into" the life and verses of Hidas even more poetry, more goodness, and more generosity. Imbedded in this manuscript was a portion of our shared past as well. A past that had not completely vanished (could it ever completely vanish?).

During the time of this work, in 1965–1967, we grew more intimate with them in a new way. They would arrive at our home, we would prepare meat dumplings, Hidas's favorite dish. My mama treated them very well; they belonged to her past, and they were gentle and tender toward her. We would eat with them, not in the kitchen (where we fed all our guests, including all the foreigners), but in the main room. They would bring whole boxes of medicines for our numerous relatives, friends, and acquaintances. They would also bring presents. To this very day I am wearing shoes that Agnessa gave me as a present.

I would send them my books. Invariably I would receive either written or oral reviews from these well-wishing readers. With critical comments. We would argue as we always had before.

And we would spend time at their home. There we would meet friends from the institute days. Disagreements would crop up.

"Is it true that you wrote and spoke out in defense of Daniel and Sinyavsky? Lev, you are shockingly naïve. You're going gray and yet you're still a mere child. Isn't it finally time to grow up?"

You don't notice the way those close to you change. Six to eight months would elapse between our meetings and at times I would note how Agnessa's chin would be sagging, how the traces of her illnesses were beginning to show through more and more (she was getting sick more and more frequently). And simply the traces of time. But then we would sit around talking, and it would be that same old Agnessa and the decades would be erased.

Even now I believe that the Agnessa of my youth has not completely disappeared in the new stately lady. In August 1970 our close friend Abram Aleksandrovich Belkin* died. Agnessa wrote to us: "It's really us who are departing, only gradually. Can you say that it's easier that way? Hardly—in my opinion it's more difficult . . . But then I wasn't as close to Abram Aleksandrovich, so frequently close, as you probably were. I even disagreed with him in lots of things and at different stages of our lives. For instance, in the Institute of Philosophy, Literature, and History, when he posed the question: in what way is Fadeyev greater than Tolstoy? (I never suffered from that kind of dogmatic naïveté) and later when he would make a hundred-and-eighty-degree turnabout on many questions. But that's not what was essential. It was his honesty, goodness, and humanity at all times, both then and later.

---

* A literary scholar (see Chapter 32). He had been one of the witnesses for the defense at Lev's trial in 1947.

"He was one of those people to whom I shall be grateful all my life, because he treated me with such active kindness during the most difficult moments of my life . . . It's difficult for me that fewer and fewer people remain to whom I can be grateful all my life . . . And what's more, I loved his naïveté. For all his intelligence and ability for abstract thought, he was constantly committing recklessly naïve acts, and simply for the reason that it never entered his head that there could exist the possibility of a mean reaction against them."

I no longer heed everything that Agnessa says without protest; more and more often I oppose her openly. The words in the cited letter "he would make a hundred-and-eighty-degree turnabout on many questions" refer as well to our arguments from those days, which even upset her. ("Rayka, at least write, otherwise who the devil knows what I'll think of the change in our relations." Letter of 1965.)

Even earlier there were many who tried to "open our eyes" to the Hidases. A futile undertaking. Ties with people, particularly ties that stretch all the way from one's youth, are something organic. And whatever must die will do so in its own good time. In its own way. If you live long enough.

Throughout my long life I lost friends and acquaintances. For good reasons and for no reason. Life separated us. In the case of the Hidases the decision was made by them.

The Hidases disappeared from our lives in 1975, when Lev's book *To Be Preserved Forever* was published abroad. They came on a regular trip, but they didn't telephone or try to contact us. I asked a mutual friend what had happened.

"Raya, their relationship with you has long since been an embarrassment."

There was nothing essentially surprising in the fact that the Hidases had ceased to see us. Lev had committed acts that were capable of separating him from acquaintances and friends, even good friends who had remained behind in our former world. But the disappearance of the Hidases shocked and wounded me as a fact in itself (even though we had sensed the growing alienation from time to time) because there were few who did in fact abandon us.

At that time I felt bewilderment, although it passed, whereas the pain did not.

Even now I shudder whenever anyone talks about the Hidases in my presence. It torments me to hear that he can no longer leave his bed, that they are thinking only about the end and how the second partner will follow immediately and voluntarily after the departed one.*

One of Agnessa's letters from 1942 ended with the words: "Don't forget me, Rayechka." A great deal later she said to me: "Your urge to remember, to tie together endings and beginnings, to attempt to uncover a unity, is a destructive urge. A terrible urge in its consequences. In a tragic world it is impossible and unacceptable to strive for harmony."

Once more she is right, and at this very moment I am striving to bring together the beginnings and endings. Because the person who has disappeared from my life cannot disappear from my memory.

Inside of me an aching lives whose name is Agnessa.

---

* Antal Hidas died in 1980.

XII

The All-Union Society
for Cultural Relations with
Foreign Countries (VOKS)

1961–1980

When I first came to VOKS, I found a young man in an unbuttoned shirt and without a tie in a large mahogany-trimmed office. He wasn't sitting in the carved chair but on the edge of a desk, with his feet dangling. It was the first time that I saw that sort of director.

Up until that time it had been faceless, condescending, and suspicious people who had talked to me (after an assiduous examination of my application). For the suspicious, I had been a nobody. Perhaps I was only exaggerating the difference. Although even now I believe that Vladimir Kemenov in those days was not to be compared with the people in front of whose desk I had stood in the People's Commissariat for Foreign Affairs, in the Council of People's Commissars, and at the Party Central Committee. At those places you found a bureau for passes and a long ladder of obstacles leading from one to the next. But at VOKS you went immediately and directly to the director of the institution without all kinds of red tape. (It never occurred to me that the elegant doorman with epaulets knew the entire staff there by sight and would be informed in advance about new arrivals.)

I timidly inquired: "What do people do here? What would I be doing?"

"You have to get in touch with Romain Rolland. He's somewhere in the unoccupied French zone."

I gasped. Me? I was going to write to my favorite writer?!

"Furthermore," Kemenov continued, "you'll have to try to restore the publication of a newspaper in China in which Russian culture could be presented."

He saw the kind of impression his words were having on me.

Vladimir Semyonovich Kemenov (like all of the older people, we called him V.S.,) always, or almost always, believed in what he was saying to us. For that reason, we too believed him.

I never wrote any letter to Rolland.

The heroic achievements I had always dreamt of had all been postponed. Until after school. Until after the institute. It was high time for them to begin. Was it possible at VOKS?

I had wanted to be together with everyone else. I wanted the most widespread profession—that of being a teacher. ("I'll be leaving here," said a girl friend of mine from the institute and VOKS. "When people ask my daughter where her mama works, she's not going to be able even to pronounce VOKS. Mothers work at school, in a hospital, at a factory." But she left later than all the rest of us.)

I wanted to be like everyone else. Instead, I entered an elite institution. Even the title was incomprehensible to everyone.

All-Union? Yes. *Society?* No, a government institution masquerading as a society (because similar organizations in other countries were nongovernment, voluntary ones). *For Cultural Relations with Foreign Countries?* Partly. After all, "relations with foreign countries" was a sinister phrase in those days in newspaper articles about vigilance and records of trials. (Later I found out that it came in judicial verdicts as well.)

But our relations were officially permitted ones. We were trying to establish contact between good people here and good people there. To help them understand one another.

Thus, I was assigned the task in the theater section of giving an account of new American plays. The best actors and directors gathered. I was afraid. I had assiduously prepared myself. I was unable to answer all the questions.

It was, after all, a time when there was a hunger for information. Even our meager reports gave at least some kind of information. For that the audience thanked me. And I was learning.

A significant part of the work was quite ordinary and simply boring. We sent exhibitions, books, photoalbums, and articles to various countries. We furnished friendship societies in the USSR with propagandistic materials. In the USA (I worked in the department for Anglo-American countries) they were called American-Russian Institutes.

The majority of the staff members at VOKS were young. We enjoyed ourselves, frequently got together after work and sat for long hours, with or without good reason, in a luxurious house on Bolshaya Gruzinskaya Street, where the embassy for the Federal Republic of Germany is now located.

The president of VOKS, Kemenov, still had close ties of friendship and ideology with the Lukács group.

Before VOKS, Kemenov was director of the Tretyakov Gallery. A year later many of the Lukácsists had gathered at VOKS.

Kemenov didn't bother at all with formalities. He wanted to surround himself with people who could comprehend and embody his projects, people who were keen listeners, the kind of people that he wouldn't be ashamed to show off both to our own masters of culture and those from abroad. He believed us when we brought along our friends to be hired.

At VOKS I had the opportunity of hearing people who were truly remarkable. I proved to be a poor listener and I memorized little. But the brilliant fireworks of the mind and talent of Sergei Eisenstein (he constantly came to us for books) or of Solomon Mikhoels* could not pass by in vain.

Long before the novel *The Fall of Paris* was published in the USSR, I had once listened to Ehrenburg at VOKS in 1940. For about four hours he gave his account, and before me arose the victorious entry of the Germans into France, the evacuation, the dead people, and the unmilked cows.

But I received the most from my colleagues. Many of them, like myself, were ignorant, and we jointly tried to eradicate our cultural illiteracy.

As in our days at the Institute of Philosophy, Literature, and History, we argued desperately, we wanted to understand, and we were frequently led astray onto false paths.

Obviously, it was not a coincidence that more than a dozen doctors of sciences came out of VOKS (I'm not talking about the academic degree but about a genuine contribution to science; I'm talking about

---

* Solomon Mikhailovich Mikhoels (1890–1948), one of the best modern Russian actors, head of the Jewish theater. He was murdered on Stalin's orders.

the specialists). Neither is it a coincidence that people from VOKS have remained among my very closest friends, with whom I have spent my life.

At VOKS I was schooling and unschooling myself simultaneously. The process of my unschooling was primarily moral.

We would send an article abroad—let's say about literature. Among ourselves and together with the author we could talk about whatever we wanted to: was it well written or poorly written, talented or untalented? Was it suitable for publication abroad? But I do not recall an instance where an argument arose as to whether the article was honest, whether it corresponded to reality.

None of us in those days strove to be, strove to become, ourselves. We didn't concern ourselves with self-perfection. There was no such idea, and the need never arose.

And we were all freer than our superiors, like Lidiya Kislova, who was in charge of my department, or Kemenov himself ("I don't want to head VOKS in the least. I want to write about Surikov,"* he said to me more than once). He wasn't deceiving us, but rather he was deceiving *himself*. He was very ambitious; he was delighted, for example, when he went to the Teheran Conference (1943). He wanted to be on top. I believe that his unmistakable erudition (which we valued a great deal and were very proud of) prevented him from rising higher than the post of deputy minister of culture. But that was much later.

We reviewed the foreign press that came to the special depository at VOKS. We compiled special bulletins. We wanted to introduce a certain rationale into the procedure: bulletins came to us from other institutions, from TASS during the war, and from the Soviet Information Bureau. We repeatedly suggested the removal of duplication so that VOKS, and only VOKS, would concern itself with cultural life abroad. But all of that was in vain. I was in a privileged position—I was able to read in foreign books and articles about what had happened in our country during the first years of the Revolution, in the early thirties and 1937–1938, as well as during that wartime period.

Thus, even before the war I started to read the original texts from the speeches of Ley, Hitler's chief of the Arbeitsfront. I was amazed

* Vasilii Ivanovich Surikov (1848–1916), leading Russian painter of historical scenes.

by the constant reference to the workers, to the proletariat, by the word "comrades," by the attacks on Anglo-American (and Jewish) capital. I was amazed, but not for a moment did any thought emerge over the similarity.

My privilege did not bring any realization. I read, but my mind and heart did not grasp any of it. Rather, they rejected it. The portrait of our life that was sketched by foreigners seemed to be distorted in the same way that the fun houses in the parks of culture and recreation distorted people.

June 22, 1941, a Sunday. The war had begun. A meeting in the White Hall. I hand in my application for membership in the Party. And my application to the Military Commissariat to be assigned to the front.

But while the applications are being processed, I have to do something. Now. Immediately.

The hospital for head injuries. During the day: work at VOKS. At night: orderly duty. The smell of putrefaction, the first disfigured faces of young boys. "Nurse, orderly, give me a mirror!" That was most strictly forbidden.

The hospital was evacuated before we were.

A mobilization to gather firewood. Outside Moscow, in Khimki. The beginning of October 1941. Hard work. My back aches. I don't have the necessary shoes or clothing. In any event I still have the quilted coat from August, when I was digging trenches and my girl friends and I were laughing over the German leaflets.

It was much easier than sitting at the enormous desk on Bolshaya Gruzinskaya Street. Firewood for Moscow. Our city would not freeze.

We loaded up the firewood to the racket of artillery fire. The front wasn't far off. We were working around the place where a memorial now stands (that was the closest to Moscow that the German tanks came). In those days it was an outlying area; now it's a new town with multistoried buildings. At that time the whole countryside would have seemed to be Martian.

I didn't want to go back home. I was cold and hungry, but on the other hand it was for the front, for victory.

Until I was drafted into the army (and I was irrevocably certain that I would be), I had to do what I could there. The country was at war. We, the people from VOKS, we had to go on incessantly telling, explaining, and showing: "This is the country, these are the people whom you Americans, you Englishmen, are helping; this is whom you should be helping if you don't want the Nazis to attack you." We tried to communicate our suffering.

We were involved in propaganda. At that brief, unique moment, propaganda was able to approach the truth. We ourselves were experiencing the suffering, we were living through the war: retreat, attack, seeing loved ones off, the evacuation of children, funerals, letters to and from the front.

Both in the front lines and in the rear any person understood that if the English and Americans attacked from the other side, how much easier it would have been for us.

The second front was not simply a political slogan, it was an essential necessity, an invocation, an object of belief, of despair, of jests. Yes, of jests as well. My contemporaries recall how canned American rations were called "the second front" for a long time. And incidentally, they were eaten with pleasure.

How many times we said the following to a member of any English or American delegation: "Just imagine that you are on the shore and someone is drowning before your eyes. He shouts: 'Help!' A real person would dash into the water to help him and only later would that person take a look to see whether he had on a nice pair of swimming trunks."

We had to convince them. At the beginning of 1941 a leaflet was released in the USA by the Russian War Relief Committee that said "This could happen to us!" (Several years earlier, Sinclair Lewis's satirical novel *It Can't Happen Here* had been published.) A map of the USSR of proportional scale showing the Ukraine and Byelorussia under German occupation was placed over a map of the USA. The White House was in flames. What was taking place in our country was visually brought to bear on the rank-and-file American.

This is what we were concerned with, only much less professionally.

There were few Americans who felt our suffering as their own. After the war some of them were persecuted under McCarthyism.

Soviet spies were among the activists in the American-Russian Institutes and the Russian War Relief Committee as well. I know that now that I am writing it. In those days such thoughts would have seemed sacrilegious to me.

Articles that were sent here—watches, warm clothing, children's clothing—were distributed not by VOKS but by the army's Directorate of the Rear Services. But after many memoranda, we too were allowed ("for propaganda purposes") to take at least a small part in the distribution, so that it would be possible to photograph and write about the recipients of American presents. Several times I was among those who handed over these presents to our troops and commanders at the front lines.

"Have you brought 'the second front'?"

Jokes before the festive ceremony. While the troops were being drawn up. Then the rank-and-filers and officers were called off by name. We would hand over the articles, shake hands, and deliver speeches. We told them about who was sending us these watches, about who over there in distant America wanted to help us. And was helping.

One of the educated commanders prompted us. "This is something like the movement for 'Hands Off the USSR' immediately after the Revolution, eh?"

We took it up. And the following time I myself turned to history. "When around the youthful Soviet Republic the ring was being tightened—the campaign of the Entente—committees of 'Hands Off Soviet Russia' sprang up at the rear in many of their countries."

"The ring was being tightened." Earlier these had only been passing lines from lectures, texts, and examinations. But now it was our daily life. There were maps in all the houses, on the streets. And it was apparent that the ring was being tightened.

We emphasized the similarities in aid in the years 1918 and 1941, but we did not see the difference. Meanwhile, that difference was stamped in the very title of the Russian War Relief Committee. It wasn't the proletariat, not simply the proletarians joining forces. It wasn't even the soldiers of the International Brigades uniting against Nazism. It was something different. Precisely what, we did not yet know.

From the trips to the front, from speeches that were improvised at first, a theme arose: "Soviet Culture Abroad in the Days of the Great Patriotic War." How we latched onto the response of some Englishman about "the windows of TASS": "These posters, made for the Ivan Ivanoviches, influence the John Smiths more than the works of their own artists."

Verses, songs, music (the Seventh Symphony—"the Leningrad"—of Shostakovich, the proceeds for the first American performance of

which, under the direction of Arturo Toscanni, went into the fund
for the Russian War Relief Committee), and somewhat later the
American editions of Soviet books—we assiduously gathered together
all those things and gave accounts about them. In the autumn of
1943 I traveled to the Northern Fleet with this theme.

Everywhere we were well received. We were a kind of frontline
theatrical brigade, a form of entertainment. We sensed both the
warmth and the joy. But also the fact that we were only chance guests
there.

In Moscow we organized a seminar for the study of the countries
with which we were linked and for the study of the common problems
that we were facing.

We weren't striving to work out a world view or opinions. But we
didn't simply want to carry out the dominant opinions of others—we
wanted to assimilate them and make them our own.

During the years of the war a process that had begun earlier continued
to develop further. The "USSR" became "Russia," a mighty power.
Officers' shoulder straps and officers' ranks were introduced, along
with separate education for boys and girls and a new law on marriage.
The Communist International was disbanded and the "Internationale"
was replaced by a new anthem. Suspicion of all foreigners grew
stronger and stronger.

The last cinders from the bonfires of 1917 were extinguished. The
majority of people who somehow embodied the revolutionary fervor
had been destroyed even earlier, during the time of the Great Terror.

VOKS, among other institutions, was called upon to serve this
process of change in a propagandistic fashion.

In 1943 we were given an assignment to write a memorandum
about how poorly the journal *Internatsionalnaya literatura* was operating. The entire memorandum, like all such memoranda, was made to
fit the presumed answer. Kemenov, apparently, knew only a part of
that answer: he wanted the journal transferred to VOKS. To this end
it was essential to show the higher authorities what clever, politically
minded people worked at VOKS, how much better they could understand a situation than the editorial board of the journal. Particularly,
of course, Kemenov.

Many years later, when I was working for a new journal,
Inostrannaya literatura, I asked in bewilderment as yet another mem-

orandum was being written to the Central Committee at Aleksandr Chakovsky's* request: "Aleksandr Borisovich, why on earth do we have to deal with this?" I got the answer: "Raisa Davydovna, we have to show that we know more than anyone else."

Kemenov never would have said anything like that. He was supposed to be "good," "fair," both in the eyes of others as well as his own. And he was. He was always able to convince us that "Internatsionalnaya literatura is a bad journal and you must find affirmation and concrete reasons for that in the articles." And we found them. Moreover, we outdid ourselves. The journal wasn't transferred to VOKS; instead, it was shut down altogether. There was no need to spread foreign ideas at all.

The necessity to keep us from *having ties* with other countries, to *separate* us from them, to separate us from foreign culture—that was what dictated the decision to close down *Internatsionalnaya literatura*. I am not excluding the fact that at that moment even those who were giving us that assignment did not yet completely comprehend the sense behind it.

Memory can be very obliging at times. It's only now that I recall my complicity in the closing down of *Internatsionalnaya literatura*.

In 1944 a new law on marriage and the family was issued. According to this law, one was required to receive permission at the initial stage of legal proceedings to place an announcement in the newspaper about an impending divorce. Only one newspaper published such announcements, and the waiting time could be up to two years. After that, the actual judicial proceedings would commence, and they could drag on for a long time from one stage to the next according to the wishes of any one of the parties involved.

The new law also reinstated the concept of the "illegitimate child," which had been repealed by the 1917 Revolution, and the rights of women who gave birth to such children were suppressed. At that time we had no idea, nor could we have had, what it would mean for a child to have a line drawn through the space on his birth certificate where the father's name should be. It only became clear later, when these children went to school. But the humiliation of this coercion to marry was obvious even then. Some of us were married, others

---

* Editor in chief of *Inostrannaya literatura* from 1955 to 1963 and of *Literaturnaya gazeta* since 1963.

were single, still others had lovers. Yet the norm for most of us was that people should be together as long as they were in love and should split up when love was gone. Nothing or no one should be an obstacle to that, least of all the state. Among those people close to me I was to hear conversations about "strengthening the family" by means of law much later.

So there we were, five co-workers, and we had to write an article for overseas about the status of women. And on top of it all, we had to provide a commentary, and, naturally, a justification for this utterly loathsome law. We did write that kind of article. I cannot recall a single one of our arguments now except (if indeed this might be considered an argument) Lenin's letter to the French-born revolutionary Inessa Armand. "A proletarian civil marriage with love," that was what we used to oppose "free love" to. So, in fact, we were defending this up-and-coming repulsive neobourgeois family that was based on hypocrisy and coercion.

A stream of letters (uninterrupted to this very day) flooded Party organizations from abandoned wives (and, occasionally, husbands), and people began to debate the profoundly personal aspects of life at large assemblies.

What foreigners did I meet at VOKS? Right at the beginning I was sent to a sovkhoz together with a delegation of American specialists in agriculture. I remembered my lessons in English at the institute and the lessons in phonetics: "Tune one, tune two . . ." Most of all, I was worried about whether I would be able to pronounce English phrases correctly enough. I went to the hotel. I was greeted warmly. And . . . I couldn't understand a single word. I didn't know that there was a difference between the language of the British and the Americans. Or that it was difficult to listen to conversational speech without preparation. Or that we had been taught Oxford English and ordinary Englishmen didn't speak that kind of language among themselves.

After a minute I said (terribly frightened and blushing): "I do not understand."

Later I got used to it. It would subsequently happen that specialists for whom I was interpreting would communicate with one another by means of specialized terms, practically expressing themselves with their hands and drawing sketches, almost without turning to me for my help. I finally learned how to translate from one language to another. But I didn't learn how to translate life or explain one type of life through the concepts of another.

I never asked any of those foreigners questions. Nor did I answer their simplest questions, about the family and children. That was how we were taught to behave at that time. Our relations with foreigners could only be official.

Later, after the war, a girl friend of mine was an interpreter for an important Canadian Communist. On one occasion, another one of our colleagues—who implemented the immediate ties between VOKS and the NKVD—dropped into the visiting Communist's hotel room. He saw that my friend wasn't exactly sitting on a chair . . .

She was kicked out of work. For a long time she couldn't find a position anywhere (the charge against her had been formulated as a political one), and it was precisely at that time that the law was adopted that forbade marriage with foreigners.

At the end of the war, Zoya Fyodorova, one of our most famous film stars, was arrested because of her relationship with an American military attaché. This story* has now been told in detail by her daughter, who went to live in the USA.

Just before the war, Erskine Caldwell arrived with his wife, the famous photojournalist Margaret Bourke-White. I had already read *Tobacco Road*. The interpreter for Caldwell himself was a woman from the Foreign Commission of the Writers' Union. I was assigned to Caldwell's wife. I accompanied her to soccer matches, and she would run around the enormous field with her camera, wearing an extraordinary purple coat. I had to run along behind her. She even photographed Stalin, but naturally without my being present.

The first person from the other world that I actually got to see was Lillian Hellman.

She arrived at the end of 1944. I went around Moscow with her, we traveled to Leningrad (where the blockade had just been lifted), to Kiev, and to the front. In Poland we sat in on a session (the first) of the State People's Council in Lublin. Afterward, in the evening, we attended a New Year's reception. An empty barrackslike building, long and undecorated tables. A bowl of cabbage, a bowl of potatoes, another bowl of cabbage. And full-sized bottles of vodka between them. Not quarter-liter bottles, but full-sized ones. There was no bread at

* *The Admiral's Daughter* by Victoria Fyodorova.

all. At the head of the table sat Bierut and Gomulka, the first Polish people's government. Speeches were delivered. That was how I greeted 1945. We went out on the street and Lillian said to me: "Raya, there was no Lenin among those people there, am I right?"

We had no sooner gone to bed than a fusillade of machine-gun fire broke out. It turned out that a detachment of German submachine gunners had penetrated the town and was shooting up the hotel where the Russians were living. During those moments that brought us close to death, I was with Lillian. She proved to be a fascinating person—clever, sharp-witted, and often full of anger.

When Lillian and I went to the front (it was the first time an American had been allowed to make such a journey), we were accompanied by a major from the Department of External Relations in the Ministry of Defense. He was a stupid and cowardly person.

Lillian created a story about him: "Look, Raya, like all military types, he was at the front at the beginning of the war. Let's say that he was in a platoon. There they immediately saw what kind of a bird he was. But how to get rid of him? So they decided to advance him, to 'promote' him to a regiment. Then to a division. Then to the Political Department at the front. And, finally, to the Chief Political Department. What to do with him, what kind of job to give him so that he would cause the least amount of harm? They decided to send him off to the front with this eccentric American woman."

This was perceptive. This major, armed, came running into our room when the shooting started in Lublin and screamed at me hysterically: "Why aren't you getting up, why are you in bed?"

No doubt about it. Hellman was more comprehensible to me, closer to me, more my own kind of person than this fool, boor, and coward.

The dogmas that were being pounded so incessantly into us and those that had been already solidly pounded into us did not agree with firsthand experience. But the dogmas triumphed for a long time over experience. In those years even the people like this major were "our people," whereas she was the foreigner.

I even found confirmation of the fact that she was not "one of us." She once said: "I'll start listening to the victories of socialism after you've built the kind of toilets that don't make you want to retch at all the airports from Vladivostok to Moscow." I gave her a very sharp and dumb reply about our people who had been killed, about the blood that had been spilled, and about the fact that we were protecting them, the Americans. And besides, was it possible to evaluate socialism by such lowly criteria!

In spite of this, our friendship has permeated my entire life. Her plays and her brilliant memoirs have intimacy and meaning for me.

Those who merely flashed through my life in those days, like Edgar Snow or Anna Louise Strong, and particularly those who left a manifest lingering trace, like Lillian Hellman, all bore witness to the fact that foreigners were people. Certainly they were different from us, but they were real. I was only to become conscious of these impressions later, but they were implanted then and there.

In 1944 John Hersey published his novel *A Bell for Adano*. A small town in Italy that American troops have just marched into. The liberation from Fascism proceeds slowly, with difficulty and interruptions. An American commandant helps the process along.

At the beginning of 1945 we decided to discuss the novel. It had been translated, and the manuscript of the translation was sent around to several writers and critics.

At this particular table we were more frequently obliged to drink toasts in champagne than talk about literature. But there we were, passionately and with great commitment talking about the book and life, about the Nazis and the anti-Nazis, about Americans and Russians. A revised transcript of the proceedings was sent to the author.

This event became the beginning of a profession for me. Naturally, at that time I couldn't have known that in the future I would be writing reviews of Hersey's new books, that a chapter would be devoted to him in my book *The Descendants of Huckleberry Finn*, that I would become acquainted with him (for a while he was a correspondent for *Life* magazine in Moscow), that he would be defending many Soviet intellectuals under harassment, from Daniel and Sinyavsky to me and Lev. At that time all of this was so inconceivable.

There we sat in the Red Hall, discussing the values and shortcomings of his novel. I was beginning to learn how to read American books, to understand them, and to talk about them.

For seven years, from 1940 to 1947, I was on the staff at VOKS. It was an unusual institution, and I was there at an unusual period, during the war. But at the same time, particularly in the postwar years, the more characteristic features of the system made their appearance at VOKS.

There was an ambiguity in the life of VOKS: the ceremonial exterior that was visible to the world, and the everyday reality. It was graphically incarnated in two types of rooms: the ceremonial ones (two large reception halls—one white and one red—the president's office, marble, mahogany, silk, velvet) and the minuscule uncomfortable little rooms in the rear of the building where the staff worked.

To others our life might have *seemed* an endless round of parties and receptions, but in actual fact we led a completely different and entirely prosaic existence.

For those who knew nothing of that, my work and the work of my co-workers must have seemed the pinnacle of bliss. I had shaken hands with Molotov, Tito, Benes, and Harriman. I had made the acquaintance of the writers Mikhail Sholokhov and Konstantin Simonov, the ballerina Galina Ulanova, the actress Vera Maretskaya, the tenor Ivan Kozlovsky, Eisenstein, and many other leading writers, political figures, artists, and actors. In Kuibyshev, in November 1941, I went to Shostakovich with a request for him to write a message of greeting for a solidarity meeting with the USSR at Madison Square Garden in New York.

I corresponded with many of the most outstanding figures of American culture. That is, I prepared the letters, but as a rule they were signed by the president of VOKS, Kemenov. In all of this and a great deal more there was a mixture of truth and falsehood (with a strong prevalence of falsehood). I understood even then that my part was nothing but illusion. (For this reason, incidentally, I received an innoculation against vanity that was powerful enough to last a lifetime.) But I reckoned that illusion was a typical feature only of that unique institution. Many years passed before it became clear to me that illusion was characteristic of the bureaucracy and bureaucratic government. It took the Twentieth Congress of the CPSU, the experience of an entire historic decade, and the reading of Djilas and Kafka to make me understand that.

My personal qualities had almost no significance whatsoever. For all the famous people that I met (and truly great and highly placed people turned up in their midst), I was some kind of "unknown quantity," easily replaceable and simply occupying a vacuum. It was nice if the "x" proved to be sympathetic, read books, and spoke English and French. Nice, but not essential.

At the age of twenty-four, I started to head the section for American countries. That was possible only during the war, because I had too many "negative" qualities for a member of the executive staff: I was young, female, and Jewish. Incidentally, even that high post was an illusion in its own fashion: extremely little depended on me, since I was almost never allowed to make any of the decisions. Whatever seemed the exception to me, was also the rule.

When I started to work at VOKS, I learned that we were supposed to have so-called presentable dress. Dresses were bought for us and we were provided with shoes and a coat. Indeed, we were supposed to meet foreigners. We were, in the main, very poor and looked quite unpresentable. In 1944 we were on our way to a reception at the American Embassy and one girl suddenly said: "What if someone there announces that each person is supposed to wear only his own clothing! What'll happen to us?" That was because we were wearing our "joint wardrobe." If you had to go into the White Hall, you would quickly put on some good stockings, shoes, and so forth. They'd stick someone's purse into your hands. That was nice and studentlike. And for me it concealed the main thing: we were being bribed. They were winning us over with clothing and food. Bribery demanded the strictest secrecy. They bribed us in various ways—some more, some less—according to rank. We arrived in Kuibyshev and at first we went hungry. It was normal and to be expected. Like everyone else. The country was in misery. Moreover, we were safe. No one was shooting at us. One had to feel there was a war on in some way. My first surprise, a bitter one, was the fact that we, heads of sections, were given two months' pay. For the evacuation. Up until then I had never had so much money all at once. What were they paying us this money for?

On November 7, 1941 (at that time all of the workers from VOKS were still living in communal quarters), Kemenov brought his Kremlin ration. They hadn't managed to settle people in a human fashion yet and still the Kremlin rations arrived regularly from the very first days. The ration was laid on the common table and we, about twelve of us, organized a luxurious feast. All of this wealth had been earmarked for a *single* family (that is, Kemenov's). The taste of expensive smoked fish so amazed me at that time that I can still taste it even today. In Moscow, before the war, that kind of fish was considered a rare delicacy and we never had it at home.

Before my departure for Moscow in April 1942, we had all been registered for the most restricted government cafeteria. There were two sections there, "high" and "low": with tablecloths and without. But even on the table without a tablecloth a dinner would appear that was extraordinary for those times. Abundant and delicious. Later they allowed us to take these dinners home.

Before entering the cafeteria, I would glance around like a coward. I had the "evidence" right in my hands: the dinner pans. A few of the local inhabitants clearly knew that something was being distributed behind this door. It was unbearably shameful. But I went in.

They would fill up three pots for me and I would pinch off a piece of bread and rejoice as I savored the joy of my family (Sveta would clap her hands; my younger brother, Mama, my girl friend who was living with us—we would all be sated). Then I would leave the cafeteria without looking around, so that I could take the food more quickly, careful not to slip, or to spill anything.

When I returned from Rumania in 1946 and started to work once more at VOKS, I noticed great changes. During the war, VOKS, like all institutions, was a female preserve. But now the men had come: self-confident, ignorant, and decorated with war medals. They had conquered Europe, so what did shabby VOKS mean to them? It seemed to them all the while that they deserved better than they had been given, that they had been "passed over." In a short while, the majority transferred to other more prestigious and rewarding posts. One became the assistant editor for the journal *Kommunist,* and I lost sight of the others.

Another kind of life dawned within this bureaucratic world, with its own intrigues abrewing and its own contradictions.

I had left a wartime VOKS that contained elements of a primitive democracy, that had inventiveness and a collective creativity.

I arrived from Rumania, where I had spent eight months, where I had understood and seen how badly we had been working before, with a multitude of plans and projects. I was convinced that we had to bring the truth about the USSR to the world and that that truth should be presented as it is: not simplified and artificial, but complicated and at times painful. We ought to send not dress photos and boastful articles overseas, but rather an honest account of our difficulties and how we were overcoming them. It meant that certain latent processes of which I was totally unconscious were under way in my soul at that time.

All my plans proved to be inopportune.

The authorities were demanding quite the opposite: victory, greatness, glory, and fanfare. Nothing else. Lofty words only. At that time a commission from the Central Committee came to VOKS. Kemenov, as it subsequently transpired, was in jeopardy. The head of the commission talked to me as though I were on trial. The substance of the charge was serious enough for those times: I had taken a reference book (in manuscript form) entitled *The USSR* with me to Rumania. It came in very handy for me; after all, I was giving lectures on the various aspects of Soviet life at the first courses organized for teachers of Russian by the Rumanian Society for Friendship with the USSR. But that reference text had not yet been approved by the Censorship. It meant that I had taken "secret" information out of the country about our industry, agriculture, and so forth.

Then Kemenov summoned me and said: "Hand in an application for voluntary resignation for reasons of study. I'll still be able to sign that kind of application today, but I could be removed tomorrow and then you might be in a bad situation." How many times had I submitted those kinds of applications before, during the war, but it had always been in vain.

Whenever they hadn't wanted to release me, they had always said that I was indispensable. I had wanted to believe that.

I proved to be totally replaceable at work—like any small cog. I want to flatter myself with the hope that there was something indispensable and mutually shared in the human relations we had enjoyed with one another. The years that I spent there left their mark on all that was to come afterward.

In July 1947 I left VOKS and began to study for my postgraduate degree.

XIII

"Neighbors"

1962

I respected the authorities and feared them. My friends and family often made fun of my fear of militiamen and housing superintendents. But in those years I did fear the higher authorities; it was a holy trembling before a *miracle*, a *mystery*, *authority*. And I did have a run-in with their most mysterious and most terrifying section. I was summoned to the NKVD. After the opening of the regular VOKS exhibition at the beginning of 1944, I received a telephone call and an invitation to come to the Hotel Moscow, room number such and such.

By that time we had become quite adept at distinguishing "them" as a generic and typological concept: "they" were everywhere foreigners were. We knew them as "they" or "neighbors" from their previous location near the People's Commissariat for Foreign Affairs on Dzerzhinsky Square. "They" were all dressed alike and looked the same.

On that first occasion, and from the following five or six meetings, I could remember no one, not a single *human*, specific detail remained, not even of the variety such as "red-haired," "with freckles," "brown hair." Nothing.

They wanted me to "cooperate." But after all, I was cooperating. We knew that a copy of every recorded conversation we had with foreigners was forwarded to the NKVD (although I never recorded my conversations with Lillian Hellman outside VOKS).

"No, that's not enough."

After a long discussion full of omissions, it came out that they wanted me to inform them about the behavior of other co-workers at VOKS.

At that time this suggestion seemed less monstrous and immoral than it does now. But even then, it made me feel sick.

We all called one another by our first names at VOKS, and many of us had studied together. We lived together through the war—we were evacuated together, slept on a single mattress, and shared our bread. And I was supposed to pass on information about my own fellow workers, my own close friends, to these ugly people who were indistinguishable from one another and who meant nothing to me. I was supposed to pass on the information in written form and sign it with any female name except my own.

I doltishly repeated that I would pass on everything they needed about the foreigners. In the stuffy rooms of the Hotel Moscow I was being enlisted as a "stool pigeon" (I learned the word later, probably after the death of Stalin). Naturally, everything was put into very noble language: ". . . helping the motherland in her struggle with the enemy."

During the very first conversation I was asked what I knew about Victor Rosenzweig. He had arrived from France in 1937 and had taught us French at the institute. In Kuibyshev, during the war, I had met him wearing an army coat. He had told me that he had been at the front and had escaped from a German encirclement. He was working as a translator at the General Staff Headquarters. Then he had been demobilized, and through my assistance he had been hired at VOKS. We were very good friends at that time. Victor was a first-class worker, knowledgeable and organized with his intellectual Western schooling. I related all of that.

"You can't tell us any more?"

"No."

"Write all that down."

I wrote it down; that paper couldn't do Victor any harm under any circumstances, and still, even now, it's lying somewhere, side by side with the denunciations, and I never told Victor about it. It's a page out of my life that is painful to remember. Like the following one.

New summonses again and again. There was obviously no sense to be gotten out of me. The threats started. Even though I gave a signed statement to the effect that I wouldn't divulge anything that was happening, I told everything to Kemenov, the president of VOKS. It was from him that I heard Lenin's words to the effect that if the

Cheka places itself above the Party, then it will turn into a secret tsarist-style police force. I don't recall the details of our conversation, although he did help me out at that time. He helped convince me of the rightfulness of my instincts.

But the dogmas and false ideas suppressed the instincts.

Yuri K. worked in my section. I had known him from earlier times at the Institute of Philosophy, Literature, and History. A very clever person. He seemed cynical and unprincipled to me. He submitted an application to join the Party. I was against his admission simply because I considered him to be a bad type.

A Party session was under way. My relations with both women who recommended Yuri K. were strained. I spoke out against K. The rest were "in favor" and didn't support me. Then I related the content of a conversation that he and I had had several months before that session. Our talk had been confused, protracted, about politics, about everything in the world. At that time he had said to me: "If in the Central Committee you had been ordered to hang children, you would have cried all night and then in the morning you would have set about carrying out the order." It was not only awful but also a seditious phrase: every Communist was obliged to fulfill any directives from the Central Committee (including eviction, imprisonment, and even murder), but it was not permitted to talk about such things, to mention such orders. For that he ought to have been excluded from the Party. The case went to the Commission for Party Control. I was summoned to all the departments. Yuri K. was excluded from candidacy in the Party and kicked out of VOKS. I didn't know for a long time what happened to him later. I didn't think about him. Probably he automatically entered the category of "alien."

Life isn't a rough draft: you can't rewrite a single page of it. But at least to try to understand . . . to find an answer that is more or less satisfactory to the question of why I acted as I did—I cannot do that even now. After all, today (this "today" has been going on for at least a quarter of a century) I wouldn't offer my hand to a person who had done something similar.

I didn't like Yuri. I was personally biased against him (not because of myself but because of my girl friend at that time). A merging of the "personal" and "public"? No, that would be insufficient as an explanation.

An accident? I blabbed and got carried away? Perhaps.

A profound personal injury from that very talk that became all the more incisive because it was unconscious? How could I agree to the fact that I might kill children even under highest orders? And the fact that such an order could come from my Party?

I had never replied to the customary questions of the teachers: "Who broke the window?" I didn't like to tattle. In other words, I cannot find any precedent for my action. If only I might be able to say today: "They forced me to." But no, no one forced me.

It's difficult to explain one's actions. It's more difficult when decades have passed between the action and the explanation. Objectively, it was a vile act that was unjustified under any circumstances. I will have to live with that realization. Till I die.

But when A. K. was excluded from the Party three years later by the Commission for Party Control, I reacted to that affair in a completely different manner. I was strongly sympathetic and I wanted to be with him as much as possible and to help him all I could.

There was no common moral measure. Like the one I am seeking so desperately now.

The whole atmosphere at VOKS was entirely nihilistic in a moral respect. But morality is indivisible. And if you can force yourself to agree to write an article about how good the new law on marriage is, then it is also possible to condemn and expel a person who has only just been in your midst.

In those days we frequently compiled various kinds of information and accounts "off the top of our heads." Figures were needed and there were none. And we, with nary a doubt, pulled the figures "out of the air": "In the first days of the war more than a hundred Societies for Friendship with the USSR arose in little Cuba alone . . ." The societies did in fact arise in the majority of cases. But how many there were we didn't know.

Probably in that devil-may-care attitude to moral dogmas lay the path to answering this question: why did none of the people around me condemn my action toward Yuri the way it should have been condemned? Which in no measure justifies me.

Despite my vile action, I was unreliable and alien in "their" eyes. At that time my second husband and I (we had gotten married in 1945) were being processed for a trip to Rumania. "We won't let you go anywhere!" I haven't any idea why, but they did let us go. And I had not heard from them for three years.

In 1948 I was summoned directly to the big building on Lubyanka. It was late in the evening. They kept me practically the whole night.

I was interrogated by three people in a row. They forced me to sign a written copy of the interrogation.

"How could you, a Soviet citizen and, moreover, a member of the Party, dare to accept a present from a foreigner?"

Lillian Hellman had given me a bracelet as a present in the car (Sergei Kondrashev was with us; at that time he was in charge of protocol at VOKS). She had even sent a parcel from America. This parcel came through the diplomatic mail and I received it quite officially at VOKS. The conversation about presents was obviously a mere pretext. Over and over again the main topic of the interrogation was: "Why did you refuse to cooperate with the officials of the NKVD?" That was the way it was recorded in the protocol.

They shouted at me, stamped their feet, and humiliated me in every possible way. They even asked: "Is it true your father owned a Jewish shop?" I was afraid of them.

When in the New York *Times* in 1968 I read a record of Pavel Litvinov's conversation with an interrogator, I wasn't just simply enthralled with Litvinov's responses. I further understood that a new generation of people had appeared who were not afraid of them, who would show the entire world, and especially us, that the Committee for State Security (KGB) was an ordinary Soviet institution. The mystery, the wonder, and the authority were destroyed. And it wasn't simply a matter of generations. After all, sixty-year-old Pyotr Grigorenko's famous letter to the head of the KGB, Yuri Andropov, was no less daring and no less effective in destroying the terror.

But I was afraid of them. As of yet, there was no hatred in me, no contempt, because I had no inner feeling of superiority. At some point in the middle of the night I even burst into tears. All they had to do was to suggest to me that I was an agent of the Gestapo, the "Allies," or whatever intelligence service, and I probably would have signed that I agreed. Just to end this nightmare as quickly as possible, to leave as quickly as possible, not to look at those horrible mugs and hear their boorish shouting.

I came out onto Dzerzhinsky Square at daybreak. And at that very moment my obliging mind and memory began to prompt me: "We are living in a fortress under siege, spies and enemies are all around, you can't make an omelette without breaking eggs" and so on and so forth.

It was bad for me, for me *personally*. It was at me and *only* at me that they had shouted unjustly, it was me they had accused unjustly. Was it really possible to avoid some sacrifices? And now I too was obliged to become a sacrifice as well. I had gotten off lightly.

With those kinds of thoughts and ever submissively (that was what was truly terrible, namely, that it was submissively) I would have followed the prison-camp route. The way thousands and hundreds of thousands were going. It was an infinitesimal minority that even objected, let alone revolted. The rest were submissive and confident of the rightfulness of the authorities.

All of my youth had passed in romantic fantasies: war, victory, riding into a city astride a tank, a horse, an armored train. There was even a jail cell in these fantasies, a hand with a red kerchief sticking through an iron grating. An interrogation, even with the Whites or the Nazis conducting the interrogation, but I would be standing with my teeth clenched, giving no one away, undergoing torture, and dying in the midst of those tortures.

But in real life there were bureaucratic offices, paper, pens, type-writers, and people pronouncing my words. Were they really enemies? They're our own people. So perhaps I'm an enemy too? No, it's not so. I am probably an insufficiently staunch intellectual, whereas they are the unflinching Bolsheviks. But why the mention of the "Jewish shop"? Simply an anti-Semite cropping up in their midst.

I should not have taken the purse and sweater that Lillian Hellman had sent me. A genuine staunch Communist wouldn't have taken them. But after all, our chief of the Special Department had requisi-tioned something for himself from my parcel, as well as from others. He was an exception. At these times I never linked the "exceptions" together.

How many times during the past years did I rehearse the following scene. I would be summoned to the KGB and I would immediately pronounce the speech I had memorized beforehand: "I refuse to answer any questions." If only I had had the strength to utter those words earlier, it might have turned out differently.

But you can't rewrite life, and the conditional mood is ineffective in this case. It happened to me the way I have just described it.

XIV

My Second Marriage

In January 1944 I was sent to a sanatorium after a heart attack.

Two and a half years of war, a year and a half of widowhood, the evacuation, my unrealized attempt to escape to the front, an intoxication with work, from morning to night, from morning to night. And suddenly a halt in full flight. Air. Pines. Solitude.

A man was sitting at a neighboring table looking at me all the time. We became acquainted. His name: Orlov, Nikolai Alekseevich. On the third day he said: "You know what I dreamt? That you were getting married to me."

During the ten years of our marriage he never dreamt again.

Through that man with hair as gray as the moon, through everything bad that came afterward, I am trying to catch a glimpse of Kolya the way I saw him for the first time then. Clean-cut features, a fine face that was open and perhaps even handsome. Elegant despite his stockiness and very broad shoulders. Enormous physical strength. His father had been an agronomist, and his mother a teacher (she had died young).

Among the legends of the war, the legend closest to my heart had been the Leningrad blockade. And here I was making the acquaintance of a man who had been in charge of supplying Leningrad with bread. He himself had starved; he had suffered from serious scurvy and had almost lost his sight. He had devised and sought out substitutes for that bread in which there was practically no grain. Later, in the museum The Defense of Leningrad, I saw the instructions and orders that had been signed by Orlov; I saw as well those microscopic little pieces of ersatz bread. Kolya had held a great deal in his hands, yet he had taken for himself only what everyone else had coming. No more.

In the spring of 1967 Lillian Hellman read me her wartime Russian diary. Where it dealt with our trip to Leningrad together, there was the following entry: "Raya says that everyone is starving equally." I gave a shudder. How could one use the word "equally" when there had been special rations (I heard about that much later) and even some kind of special tennis courts for Zhdanov?!*

But in 1944 I was certain that an equality in misery had reigned in Leningrad. My acquaintance with Kolya had confirmed those thoughts in me. After all, he had truly starved in the Leningrad blockade even though he was in charge of the bread.

Among my hesitant and uncertain friends, there had appeared a person who always knew firmly *how things should be done*, who was absolutely self-confident.

I had been waiting for that kind of person, I had unconsciously been prepared for this encounter—from my very first virginal fantasies about the horseman who would throw me across his saddle, from my infatuation with the heroes of Jack London and Ernest Hemingway.

I wasn't yet at all clear on whether I seriously loved him, I wasn't longing to get married, I was headed for an affair. But he was assuming responsibility, on his own behalf as well as mine, for everything that a woman at that time was expected to do on her own (and often was unsuccessful at doing). After all, a new law on marriage had just been passed.

I had no desire whatsoever for our life to begin amid ruins that were still smoldering (Lyonya was still present in our apartment—in photographs, in personal effects, in letters, in everything). For that reason we both felt the urge to leave Moscow.

I don't recall the first arguments, just as later I don't recall a single day without them. We were people from different worlds. He never attempted to take a single half step toward my world, whereas for a long time, an incomprehensibly long time, I strove toward his world, crippling myself, mercilessly smashing that personal world of mine that I had somehow managed to put together with the people who inhabited it.

He read a great deal and indiscriminately, for the most part historical

* Andrei Aleksandrovich Zhdanov (1896–1948), at that time head of the Leningrad Party organization and a member of the Politburo.

novels. He knew a great deal and remembered a great deal. When in 1950 he was sent to the Higher Party School, he studied furiously, like a person who was making up for lost time. He made a synopsis of every book, and he received only excellent grades. He treated literature like something sacred. He himself dreamt of writing and even tried to write, but he had no literary abilities. Just as, incidentally, he had no taste. He had that characteristic feature of Russian youngsters: he corrected the map of the heavenly bodies by daybreak (Dostoyevsky). *A priori*, and well in advance, he always possessed a firm knowledge of all the solutions and all the answers. So what need did he have for questions?

A personal and scrupulous honesty (not only during the blockade, but at all times) lived side by side in him with the following principle: I will not take anything from anyone else, but neither will I give away anything of my own. He never gave anything to beggars (wasn't this where our first disagreements began?). And, amazingly, he was still able to completely twist things around so that the miserable old woman sitting in rags on the corner became a shark of world imperialism. He possessed an ironclad rule and it even extended to include the old woman: no philanthropy. No indulgence of the privately employed (in his vocabulary there was hardly an expression of greater abuse than "privately employed"). He resolutely dismissed both private doctors and private teachers. As a result, to my shame, I never taught my daughters foreign languages in their childhood.

We dreamt of moving to a small town, of going to the kind of town that had just been liberated from the Nazis and building the ideal socialism there. In order to do so one needed plenary authority. Thus, Kolya would be the secretary of the city council there. He would create an efficient working organization, without any bureaucratic distortions. We and our friends would plan this new socialist phalanstery in all its details for long evenings on end. Kolya was confident that he knew what the people needed. And he was prepared to drag them into paradise by force.

The opportunity never came for an experiment with a single town. But I experienced to the fullest the way he dictated his conceptions about life to those near and far.

Some reckon that a child is a hollow vessel into which educators are obliged to pour what they consider to be necessary, correct, and useful. A child, particularly a poorly raised one, resists this treatment, but the child must be forced for his or her own good. This task is difficult and thankless ("It's a lot easier to moon over each other," Kolya would repeat mockingly), but that is a real upbringing, and the child, if one doesn't interfere with him or her, will ultimately realize that you were only wishing the best for him or her.

The opposite point of view: a child, even a small one (Sveta was five years old when I met Kolya), is a distinct individual. One must know this individual, respect her, and slowly and carefully win her over, above all with love. One must create a network of relations, of bonds, a subtle organic system, like the circulatory system. If that kind of system emerges, then a proper upbringing will be realized. That is, your words, your actions, and your counsel can at least be heard, can be assimilated. If that system doesn't exist, then regardless of how right your words are and how good your actions are, they won't produce any effect. On the contrary, they could have the opposite effect.

At first intuitively, then later consciously, I always favored the second way.

Kolya responded to his role as Sveta's father (she never called him "Papa," although he worked very hard for that) just as responsibly as to any kind of work. He carried on a bloody battle with the grandmothers, with the grandfathers, and with me over Sveta. He devoted a great deal of time to her, read to her, told her fairy tales, played with her and her girl friends. And he was unremitting in his attempts to educate her, that is, he would tediously repeat the same truisms, while I, biting my lips (I rarely restrained myself from an outburst), would count to a hundred and back again.

I myself had attempted to proceed scientifically before meeting Kolya. Today's young mothers read Dr. Spock. Whereas my pedagogical conceptions arose out of a combination of instinct, Rousseau's *Émile*, Tolstoy, a few Soviet books on child rearing, and my own experiences as a teacher. The child must not be fed at night. Sveta would scream bloody murder. I would be firm. How I wanted to take that little bundle in my arms and feed her. And how I wanted to sleep. But I would control myself. I was waiting until six o'clock in the morning, then I could feed her. Mama would come to my door. And shout. There was my meek mother screaming: "Feed that child immediately or I'll go to the militia and I'll say that you are torturing your baby!" But I was winning the duel. I did teach Sveta to eat at fixed times. But I never won anything else.

And there was Kolya, who in order to "correct" Sveta after failing to achieve anything through admonishments and punishments, spanked her. A nine-year-old girl. In my absence. He hit her several times. All my failings were insignificant next to the fact that I, the mother, a loving mother, had allowed such a thing.

I didn't protest, I didn't scream, I didn't take her into my arms. Many years have passed since then, yet it is much more difficult for me to return to this and write about it than about my political and socially immoral actions, like the story about Yuri K.

In order to understand another person, it is obviously necessary to understand oneself, to recognize something in common between yourself and the other person, not to consider yourself the possessor of some absolute truth in the final instance. But Kolya never admitted that he was wrong in anything. Both with adults and children he had papal infallibility, not in reality, of course, but in his own imagination. He never even admitted the obvious; he would not admit that he was an alcoholic.

His father had been an alcoholic and his brother drank. Kolya would constantly try to make me see that he simply liked to drink, and who didn't? He really did know how to drink, and thanks to his warriorlike health he could drink for a long time without getting drunk. Only in the last years of our life together did he begin to get drunk from a single glass. I was late and ineffectual in starting to oppose his drunkenness. But it would have made no difference even if I had started earlier. The final result would have been the same.

Three o'clock in the morning. No Kolya, and as usual, I can't fall asleep. The entry door downstairs bangs and I have this fantasy: they are carrying in his bloodied body. No, I can't bear it any longer. I jump up, dress, and go looking for him. More often than not I find him in the cocktail bar in our own building. He's sitting alone and drinking. And I keep convincing myself with maniacal stubbornness: nevertheless everything's fine for me. He's alive. He loves me.

At times it seemed to me that I was losing my mind. Otherwise, if we were both normal people, how could he, after drinking away his pay for the umpteenth time, after lying for two days in bed as a result, gloomily silent, otherwise how could he affirm: it was nothing of the sort. Again he was right, and again I was the guilty one.

For all that, what a solid person he was, like a pillar. For example, the time when I wasn't accepted for graduate studies at the Institute of World Literature in 1947, despite the fact I had received "excellent" in all my subjects. Kolya went to the presidium of the Academy of Sciences, talked sense to them for a long time, talked openly about anti-Semitism there, even about Nazism, and I was accepted. Or the time when I was failed on my dissertation defense by a secret vote in 1951, whereupon I immediately left to join him in Tallinn (he had been sent there after finishing the Higher Party School); again he helped me to get over more easily what at the time seemed to be a great bitterness.

Back in the sanatorium, where we first met, I got sick: a badly swollen cheek. He cared for me in a touching fashion, anticipated my smallest wishes. Then he was in love, so it was understandable. But nine years had passed. I had firmly made up my mind to get a divorce and had even written an application to the court. And then I fell sick: a serious attack of malaria. And again he never left my bedside, he was constantly there and so attentive. And against my will he stole back into my heart: here I was going to get divorced and I would be alone with all my ailments. Perhaps I could get over it; after all, everyone drank . . .

In 1956 I returned from a business trip and Sveta said to me: "Mama, I love you, but I don't want to live with Uncle Kolya anymore." The end began at that moment. He didn't believe that I would prove myself capable of making the break—my infinitely long submissiveness prevented him from believing it.

Nevertheless, I never became the kind of woman that would take anything, both drunken blows and drunken caresses. I kept bending over backward again and again, but fortunately I never broke completely. And even while I was still married, I started to win back, inch by inch, the free territory of my soul.

We seldom argued about political topics. He was more logical than I and for that reason allowed himself to criticize our shortcomings more sharply. He never had to prove that he wasn't an outsider.

Wasn't it nice on a day off to get in the car assigned to the house and drive off into the woods? It was. Wasn't it nice when fruit and vegetables were brought home, when fine foods were brought home and we could feed the children, our family and friends well? Yes, it was.

But at the time I was vaguely conscious of the fact that it was unjust, that it was a privilege of the ruling class. Kolya's personal qualities obscured a great deal for me. Even the fact that his wages and rations quite frequently were wasted on drink and that for that reason I suffered certain privations. There was no land of milk and honey in my life. There were constant debts, the sale of personal items, and the pawnshop. But that was personal. As the wife of a Party official, I enjoyed the additional perquisites of the Party apparatus. In judging Kolya I have no right to forget about that.

In Tallinn, Kolya, a plenipotentiary of the Ministry of Procurement of the USSR, had a serious conflict with the Estonian Central Committee, which culminated in his removal. In 1952 he was dismissed from his work, demoted in rank, and transferred to the town of Ivanovo.

At the time I reckoned that he had probably been right in carrying out his work, but that the authorities had been fed up with his truancy and tardiness owing to drunkenness. Moreover, the chauffeur, with whom they all drank with increasing frequency, smashed up a government car. Kolya had no small share of the blame in this, but as always he wouldn't recognize it.

In reality, however, the conflict was a social one. Nikolai Orlov, representing the interests of the imperial power, kept demanding more and more from an already exhausted colony. Whereas the local Estonian authorities, even though they feared the central power, kept striving by whatever means to decrease the amount of tribute paid, the amount of the deliveries, in order to leave a few things in the Estonian republic. They gleefully seized on Kolya's drunkenness (they themselves drank no less) in order to get rid of him.

My first surprise and presentiment arose when I understood that he had no friends. As my dowry I brought a great number of friends. At first they not only accepted him but also sensed his magnetism and became friends with him. However, they all gradually drifted away from him. Essentially he had no need of other people.

My inner liberation dated from Estonia. My inferiority complex, which had been instilled in me by my social development and which was being further reinforced by Kolya with complete success, slowly began to cure itself. I felt that people needed me.

I began to erect a barrier between us, a solid and impenetrable one. Frequently, very frequently, I would smash into this barrier and would want to tear it down. After all, I had been accustomed to something else, not to the stony silence that would go on for days. I had been accustomed to communication, to trust. And yet, clenching my teeth, I would live behind that barrier. What was I trying to preserve? Apparently, what was left of me. I had already long since begun to rejoice over his trips away from home, to rejoice over my freedom.

I didn't know that this was merely the introduction to that great joy I experienced when in June 1956 I was freed once and for all.

XV

Books

"I began my life as I shall no doubt end it: amidst books," Sartre wrote about himself, and I too could repeat those words. I read a great deal, beginning in my childhood; everyone in our family read a great deal. I studied in the faculty of literature. The whole circle of my interests, both personal and professional, was, is, and will be once and for all connected with books.

For all my faith in the word, I understand that a person's behavior is determined by many things, not just by the books he has read or the one's he hasn't. But my behavior has been determined to a significant degree by books.

In my childhood it seemed to me that if a person read a lot (and even more so, if he himself wrote), then he would belong to the intelligentsia and his spiritual and moral code would derive from this. Professor Roman Samarin, an unprincipled careerist who was in charge of the philology faculty at Moscow State University, was a highly educated man and read a great deal. Yakov Elsberg, a longtime *agent provocateur* for the State Political Directorate (GPU) and the Ministry of State Security (MGB), was the same kind of tireless reader. People who knew Stalin said that he managed to read 600 pages a day.

But what is most important is what a person reads and how his reading is connected with life and with behavior.

We had a lot of books in our home. My parents were constantly reading and buying books. I remember Mama in her later years lying on the sofa and reading tirelessly. When Father was a member of the board at the State Publishing House, he was offered books as a supplement to his salary. We had the multivolume collected works of Chekhov, Jack London, Guy de Maupassant, Stefan Zweig, Aleksei Tolstoy. These books disappeared very quickly. Thanks to us children and our many friends.

Only father's bookcase was locked. There was a peculiar odor in this bookcase: the compound odor of tobacco, leather, and old books— the odor of my childhood.

In my early years I was sick a great deal and Mama would bring me books from the secondhand bookstores.

My very earliest recollections of reading matter were books from the series Golden Library: *Exemplary Girls* and *Sonya's Pranks*. Later I read these books in French and very much amazed my teachers with my rapid achievements. In actual fact, I simply recalled entire pages by heart from the Russian texts. *Hans Brinker or The Silver Skates, Little Men, Little Women . . .*

Along came Lidiya Charskaya, our Louisa May Alcott. Probably even now I could relate the misadventures of her heroines. Yet how many books there are that I read not thirty-five years ago but only in the past month and that haven't left a single trace. Naturally, it's a matter of the quality of a child's receptiveness and today's impoverished memory. But that's not all there is to it.

When I was fourteen years old, a literary trial of the works of Charskaya was organized in my school. Charskaya was sternly judged and condemned. This is probably where the tiny roots of that double standard emerged, which has already brought and continues to bring us innumerable misfortunes. For yourself you can rejoice, get carried away, weep tears, and laugh. But then you act "the way you should." And it turns out that you must condemn.

Probably Charskaya is a sentimental writer. I haven't reread her books. But I am quite certain that for all of us, the boy and girl pupils of that distant era, it would have been much less harmful to continue to weep over the ill-starred fates of the girls in tsarist Russia's private schools than to weep in private but to condemn aloud. For me, as for many, both a cynical attitude and an acknowledgment of hypocrisy were impossible, given the makeup of my character. It meant that a choice had to be made. And so, for many long years I attempted to convince first myself and then others of things against which everything inside me was rebelling.

No one directed my reading. It seems that once I was forbidden to read *A Thousand and One Nights* (*Arabian Nights*). For the very reason that I had been forbidden, I got hold of the book (brick-red volumes with gold engraving) and my boredom knew no limits! I gave up somewhere in the middle of the first volume.

Turgenev, Cooper, and Dickens came into my life in childhood. Even now I gaze at the thirty-volume collection of Dickens's works and calm peaceful thoughts about old age, about a deep armchair and spectacles descend upon me. About how once more Oliver Twist, David Copperfield, and the little girl Dorrit, those kind and unfortunate heroes and heroines of my childhood, will close in around me. Even now, my notion of the most bitter, the most irreparable injustice is still the unrequited love of Florence Dombey for her father.

I can still clearly visualize it as though it were taking place before my eyes: Eliza jumping from ice floe to ice floe with little Harry in her arms. I hold my breath: will they actually catch up with her? How can I help her reach the other shore? And however many clever and convincing articles I was later to read about the limitations of Harriet Beecher Stowe, articles about slavery and the social problems of America, I will never forget that childhood sensation: first the cold of those ice floes, then the grief of others.*

I wanted to be like Cooper's heroes: to shoot accurately, to walk through the forests together with Natty Bumppo, to be courageous, strong, and hardy.

When I was about fourteen or fifteen, Jack London superseded all the rest.† He brought with him that breath of travel that apparently will always make me feverish. The collected works of London were printed on poor paper, and they were stitched together in such a fashion that a book might end in the middle of a paragraph or even a word. In those days it was a marvel, it was a world that was much more real than the one in which I actually lived.

I read with unusual speed, and this could be explained very simply: I skipped a great number of pages at a time. Faster and faster through the descriptions of nature, past the fighting—just the plot, the action, and the dénouement. I read at the same tempo as I lived.

One "reading day" in 1931 is very clearly imprinted in my memory. I was given Zola's *Nana* and Chernyshevsky's *What Is to Be*

---

* In 1971 I published a book about the life and work of Harriet Beecher Stowe, and then in 1975, another one.

† In 1967 I published a book about *Martin Eden*.

Done?* And in a single Sunday I gobbled up both books. I was left with a feeling of complete indifference to Zola's novel. But Chernyshevsky's book provided me with an answer to the question posed in the title *What Is to Be Done?*: a social revolution. The creation of communes. And as far as one's personal life was concerned, one must love only with sincerity. A mistake in love can be corrected: husband and wife can separate and can and must do so in a humane fashion.

That is what I took away with me from that book, together with a generation of my predecessors and contemporaries.

I can now see how artistically unsatisfactory the book is. I was annoyed even then by the author addressing the "perceptive reader" and by the inordinate repetition of the word "dearest." But what trivia when compared with the rest!

Many years later I read Nabokov's *The Gift*. This book assumed the greatest importance for me. Long periods of not rereading it leave me feeling empty. But even now I am not entirely in agreement with Nabokov and in disagreement with Chernyshevsky. It seems to me that Nabokov (although it contradicts his character) feels a human pity for Chernyshevsky, particularly at the end of his life. And a kind of restricted esteem.

In all of the favorite books from my childhood, all the loose ends were tied up, virtue invariably triumphed, and vice just as invariably was punished. The world was strictly divided into bad and good. Later this division came to signify the following: those who were "against us" and those who were "for us."

In 1930 I read *At the Top of My Voice*—that was how I got started on Mayakovsky. One of the first disquieting and unanswered why's came a few months later. "Why did he shoot himself?" I asked, but I received no response. I was tormented for a time by the question, but later I forgot about it. I forgot about the question.

I memorized mediocre contemporary Soviet verses and zealously hid my love for Pushkin and Nekrasov.† Once, I timidly started to stutter something about Nekrasov, and our leader, a young fellow

---

* A novel in which Nikolai Gavrilovich Chernyshevsky (1828–1889), a major Russian political thinker, economist, critic, and writer, deals with, among other things, the social and economic emancipation of women.

† Nikolai Alekseevich Nekrasov (1821–1898), Russian poet, known for his realistic verses on social and civic themes.

from a factory wearing a leather jacket, burst into loud laughter. "Nekrasov . . . I can see why you're wearing braids, you're a real leftover." Covered in scalding tears, I cut off my braids the following day. They were long, ever so long; it was such a pity. It was more difficult to "cut off" Nekrasov and Pushkin, and fortunately I never did that.

At the age of sixteen I discovered Blok. I always repeated his verses and I said that I didn't need any other lyric poetry. So not only did I miss Yesenin in my youth (he remained alien to me), but Akhmatova as well.

Blok took over some secret abode in my soul and the doors to that abode would open at every emotional shock: love, death, war. In fact, during the war it was Blok that I read most frequently. The walls of this abode were thick and impenetrable. Verses did not apply to my other real life. That life followed its own course.

At sixteen the one and only penetration into a world of chaos appeared with the simultaneous onslaught of Dostoevsky, Freud, Nietzsche, Spengler, and textbooks on psychiatry.

I could not withstand this contact with tragedy, with the primordial tragedy of human existence. Peering into the abyss, I leapt back in terror and returned to the undeviating universe of the bayonet charge, red kerchiefs, the two worlds, and that bookish sea that was continuously evaporating.

I never acquired a taste for high satire. I had read Swift and Shchedrin* but really never read them again.

Once again, I never had, and still don't have, the courage to accept certain bitter truths about the very essence of human nature, about its primeval wickedness. At times I continue to doubt whether they are the truth or not.

I was studying at the Institute of Philosophy, Literature, and History in those very years when Russia was being thrown into the prison camps.

The removal of each category of people, including those who are leaving the Soviet Union now, meant that a certain category of books would be proscribed and withdrawn. This practice continues.

* Mikhail Yevgrafovich Saltykov (1826–1889), leading Russian satirist, who wrote under the pseudonym N. Shchedrin. Author of numerous works, including the novel *The Golovlyov Family*.

In 1975, for example, the books of Viktor Nekrasov, Vasilii Grossman, Yulian Oksman, and Yefim Etkind were withdrawn.*

In the card catalog of the State Library for Foreign Literature, I came across file cards that were old and frequently faded, where the names of literary specialists who had been suppressed during the thirties had been neatly crossed out.

In 1977 an excellent work was published entitled *American Literature in Russian Translation and Criticism (Bibliography: 1776–1975)*. All of Lev Kopelev's articles were missing from it. The articles that he and I had published jointly under both of our names were ascribed to me alone. When I saw that, I sensed the same kind of danger that the terror might be repeated as when I found out about the new arrests.

They stoked up bonfires for books in our country as well; but in contrast to the openness and theatricality with which books were burned in German cities, they were burned in Russian cities in secret.

It was as though Russia and Germany had exchanged national characteristics: it was from the Germans that one might have expected accurately compiled lists of inventory numbers for books destroyed and not a dance around the sinner-books writhing in the bonfire.

In Uzhgorod in 1964 we were told that in 1949 books were being destroyed so frantically that there was not even time to record the names or titles, only the numbers.

At an evening dedicated to the memory of Isaak Babel, I heard Babel's words of 1938 quoted in a speech by Ehrenburg: "I was at a factory where books are being turned back into paper. Hefty wenches sit there and sensually rip off the covers."

From 1935 to 1940 I was studying literature. At first I was studying how to sit in judgment, how to pass sentence, and then only later, to know, understand, and love. Frequently, the second step of knowing, understanding, and loving was omitted altogether. I had to judge, of course, not according to my own criteria but those of others. The fact that the ideas of others became practically my own made it even worse.

---

* Since being deprived of our citizenship in 1981, neither Lev Kopelev nor I exist as authors in the USSR. Our books are banned, as are those of Vasilii Aksyonov, Vladimir Voinovich, Aleksandr Zinoviev, and others.

Speaking on the eightieth birthday of Pereverzev* in 1962, I said that he had started out for me as "Pereverzevism." There had been no individual person, no scholar Pereverzev. There had only been "isms," and these had suggested something "alien." And had Pereverzev been the only one? He, at least, had survived, returned, and could hear voices of support. And what of the others who hadn't survived, those who had existed for me in my student years only under those terrible rubrics of "isms"?

There was a fanciful admixture in my head of *Das Kapital*, Veselovsky and Taine, Paustovsky, Ilf and Petrov's *The Twelve Chairs*, and Rolland's *Jean-Christophe*. In all the corridors verses rang out, classical and contemporary, by poets who were both recognized and still unrecognized. Today on my shelves I have books by many of my fellow students. Sometimes it seems to me that even today I can hear those voices . . .

I was gasping from the sensation of human riches, from the intelligence, beauty, and radiance I found in books. It seemed to me that people around me were pure, radiant, and beautiful. The concepts of free and unfree merged simultaneously in my unformed mind and heart, they overflowed into each other, became synonymous. The unfree had hundreds of pseudonyms that were attractive and romantic.

For a long time I had no feeling for the literary word, no understanding of form, and I didn't know how to read the inner language of a work, to penetrate into its artistic logic. I knew that I was lacking in this. But I never imagined *to what degree*. I never imagined that I was lacking the most important and the most essential thing. It's probably too late to make up for the deficiency in those beginnings.

The principal idea of B. Sarnov's clever article "A Book that Is Read at the Right Time" relates not only to books. There are forms of knowledge and discoveries and entire artistic worlds that must come at the right time.

Having graduated from the Institute of Philosophy, Literature, and History and having become a doctoral candidate in literary science at the Institute of World Literature, I was nevertheless sleepily ig-

* Valeryan Fedorovich Pereverzev (1882–1968), Russian literary scholar, proponent of vulgar sociology, which held that the class a writer belongs to determines his ideas and style. Pereverzev spent many years in prison and exile, and was later rehabilitated.

norant of my own native literature. The names of Akhmatova and Tsvetaeva, Mandelstam and Bulgakov, Voloshin and Khodasevich, Berdiaev and Belyi, meant nothing to me.

But it wasn't simply a matter of names, of these names and many others. It was a matter of unknown layers of culture.

Fortunately, my earlier conceptions apparently had not yet had time to atrophy. My receptiveness was still preserved (naturally to a much lesser degree than in a normal youth). I wanted to know, I searched voraciously, and the manuscripts flowed into our house, were copied out and shared with friends.

The summer of 1963. We became acquainted with the German poet Hans Magnus Enzensberger and took him to Zhukovka.* He asked about Tsvetaeva. We got out a black portfolio in which there was some unpublished poetry. We read it to him.

"Is that how you keep it?"

"Yes, for the time being."

Small volumes published in the USSR stand on our shelves now, along with a great many foreign editions of Tsvetaeva's works. Quite recently I saw again some thick notebooks where the verses of Tsvetaeva had been copied out by hand.

Islands, continents, mainlands of prose and poetry that had been submerged in the void were discovered. Some of the manuscripts became books. A new knowledge was being born and a new attitude to the world.

In Nadezhda Mandelstam's first book, *Hope Against Hope,* we find the following episode. In 1949 she met an old Bolshevik woman in Tashkent. "She must have felt instinctively that we had something in common," writes Mandelstam, "—the fact that in those years nobody was reading either my literature or hers. Both had gone out of use, and we both hoped that they would come back again. We both believed that our respective values were indestructible—though mine have now gone 'underground,' while the underground literature she had read in her youth had been canonized by the new state. Both her literature and mine had lost its readers."

The literature that Nadezhda Mandelstam was talking about wasn't making a return for me; rather, it was newly revealed. It forced itself on me (not without opposition on my part) and at first coexisted peacefully with the literature I had been raised on. But later it began

---

* A village 30 kilometers from Moscow, where we rented a dacha for twenty years.

partly to displace the earlier literature. It came at first as an artistic enrichment, as a new aesthetic. But later it was transformed into a new ethic; it became not simply a refutation of my earlier literature, but a refutation of my former world as well.

In September 1935 Ehrenburg brought Malraux along to us, the first-year students. The French writer asked us whether we recalled Pasternak's lines: "On that day when all of you, from head to toe . . ." Not a single person responded, everyone was silent. Perhaps they were too shy to answer.

Lyonya and I took a book of Pasternak's poems and tried to read it. It was very difficult, at times quite incomprehensible. The joys of discovery have remained from those days: "The lilac branch bedewed by a sparrow"; "If at some point over the years in a concert hall"; "It's the sharp outburst of song"; "Oh, had I known that such is the case." Somewhat later came the narrative poems *Lieutenant Schmidt* and *The Year 1905*. But both then and later I had no spiritual urge to read Pasternak the way I read Blok, Mayakovsky, and Pushkin. I didn't go to his readings, I never heard the way he read himself.

In 1954–1955 his works were caught up in the thaw as well. Verses from his novel started to reach us. A verse cycle was published in the journal *Znamya* (The Banner) in 1954. In March 1955 I heard the poem "August," and this poem implanted itself in my memory all by itself. That was something that hadn't happened to me in a long while. And fresh lodes and strata keep revealing themselves in this poem. At first it had been the rhythm and the waves that made your heart stop beating. This poem both arouses and is aroused by thoughts about death. Ten years yater, in 1965, "August" was published for the first time in the USSR.

In 1956 we read the manuscript of the novel *Doctor Zhivago*. The book about our Revolution was written from the outside. It was alien, at times distressing. This book contradicted what we thought, dreamt, and argued about in that stormy year of 1956. In this regard his *Autobiography* made a much greater impression on me. At that time I couldn't see in his novel the eternal values—goodness and truth— which now draw closer and closer. A doctor who not only abandons medicine, but a doctor who ceases to help people even though he could—all of that was unfathomable to me. The prose reminded me of the end of the nineteenth century, a prose that was very distant from me in its artistry.

We argued with friends. We weren't yet mature enough for this novel. More time had to elapse.

On the first reading we were attracted by the description of nature; no, one must not say "description" when dealing with Pasternak, it was nature itself. And then there were those scenes when Yurii Zhivago was writing his poetry.* The verses themselves became a part of our life on the first reading.

In 1957 *Doctor Zhivago* was published in Italy (the book was supposed to appear in the USSR as well), and shortly afterward, in other countries. At the editorial offices I opened the foreign journals and newspapers and read one article after another on Pasternak.

Afterward, the Nobel Prize was awarded. Then came the shameful scandal organized by our press. Once more fear was being pumped into us, once more mass psychosis was operating and the base instincts of the crowd were being stirred up.

On November 8, 1958, Lev and I were in Peredelkino and found ourselves for the first time in the home of the Ivanovs. They proved to be right in the eye of the hurricane, both because they were Pasternak's longtime friends and his next-door neighbors. Tamara Vladimirovna Ivanova was among the few people who would visit Pasternak in his home during those terrible days. Moreover, her son, Vyacheslav Vsevolodovich Ivanov, was, despite a forty-year age difference, a close friend of Pasternak's. He was the one who refused to shake hands with the critic who had attacked Pasternak.

Lev and I weren't at the writers' meeting (we were not yet members of the Writers' Union).

At the beginning of 1960 I saw Pasternak for the first time. It was at the Ivanovs' and we were listening to Tamara Ivanova's story of their trip to India. Pasternak came in with his wife and with the widow of Tabidze.† He sat at the table, drank vodka, ate cabbage, and asked questions. But I couldn't escape from a sense of the fantastic in what was going on: here was a face that I had seen a thousand times in newspapers and magazines in every language; here was a person who was still a worldwide sensation.

---

* In her remarkable article "The Epic and the Lyric in Contemporary Russia: Mayakovsky and Pasternak" (1930), Marina Tsvetaeva asserts that the epic is alien to Pasternak and that in distinction to Mayakovsky, he is thoroughly lyrical.

† Titsyan Yustinovich Tabidze (1895–1937), Georgian poet and friend of Pasternak; shot in 1937.

Afterward, we argued for a long time about whether Boris Pasternak was happy or not.

Lev believed that if the attitude toward Pasternak that had been initiated by Bukharin at the First Congress of Writers—where he was immensely praised—had been continued, then Pasternak's fate would have turned out differently. But David Samoilov and I, with the support of Vsevolod Ivanov, objected. We said that Pasternak had lived a very fortunate life: in spite of all the difficulties he had remained true to himself and equal to himself. It isn't often that such a destiny befalls a Russian poet.

In the announcement of his death—May 30, 1960—which was published in the newspapers, it was stated that he was a "member of the Literary Fund (Litfond)."*

There were about 2,000 people at the funeral. Only Paustovsky was there from among the well-known writers. You could hear music in the house all the while. Famous musicians—Heinrich Neuhaus, Sviatoslav Richter, and Maria Yudina played. He was very handsome in the coffin, statuesque and with a resemblance to Dante.

In Pushkin's Leningrad apartment there is a drawing of Pushkin in his coffin, drawn by the artist Bruni. In Moscow there is a drawing of Pasternak in his coffin, drawn by the artist Bruni, a descendant.

Before the body was carried out, the relatives requested everyone to leave the house. I stood by the porch, and on the other side was Olga Ivinskaya, the heroine of his later lyrics, the heroine of *Doctor Zhivago*, his final love. In her humiliated position, she seemed overwhelmingly beautiful despite her age at the time. She was straining toward the closed window.

The people wouldn't let the coffin be put into the waiting bus. They carried it to the cemetery. He himself had chosen the place by the three pines, from where the house was visible. A eulogy was delivered at the graveside by the Moscow University professor Valentin Asmus. He spoke about this genius of a Russian poet, about his abiding place in Russian poetry. (Later a commission at the university "investigated" Asmus's speech. He was asked on what basis he had called Pasternak a "genius." He replied: "In my lifetime I have used this word a multitude of times and never asked anyone for permission.")

* Formed under the auspices of the Writers' Union in 1934, the fund provides financial and household assistance to writers.

After that, someone shouted: "He loved the workers." Another cry: "He spoke the truth, but all the other writers are cowards." "The mighty service rendered by Pasternak is that he was a bridge between West and East, he preached a Christian humanism."

A young physicist read *Hamlet*. We left when they scattered earth over the coffin while the young people read his verses by candlelight into the night.

After Pasternak's funeral, the Peredelkino cemetery, which up until then had been a deserted village plot, became "prestigious." A lot of people made an effort (and still do) to have their loved ones buried there.

All these years I have been slowly advancing toward Pasternak. I have read his novel three times and have become more and more deeply immersed in it. With each reading I have grown more attached to it, and I find I can't do without it. Only the beginning has remained alien to me (except the first meeting between Yurii and Lara and the candles on the table). I have been unable to accept Yurii giving up treatment of the ill—even though I understand that he was pre-destined to be a poet and not a doctor and I have been encountering this situation more and more in life. And I have found increasingly that I can't manage without Pasternak's verses. Particularly, most especially, the Biblical ones—"Christmas Star" and "The Miracle."

From childhood I have loved Kramskoi's painting *Christ in the Desert*. I fell sick, and while at home alone I read in silence the Gospels together with Pasternak's verses. And I could imagine so vividly the humaneness of Christ, the commonplace nature of that entire story, the contemporaneity and eternal and prophetic nature of it, and the pure faith. That was how the revelation suddenly came to me—not in a religious but in a humanistic sense. A man for the people. An ideal. A righteous man. And how excruciating it all is, and yet there is nothing more mighty in the world.

Yet in Pasternak there does exist that path from "I" to "we," from an extraordinary plenitude of happiness, a happiness that is almost biological, to an understanding of pain and suffering. Without all of that there could probably be no great poetry on earth.

I had such a sudden urge to share all these entirely old "revela-tions" that I called Masha (Sveta wasn't in Moscow) and told her the story of Christ, the way I had told my daughters fairy tales in their childhood. But then this was one of the most important tales in the world.

The fresh literary interests that I later developed became steps in my re-education, the acquisition of a great culture. Becoming involved in the verses of Akhmatova and the prose of Bulgakov and Platonov proved to be truly fortunate for me.

However, several no doubt very important encounters never took place, whether because it was too late or for whatever other reasons. I never became involved in the books of Zoshchenko* (even though I exerted a great deal of effort to that end). Andrei Belyi† never became part of my life (with the exception of his memoirs), just as many years before, Afanasii Fet‡ did not either . . .

---

* Mikhail Mikhailovich Zoshchenko (1895–1950), popular Soviet satirical writer and humorist, whose works often dealt with everyday Soviet problems.

† Real name Boris Nikolaevich Bugaev (1880–1934), leading symbolist writer.

‡ Afanasii Afanasievich Fet (1820–1892), Russian aesthete and member of the Parnassian poets.

XVI

Fear

So what was I afraid of in my childhood? Contemporary psycho-analysis teaches that if you want to understand a person, if you want to understand his present-day fears, then you must return to his childhood, to those sublimated complexes of childhood, to the fears of childhood.

A mindlessly courageous young girl emerges out of my childhood.

Whenever I come out of the house, very rarely do I stop in the courtyard and gaze up at those eaves along which I used to go crawling after the young boys, having tucked up my braids any old way so they wouldn't get in my way. I even feel awkward showing those eaves to my close friends—they would think I'm just fibbing and boasting. But in fact, there are still old ladies around who used to call that young girl the roof climber.

I'm nine years old, and we are living in a Ukrainian village near Poltava. Outside the village the highway goes past the woods toward the cemetery. The kids are arguing.

"Who's not chicken to go walking through the cemetery alone at midnight?"

"I'm not chicken!"

Once it's said, there's no way back. I have to put a stone on a grave. And they'll check it in the morning. Around eleven o'clock at night I crawl out the window. Everyone in our family is already asleep. I run down the road to the cemetery. I'm terrified; I hum songs under my breath and I recite verses. I lay a stone down and triumphantly return. I can't wait till morning. The only pity was that my "feat" was performed right before our departure for Moscow so that I only had the opportunity to bask in the rays of fame for a mere week.

Another summer, in 1930. Kislovodsk. I'm twelve years old. And I know with utter certainty what a person needs to make him happy: to go galloping on a horse. Probably I got it all from books: Gustave Aimard, Cooper, Lermontov's *A Hero of Our Time*, and, of course, Jack London's Paula, the little lady of the big house. But then right here in Kislovodsk I see live horsemen all the time. I make my way to the stables.

"Let me."

"How old are you?"

"Fifteen," I say, without batting an eye.

"Well, okay, I'll let you. But you're lying [I turn completely crimson and I'm on the verge of crying]. Just remember, if you get scared, I'll chase you off."

If only I don't get scared. If only I don't get scared. I climb up on the horse, I'm all covered in sweat, I fasten convulsively onto the reins. At a walking pace. A canter. A gallop. Through all the hazards. I'm so afraid that I'll be chased off that I'm not afraid of the horse, of falling, of being crippled.

I'm small in build and I always stood last in physical education. There I am in badly fitting baggy pants and a sports vest. On a big horse I'm just a pip-squeak, not the least resemblance to my fictional and real-life heroines. But still I go galloping on a horse, in real life, along the narrow Caucasian roads.

I'm writing in Peredelkino at a writers' retreat, where I'm being crowded by sticky, shameful fears. There are plenty of them; they won't let me sleep, and it's impossible to sit down at the desk before they've been chased away.

I am ashamed of fear, and yet I still suffer from it. During the entire winter of 1965–1966 I was afraid of the letters that Lev wrote in defense of Sinyavsky and Daniel. I was afraid of the upcoming meetings. Those were genuine fears. But to recognize the reason for fear is already a way of beginning to cope with it. The most important thing concerns the kind of fears that are left unspoken, that have no cause, that have settled in somewhere deep down, and that you can't tell anyone about: I am afraid because I am afraid.

From childhood I despised what was puny and cowardly, what I used to call Jewish. I had to squeeze it out of myself, I had to root it

COLLEGE OF THE SEQUOIAS

LIBRARY

out so that nothing remained. To swim, to leap, to work on the balance beam, to exercise on the horizontal bar, on the rings, to hurtle down from high mountains on skis . . .

I was simply thrown from a boat into the sea and I started to swim.

No sooner did I tie on my first pair of skates and go on the ice than I fell down and broke my arm. No sooner was the sling removed than I went secretly (my parents still wouldn't allow me) back to the skating rink, fastened on the skates, went on the ice, fell down, and broke the very same arm. Not in the least discouraged, I waited until I could once more go back to the rink, get up on the ice, and learn how to fly so that the wind would whistle in my face. I waited and I did learn how.

I was firmly convinced that this was the only way to live. I didn't have a bit of sympathy for those who couldn't. If you want to, then you can do it. There is no such thing as "I can't."

So when my little daughter Sveta used to cry because she was afraid of jumping off a tiny mound, I was ashamed that I had raised such a little coward. Whenever I myself retreated in fear before whatever danger, I despised myself.

There was a woodshed in the yard of my school, and it was possible to crawl out the windows of the second floor from the physics lab. The young boys crawled out and jumped. I crawled out too, but stopped. I was frightened. It was particularly repulsive because the rest of them were punished. But not me.

One of the boys later confessed that he fell in love with me precisely at that very moment when I refused and didn't jump. But he went ahead and jumped while I watched.

I frequently heard and read in books that fear is becoming to a girl and a woman, that to be afraid is a sign of femininity. I'm a flirt, I always wanted people to like me, but I never pretended to be a coward in order to give some timid man the possibility to stand out and show off his valor. And anyway, I don't have much faith in all this kind of talk. I believed that if someone liked you *for something,* then it should be for your valor and not for your cowardice.

But more frequently, much more frequently, I did jump.

I made a parachute jump. I wasn't afraid of the bombings, and no sooner had I sent my daughter off with the evacuation than I never went down into the bomb shelter again. I was not afraid of giving birth, I was not afraid of my numerous operations.

As in some primeval magic cosmology, fears took on substantial forms and became animate. In my childhood I suffered from a serious case of scarlet fever, with complications, high fever, and delirium. I used to cry out to my uncomprehending parents: "The serum, take the serum away!" "Serum," a new word that I had heard in my delirium, was what I named the mask, the brown doll's mask of the old gnome. I was afraid of that mask and for me it was converted into the nucleus of pain and illness. In cases of adult illness there was no longer any "serum." But for a long time the conviction did not leave me that everything was external and all one had to do to get rid of the pain or badness was to eliminate or change that external manifestation.

When I was studying in the seventh grade, we did our practical training at a factory. In was hot, and mostly we just hung around without anything to do. It was a very rare event for anyone to explain anything to us or let us touch anything. In return, we were "tempered in a factory cauldron." And we stuffed our pockets full of the "rejects": the razor blades that it was so much fun to break up and turn into metallic crumbs in our classes.

Somehow or other almost all of us managed to miss out on our practical training. I was accused of being an instigator. At that time I was caught up in love games that were spent in furious correspondence (even though the "object" of affection was sitting at the neighboring desk) and I would answer questions sluggishly. Then suddenly the senior Pioneer leader said: "You, Raya, are the daughter of a white-collar worker. You're from the intellectual classes, so how could you understand the working-class soul? That's why Polya here didn't pass; she has been nurtured on her mother's milk with a love for work, she's a worker, body and soul."

I fell into a shamefaced silence. Polya was the daughter of our school cleaning lady. That very morning I had been drilling physics with her for the umpteenth time, I had explained the construction of the electric motor. She was incredibly dense, although she seemed quite goodhearted to me. And every time I visited them in their room with the window at sidewalk level, where eight people lived (how did they sleep? where did they all find space?), I experienced a poignant shame because of the prosperity of our home. The Pioneer leader continued talking, while fear crept into my heart. Does it mean that I'm not worthy to participate in the revolution? Does it mean that Polya is suitable for this and I'm not? At night I would imagine how I would go away to join up with the underground somewhere in Germany, how I would take part in the battles, how I would carry the banner at the demonstration, or how I would run away from home to build the city of Komsomolsk in the Far East.

No, no, I'll go to the factory, I won't skip out on it anymore, I'll do what's necessary so that no trace of the white-collar worker is left in me.

The war. Who'll go on a dangerous assignment? Who's not chicken?

There was nothing of the sort. Because I was afraid to go against the rules, the regulations, the statutes.

On the accursed day, October 15, 1941, when the wet snow was mixed with black smoke (they were burning the archives), I ran to the district office of the Party to get permission not to leave with the evacuation so that I could stay and defend Moscow. There I was firmly told: "Everyone must stay at his post; you are doing important work, you are purposely being evacuated together with the executive staff of the People's Commissariat for Foreign Affairs and that's how you'll help the front lines. You have been accepted as a candidate for membership in the Party, so please submit yourself to Party discipline. The more difficult the situation, the stricter must be the discipline. You do understand what would happen if everyone started to act independently!"

A Communist battalion was being organized, one floor below, in that same building. I ought to have acted independently, I ought to have obeyed myself. But, no, I showed up under orders and left for Kuibyshev.

Once Lyonya was buried, I wrote an application to the Military Commissariat requesting to join the army. I was refused.

In the summer of 1943 I was with a delegation at the front near the city of Orel. I was invited to stay till the end of the war. True, it was a somewhat timid invitation and all the while the commissar kept repeating the question: "But won't I get into trouble for this?"

There was one further opportunity. In October 1943 I visited the Northern Fleet once again to give lectures. And I could have remained there.

It wouldn't be true if today I said that I didn't go to the front because I had a little daughter and I was obliged to stay with her. Or I didn't go because I was afraid of the shooting, of the bombardments, and, ultimately, of death. In actual fact, I was afraid of the authorities, I was afraid of something worse; there was perhaps less dignity in this kind of fear.

Given the entire makeup of my life, my soul, my youth, I should have been at the front. My wartime letters to Lyonya were a cry specifically for that. It's an old wound that essentially hasn't healed. Even now, every wartime song or poem echoes painfully with my unrealized dream.

And thus my physical bravery became of no use to anyone.

For a long time I refused to accept the inevitability of death. I existed for such a long time in an illusory world, where immortality reigned. So then there was truly nothing to fear once the main fear was lacking. In August 1942, when the airplane was shot down and Lyonya perished, my world of blissful ignorance was shaken for the first time.

A friend of mine once said that people around us move along parallel paths, and they simply find themselves at different points. If you look back, you'll see yourself, the way you were yesterday, at such and such a point. And someone close to you will be at that same point today where you saw yourself yesterday.

And so I was afraid when in 1960 Lev wanted to send something to the *Literaturnaya gazeta* in the nature of an obituary on Pasternak. But I wasn't afraid to go to the funeral. That sounds ridiculous today, but how many of those around me who loved, understood, and worshiped Pasternak were afraid to go to the funeral at that time!

After the March meetings of the intelligentsia with the government in 1963, after Ilichev (who at that time was in charge of the Department for Propaganda in the Party Central Committee) accused Lev of "abstract humanism," I was walking along the paths in Peredelkino fearing that everything would return once again. But now I have no shield—the shield of deafness and blindness. Now I'm living "after the fall," I cannot accept anything, I cannot justify anything.

I'm afraid of getting involved in the Brodsky* affair, but I am getting involved in it.

In September 1965 Lev and I were in the Caucasus and there we

* See p. 276 ff.

learned that Andrei Sinyavsky had been arrested (we had read his articles) and someone else as well (the name of Yuli Daniel was totally unfamiliar to us).

Koma (Vyacheslav) Ivanov and I were swimming in the sea and I said to him: "Koma, I'm afraid."

"What are you afraid of?"

"I'm afraid for Lev, for his heart."

That was the truth, the real truth, but not the whole truth. I did not doubt that Lev would somehow get involved, that he would start to intercede, and that naturally trouble would follow. But there seemed to be less and less strength, and with each year it all became more and more difficult. The Brodsky case had just barely finished, and without a pause a new case was beginning.

It was the same kind of fear that made me afraid for my father during those nights in 1937. And the same kind of fear that made me afraid in the Lubyanka when I was forced to spend the night there in 1948.

But in addition to all these logical considerations, there was another kind of fear as well. The kind of irrational, sticky fear that makes you want to crouch in a corner with the cry: "I don't want to!"

In 1976 Lev was recovering from a serious operation. His book *To Be Preserved Forever* was published abroad. He wasn't gaining in strength. Fears. Yet those fears of a decade before seemed almost laughable. And that helps a little in suppressing my current fears.

Merely by reason of my technical ignorance I'm not afraid that the conversations in our apartment are being recorded. It's simply that in the depths of my heart I can't believe that something could possibly be recorded on a tape recorder.

I look around: where are my friends right now? People are freeing themselves from fear. And here is just one example of that fact. In 1958 no one, not a single person, spoke out openly in defense of Pasternak. Yet many, a great many, considered Pasternak a great poet and had known him for years and even decades.

Seven years passed by. More than a hundred literary people, as well as many other people from various sectors of society, spoke out in support of Sinyavsky and Daniel. Their works were practically unknown and few were acquainted with the authors. Letters were written to newspapers, the government; letters and telegrams were written to the Party congress; people spoke openly of their disagreement. People freeing themselves from fear. In this case I was not in the least frightened when I was summoned to Party headquarters in connection with our letter in defense of Sinyavsky and Daniel.

On March 9, 1966, I spoke out at an open Party gathering and talked about the manuscripts that had not become books: Valentin Katayev's *Holy Fount*, Aleksandr Bek's *The New Appointment*, Lidiya Chukovskaya's *Sofia Petrovna*, Evgenia Ginzburg's *Journey into the Whirlwind*, Anna Akhmatova's *Requiem*, and Vasilii Grossman's novel *The Life and the Fate*, which was confiscated by the KGB. I was congratulated, thanked, recorded, and quoted. People were enthralled by my courage. But I felt awkward because my speaking out was a queer mixture of courage and fear. I was afraid to get up on the stage and yet I went. I was afraid to name Grossman's novel and yet I did. But I never mentioned a word about Sinyavsky and Daniel. Yet they were sitting in Moscow jails awaiting transportation to prison . . .

How did this adult coward grow up out of that courageous little girl?

I hardly could have gone through the entire torturous process of the meetings, newspapers, journals, and resolutions without there being any trace of fear.

I was still striving for approval all the time. So that my audience would applaud, so that I would seem brave to everyone, so that I could show off—on the podium or on a horse.

How could you follow your own path when no one approved of your path? Perhaps it wasn't the right path at all? No, one had to proceed along the broad avenue, three abreast and keeping step. That avenue had been laid out by those who were in the forefront. They knew better; they were thinking about you and for you.

The really frightening thing was to swerve off to the side, to break away from the path, to become an outsider. That accursed intellectual core and upbringing of yours would at times draw you off into byways, would draw you off to seek out things on your own. No, no, don't give in, fight against it, the way you did against cowardice in your childhood. And stay with the rest of them, with nobody but them.

Perhaps I'm rationalizing too much now. That's just more of my character showing through. But then perhaps that's what my character mainly is.

> From childhood I never loved ovals,
> From childhood I always sketched angles.
> —Pavel Kogan

> But then I always loved an oval
> Because it was so perfect.
> —Naum Korzhavin

I agree with Korzhavin. I never drew angles, I avoided them, I was afraid of them. And so it is to this very day.

My grown-up daughters frequently say to me even now that we have ghosts in the apartment. They don't like to stay alone there; they insist that the floorboards creak and someone is walking around. I laugh at them because I never experienced anything similar, either in my childhood or later. Probably I'm laughing in vain. Probably my daughters are more keenly aware of a world filled with dangers than I am, a world that is hostile to man, where fears hover about from birth to death.

Both fear and fearlessness existed side by side within me.

The fact that I was so fearless in the face of life made my childhood and youth richer. With my every fiber I sensed utterly and completely the untroubled happiness of the beginning and the immensity of it all. But it also deprived me of a great deal and made me a hardened person. There doesn't have to be a causal relation here, but that is the way it was with me.

Later on, it limited my literary possibilities, it didn't afford me the opportunity to perceive with depth that sphere of phenomena that I was called upon to concern myself with professionally: contemporary art. Art can't be understood without knowing fear, despair, the absurd, and the terrifying impossibility of communication.

Together with the advent of fear in my life, a conscious fear, I began to comprehend other people better, I became more compassionate; sounds and shades were multiplied in the world.

Tragedy purifies by means of fear and compassion. These concepts are related but not identical. A fear for someone close to you isn't undignified as long as it doesn't envelop the entire world. A fear for oneself, no matter how natural it may be, can be undignified.

From time to time I come back to that place in Nadezhda Mandelstam's first book where she wishes that she had wailed because of the abuse, the horror, and the pain. Now I regret that earlier I feared so much less for Mama and my daughters than I might today. But I do not in the least regret, for example, that even though I made my hands bleed from biting them, I never once cried out when I was giving birth. No, even now I feel it is undignified for a person to wail. But then I have never experienced the kind of circumstances that would compel me to do so.

I keep repeating, just like an ancient charm: "I will not be afraid!" I was studiously sticking a toy arrow into a toy bear so that the real one would die.

Or perhaps I was banishing fear somewhere off into the depths, into my subconscious. But when people say to me now that "their" cars are often standing near our doors, particularly when foreigners are here (and more and more of them come to see us), I am not in the least frightened.

How can you get rid of your fears? Contemporary psychoanalysis teaches us: return to your childhood. Alas, a return to childhood does not help.

XVII

Bucharest

1970

In our dreams during the final year of the war we were traveling to some Soviet city that had been freed from the Nazis, and in that city we were going to build socialism, the genuine variety, what today we would call socialism with a human face. My husband, however, was sent to the Allied Control Commission in Bucharest. The victorious armies were establishing order in the conquered countries. Once more there would be a new order. An antifascist one.

Our train stopped for a few hours in Kiev. We walked along Kreshchatik Avenue and there wasn't a single undamaged house. German prisoners of war were clearing away the stone rubble. Sveta said in amazement: "Mama, they look just like normal people."

Our first Rumanian city, Constanţa, greeted us with a warm rain. We were in our heavy fall coats, but the people in the streets were wearing raincoats. Nowadays there isn't a single little village in our country where these transparent raincoats aren't worn, and they are frequently being replaced now by nylon raincoats. But at that time I looked on these raincoats as otherworldly material, as a symbol of a luxurious "abroad."

For several days we had seen through the windows of the train a Russia that was impoverished, ragged, and shattered. I had spent the entire war in the midst of a dark-gray color. In Bucharest the summer-time crowd shocked and outraged me with its fashionable colorfulness: red, yellow, and blue dresses everywhere. I immediately wanted that kind of dress and I was ashamed of wanting it. I condemned the frivolous Rumanian women. Of course they knew nothing of grief. And I condemned the men in their patent-leather shoes.

We lived in the Hotel Union, a third-class Soviet colony. More important officials lived in the Palace Hotel, while the most important ones were in private dwellings.

I came to Rumania six months pregnant. Before I gave birth, I was busy at work: holding consultations, looking over the exhibition devoted to the USSR, then compiling outlines for lectures. But my main life was at home. How unusual that seemed after being so busy in Moscow—the constant rush, without a moment to myself. "Lipstick is put on at the expense of the state," as my girl friend used to say when she sat down at her work place and took out her lipstick.

In Bucharest we had breakfast and lunch in a restricted cafeteria, but we ate supper at home (bread, milk, and grapes).

On May 8, Kolya suddenly came home from work in the middle of the day with roses. He kissed my hand and congratulated me on Victory Day. In the evening we walked through a drunken Bucharest. The following day we went outside the city to celebrate.

How many times, like everyone else, had I imagined that day, dreamt about it, longed for it, and waited for it. I remembered Lyonya and his verses dedicated to the future day of victory.

I burst into tears later, when a whole packet of letters arrived from friends in Moscow. They gave such a detailed account of everything. One letter supplemented the other so that it later seemed as though I myself had been there, in that crowd of *mine* on Red Square. I saw the way the soldiers were treated to vodka on the streets, the way some Americans were tossed up and down in the air near the Hotel National, the way people were suddenly different and for an instant felt like a single family caught up in the joy of humanity.

That great celebration was a very bitter one for me in the midst of the drunken revelry of people who were both foreign and alien to me. Naturally, everything is relative. When Lev related how he had been forced to celebrate Victory Day in a jail cell after fighting through all four years of the war, I felt not only an agonizing pain for the right that had been denied him to be in Berlin on that day, but I also felt ashamed of my own sorrows.

I had no one to reminisce with on May 9. To reminisce about those four whole years, day by day. The most bitter and the most joyful days.

To recall June 22, October 16—the evacuation from Moscow—and the return to Moscow. Stalingrad. And the first fireworks.

I was grateful for the roses, but Kolya and I had no memories to share together.

Life in Bucharest was broken in two, not when I gave birth but when Kolya left. He fell ill and was sent back to Moscow. For more than three months I lived alone with two small children. I was working a great deal. During those months I experienced peace and freedom if not happiness.

When Kolya was around, we never had anything left over to make purchases. The money went for drink. But when he left, I gradually began to clothe myself. That most inaccessible of raincoats made an appearance, along with a suit, a handbag, a hat, and a long cherry-colored bathrobe.

In my childhood I formed an ideal of beauty that more closely resembled the illustrations in the series Golden Library than anything else: a wasplike waist; small feet in heels peeking out from underneath a dress; long blond hair that was worn loose, in a braid, or a bun; a veil and a broad-brimmed hat. (Nowadays this old ideal has become the most contemporary of styles: "Retro.") For my first twenty-five years I had worn jackets with a leather belt and shoulder strap, white sweaters, short dark skirts, berets, and oxfords. And suddenly my childhood dream was coming to life.

There are very few photographs from the Bucharest days. A woman in a bright-colored dress holding a white bundle all rolled up. A woman in a severe blue suit with a stern face, giving a lecture. A woman and a little girl, Sveta, with close-cropped hair and holding an enormous teddy bear. Another little girl, the newly born Masha, in flannelette diapers, white with blue polka dots. How beautiful that soft flannelette was! And during the war I had been used to seeing unweaned children bundled up in old rags. I had seen a little boy in diapers of coarse black cloth, the material handed out to his mother in Kuibyshev.

For the first time in my life I had ten pairs of stockings lying in my wardrobe. The only luxury item that I bought in Rumania was a dinner service for twelve people. A single plate and one gravy dish have survived from it. And Sveta's doll that could close its eyes and had eyelashes on its lids. That doll had also come from my childhood imagination.

In Rumania I heard about our rapaciousness abroad. Rumors circulated about trucks and planes on which foreign goods were being transported off to Russia, both officially and unofficially.

Naturally, I was indignant over these pillagers. They were besmirching the good name of the Soviet people.

An old friend came to my hotel in a military uniform. This was the first person who told me about the pillaging and violence that Red Army soldiers had committed against the populace. He was finishing up the war in Czechoslovakia and he told me about what he had seen with his own eyes. I knew that he was an honest person and couldn't have made anything up. But I retained nothing of his stories; they made no lasting impact on me, and my heart, by its very makeup at that time, rejected the possibility of such things. Naturally, there were isolated and atypical scoundrels everywhere, even in the Red Army.

The Rumanian art historian Mircea Nadejde related how he and his friends had been waiting for the Red Army, how fervent his hopes had been. The Russians would come and night would be changed into day. "But your soldiers took my watch away by force. How they took it, that's what was really insulting. I myself would have given it at the first request." He told me that as he accompanied me home after my public lecture "The Countenance of the Soviet Man."

Before me are three verbatim steno reports in French. With literateness, with skill, and at times even with sophistication, I defend the Soviet state, the system, and the people.

One poster in Rumanian has been preserved: "Some Aspects of Soviet Culture," and lower down, "Raisa Orlova, ARLUS, No. 115 Victoria Street, Sunday, 18 November 1945, 11:00 A.M."

A young woman appears at the lectern. I am introduced to the audience: "*Domna* Orlova." Someone's outburst interrupts the chairman: "*Domna* or *domnisara*? Madame or mademoiselle?" I myself reply: "A *domna* who already has two *domnisaras*." Laughter, smiles, and gratitude for the fact that I gave a human response and had, moreover, learned a most elementary Rumanian word. And I'm pleased with myself, pleased with my response, happy that I looked young.

My public lectures were "The Soviet Person," "Soviet Culture," "Popular Education in the USSR," and an evening of questions and answers.

Three steno reports. They're like that same canvas on which other *domnas* even today embroider the advertised patterns in Bucharest, in Paris, in Cairo, and in Tokyo. Today the world has already learned a great deal about us, a very great deal. But in those days the Iron Curtain had only just been torn asunder by a bloody war. We had been attacked, we had defended ourselves, our army had left Russia behind and entered Europe. And so now we had to explain what in fact had happened. Perhaps it was necessary to cast off all attempts to understand Russia intellectually and one simply had to believe and speak about a miracle; or it still was possible to understand and explain.

I set about explaining, completely oblivious to either the enormity of the task or its infinite difficulty. The street where I was speaking was aptly called Victoria Street. In this city, as was the case throughout all of Eastern Europe, units of the Red Army, a victorious army, were stationed.

Naturally, I was not aware of that, but an army was standing behind my explanations. "There are two views of the Soviet person. The adherents of one view, which was widespread before the war, insist that the Soviet people are beings of a particular species. Both our friends and our enemies share that belief. Our enemies take us for devils. According to their conception, the USSR is a hell where people die from hunger, where people are tortured and so forth.

"Our friends take us for angels. According to their conception, the USSR is a paradise, a dream come true where there is nothing more to wish for.

"But neither the ones nor the others consider us to be people, with all the virtues and vices typical of the human race. They cannot conceive that the USSR is neither hell nor paradise, but a constantly developing society, an experimental arena for great achievements, a society that is seeking and finding new paths for mankind. And if in the process of these searchings it happens to go astray, then this society retraces its steps and begins its searchings once more . . .

"The adherents of the other view (there are an especially great number of them now after the war) say: the Soviet people are not different from us, they are the same as we. Their attempts to have supposedly discovered something new have suffered failure . . .

"Both views are untrue, although there is a grain of truth contained in both."

There's nothing, to be sure, that is as amazing and repellent today as the confidence of that self-confident *domna* on the stage: she possessed the absolute truth.

Brave enough by the standards of those days, for after all, I did touch on both hunger and torture, naturally in order to "give a rebuff" to them, but in those years one was not even supposed to mention such things.

The majority of the people sitting in the overflowing hall knew what hunger was. Some of them had passed through fascist jails. They understood that the fate of their conquered country was now irreversibly connected with their powerful Eastern neighbor. It was vitally important for them to find out what kind of a country Russia was. It was still possible at that time to choose—Rumanians could still get themselves out to other countries.

My audience, like all Western people, reacted suspiciously to an aggressive propaganda, to that self-praise that our newspapers, journals, books, and lectures were full of.

But the woman on the stage did not seem to be propagandizing. She was posing questions. She was formulating their doubts, those of the audience. She was trying to put herself in tune with them. They were beginning to believe. And when a little later she would start to prove that the USSR was no paradise yet but still a beautiful country, how easy it would be for them to believe what they wanted to believe, because from time immemorial it has been characteristic of people to believe in something better.

With each page of the old steno report, that woman becomes more alien and one feels increasing shame for her.

How did she, then, define the features of the new man? The revolution liberated human relations from the power of money. "Money no longer determines a person's role in society. Money no longer plays any role in the relations between parents and children, between husbands and wives, between friends."

The year is 1970. A passing grade in the university in Georgia costs 25 rubles. One student had the following experience. He put 30 rubles inside his grade book, and when he received his passing grade, he said to the professor: "You owe me five rubles." Without a word, the professor gave him the change. Before an operation in a hospital, the nurse and nursing assistant are each given 5 rubles. For the operation the surgeon receives hundreds, sometimes thousands of rubles. The cashier who hands out the honorarium in a publishing house is given 3 rubles. Everything is sold and bought. It's precisely money that determines human relations in many cases.

But there in Bucharest in 1945 she, that is, I, continued. "A Balzac of our times could not create the kind of models like Grandet, like *le père* Goriot, like Rastignac.

"I do not mean that we don't have any misers. We do, unfortunately, and a great many. But in our country there is no basis for a Grandet as a social type, in our society it is impossible to find thousands of small Grandets."

I was uttering these words at the very time when the careers of thousands, perhaps even tens of thousands of Rastignacs were being established.

For the most part, those who were sitting in front of me were intellectuals. Of course they knew Balzac. French culture had always been a native culture for Rumania.

Thus the ties between the lecturer and the audience were strengthened even more. Now one could pass over to the offensive. "It is in your country that I have heard about the problem of a 'dowry' for the first time. People felt sorry for me here because I have two daughters and no sons, and it will be difficult to marry them off without a dowry." In this case, as in all the rest, I was sincere. I had never heard of a dowry before. And I was amused by the misgivings of compassionate Rumanian women in regard to the future of these two little girls. They subsequently did get married without a dowry, which, incidentally, would have greatly alleviated their complicated lives.

With winning sincerity I admitted that we had a lot of deficiencies: "The majority of our women do not have silk stockings [this was still the prenylon era!] . . . we had to produce everything not for the select, but for two million . . . But despite the fact that we still are lacking in a great deal, we are happy. We are happy today . . . our world is still not very comfortable, but it is just and beautiful, and that is much more important."

I told my audience about Oleg Koshevoi (the hero of Aleksandr Fadeyev's novel *The Young Guard*, which was just coming off the presses). Oleg wanted peace, happiness, harmony, but agony, torture, and death had fallen to his lot. "The fate of our country can be likened to the fate of Oleg Koshevoi. A peaceful, industrious country was striving for achievements not on the battlefields, but in art, science, and labor, in the improvement of human life, yet circumstances had reduced Russia to a fortress resisting barbarism."

People applauded, presented me with flowers, and shook my hand. But there was also an insulting amazement in their reaction to me that seemed to affirm the questions that I had posed at the very beginning. Translated into words, those amazed looks must have sounded something like this: "A Soviet woman has come here from there, and she's civilized, doesn't wipe her nose on her sleeve, and can even express herself in French." I was indignant. It was unjust. What right did those Rumanians have to be amazed at the fact that a person from Russia was civilized? After all, I knew that I was far from being above the average level.

Now, when I recollect and read it over, trying to attune myself to that time, I still ask myself: perhaps it would have been better if on Victoria Street a fat-mugged colonel had appeared before them speaking in Russian, who, without any refinement, would have declared to them that the Soviet people had long since achieved perfection in everything and so all they, his audience, had to do was to arrange themselves into two ranks and march off after the Soviet people straight into paradise. Then a great deal would have become clear immediately, and those Rumanians who knew how to think would not have been led astray . . . But perhaps this is idle speculation. There are many paths to truth, and those who wish to traverse those mined paths have to do so by themselves, on their own.

I was homesick for Moscow, for my relatives, my friends, but it was not a real nostalgia, only a subdued one. I felt like being alone. I needed to be—it was a kind of pause, an intermission.

The sun was no longer an enemy, as in the summer, when I could escape from it only by curtaining off the windows with wet bed sheets. I was basking in the caressing autumn sun—and I was my own mistress. Masha was sleeping calmly. I was laying out her diapers in the washbasin under a stream of hot water. Soon I finished the daily ironing. The children weren't ill.

In the evenings, after the children had been put to bed and I had read what I had to, I would sit down by the open window, turn out the lamp, look out at the cheerful Bucharest square and ponder. I was at peace with the world and with myself. For the first time in a long while and for the last time before a long period of being in crowds, I was left alone with myself. And unconsciously I wanted just that. But I still didn't know what to do with myself.

On a December day, when I returned from a lecture, I learned that Kolya had returned from Moscow. The initial prophetic reaction in my heart: "I don't want this." Unfortunately, I came to terms with it in an instant and a minute later I was embraced and felt happy. On December 30 we came back to the USSR.

XVIII

My Graduate Studies

I enrolled in graduate studies at the Institute of World Literature in 1947. Graduate studies became the next stage in the process of priming that had begun at VOKS. Here I learned dogmatism, non-independent thought, and literary criticism by means of illustrative quotation.

I read a great number of books and sat through a great many works, chapters from dissertations, lectures, and reports prepared by others, maintaining only the vaguest distinction between what was good and what was bad. Any criteria of what was artistic remained extremely muddled.*

I began to study American literature in a professional way. My supervisor was Anna Elistratova. She was a person with an encyclopedic education, a serious scholar.

I enrolled in graduate studies immediately after a vicious attack on the first volume of the history of American literature. Elistratova was one of the authors. She was beset by fear for a long time after the attack, particularly because her friend, the specialist in American literature Abel Startsev, who had written the greater number of chapters in that volume, was dismissed from the institute and then arrested.

Roman Mikhailovich Samarin was in charge of graduate studies. From the point of view of human qualities, it was impossible to compare him and Anna Elistratova. But even she had a hand in the

---

* I was repelled by the novels of very bad writers, such as Fedor Panferov, Mikhail Bubennov, and Arkadii Perventsev, and liked those of Vasilii Grossman, Emmanuil Kazakevich, Konstantin Paustovsky, Vera Panova, and Viktor Nekrasov.

overall affairs and the dealings of Samarin. I was taught to do likewise. And I proved to be an exemplary student. Our assignment was laid out: to "expose" the Americans, to "expose" their literature. This is what I studied and nearly mastered during my graduate studies.

At that time my articles were starting to be published. It was amazingly easy for me to write in those days. There were orders for a number of topics and I filled those orders precisely, on time. Everything I had to I wrote smoothly. It was completely natural that at first my articles were hardly even edited. Now, fifteen years later, the tiniest review is nothing but agony.

I didn't like what I was writing in those days too, but there were no inner torments.

Elistratova taught me one thing: accuracy in the treatment of facts. Everything should be checked and rechecked over and over again—the names, the titles, the quotations.

But beyond that, no objective standards existed at all. The entire methodology of scholarly work was completely fallacious: to force things to fit a ready-made answer. Not to deduce the idea from the material, from the diversity of what had been read and pondered, but on the contrary, to adjust the material to a thesis that was known and approved beforehand. There was no journey to a land of the unknown. This became all the more obligatory the closer the material was to our own time. In the realm of the classics it was still possible to work differently. But I was attracted only to contemporary themes.

I was in graduate school at the Institute of World Literature at the same time that Mikhail Bakhtin's dissertation "François Rabelais and the Comic Culture of the Renaissance" was all the rage. (Nowadays it's a classic that has been translated into many languages.) But I never heard his name mentioned at the institute.

A scornful attitude toward the intelligentsia had emerged and grown in me during the VOKS years. At that time I spoke ironically about those few of my fellow classmates who went into scholarship. I didn't really consider myself suitable for scholarly work, and even the work itself, as well as its practitioners, did not prompt any respect. Incidentally, anyone could have done the scholarly work that I did in 1947 as long as they didn't possess a free mind. A free mind was no burden to me then.

Much more important, however, were not my personal opportunities but rather the quite widespread anti-intellectual atmosphere that

I detest so much now. That atmosphere permeated my own heart, and whenever I imagined the person whom I might fall in love with, I kept repeating like an incantation: "If only he's not a four-eyes!"

I turned my back on history, on art, on "intellectual" conversations. I rejected the most beautiful things that united, unite, and will go on uniting man with the past and the future.

As in a great deal else, I was going counter to myself, counter to what had been instilled in me in my childhood and youth, counter to my heart.

In a conversation about one poet, I heard: "He lives to spite himself. He torments himself, he forces himself into an uncharacteristic form." That defined my condition very precisely at that time. Japanese trees that are twisted and constrained into an uncharacteristic form grow up into marvelous curios. They have nothing of the joy of the free and natural tree.

The thing that attracts me most in people now is a freedom and fidelity to oneself. The ability to find one's own form, to be aware of it, to be faithful to one's predestined nature. Whether one will be able to fulfill oneself or not is something different that doesn't depend on the individual. But to follow one's own path does.

That's why the book *The Italics Are Mine* by Nina Berberova* (which I read in 1975) proved to be so important to me. Above all, the ability to divine the symbols, the signs, of one's own destiny. And, what was vastly more difficult and therefore to be encountered much more rarely, the ability to act in accord with these signs.

At that time I strove for self-education, which in fact turned out to be self-suppression.

In 1962 I read in the diaries of Olga Berggolts† some entries that were kindred in spirit: "A novel where the main thing will now be about the rights of an individual to self-determination, dealing with that individual's vital and primordial rights, with his tragedy of self-restraint and even self-annihilation—in the name of our mighty ideas" (February 15, 1940). And further on: "I'm reading Herzen with a gnawing envy of people of his type, of the nineteenth century. O how free they were . . . And even here, in my diary (I'm ashamed to admit

---

* An émigré writer who left Russia in 1922.

† Olga Fedorovna Berggolts (born 1910), Russian writer. A survivor of the Leningrad blockade, she dedicated a number of works to the heroic people of Leningrad.

it!), I am not recording many of my musings simply because of the thought that an investigator will read it and will put me on trial" (March 1, 1940).

I came to my senses (I can't say it any other way) over my anti-intellectual psychoses before 1953, in Tallinn, when I myself began to teach.

For my dissertation at the Institute of World Literature I selected the topic "The Image of the Communist in American Literature, 1945–1950." The material used for research always affects its character. It was no different in this case. Essentially there was nothing to examine. I was involuntarily led off into history. In the second chapter (about the thirties) and at the beginning of the third chapter (dedicated to the history of progressive journalism), there is some interesting material, and new facts are introduced. In the twenties and thirties in the United States there was a powerful and unique left movement, in which communists played a large part. This movement had varying effects on a broad circle of writers: on John Steinbeck and Ernest Hemingway, on Lillian Hellman and Dorothy Parker, and on many others.

That kind of thing was going on not only in America. The seductiveness of communist ideas, their attractiveness, drew many writers of varying talent and varying views. Among them were also those whose names were banned from mention in our country, like Spender, Auden, and Orwell. Even the author of the prophetic 1984 had not remained alien to leftist influences (in the broadest sense of this word), both in his essays of the thirties and in his book *Homage to Catalonia*.

While working on my dissertation, I naturally thought, that is, I repeated other people's thoughts, that communism's effect could only be fruitful. Then years later, as I set about writing this book, I repeated in imitation of others that this effect could only be corrupting.

The truth is far from being in the middle. I am attempting to come closer to an understanding of history, to come closer to its cunning and its complicated, devious path. The inherent depths involved in such a study still exist today. For the writer the attraction to the universe of the "underdogs," of the starving, is a natural one, the attraction to what today bears the name of the Third World.

One might have reflected some on this, but not at the intellectual level at which I found myself at that time. Instead, I made a selection of weak, schematic proletarian novels and spiced them up with theoretical constructions on socialist realism in American literature. It was the purest kind of scholasticism.

In 1956 Lev started work on his book *The Heart Is Always on the Left* and suggested that I compile my articles. I refused: not a single one of the articles written by me and published from 1947 to 1953 deserved to be reread.

My first appearance in print of which I am not ashamed is my review of Martha Dodd's novel *The Searching Light*, which was published in *Inostrannaya literatura*. But by then it was already 1955: a new era in my life and in the life of my country.

I was in the middle of my graduate studies in 1949, the year of the fight against cosmopolitanism.

In essence, though, it began earlier—probably when Stalin raised a toast to the Russian people after victory, in the summer of 1945, to the effect that any other people would have gotten rid of such a government. And that the Russian people were "the first among equals" in the Soviet Union.

A mass psychosis was rampant (the second round, after 1937), with theatrical effects, mob zeal, howling, and outcries. All of that demanded a suppression of will, intellect, conscience, and honor.

The principal enemy was "across the border," the world where our army had been at the end of the war. The disparity between Soviet newspaper articles and actual reality, even in such poor countries as Poland and Rumania, made a deep impression on the awareness of hundreds of thousands, even millions of people.

A flood of prisoners flowed into jails and concentration camps.

Who was guilty for the fact that we lived so badly, worse than anyone else? At first the spies were the guilty ones. Then the foreigners. Various internal aliens followed: the Crimean Tartars, the Chechens, and the Kalmyks. And, finally, the most popular and time-tested formula in many countries and for many generations, and certainly time-tested in Russia: the Jews were guilty.

Once, not long ago, I had to take a look through *Literaturnaya gazeta* for 1949. It's impossible to comprehend now how I could have believed that. In effect everything, the choice of the authors for the vicious articles, the style, the vocabulary, to say nothing of the content—all bore witness to the filth, falsehood, and repugnant comedy of that time. I believed it, even though I had reservations and many personal disagreements. Perhaps, if at that time I had summed up those personal differences of opinion, something different might have happened.

In *Novy mir* (No. 9, 1961) I read in Ehrenburg's column that the Jewish poet Perets Markish had been arrested on January 27, 1949. An article appeared the next day in *Pravda* about the "critics-cosmopolitans." It's difficult not to make a connection between these phenomena.

In 1961 readers could still find out from the newspapers and journals who had been arrested. For a long time it's again been impossible to find out such things. Authors who are striving for the truth give us to understand by using various forms of Aesopian language, such as "his father disappeared" or "he was raised by his grandfather and grandmother," that the parents had been arrested. But more and more often it seems to me that phrases that mislead the censor can also mislead hundreds of thousands of readers, particularly the younger generations.

At the very beginning I spoke out at one of the meetings when that article in *Pravda* was being discussed. I did not simply cast my vote passively. No, I spoke out in support of that entire loathsome business.

Before continuing, I must make one digression. During my work at VOKS I witnessed genuine and unfeigned obsequiousness in front of foreigners. It inspired and still inspires repugnance in me.

On Sundays in Rumania an organ-grinder used to pass by beneath the windows and a parrot would pull out "fortunes." I didn't like fortune-telling, but I always listened to that painfully monotonous organ-grinder and felt lonely in an alien world. I was very tied up in Rumania: five-year-old Sveta and the newborn Masha. But a decade after that, in 1956, in Poland, where I spent all of two weeks, in a world that I found unusually interesting, where everything corresponded to my own agitated state, even there in the evenings, when I was very tired, I longed for Moscow, the Moscow outskirts, Russian speech, for what was my own . . .

Now, thirty years later, thousands, if not tens of thousands, want to leave, depart, flee. Jews and Germans. Russians and Lithuanians. You keep hearing that a director defected, a chess player defected, a sailor defected . . . For many—who eagerly want to leave at any price, who struggle to depart and are arrested, banished for this wish—my attitude will be completely alien. But I haven't changed in this. No proofs, whether logical or emotional, can shake me: I love because I love. Because the one life that was given to me has been spent here. (And as old age approaches, that love has merely grown more acute just as everything else grows more acute [1979]. And that hasn't changed even today, in 1982, my second year of living in a different world.)

In 1949 it seemed to me that the people speaking at gatherings were also protecting our native land, Russia, and that vague feeling that one doesn't care to call by the abused and worn word of "patriotism." Probably I was attempting to speak about patriotism as well. I cited examples (negative!) from articles about America that had been published in *Internatsionalnaya literatura* during the war. One of those articles belonged to Abel Startsev, who had already been arrested by that time.

How obvious it seems to me today, and to all the decent people around me, that it is vile to carry on polemics with someone who is imprisoned, with a person who has a gag in his mouth. But that was exactly how I acted at that time. I have no right to forget about that.

Another theme of my speech was Jewish bourgeois nationalism. On this point, thank God, I managed without any Soviet examples (I made mention of Howard Fast). I spoke about the fact that from the very beginning of the Revolution the Party conducted an incisive battle against anti-Semitism but not at all against nationalism (an excellent illustration of the "absence" of anti-Semitism was this very meeting itself). I spoke about the fact that bourgeois nationalism had been allowed to develop into a major danger.

Everything was logical and in contradiction to reality. What I did say about nationalism I felt both before the meeting and for a long time afterward. Not only did I not think of myself as Jewish, but while it was still possible to do so, I called myself anti-Semitic and with justification.

If we had lived in a normal society, which does not yet exist on earth, the process of assimilation probably would have been completed in me. In effect, it was essentially completed in me. I am living in Russia, my native language is Russian, my native culture and literature are Russian. I don't know a single Yiddish word. Many of the world's cultures (French, American, Italian, Spanish, German) are incomparably closer to me than the Jewish culture. I never sensed the call of blood. Both the massacre at Babi Yar and the Nazi humiliation of the Ukrainians, Poles, French, and Russians were likewise genuinely unbearable and despicable.

. . .

Since the time when these pages were written, a generation of people has grown up in the USSR who feel that they are Jews. A third emigration has appeared. I don't mean the émigrés or the ones who simply want to leave the Soviet Union. I mean the "repatriates," those who want to leave or who have already left for *there*, for Israel. There are a great many of them. This movement has become an important factor in international politics.

These new Jews hate and despise people like me no less than anti-Semites hate us (who, incidentally, have grown relatively in strength since 1961).

But I continue to feel the same as I did then. I feel like a Russian. Even though I am not recognized as one.

There had been talk about anti-Semitism before the war. At that time the story was told (whether fact or fiction) of how it had been suggested to the talented journalist Mikhail Rozenfelt that he sign an article with a pseudonym. He had replied that he would agree to only one pseudonym: Purishkevich.*

Anti-Semitism grew stronger during the war. Defensive reactions grew as well. I, for instance, was told that it was shameful for me to change my maiden name of Liebersohn to Orlova. Furthermore, I was told that it was inadmissable to change my daughter Sveta's name.

In 1942 I had a conversation with Kemenov on this topic. He made an attempt to explain and partially justify what was happening. He told me that the best Jews, the intellectuals and the active Party members, had broken away from their people, from their roots, whereas the urban bourgeoisie, or more specifically the small-town bourgeoisie, remained the champions of nationalism as such. They were the old people. Nationalism was supported only by what was old, prerevolutionary, and ingrained. Among other nations that held territory, the Georgians and the Armenians, a new form of Soviet nationalism, had emerged, but not among the Jews. It all seemed to me to be abstract theorizing even at that time, when I was in awe of his mind and erudition. Why then in the Soviet state, where we prided ourselves so much on equality and fraternity, why were anti-Semitic statements and anti-Semitic practices becoming more and more revolting, more and more obvious?

---

* Vladimir Mitrofanovich Purishkevich (1870–1920), a right-extremist deputy of the Duma, a known anti-Semite, who took part in killing Rasputin (1916).

There were intensified conversations about "family relationships," "kinship," and so forth.

It was in a line for flour that I first encountered anti-Semitism on a lower level. A husky, tipsy young fellow butted into the line ahead of us. We tried to stop him and I heard the words "Jew-face." Without thinking, I slapped him across the mouth and was practically hauled off to the militia.

I experienced the opposite, too. There was no milk in Kuibyshev during the evacuation. The line at the market began at five o'clock in the morning, and the price was 30 to 40 rubles a liter. My little daughter needed milk. The milkwoman arrived around seven in the morning, and by that time we were all numb with cold. Suddenly a plump, ruddy-faced woman appeared, who, judging from her accent, was clearly a Jewess. She jumped the line with a shout: "Give it to me first, I'll pay you more!" I ran up to her and said quietly, but very distinctly: "Clear out at once or I'll kill you." I have no idea of how I was about to kill her, but apparently there had been something convincing in my tone. She shrank back and disappeared immediately.

I cited some words by Lenin at the Party meeting in 1949: a Communist from a nation that was a former oppressor must struggle above all against the chauvinism of superpowers, whereas a Communist from a nation that was formerly oppressed must struggle against a local nationalism. But not a single Communist from an oppressor-nation spoke out publicly against anti-Semitism. In order to do so at that time one would have had to possess an outstanding clarity of mind, a rare courage, and a rare nobility.

Eventually, this kind of person did turn up: Sergei Obraztsov, the famous director of the puppet theater. At a large meeting of the intelligentsia, where a party hack delivered a pogrom speech, Obraztsov said that his father, a former nobleman, a member of the Academy of Sciences, an expert in railway construction, had thrown anti-Semites down the stairs.

In private homes the majority of people sharply criticized the campaign against cosmopolitanism. That included people who were by no means faultfinders.

At that time I was defending villainy. But I began to sense a few things immediately when it concerned certain persons.

At the Institute of World Literature four sacrificial lambs were selected (much later I was told that the organizations had drawn up and agreed beforehand upon the lists of cosmopolitans among themselves): Valerii Kirpotin, Boris Yakovlev, Tamara Motyleva, and Boris Byalik. All these people were unknown to me at that time.

The question of Kirpotin's exclusion from the Party was put forward. Several people spoke out, including Yelena Rossels, a translator from the Ukraine. She related how Kirpotin, then director of the Writers' Union, had abandoned women, children, and invalids in 1941 during the evacuation. Perhaps it had been true. But he was charged with something completely different. And why did the most obvious thing never occur to me at that moment, namely, who in fact were the judges? Uspensky, one of the principal judges, was a mediocrity, a drunkard, and a scoundrel. Ivashchenko, a capable person, was straight out of Dostoyevsky's underground!

Kirpotin was dismissed from the Party organization at the institute. But the district committee did not uphold the dismissal: Fedor Panferov interceded on his behalf.

The next one to be accused was Boris Yakovlev. Incriminations were brought to bear against him because his father, Holtzman, a doctor, had been among Gorky's "murderers." Further, it was charged that some paragraphs in his articles were erroneous. He was accused of tangled amorous intrigues with wives and girl friends.

If Yakovlev had not by chance been born a Jew, he might even have been among those who were conducting a campaign against cosmopolitanism. In 1948 he had published an article in *Novy mir* about the modernist poet Velemir Khlebnikov entitled "A Poet for Aesthetes," whereas in 1979 he had loudly reviled the anthology *Metropole*. All of that, however, had no bearing on the reasons for excluding him. Rather, the fact that he had real shortcomings helped me and those like me to justify what was happening: "They acted correctly in excluding Yakovlev. There's no point in keeping people like him in the Party."

The case of Tamara Motyleva was more complicated. I didn't know her personally then, but I had read her works and I had a great deal of respect for her. She was accused of cosmopolitanism as manifested in her books and in her ties with the literary scholar Isaak Nusinov, who had been arrested a short time before.

Tamara Motyleva was sitting in our place in 1968, after Lev had been expelled from the Party. The phone was ringing ceaselessly. And I was saying frivolously that I couldn't bear any more demonstrations of solidarity with Kopelev. She recalled: "In 1949 the tele-

I am seven; my sister, Lyusya, is two

Graduation picture from the Institute of Philosophy, Literature and History, 1940. My first husband, Lyonya Shersher, is in the top row. I am in the second row, directly below him

The beginning of the war, 1941. Inscribed to Lyonya, who was leaving for the front

With my third husband, Lev Kopelev; our first summer in Koktebel, Crimea, late August 1957

With Konstantin Paustovsky, Tarusa, 1963

With Sveta and Lev, on the hill near the Moskva River in Zhukovka, summer 1958 or 1959

The Writers' Union's House of Creativity, Maleyevka, 1967

With daughters Svetlana and Masha, and granddaughter Marina, 1972

With Sveta and Aleksandr Galich at our house in Moscow, March 13, 1974

With Masha and Marina in Komarovo, Leningrad, 1979

Ussugli, 180 kilometers from Chita in Siberia, 1972: with son-in-law Pavel Litvinov and daughter Maya, holding Lara

With Anne Marie and Heinrich Böll, Eifal, West Germany, November, 1981

Opposite: With Lev at the Allah Verdy Church, Kakhetia, Georgia, spring 1979

phone was silent. That is, it did ring. A maid was living with us who had a great many admirers. But I stubbornly kept going to the telephone myself, always expecting that perhaps someone would phone me." That was the obvious difference between 1949 and 1968. For the time being that difference does exist.

At the meeting dealing with Motyleva a great deal was said, most of it bad. One colleague declared that all her life Tamara Motyleva "had easily jumped from one pulpit to the other, but had always avoided difficulties." Another recalled that she had refused to go out on woodcutting parties during the war. All these facts and semifacts were offered in support of the raucously hysterical speech by Ivashchenko, in which Motyleva's works were declared harmful and obsequious.

When, in 1955, Tamara and I began working together at *Inostrannaya literatura*, I initiated, with great difficulty, a conversation with her about 1949. I was simply guilty before her because, after all, I had raised my hand in favor of her exclusion from the Party.

In 1956 I had been briefly on friendly terms with the widow of the writer Bruno Jasieński, Anna Berzin, who had at that time returned from a concentration camp. She said that she hated Motyleva after her article appeared in *Pravda* in 1937 against Jasieński (published after his arrest).

Later, when we became more intimately acquainted, I myself grew convinced of how many people Tamara had helped, how many books had been published through her direct participation (including Lev's book *The Heart Is Always on the Left*). She helped also when she didn't agree with the author, when she held completely different views.

We paid her a visit in 1957 and she recalled a great deal about the Comintern (she began work in the Communist International of Youth and later was Dimitrov's secretary). I said that all of that should be recorded in writing, that soon no one would be left behind who knew about it. But she replied that for too many years she had forced herself to forget and she actually had forgotten. And now it was impossible to remember.

In 1977, after Motyleva had read Lev Kopelev's *To Be Preserved Forever*, published in the United States, she returned the book with tears: "I can't accept that." We haven't met since then, but my attitude toward her hasn't changed. She is one of those who doesn't have the strength to review her life, something she stated honestly in her very first frank conversations.

The fourth victim at the Institute of World Literature was Boris Byalik: brilliantly witty, clever, and capable.

Kirpotin, Yakovlev, and Motyleva had all defended themselves from a rational point of view. They had admitted a few things, but for the most part they had denied the charges, proved them absurd, compiled quotations, and tried to prove that there had been a juggling of facts. But all of that was completely in vain: the majority had suppressed any perception of what was rational.

Byalik attacked. He attacked himself. He utterly disarmed his accusers and they simply had nothing left. He spoke with outward brilliance, with wit and detachment, as though the discussion concerned someone else. He exposed the Leningrad school, the Leningrad University of the thirties, the dominance of the modernists and formalists, and the devotion to Hegel. Byalik's calculation (even at that time I had a vague apprehension that there was no sincerity in that speech) proved successful. The meeting, like all the meetings at that time, thirsted for repentance. Byalik was repentant and received a lesser sentence than the others: just a reprimand.

The psychologists, sociologists, and writers have long known that a person in a crowd acts differently than when he is alone. Mass psychosis.

"A general willingness," of which Pasternak spoke, was paramount in our behavior at the meetings in 1949. If required by Soviet authority and the Party, we were willing to do anything. We were ready to declare our loved ones as well as ourselves to be spies, traitors, and *provocateurs*. And we did so either sincerely (erring with the best of intentions) or like Byalik, comprehending that it had to be done thus so that things would be easier. A sacrifice had to be offered.

The year 1949 invaded all areas of science, ideology, and the entire life of society. As a result of the session of the Lenin Academy of Agricultural Sciences in 1948, the "Mendelian-Morganists" were put to shame, and Trofim Lysenko* was promoted (and it has been impossible to remove him since then). Obscurantism triumphed. Nikolai Vavilov, who had laid the foundations for the "green revolution," died

---

* Trofim Denisovich Lysenko (1898–1976), leader of the Soviet school of genetics that opposed the theory of heredity and supported the theory of acquired characteristics.

from hunger in prison. And that same revolution had been successfully realized not in our country but in Mexico and other Latin-
American countries.

At that time cybernetics was declared a bourgeois pseudoscience.
But in a special prison in 1949 Lev translated Wiener's *Cybernetics*
on the personal orders of a deputy minister of State Security. A
"pseudoscience" for the masses, but the initiated were supposed to
know it.

From the first days of the October Revolution the intelligentsia
proved to be foremost in jeopardy. It was natural that during periods
of intensification in punitive politics, during periods of particular outbursts of terror—in 1921, 1937, and 1949—it was the intellectuals
who were primarily destroyed.

In 1937 I was still trying to protect the persecuted. Twelve years
later I had joined the persecutors. There was no more shameful period
in my life.

But the persecutors did not hasten to "adopt" me. On the contrary.

The failure of my dissertation in 1951 (everyone praised it aloud,
but the secret vote was seven in favor and eight against) probably
was tied to that same campaign against cosmopolitanism.

Meanwhile, at home the table was laid out, and a long skirt and
blouse of pink organdy lay ready. All my comrades (they were practically feeling guilty over me) came to visit me. Even though we
were sad at heart, we even ate, drank, and made merry. Well do I
remember the faces of Yuri Gaziev and Sarik Saryan, the son of the
painter.

A year later, in November 1952, after my return from Tallinn, I
successfully defended that same dissertation in the same institute and
before the same academic council. Nothing had changed in the world.
Even now I don't know why I was allowed to defend it.

Fortunately, an external turnabout occurred once more in my life:
I left Moscow and dropped out of that circle where people spoke out,
criticized, repented, attacked, and renounced. I dropped out for almost three years.

Today, in turning back to 1949, I ask myself many questions.
Perhaps it was the terror that I had experienced a year before at the
Lyubyanka that had propelled me onto the podium of the Party
meeting? I tried to forget that night, to strike it out of my life. Whether
I succeeded in doing so completely, I cannot say.

Where had that internationalism disappeared to that I had felt and now feel so poignantly and desperately? Where had that world disappeared to where there had been no nations? That enormous, boundless world of culture, art, and simple humanity, a world that had permeated both my childhood and youth and that only returned to me at the time of my awakening. Where had it disappeared to? How had I let it dissolve, conceal itself, and cringe? How could I have existed in a false, villainous, and vulgar world from which universality had been banned?

I couldn't answer these questions.

Why hadn't I been saved? Why hadn't those around me extricated me? There had been many who thought and spoke differently about cosmopolitanism than I did. Why hadn't Shakespeare, Pushkin, Tolstoy, and Mayakovsky come to my rescue?

They didn't extricate me. I wasn't rescued.

The guilt is mine.

XIX

Tallinn

In 1951 I left to join my husband in Tallinn, where I was accepted for work in a pedagogical institute.

The trips back to Moscow during the years of work in Tallinn were special: a hungry provincial would arrive, and there was no need to put a checkmark in her notebook to indicate where she had "been," what she had "seen" and "heard," for being in Moscow truly meant being, seeing, and hearing. Not only for myself, but also in order to tell my beloved and grateful girl students.

I was obliged to give lectures on all the courses in both the Russian and Estonian departments: folklore; the eighteenth century; Russian and Soviet literature; a course on foreign literature; and an introduction to literary studies. In the Estonian department I taught the course "An Introduction to Literary Studies," and it turned out that no one understood those obscure words. The level of instruction willy-nilly became that of elementary school in much of what I did.

Our Russian department was nothing more than a minuscule islet in the Estonian sea.

Just as in Bucharest, there was a mighty power standing at my back. There was the Red Army. And just as in Bucharest, I was unaware of it.

We lived in such isolation from the Estonians that I had no knowledge of their moods and animosity. At the market my friends occasionally heard: "When the White ships come, then all of you will be driven out of here." They were waiting for the White ships* and they're waiting for them to this day.

* The White Guards.

Not a single Estonian home opened its doors to us. This fact brought our small group of teachers closer together.

As head of a department, I was present at the pedagogical council meetings. It was natural that the meetings were held in Estonian. I used to feel annoyed—it was stupid to sit there without understanding a single word. Several years later Lev taught me a lesson about that: "In whatever country, however small, whose bread you are eating, you are obliged to learn the simplest words."

Our awkward students were the future teachers of Russian in Estonian schools.

What did I teach? How did I educate both the students and the teachers in Tallinn? One of my former students asked me to telephone the first secretary of the district committee (in Moscow!) in order to get pedagogical work for her and provide her with living quarters. Ten years later I simply would have shrugged my shoulders. But at that time I telephoned, and judging from her letters and subsequent events (I completely forget the circumstances), she was given work immediately, though she had to wait a long time to get living quarters (the standard length of time that was normal in our circumstances). The confidence that it was possible to achieve justice, or rather that it was necessary to do so, truly helped in some situations. I had no idea of the extent of the obstacles, I did not sense the thickness of the wall that I had to smash my way through. That was because everything seemed possible to me as it had in my youth. I'll cite lines from letters I received.

"It's difficult for you to comprehend why the world doesn't change quickly enough for the better. But what can you do if historical time seems painfully slow for a single human life?"

"You never seemed to be a fighter to me. You had a different effect on people and life: you aroused everything good that was in a person, you knew how to emphasize that good and rejoice in it, and everyone strove to do better, somehow seemed to blossom next to you, wanted to go on perfecting themselves, to manifest themselves in a creative fashion."

Apparently in my lectures I tried to inspire people to be kind, generous, and noble. That was precisely where the great lessons lay in Russian and world literature. And they completely coincided with the lessons of communism. Probably I myself tried to act in such a fashion that my behavior did not contradict my words (as far as it was possible).

To enlighten—that was what I was supposed to do all my conscious life. That is what my vocation is. (Perhaps that should be in the past tense: *was*.) That is what I sensed for the first time when as a twelve-year-old schoolgirl I walked into the barracks on Strastny Boulevard where courses for the liquidation of illiteracy were being held for soldiers. And they, imitating me, would reproduce in chalk on the board: "Masha ate kasha," "We are not slaves."

To enlighten means to bring light. I cannot give a simple answer today as to whether I brought any light or whether I spread confusion in young and unformed minds. It is just as difficult to separate truth and falsehood, the good and the bad, in this instance as in all of our life. I taught them what I myself believed in at that time.

I taught them how to read books. It is not at all the same as the formation of words out of letters, but an important, special ability. I taught students how to read poetry. When I went with them to the kolkhoz to help in the harvesting, I would recite Mayakovsky in the evenings. I recited from memory and we discussed the poems line by line.

At the kolkhoz the girls worked very well, with rare exceptions. The exceptions were swiftly and energetically scrutinized. In every possible way I tried by word and deed to promote the very joy of common labor. But there were the normal questions: "What's all this for?" "Why are there only women out in the fields?" "Why aren't the men from the kolkhoz working?" I considered such questions to be an attempt to evade work. Moreover, it was the lazy and "bad" ones who asked these questions—or did it only seem so to me?

When we were eating, sleeping, singing together (and most importantly, working together with students), we became practically like family. After fulfilling my own personal quota I would walk 15 to 20 kilometers a day to make the rounds of all the work brigades. And it was I who did not arouse but rather suppressed and extinguished any glimmer of displeasure, any glimmer of political thought, of political consciousness.

Probably it was somewhat more complicated. In 1967 one of my former students reminded me of the following conversation we had around 1950.

"Raisa Davydovna, can an innocent person be arrested in our country?"

"I don't know. I can't answer your question." She claimed that it was from that moment that she began to think.

I recall one debate in the classroom on the painful topic of nationalism: the Russians and the Estonians. The students expounded a variety of claims in which everything was mixed up, both the important and the secondary: "Why isn't our language being taught?" "Why do girls go out with sailors?" (In a port city this was considered immoral.) And a great many other whys. Now I realize that this was a protest against the Russian invaders, a protest, perhaps petty, twisted in form, and a bit eccentric, but still a protest. Cleverly and sensitively, with a thousand proofs and by relying on my authority, I defended chauvinism. Of course I named both chauvinism and nationalism, but in thinking that I was defending internationalism, I was supporting the authority of Russian bureaucrats over the Estonians.

Immediately after my departure, that tiny world that I had created, or thought I had created, collapsed like a house of cards.

"It's a bit strange that in idealizing a large portion of the people you did not idealize life in the least! Don't take offense, please . . . without you here, that is, in our department, something has been broken off, there is no common link; rather, everyone is pulling in his own direction."

Rereading the letters written to me from Tallinn after I left, a thick packet that I haven't touched for twenty-five years, I have the feeling that I'm watching a serialized television film. The film is old, faded, has lost its color.

One and the same situation stands out in the letters of various correspondents (who are at odds from time to time). There are no men, only women and girls. Holidays, classes, parties, New Year's gatherings, subscriptions to new collected editions, appraisals of public lectures—who is lecturing and how well—that's what they write about most of all. Getting married, affairs, divorces, friendships and fallings-out, intimacies, and spats.

Somewhere in Moscow is the court of arbitration.

Questions are asked. God, the questions they don't ask! And apparently I must have given answers . . .

"How should I spend my leave?" "Should I enroll for graduate studies?" "Should I get married?" "Should I get an abortion?" "Should I demand alimony?"

They make requests of me: "Recommend a topic for my diploma." "Be the supervisor for my thesis or dissertation."

They ask me to bring sugar. Apparently I used to ask for a few things as well: "I can't find you any lace material for curtains . . ."

They inform me of many details in their lives: "I have decided to take communion with you before the trial I have to face next week. Perhaps it will prove to be insignificant, but I can hardly believe so right now. Tomorrow the student teachers from the fourth year at the institute are coming here for an entire week."

"Not a single Russian book." "What a scourge, several classes in one classroom." "What a long way the children have to walk to school . . ."

The process of rehabilitation was starting, but faintly and slowly. For my favorite student I offered to go to the prosecutor's office to find out about her father, the director of the Estonian Theater in Leningrad.

"Don't bother, I'm afraid of the consequences for you." (I did go, and it turned out that her father had been shot in 1937.)

The husband of a former student of mine, a department head, was convicted of a major crime. I'm looking for a lawyer for him in Moscow.

I comprehend all the more profoundly now that for me Tallinn became a refuge from that era, from all the filth, the baseness, and the crimes, from what was going on right next to me. My eyes were blinded by the good things, but nonetheless they were blinded. I was very much needed there, as, to be sure, I never was anywhere else for my entire preceding and subsequent life. That happened, doubtless, because I found myself in very weak pedagogical surroundings, where my insignificant knowledge seemed to be broad and deep. And because I was living in accord with my vocation. Probably some furrows and some traces remained in those young souls. In pedagogical work you cannot measure the harvest.

In the summer of 1958 Lev and I made a trip from Leningrad to Tallinn. Musing over a military relative of his who had always complained about the Estonians and their lack of goodwill toward the Russians, Lev said: "But why should they, strictly speaking, be friendly toward their invaders?"

New convictions constrict us at first, like a new pair of shoes, and how one longs at times to go back to what is familiar, well worn, and comfortable. I flared up strongly in response. "So then, according to you I was an invader?"

In 1960 Lev and I were in Riga on a business assignment. Several months before our arrival there had been yet another official purge of a nationalistic alignment. As was typical with any purge, a multitude of circles, both large and small, were dissolved.

June 24, St. John's Day, is a traditional holiday throughout the entire Baltic region. In Latvia it is celebrated with particular solemnity —half the male population is called John. *"Ligo"*—"Let Us Rejoice"— this is how that day is poetically named. The authorities decided to suppress the holiday. After a Communist labor brigade at the enormous Riga Electrotechnical Plant refused to report for work as a sign of protest, permission was given at the last moment. Upon our return, we managed to appear in print in the journal *Nauka i religiya* (Science and Religion). This is what we wrote: "We are convinced that the Latvian *Ligo* will shortly be just as nonreligious a holiday as the New Year's fir tree. And only the elderly and the historians will be able to talk about those 'dogmatists' who in our time were attempting to 'shut down' this national holiday under the pretext of intensifying antireligious propaganda."

We were wrong. *Ligo* is a national holiday, both secular and religious.

Here again I entered the fray because of my innocence, because of the *incompleteness* of my insight.

In 1961 the *Ligo* in Latvia was suppressed for good. In 1965 people began to celebrate it sporadically once again. The prohibition was, of course, "attributed" to Khrushchev: subjectivism and voluntarism. In 1966 Lev received an urgent request for an article on the *Ligo*. It was published in *Druzhba narodov* (Friendship of Nations; No. 7). Supposedly the secretary of the Party Central Committee of Latvia wrote an indignant letter to the editor in which the authors—Lev and a Latvian specialist in German studies—were accused of "Latvian nationalism."

In Tallinn I helped many students, but I did teach that the Soviet order was the very best, that the world in general, and ours in particular, was good, and everything in it was basically organized in a just fashion. All one had to do was to know how to see that, to discern that, even if your personal fate had crippled you.

One of my students wrote to me before her departure for the countryside: "I know full well that there is a mass of difficulties ahead, but I shall never forget those lines that you once read at a

Komsomol meeting: 'Even if the roof on top of your house is caving in, that still doesn't mean the entire world is caving in.'"

I taught that the common good is higher than the personal, that no man is an island, and that there is no purer and more beautiful joy than the joy of participation. And I studied together with them.

Many years later I was told about one good teacher from the Vladimir Pedagogical Institute who had received the following letter from a former student: "I, like almost all of us, did not believe in anything until I met you. Your lectures became a turning point for us. But now I come to a countryside where there is hunger and poverty, falsehood, and humiliation—and I curse you, you specifically, because I did not believe the others but I did believe you."

My girl students from Tallinn had every reason to think that kind of thing about me.

The clouds that were gathering worldwide hardly penetrated through the thick walls of my Tallinn refuge, through the wall of love and elation with which I was surrounded. In January 1953 we heard about the "doctor-murderers."*

In February 1953 I went on leave, and Kolya and I met in Moscow (he was working in the town of Ivanovo and I was alone during the winter of 1952–1953). My daughters were living in Moscow. It was a terrible month. By that time I already had the feeling that something incredible was going on. Every day there were satirical anti-Semitic pieces in the papers. Arrests. And the rumors grew more terrifying each day about the forcible deportation of Jews to the Far East, which was to commence on May 15, 1953, after the public execution of "Zionists" in Red Square.

Kolya was drinking heavily, but when he heard about the deportation that was to take place, he kept saying ceaselessly: "Don't worry, either I won't let you go or I'll go with you."

I grew exhausted by the daily discussions and the conjectures about what lay ahead. My leave terminated March 6. We decided that I would go to visit Kolya for three days in Ivanovo.

He was sick. In the evening at the hotel we heard about the death of Stalin on the radio. It was quite terrifying. I wept in the midst of strangers. I was thinking about how some Balzac would describe what

---

* The "doctors' plot" involved the arrest of a group of leading physicians, most of them from the Kremlin hospital and most of them Jews, on charges of trying to murder members of the Politburo and Stalin himself.

was going on around Stalin's deathbed. (For a true believer like me these were thoughts that were very strange. But thoughts did arise at that very time about how those surviving leaders would share the power.) The name of Georgii Malenkov was being mentioned most frequently, but people were saying bad things about him. For me Stalin's death caused enormous grief and seemed like the end.

Moscow was closed to entry. I returned only on March 9. There were the stories about the mad mob at the funeral and Sveta made me very angry: my little daughter said she *saw* a teacher whose leg was crushed. I replied to her: "Don't you dare repeat that philistine gossip." I still didn't want to see the reality.

When I got back to Tallinn, I was once again overwhelmed with the familiar warmth: my dear students were waiting for me at the railway station. Later I was asked to speak on the radio. This is what I said.

"The agonizing days of mourning have passed, probably the most difficult days in the life of our generation . . . There is a mighty human sorrow that must become, and is already in the process of becoming, a mighty force . . . Soviet pedagogues have been handed the keys to the future of our native land by the Party . . . A heavy grief has fallen on our shoulders. But this heavy grief cannot break or bend the people who have been forged by Lenin and Stalin. We have grown older during these days. And the responsibility of each person has grown. The mighty burden that the giant Stalin bore upon his shoulders now falls on all Soviet citizens."

That was what and how I thought then. The crumbs of human emotions drowned in a broth of memorized formulas, in those primeval elements of Church Slavonic, our Church Slavonic language in which people spoke on the radio and from podiums and wrote in the news-papers and journals.

The solemn reception organized for me by the students had apparently caused the authorities' cup of patience to overflow. I was summoned by the director, and he suggested that I hand in my resignation "for personal reasons." "Why?" I asked. "After all, there are still three months to go before the end of the academic year!" He replied that it wasn't on his initiative—the Central Committee had demanded it because my husband had been dismissed from work after a scandal.

Once more, loyalty was not rewarded. After I spoke out earlier at the meeting in 1949, the failure of my dissertation had followed. After this speech came my banishment from the institute in Tallinn. But I was not speaking out or writing in the least for the sake of whatever forms of reward.

I fell ill—angina with heart complications. My girls looked after me unceasingly. Lying in bed, I read in *Pravda* on April 4, 1953, the following communiqué about the doctors: The Ministry of Internal Affairs "has conducted an exhaustive investigation . . . As a result of the investigation it has been established that the defendants . . . had been falsely arrested by the former Ministry of State Security, without any legal cause. The investigation proved that the charges . . . had turned out to be false. It has been established that the testimony from the defendants . . . had been obtained by officials of the investigative department of the former Ministry of State Security through the application of unacceptable and strictly prohibited methods of investigation . . . The defendants have been released . . . The guilty parties have been arrested and brought forward on criminal charges."

The building that had been erected in my heart so assiduously, so firmly, for so long, showed a crack. The crack widened and widened until I suddenly found myself under the rubble.

I went back to work and no one breathed a word about the fact that they had wanted to dismiss me.

Postscript. Now, in December 1975, I am reading the following communiqué: "The ambassador from the USSR to Japan, O. Troyanovsky, greeted the delegation from the Supreme Soviet of the USSR with A. Vader at the head . . ."

I studied with Oleg Troyanovsky at the Institute of Philosophy, Literature, and History. In the fall of 1941 he attended courses for military translators along with many of our students. A beautiful girl was living with his nice parents, and he used to sign his letters to her with some perception: "Your first husband." Oleg became Stalin's personal interpreter, the Soviet ambassador to Japan, and the Soviet representative to the United Nations, but then I lost sight of him.

Vader. Back in December 1952, when Kolya was leaving, we decided that we had to give up our apartment in Tallinn, despite the fact that it was not attached to a government office. At City Hall they looked at me with disbelieving elation. (Those are the words of my friend who went along with me. It all seemed to me to be completely in the order of things.) "You're giving up your apartment?"

I stayed for half a year in a single room (I only slept at home).

A. Vader, a graduate of the Higher Party School, moved into the two other rooms with his family.

Coming into the apartment, he solemnly declared: "You have acted like a true Soviet person."

But I acted like an idiot. If I had but for a moment thought of the future, not about the "radiant common future" but about the immediate future of my family, my parents, my daughters, Kolya, and finally, even about myself, then I would have understood that I should have exchanged the apartment for another in Moscow. How many woes I might have avoided.

And they would have managed to find a place for Vader even without me.

The academic year came to an end, my Tallinn came to an end, and something else that I never suspected had also come to an end: a whole era in our history.

XX

Awakening

In the summer of 1953 I returned to Moscow, and in the fall I started to teach foreign literature at the Moscow Regional Pedagogical Institute. We planned an evening with my students on the theme "My Favorite Poem." It became clear, to my amazement, that Mayakovsky was not among the favorite poets of my students. And, in general, there were few people who had genuinely favorite poets. Nevertheless, the evening didn't turn out badly. They read Lermontov, Tvardovsky, Simonov, and Shchipachev.

Tolya, one of the students, read an excerpt from Tvardovsky's narrative poem *Vasilii Tyorkin*. At the end of December my girls begged me to have a talk with Tolya: he had a failing grade and was cutting classes. And the most terrible thing was that he said he was going to commit suicide.

At that time, in 1954, a conversation took place that played a significant role in my fate.

He and I stayed behind at the institute and were the last to leave. The night watchwoman gave us a suspicious look. At first our conversation faltered. I was taciturn, and Tolya, apparently expecting a sermon, was prickly and uncommunicative. We sat there about an hour, exchanging phrases halfheartedly, and then at some point a spark of contact was ignited. Then a flood was let loose on me.

"What's the point of living?" he asked, staring at me with his clear, honest eyes. He had no parents. His grandfather was in a village and starving like everyone else. He said it calmly, as though it were something matter of fact.

Tolya had gone off to Smolensk and become an active member of the Komsomol. He wanted to understand why the newspaper said one thing whereas in life everything was completely different. He spoke out at a meeting of Komsomol activists and shared these thoughts. The secretary of the Komsomol district committee ("For me at that time, Raisa Davydovna, the secretary of the district committee was the same as God") said: "What have you been hiding, I didn't know that you're a Jew; it's the Jews who are dissatisfied with everything. Just look at the doctor-murderers among them." Tolya came from a long line of Byelorussian peasants and had wavy black hair. He hurled himself on the secretary with his fists and honestly admitted himself that he almost killed him. He was dismissed from the Komsomol for rowdyism, and evaded—with difficulty—prison.

"I then decided that all you could find there would be injustice and despotism, but that it wouldn't be the same elsewhere. Moreover, Stalin didn't know anything about that. I've been in Moscow for four months and I see the same things here. There is so much falsehood and deception at the institute. Words are one thing, and action, another . . . What a lot of self-satisfied and sleek people there are here. I eat in the student cafeteria [the cafeteria was very bad], and I keep imagining that I see my poor hungry little sisters before my eyes. And for that matter all the children on our village street. They never saw sugar. I went to Vitka's apartment [the son of a deputy minister]: six rooms, one bigger than the next. Real gentry. Vitka is a sucker. He doesn't know anything, he doesn't understand what hunger is. He's not really a bad guy. But what kind of socialism is that: everything for some people and nothing for the others?"

How could I answer? Bitter shame and complete impotence—that was what I felt. Had I the right to teach? Didn't it really mean teaching about life? I myself was no longer under any delusions and could not, as I once did in Tallinn, clarify and convince. These were formidable questions and one had to search for the answers. But they, the young, the honest, they couldn't wait until I found the answers.

I don't know what eventually happened to Tolya.

In the winter of 1955 I was offered a position on a new monthly, *Inostrannaya literatura*, and I left; at first I worked part-time, and then in the summer I gave up teaching entirely.

Beginning in 1953, I kept coming across rotten things all the time. Perhaps I'm simplifying somewhat now—it began earlier. After all, in

1946 we were prepared to go off to a war-torn town in order to build genuine socialism. That meant we must have been living in a *non-genuine* one. It was just that we couldn't yet bring ourselves to pronounce these seditious words.

But after the death of Stalin, the floodgates were opened.

In 1954 the play *Guests* by the young playwright Leonid Zorin was published. The standards of the times were illuminated in three generations of the same family: the grandfather is a decent person, an Old Bolshevik, an anachronism; the father is a degenerate Party functionary; the son is close to the grandfather and ashamed of his father. He is repelled by the hypocrisy that he comes up against in his own family at every step.

A special expanded session of the board of the Ministry of Culture became involved in the criticism of this play. Georgii Aleksandrov, the Minister of Culture at that time, declared Zorin's play to be "hostile." A few months later, there was a secret letter to the Central Committee in which Aleksandrov was unmasked as the head of a bordello where orgies took place. After that he was sent to Minsk, to the university, to teach Marxism to the students.

Academician Aleksandrov was receiving at that time 30,000 rubles (in old currency) per month, whereas the cleaning lady at his institute was getting 300 rubles. That was called socialism.

Beginning in 1955, I spent every summer in the village of Zhukovka. Earlier, Stalin's dacha had been close by and it was a prohibited zone, inaccessible to mere mortals. Even to this day a special pass is required —this is now explained by the proximity of the Rublevo Reservoir.

You only have to go a hundred paces away from the village and you'll bump into fences. Nothing but a string of long gray or green fences. Sometimes there is barbed wire on top of the fences. Of course, the fences had been obvious to anyone sharp-eyed enough to discover them earlier. But it's only now that I find myself running into them everywhere.

But who would cut himself off from the people behind these fences? Whose grounds are these? What kind of a special caste is this? What kind of a special stratum? And while I searched for the answers, there arose implacably before me that same familiar, homegrown word of ours: *class*. A whisper, softly, from somewhere out of the depths: *class*. To pronounce, utter, and conceive of this word was a terrifying thing. It wasn't a matter of fear in the face of repressions. It was terrifying for one's belief. The new class. Degeneration.

Beginning in 1956, people started to talk aloud about this not only in their apartments but from the podium at meetings as well.

We heard about Bonifatii Kedrov speaking out at the Institute of Philosophy. The letter that his father wrote just before his execution, when he had undergone torture, was quoted by Khrushchev in his speech at the Twentieth Congress.

We heard about the speech of the chess grand master Mikhail Botvinnik.

About the speech of Yuri Orlov at the Institute of Theoretical Physics.

About the speeches at the Institute of Eastern Studies.

People talked about the social basis for "the cult of personality," about the kind of system that was capable of producing this cult.

Dating from those times, Kedrov became the director of the Institute of Philosophy, and now he is in charge of the section of natural science at the Institute of the History of Science. In December 1979 he spoke out once more at a Party meeting. He spoke about the economic catastrophe facing our country.

Yuri Orlov, a corresponding member of the Armenian Academy of Sciences, founded and headed the Helsinki Watch Committee in 1976. He's been in jail and then in a concentration camp since 1977.

Historical materialism was being professed in words, but it was pure idealism in actual fact. Why did the cult arise? Because . . .

I started to reread Lenin's articles from 1920 to 1922. They were filled with alarm. Lenin had foreseen that very possibility when bureaucracy, when the power and authority of the apparatus, would change the course of the revolution. Degeneration . . .

In 1955 I heard for the first time about the state dachas—the dachas of Stalin and other members of the government. The luxury there could be compared to that of the palaces of the Russian tsars. They had chopped down ancient trees. Special roads were laid down.

The visage of the new class was evident for me above all in its so-called everyday life-style. Luxury. "Communism for forty people," as they used to quip about the sanatorium at Barvikha. The restricted government store in Zhukovka was named "Greece" by the entire village: "There's everything in Greece."

Cowardice: everything concealed behind fences. Falsehood. Hypocrisy. Impunity. It was later that I read Milovan Djilas's book *The New Class*.

At the beginning of the 1960s this is what I had come to understand. During the Stalinist period, in our country there was a great pyramid resembling the pyramids depicted in the old social studies textbooks. At its base was the class of slaves. Millions of them—to this day we do not have the exact figures. It was by means of slave labor that the north and far east had been assimilated, the canals dug, and the mightiest hydroelectric power plants erected. Even Moscow University was constructed this way.

The second class was the peasantry. In essence it was a semiserfdom. Even to this day a member of a kolkhoz does not have a passport, or identity card.* In other words, he is deprived of the right to move freely about the country. He is under the most complete authority of the kolkhoz chairman.

In 1960 in a small town in eastern Latvia we were told the following story. There were not enough people in the kolkhoz. People were sent to recruit workers in neighboring Byelorussia. The Byelorussians were more than happy to accept, for they lived in utter poverty. Several families arbitrarily left Byelorussia for Latvia. They had not been given any permits. In essence, the Latvians had simply stolen those families. We saw one of the "purloined": a downtrodden fellow right out of nineteenth-century pictures and poems. He was on his way to send a money order to his son somewhere near Leningrad so that the latter could visit him. He had never held that kind of money, 300 rubles, in his hands before.

Our friend the writer Frida Vigdorova once said that she always felt ashamed when she returned to her comfortable large Moscow apartment after her traveling assignments. I too began to share that sense of gnawing shame over my prosperity, abundance, shelter, and freedom. Yes, for all our restrictions, in comparison with that Byelorussian peasant, we lived in relative freedom. The bread that we were eating represented, in fact, his sweat, his oppressed, slavelike existence.

In September 1961 I was sitting at a meeting of the American-Soviet Institute. All around me were well-known and honored colleagues. VIPs. I too was a sort of VIP at the time. Sitting beside me

* This was changed in 1974.

was the young philosopher Yuri Zamoshkin, who had just returned from America; Ruben Simonov, a theater director; Aleksei Shakhurin, a Hero of Socialist Labor and a former minister in the aviation industry; Nikolai Blokhin, the president of the Academy of Medical Sciences; and Nina Petrovna Khrushcheva.

And suddenly, a painful thought: what about them, all of them who were gathered there, did they know that the peasants who were feeding them had no rights whatsoever? They ought to have known. But they did not want to know. The way I too had not wanted to know earlier. What an abyss between them and that Byelorussian! But wasn't there an abyss between the Byelorussian and myself as well?

I knew very little about the working class, but I did know for certain that it was not a leading force in society. And without a doubt it was not a progressive one. The workers at least did have passports.

The apparatus and the leadership were higher up in the pyramid. And finally, on top of all of this was the summit, the peak, Stalin.

In the years 1953–1956 the base, the class of slaves, was significantly decreased. The very top, Stalin, had been removed. Several changes took place in the situation of the kolkhoz workers. Their debt payments were wiped out. Their taxes were decreased. A portrait of Malenkov hung in the huts of kolkhozes over a period of several years. Many of the less productive kolkhozes became sovkhozes. However, in September 1961, Fedor Konstantinov, the editor of the journal *Kommunist*, gave a report on the program of the CPSU. He declared that the tendency to convert kolkhozes into sovkhozes was a mistake, because all the kolkhoz workers of an advanced age immediately started to retire on a pension. "Could our government really support them?" This was said from the podium by the editor of the theoretical organ of the Party. This was a cynical and frank admission about citizens of two grades: the state would support some, while others were compelled to support the state.

The apparatus had wavered for a bit, but not significantly and not for long. The "fringe benefits" had been taken away. These were the outright perquisites, enormous and secret, over and above the salaries. And the quantity of personal executive cars diminished. In the summer of 1965, after Leonid Brezhnev came to power, the salary of Party functionaries was *significantly* raised, and many of the personal cars were returned. Furthermore, subsistence benefits were significantly increased in the following years.

But what place did we, the intellectuals, occupy in this pyramid? Many times in conversations with foreign writers we would relate with pride how well our intelligentsia lived. Too well. By means of the tried-and-true stick and carrot the intelligentsia had been dragged into the service of the ruling class. Into shameful silence about the situation of the people. Into a whitewash. Into odes and panegyrics.

A group of Moscow poets was in Azerbaijan. There, the sovereign, independent prince, the secretary of the Azerbaijan Party Central Committee, Bagirov, unexpectedly came to the home of the poet Samed Vurgun, where friends and the visiting Muscovites had gathered. They sat down at the table. Pavel Antokolsky began to propose a toast. Bagirov said in a voice that would tolerate no disobediance: "Sit!" Antokolsky sat down. But then immediately: "Stand!" And Antokolsky stood up. So it went about ten times in a row. That happened, of course, back in those years, in 1951.

Pavel Antokolsky was already an elderly man, a poet, who had buried his son at the front. He told the story himself, and in reply to the very cruel question "But why did you obey?" he replied: "How could I act differently; after all, I am a Party member." If only he had simply said: "I was afraid, I already knew so much about Bagirov, about his willful tyranny, his cruelty, which could compete with all the horrors of the Middle Ages." But he didn't say that. Instead, he tried to pass off even that kind of humiliation of human dignity as service to the Party.

In 1956 that same Antokolsky wrote the following verses:

> *We are all the laureates of prizes*
> *Dispensed in his honor.*
> *We who have passed through an age*
> *That was moribund.*
> *. . . And it is not the corpse we despise,*
> *but rather our own muteness.*

Even in the most difficult times this was not always the case with everyone. There were "dissonant" voices. Now they are growing ever greater in numbers.

Many books that sharply criticize our sins, both the published and the unpublished ones, the books wherein is contained the greater or lesser part of the truth, are mostly within the boundaries of Soviet ideology, within the boundaries of a socialism that has been purified, purified in a utopian fashion from the vileness of bureaucracy.

At various points over the years this particular assertion of mine has received a stern rebuff, for me personally at least, in the works of Aleksandr Solzhenitsyn, Arkadii Belinkov, and Varlam Shalamov.

The authority of the ruling class, which even today brings countless woes to the people, is maintained primarily through force. Leaders will not surrender their might willingly. But violence in our country, be it even with the most noble purposes, will bring only new evil. We must come to our senses in this chain reaction of evil.

How can we break out of this vicious circle?

XXI

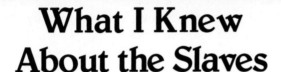

What I Knew
About the Slaves

1962

The class of slaves. The land of GULag, which we were also calling the "other world."

The summer of 1955. We went off into the woods of Zhukovka and built a campfire. There were six of us—old friends.

And in the woods for the first time I heard the folk song:

> *The zeks suffered from the pitch and roll,*
> *Clinging to each other like brothers dear,*
> *And only infrequently from their tongues*
> *Did they let muffled curses break away.*

Subsequently, this song, "Magadan," was repeated innumerable times and is still being repeated at many parties. But after I heard it for the first time, I kept spending long nights seeing, no, feeling, the pitching and rolling, Kolyma, the holds of ships, the *zeks* . . .

That song prepared me for reading the chapter in Evgenia Ginzburg's *Journey into the Whirlwind* where the story is told of how she was transported half-dead to Kolyma.

"The *zeks* suffered from the pitch and roll . . ."

Over and over again with a terrifying repetitiveness. Only now has the word *zek* shed its anonymity. Here she is, Evgenia Semyonovna Ginzburg, this pretty woman walking alongside me, with the handbag that she never parts with (it contains her passport and Party card)—she is the one who was in that monstrous ship's hold . . .

There was not the least bit of politics in the words, and that song might have been composed by and about criminals (and it's not excluded that in fact it was), but in 1954–1955 the song was understood differently. At that time everything was adding fuel to the fire. People even came from a performance of *Macbeth* with eyes opened wide—"about the crimes of the band."

In December 1954 I found out that Lev Kopelev, a friend from my student days, had returned from the camps. And I dashed over to his home. My first sensation was that he had not changed. He began to tell me much later the story of how it had been for him.

In September 1956 Lev took me to look at the places where he had been imprisoned for seven years. A large brick building stands opposite the Botanical Garden, and this was the scientific-research institute where they had worked. Alongside were strange-looking structures: yurts—real yurts, just like in Central Asia. In 1956 ordinary families were living in them. We went in, apologized, and said that Lev was a former convict here. The women clearly did not believe us. I tried to look at Lev through their eyes. He was decently dressed, wearing a hat, smooth-shaven, tanned. No, he didn't resemble a prisoner in the least.

There were no longer any fences. But earlier there had been a solid wall. This is what the denunciations had led to, that was what the least little disobedience had ended in. You were locked up.

Where the *sharashka** had once stood everything was now disturbingly ordinary. There was no monument to the terror, the wickedness, the debasement of man. Diapers were drying. Many of the former prisoners were working at the research institute, only now they were free. Posters were hanging: invitations to something, appeals to something. Just as though nothing had happened.

When Shostakovich's *Katerina Izmailova* (or *Lady Macbeth of Mtsensk District*) was resurrected, the newspapers said that this opera had been unjustly criticized. "And forgotten." That's exactly what they wanted to do with people—to forget. We used to smile condescendingly when we read in Feuchtwanger's book that during World War I his uncle used to sleep on the floor because the soldiers were sleeping on the bare ground in the trenches. But it wasn't at all funny.

---

* *Sharashka* is a word designating a special prison institute where the prisoners are trained specialists or technicians. The conditions are much better than in ordinary prison camps (see Solzhenitsyn's *The First Circle*).

Meanwhile, right here beside us, our friends had been forced to live as other than people, and we, unfortunately, had not slept on the floor. We had been weaned away even from ordinary, age-old compassion, and we had allowed it to happen to us. After all, at one time the Russians used to put bread out on their windowsills in Vladimirovka for the prisoners, who would come by and take it. Whether they were robbers, rapists, or murderers, all the same they were people.

One of Lev's friends was working, while he was imprisoned, on a building on Kaluzhskaya Street. A five-year-old boy, the son of a guard, came up to him. The convict reached out his hand to the boy, but the child jumped back as though from some wild animal. "You are an enemy," the little five-year-old person uttered firmly. What has he grown up to be?

After visiting the yurts, we walked for a long while; it was difficult to regain one's senses. And then I begged Lev to tell me in detail, day by day, the way it was, to tell me all about those ten years. That story was essential to both of us. He continued, with interruptions, for about three months—it was almost impossible for him to go on telling the story, and for me to hear it, for any length at one time. But I did not relent. "Everything, everything that you can remember." And then he would remember almost everything.

In 1960 he started to write the book *To Be Preserved Forever.* That was my main road to that "other world."

In the spring of 1956 I heard the verses of Olga Berggolts. Some of them had already been published in *Novy mir.* Gradually, a few verses began to appear in print after the Twenty-second Congress. But the most powerful ones, up until now, are the verses that are passed on by word of mouth.

> *Here I stand, I cannot do otherwise.*
> —Martin Luther

> *No, not from our meager little booklets,*
> *Created in the likeness of a beggar's pouch*
> *Will you learn how difficult it was for us,*
> *And how without hope we did live.*
>
> . . .
>
> *And in the darkness of airless cells*
> *For days and nights on end,*

Tearlessly, with lips all smashed,
We whispered "O motherland! O native people!"

And we found justification,
For that cruel mother of ours,
Who to futile suffering did send
Those very best sons of ours.

Not suffering (there's nothing new in that—humanity has passed it on well enough from ancient times), but precisely the fact that we *"found justification"* and *"whispered 'O motherland! O native people!'"*

In June 1956 there was a meeting at the Writers' Union about the state of culture in the East European countries. Olga Berggolts was invited to speak. From far away she seemed to me attractive and unusual on the stage. She spoke in a casual fashion, and people listened to her in dead silence. "Now everyone is looking for an author or authors of the theory of nonconflict. I am about to remind you where everything started." And almost without commentary she read excerpts from the resolutions of the Central Committee concerning the journals *Zvezda* (The Star) and *Leningrad* and concerning some films, excerpts vilifying Akhmatova and Zoshchenko and quoting Zhdanov's speeches (1946–1948). From time to time laughter broke out in the hall, a suppressed laughter. In actual fact it might have been quite humorous had it not taken place so recently and had been so terrible. Berggolts spoke about the camps. One could sense a kind of maximum degree of personal emotion.

A short while after that evening, friends took me to the Hotel Moscow, where Berggolts was living, and introduced me to her. We found her after a really heavy drinking bout. She lay there, read poems, and told us a lot about herself. It was then that I learned for the first time that Nikolai Lesyuchevsky, the director of the Soviet Writer Publishing House, had been an accomplice in the arrest of the poet Boris Kornilov, Olga Berggolts's first husband, who perished during those years, and it was then that I learned about the death of her child when she had been imprisoned. From close up she was not as attractive as she had been on the podium, but she was for some reason more endearing and warmer.

Olga Berggolts personified naked human suffering and grief. And even though it was immeasurably painful to see her drunk every time, bereft of her human guise, yet how else could she have saved herself from the past, from her recollections and her loneliness?

For me her verses, diaries, and stories became yet a new road into that "other world."

Here was one more road to the camps, to the truth about the past, a road that had become universal.

In the summer of 1955 Lev came to Zhukovka for the first time, together with his enormous black briefcase, from which he was always pulling out some interesting books, newspapers, and articles. He read a letter to me from Aleksandr Solzhenitsyn, a friend of his from the *sharashka*. At that time Solzhenitsyn was in Central Asia, in exile after his imprisonment. He was writing about his illness, about his desire to stay there in the village, where he was working as a teacher. One immediately sensed a person who was out of the ordinary, and tired. The letter—so it seemed to me—was permeated with what practically amounted to an Oriental resignation.

In 1956 he came to Moscow and showed up at *Inostrannaya literatura* with Lev. Afterward, he settled near the Torfoprodukt station and worked as a teacher there as well. When Lev and I were knocking about in search of living quarters, he invited us to stay at his place.

We saw one another over the course of eighteen years (1956–1974). Our ways converged and diverged. But I am writing here only about how the road into the "other world" was revealed to me.

In the early spring of 1961 he brought us a novella, typed single-spaced on both sides of the page in the faintest of scripts, on an old typewriter. At the top was written "ZEKA ShCh 854." Now it is a world-renowned work: *One Day in the Life of Ivan Denisovich*. I am trying, difficult as it is, to re-create my feelings from the previous year without mixing in what happened afterward.

It was terrifying to read it. At that time I was not in the least thinking about the author, his talent and literature. The same thoughts kept pounding away: how to get people to read this, reprint it. But that would be very dangerous. He didn't want to do that either. He was a conspirator himself.

In the summer he came to our dacha. Our friends had read it. Lev Ospovat was the first person who said: "Brilliant!" A small list was compiled of people to show it to among the writers. For some reason, nothing came of it. Lidiya Chukovskaya could not read such faint script. The Ivanovs weren't in Moscow. We weren't seeing the

Tendryakovs. We had no direct access to Tvardovsky, the editor of *Novy mir*.

Solzhenitsyn came again in November 1961, immediately after the Twenty-second Congress. We had just returned from the Caucasus, and we tried to convince him to submit the novella to *Novy mir*, to Tvardovsky, without hoping for a moment that it would be published. I took it to Anna Bezder—we had been students together—with the request that it should go only directly to Tvardovsky. A wet snow was falling. I briefly explained to her what it was all about. She looked at it without hope. "After the congress there's been a whole flood of manuscripts like this, and I'm afraid that not a single line will appear in print." First Tvardovsky was going off somewhere, then he was very busy. Anna herself read through it and was shocked, but she reckoned, like all of us, that publication was impossible.

On Sunday at eight o'clock in the morning there was a ring. It was Anna, forewarning us that Tvardovsky was going to telephone. He had read it and was in utter ecstasy. He spoke with Lev for a long time and said that he would summon the author. That was how it started.

A myth was immediately created around this affair, which became continually embellished with fresh details. Samuil Marshak said that the novella arrived "on its own" (he could only have heard that from Tvardovsky himself).

On the edition presented to us by Solzhenitsyn is the following inscription: "To my dear friends, Raya and Lev, who initiated the unforeseen course of this novella. November 1962."

But what surname to write down? On the manuscript Lev wrote "A. Ryazansky."*

Tvardovsky conducted a brilliant battle on behalf of the novella. He collected reviews by other established authors: Ehrenburg, Chukovsky, who called it "a literary miracle," Marshak, Fedin. He submitted everything to the Central Committee. A few things were edited in the manuscript, but very little. There was a long wait for permission, and in the meantime, a great many Moscow literary people read the story. Its growing reputation very much upset *Novy mir* and the author. Our copy was locked up in the safe at the editorial offices.

In my life I can't recall a literary event to equal this. Even before publication, writers were saying, one after the other, that it would be

---

* Solzhenitsyn at that time was a schoolteacher in Ryazan.

impossible to write in the old way after this kind of thing. The novella was printed and everyone, all the literate people, were able to find out the way it was in the concentration camps, and, perhaps more importantly, the way it was in this world. Because it was not merely a story about camps. We read not only about the way prisoners lived, but the way we lived as well.

In distinction to other "prison-camp" works, which kept multiplying, *One Day in the Life of Ivan Denisovich* aroused not only feelings of guilt over those who were imprisoned, but something more profound as well: a feeling of historical guilt over the peasant.

Why was it that I came to share these roads so late, when the gates to the prison camps had begun to open?! How is it possible to comprehend that many of us lived without knowing, without sufficiently realizing, that the prison camps existed?

There is a kind of tentative explanation. Among the inhabitants of the American South before the Civil War, there were various kinds of people. But even for the best of them, morality did not stretch as far as the blacks. Everything was permitted in regard to the blacks. It was the same thing with the Russian landowners. All the standards of chivalry, nobility, and honor were exercised among themselves. But the peasants were excluded from that. This is what Tolstoy shows in his story "After the Ball." ("He is a colonel, he knows something that I don't. Otherwise he couldn't have acted in that fashion.") The hero of the story in the second part turns out differently because he doesn't consider those before him to be people.

A conception of different moralities—for different groups of people—was cultivated from the first years of the Revolution. Lenin's formula at the Third Congress of the Komsomol—whatever is useful to the proletariat is moral (taken straight from Nechayev*)—contains in itself everything that was to follow.

At first it was necessary to cease treating each person as an individual. It was necessary to acquire a way of thinking in categories—and not only a way of thinking but an attitude toward the world as well. The circle of categories that were excluded from the concept of "people" was continuously widening. The members of the landed nobility are not people, the rich peasants are not people, and the children of "nonpeople" are not children. Once it was possible to

---

* Sergei Gennadievich Nechayev (1847–1882), Russian terrorist, author of *Catechism of a Revolution.*

shoot the children of the tsar, to banish the naked and unshod children of the kulaks (or pseudokulaks), then everything was permissible in regard to children of the "suppressed" categories. And finally came the era of the all-embracing rubric "enemy of the people."

There is probably no treachery committed by Soviet writers more bitter than the treachery over the very concept of the individual. Yes, I mean precisely what Soviet official terminology considers to be an abstract concept but which, in fact, is all the more concrete. That one person you have met, that unique one with his joys and, particularly, with his sorrows, it is only through him, that ordinary person you have met, that you have the right to measure all else! At the Institute of Philosophy, Literature, and History I heard in a course on Greek philosophy that "a man is the measure of all things." I heard it and forgot it, and it did not become a foundation of my world view.

All the time I keep seeking rational explanations, I keep seeking a comparatively simple, in any event, basic, connection among the facts. Yet there is always something more important out of the realm of the irrational that does not submit to any "computation." There are some kinds of profound abysses in a person that Dostoyevsky knew about and that contemporary writers and artists know about.

In our falsely rational world we have denied this and continue to do so. I know that this world abyss does exist. I know it in my mind. And I don't know how to live with the knowledge that it does exist.

If we can't conceive of this as well, then it is impossible to comprehend the horrible cells and the sadistic interrogators and the entire sea of our woes.

The GULag Archipelago (I hadn't known the words yet) came into my life in the middle of the 1950s, never to leave it again. And that became virtually the most important part of my awakening.

XXII

In and Of the Party

I was never a non-Party person. I cannot recall either reflection, vacillation, or doubt. It was all matter of fact and natural: from the Pioneers into the Komsomol, from the Komsomol into the Party. It was a direct, well-trodden path. Probably I would have entered the Party as a student if I hadn't been reprimanded for a "lapse in vigilance."

I was proud of the date of my application, June 22, 1941, the first day of the war and the date of entry into the Party. I was confirmed as a candidate member at the district Party office in October 1941, when Moscow was being evacuated. And I joined the ranks of the Party in October 1942, when the Nazis were at the gates of Stalingrad. Country and Party were in bad straits when I was joining up. Twenty years have gone by since then. The terrible Party meetings of 1949 have passed, and they were particularly terrible because at that time everything seemed basically correct to me. In any event, it was unavoidable.

Beginning in 1955, there were the classified letters of the Central Committee, which I listened to in the White Hall on Vorovskaya Street, in that same hall where Natasha Rostova, the heroine of *War and Peace*, had danced. In those letters the "errors" were revealed one after the other: in the management of agriculture, in the management of industry, in foreign policy . . . It was there as well that I listened to Khrushchev's secret report at the Twentieth Congress.

There was also our three-day-long Party gathering in March 1956, where people, one after the other, spoke the truth. Either they only realized it then or they had known about it and kept quiet for years.

Of course, we heard the empty phrases and empty speeches as well, but they were amazingly few in number. The majority of people spoke about the most important things, about the most painful things, about how people had lived all those years, and about what had to be done now.

I will quote the words of the author of the first revolutionary film, *The Little Red Devils*, the old Communist Blyakhin: "I do not agree with Mikoyan* [that is, with his speech at the Twentieth Congress]. No, the Leninist norms, the Leninist principles, have not yet been re-established. There is no point in mistaking wishful thinking for reality.

"Lenin dreamt about the creation of a socialist apparatus not in words but in deeds. How has this behest of Lenin's been fulfilled? Instead of a socialist apparatus, a bureaucratic apparatus has been created and nurtured that is based on petty officialdom, heartlessness, careerism, and the pursuit of cushy jobs.

"The foundations of the Constitution, the fraternity of nations, and socialist legality were put in jeopardy by the Stalinist era. Mention has already been made here about the Kalmyks. And what can be said about the sufferings of the Jewish people! [His voice started to break and the hall froze.] The Beilis affair† brought shame on the tsarist autocracy before the whole world. The shameful doctors' plot was a shameful blot on the Party and, above all, on us Russian Communists . . .

"There are people who are surreptitiously putting the brakes on all changes, and putting the brakes on rehabilitation. Only seven to eight thousand people have been rehabilitated. Khrushchev's words at the congress about the number of imprisoned people produced a distressing impression. For how many more years will our innocent people languish in prisons? A series of measures is required in order to carry out a massive rehabilitation in the shortest possible time. [This actually took place in the succeeding months, although the Stalinist apparatus was applying the brakes to rehabilitation in every possible way.]

* Anastas Ivanovich Mikoyan, at that time the first deputy chairman of the Council of Ministers.

† M. Beilis, a Jew, was falsely accused of the ritual murder of a Russian boy. The jury acquitted him in 1913.

"It's hardly worthwhile naming the names of the guilty ones and the toadies. Many are guilty. But it is impossible to forget the terrible sin, and we dare not diminish its importance!"

At the end, Blyakhin said that the sole guarantee against any repetition was a Soviet Leninist and Party democracy.

The third day of the gathering was under way. This is what and how I thought and spoke out in 1956.

"The days we are living through somehow remind me of the first days after the October Revolution. The same kind of democracy filled with meetings and bursting with the spring torrents. Everyone is striving to speak his or her mind, both those who were silent for so long and those who never told the truth. And those who sincerely believed but now are painfully discovering that they believed in a lie. Now we are involved in assessing our own conscience. Everyone should be answering the question: and where were you? I too am asking myself: how could I have voted for the exclusion of worthy people, honest Communists who are sitting in this hall?

"But we cannot allow ourselves the luxury of halting at this stage. We are not repentant nobility but members of a militant Party that answers for the fate of its native land."

But as things have turned out, everything was totally outside our control. We were not allowed to pause at that stage. And today I would no longer be speaking in such a manner.

The congress took place beneath the symbol of a restoration of Leninist norms. In connection with this, I posed two questions:

"The soviets [councils] were the great achievement of October. But in the work of the soviets—this was already discussed both at the congress and at our own gathering—there is a great deal of window dressing. This happens for the reason that the deputies frequently do not feel any responsibility to their electorate. Comrade Voroshilov talked about the utilization of the constitutional right to recall a deputy. This is important but insufficient. What we really require here are several candidates so that there would be *elections* and not a selection.

"The second problem concerns the departments of qualified personnel. This is the most undemocratic and senseless portion of the apparatus. After all, every director selects his own people for himself in any event, and the personnel departments are simply a hindrance. The entire system must be re-examined. (This has to be done, of course, with the entire system and not just the system of qualified personnel departments.)

"One of the most serious consequences of the cult of personality was the double standard. One thing was said, but something different was done. Hypocrisy and bigotry were nurtured. An enormous gulf existed between public opinion and the press. This has not been completely eliminated."

Then I gave a number of examples of this double standard in literary life.

Neither at the time when I was speaking out nor when I was writing about this or correcting my manuscript many times did I realize exactly what I was proposing. I was not thinking about the implications, not even the most immediate, let alone the more remote: namely, that the existence of several candidates in an election would undermine the basis of the monolith. The very possibility of a choice is a negation of the system. The abolition of the qualified personnel departments is another infringement on the holy of holies.

But then Khrushchev, the leader of a great country, had blurted out a few things without in the least stopping to consider what he was saying, and earthquakes followed his speech. So, without stopping to consider, a few other people also took action, and I did likewise.

The record from this gathering was published abroad in the *Political Diary* in 1972. In March 1976 my speech was broadcast on Radio Free Europe in connection with the twentieth anniversary of the Twentieth Congress. I have strangely mixed feelings: joy, because it meant that something had endured, and sorrow, because how could I have not understood anything? For that reason, I, as I was at that time, was able to utter these words without comprehending their consequences.

At the end of the gathering, the "Internationale" was sung, sung as I have never heard it sung during my whole life. The hunched back of Aleksandr Chakovsky, the crooked smirk of the film director Sergei Gerasimov, none of that had any significance. A new era was beginning. Here it had come at last, the real, genuine, revolutionary common cause that one could devote oneself to entirely. And how many people there were of like minds, how many people who were strangers, yet who were close to me and who thought and felt exactly the same as I did! How simple it was to find out about a person: "What do you think of Dudintsev's novel *Not By Bread Alone*? What do you think of Anatolii Sofronov and Nikolai Gribachev?" A few malicious responses or, on the other hand, defensive ones about the apparatus and the character reference was complete. "One of us" or "not one of us." Once again the world was becoming simple and black and white.

What is party spirit (*partiinost*)? Party spirit means acting at all times, in all places, and in all things as a party, as a group, a mass, a very great mass now. But how can one know how a mass thinks? In other words, party spirit means acting the way the Central Committee deems necessary. That is what party discipline is about.

During these years the following argument kept flaring up more and more frequently: wouldn't it be better to be outside the Party?

Here I am speaking simply about the ideological and ethical aspects of the question, because in practical terms people do not leave the Party out of pure fear.* If I am not to lie but to give my genuine reason, then I want to leave because I do not agree with the intervention in Hungary, with the new cult of personality, with the disgraceful things going on in the countryside, with the old lack of rights for the kolkhoz workers, with nuclear tests, with the new and the old falsehoods, with the new and most recent lawlessness, with the kind of "backlash" in the newly instituted harsh laws hitherto unseen even in the times of Stalin. I'm not even talking about our literary affairs. You might not perhaps be imprisoned for any declarations of that type, but undoubtedly they would cease to publish you, and your professional work would be lost.

So then it's a matter of something different: would it still be possible and easier to carry on the struggle for a *genuine communism* from within the Party or outside it?

Honestly speaking, during all these years after 1954 I was never once forced to be aware of the burden of my Party membership, the type of question did not arise in which I was *forced* to vote against my conscience. (After the trial of Sinyavsky and Daniel in 1966, I did feel the weight of my Party card.)

I felt then and I feel now a complete equality with non-Party people. (Naturally, I mean an equality and not a superiority.)

A minor event in November 1962, when I am writing this, forces

* In the years 1974–1979, of the people I knew the following left the Party of their own accord: Yelena Bonner, Iosif Bogoraz, Evgenii Gnedin, and Sonya Sorokina.

me to look at everything somewhat differently. The elections for Party office are approaching.

Suddenly people were telling me that they were about to elect me deputy secretary. I was in the most terrible panic. All I could hear inside me was a voice saying "I don't want to!" And I believed that voice. Strictly speaking, what did I mean that I didn't want to? Was it the work? No, it wasn't that. I was carrying a whole load of social duties and fulfilling everything honestly. And if the following day they had dumped yet again as much, I would have borne it joyfully.

I did not want to be going to the district committee offices, to the Moscow committee. I did not want to be going to "the council of the profane." But why? There was a disparity here. Here are my friends, people of exactly the same frame of mind as I, secretaries of Party organizations, Party organizers, members of the Party bureaus. And whether the people holding positions in those Party bureaus were bastards or decent people made a great deal of difference for the fate of individuals. Had it not been for the Party meeting of the section for literary criticism in December 1961 and the fiery activism of the literary critic Ivan Chicherov, the Elsberg affair might not have been raised and this informer, Yakov Elsberg, the perpetrator of so many arrests over so many years, might not have been publicly unmasked.

So, then, why did I not want to take part in this and similar work? I cannot even answer that question today. But if I had been expecting answers, I would not have written a single line in this book.

Perhaps a possible answer can be found in what Leon Trotsky said: "None of us wants to be or can be correct in opposition to our Party. In the ultimate instance, the Party is always right . . . It is possible to be right only in concert with the Party and by means of the Party, for history has not devised other ways for the realization of being right. The English have a historical saying: 'Right or wrong, it is my country.' With an even greater historical correctness we can say: 'Right or wrong in separate, particular, and concrete questions at separate moments, it is still my Party' . . . And if the Party carries out resolutions that one or the other of us considers to be unjust, then one says: 'Just or unjust, it is still my Party and I bear the consequences of its resolutions to the fullest.' "*

* *Twelfth Congress of the Russian Communist Party (Bolshevik): Stenographic account,* Moscow, 1963, pp. 158–159.

He survived only a few hours after Ramón Mercador struck him a blow with an alpenstock. As directed by a Party resolution.

Generations have repeated this formula.

If you are a part of that machine, you don't dare to be anything else. Just a small screw. Just a lever. Or just a means of putting those levers into action.

Is there an inevitable hypocrisy inherent in the very principle of the Party organization? People have differing opinions, but they must say the same thing. It's not a matter of a calculated hypocrisy: I'll just hide my own thoughts and express something contrary because that will be more advantageous to me. No, it's an unconscious hypocrisy that has become habitual and has been organically assimilated, a hypocrisy that has been depicted best of all by Aleksandr Yashin in his very important story "Levers."* People who are good, honest, and responsive turn into the levers of a soulless machine. We know that this machine was capable of serving mass destruction as well.

For a long time it seemed to me that the alternative to the Party was solitude. I am not in favor of solitude. A man needs to feel the shoulder of his comrade, of a like-minded person. To live for others. That was how the Party once was, though not for very long and not in all ways.

Perhaps there should be many parties? Am I really in the same party with hacks like Vsevolod Kochetov and Anatolii Sofronov now? Just to mention writers. No, we are in different ones. In all respects. Yet, formally, we are in the same one.

Perhaps the Party isn't the answer at all and Isaak Babel was right: an International of honest people is what is required. Of good people.

Today, in 1968, this entire chapter is an anachronism for me. There's only one thing I want. To rid myself of it. To leave.

Appendix (1980)

To the secretary of the Party committee of the Moscow
   Writers' Organization

Respected Comrades!

An "examination of my personal case" has been assigned for February 12. In order to facilitate that examination, which is extremely painful for me and, perhaps, not so very easy for you, I shall not come to the

* See Chapter 29.

session. And for the further reason that in the summer of 1978 I set forth my views in a protracted conversation with the members of the Party committee, listened to the objections of my comrades and have given them my consideration.

This impending dismissal is difficult for me. I submitted my membership application to the Party on June 22, 1941. For the first fifteen years I unequivocally fulfilled all resolutions, with a sincere belief in their necessity. If doubts arose, I suppressed them, reckoning that it was not I who was right, but those who carried out the resolutions. For that reason I was forced to commit actions of which I am ashamed.

After the Twentieth and Twenty-second Congresses, after the "unmasking of the cult of personality and its consequences," I, along with many others, hoped for fundamental changes in the country and in the Party. It was precisely at that time that I made a vow to myself: not to join in any resolutions if they seemed unjust to me, regardless of what departments they were issued from.

Today, I am attempting to proceed from the principle of goodness and justice in my attitude toward people and events. For that reason I find persecution of dissidents unbearable. The persecution of A. D. Sakharov, the best person I have met in my life, is unbearable. Even though I have remained silent and aloof from this persecution, I am aware of my fateful responsibility. It always seemed to me that the duty of a writer in Russia is not to attack but to defend.

In the Party organization, with which I have been connected for a quarter of a century, there are many wonderful writers, kind friends, and comrades. I am grateful to them for a great deal.

I am requesting you to examine my case without me, the conclusion of which is predetermined (I have become convinced of this once again after reading the slanderous article about my husband in *Sovetskaya Rossiya* [*Soviet Russia*]).

I am handing over my Party card No. 06100731.

R. Orlova-Kopeleva

February 5, 1980

XXIII

How I Was an Invader

1968

I don't want to write this chapter. But it has made up its mind to be born today and I cannot resist.

Thirty years ago I went through a great deal of what one hears nowadays about Czechoslovakia on the streets, in the subway, at tea tables. I covered all the laps and all the stages.

On September 1, 1939, we were leaving the Crimea. Courses were already under way at the institute and we had to get back to Moscow quickly, but we had no tickets. World War II had begun. That did not concern me in the least; only getting on the train in Simferopol was difficult and I was pregnant. The world war was under way not in our world, but in their world. And if the imperialists were warring among themselves, that was just fine: they would weaken one another. In my consciousness the division of the world was the clear-cut line of the frontier.

When Lyonya left for Lvov (1940) he wrote to me: "Perhaps it seems funny, but earlier the frontiers of our country seemed to me to be the frontiers of the world that I had imagined to myself from childhood: with a blue sky, with white snow, with the black edging of the forest on the horizon. Did I imagine that 'there' the sky was black, the snow blue, and the winter forest orange? Of course not. But if you just think for a moment and try to recollect, then you'll understand that your impression of 'there' is approximately the same. That's how much we've become accustomed to 'over there . . .' and 'over here . . .'"

On September 17, 1939, German and Soviet troops entered Poland. We were sitting at the table in our home excitedly discussing the news. We argued. We rejoiced. But I was very ashamed. After all, the very moment had arrived for which I had been preparing myself all my life. The revolution was becoming a reality and the red flags were being hoisted while I was tied up at that time. I had gone off into my own "little world" (in those years people always said precisely "little world" and the derogatory adjective was underlined because one life seemed insignificant in comparison with the grandeur of the whole). I was ashamed that, tied up with my pregnancy, I would not be able to, I would not be in time to participate!

People lived very badly in the places where our army came. A single match would be shared four ways. I felt sorry for those unfortunate western Ukrainians and western Byelorussians. Let them live better from now on. Let them be as well off as we are. Let each of them have his own match.

The frontier was pushed back. By agreement. But I felt uneasy in my heart. Moreover, the pact of friendship with Hitler was a thorn in our side. After all, that very simple, childlike question had not disappeared: for us or against us? So, if we were for Hitler, then what were we supposed to do about the antifascists, the novels of Willi Bredel and Feuchtwanger, the stories about the tortures and the staunchness of the Communists, the Jewish pogroms, and bonfires of books?

Now the Red Army had entered the western regions and had won over the people. Otherwise those people might have remained under the Nazis.

Our older fellows who had finished the institute had to go into the army. Some didn't want to go. But how could they not want to go into the Red Army and particularly at such a time! "It's foolish," they said. "Why graduate from the Institute of Philosophy, Literature, and History in order to serve as a private? We could be interpreters or political instructors." I tried to argue with them, and I made a vow to myself: the following year Lyonya would go into the army and I would not even show that I was sad to part with him.

An honor student in the fifth year, I continued to be densely ignorant. I knew practically nothing about the earlier partitions of Poland. I had run across some relevant paragraphs in history texts, but they made no impact on my heart. I had absolutely no understanding that in 1939 the country of Poland had been wiped off the map of the world. And we had been co-participants in that act. Herzen's *My Past and Thoughts* was one of my favorite books, but

I had not read his articles on Poland and the Polish uprising of 1863. If someone had told me at that time that it was immoral to force your way into someone else's country, that every nation had the right to decide its own fate, I would have repeated what I had learned: everything that serves the proletariat is moral. The seizure of the western regions serves the proletariat, therefore it is moral.

And still, as it turned out, I needed justification, I needed answers to the unasked questions . . . And I found those answers and justifications in Tiutchev.

In Agnessa Kun's room we read Tiutchev's verses that were written after the suppression of the Polish uprising of 1831.

> *And so to woeful Warsaw thus*
> *We dealt the fateful blow,*
> *To purchase at this bloody price*
> *All Russia's peace and unity.*
>
> *Away you wreath of infamy*
> *By slavish hand entwined and weaved!*
> *Autocracy was not the end*
> *For which our Russian blood did flow!*
>
> *In Russian hearts there surely beat*
> *A different thought, a different faith:*
> *To save the oneness of the state*
> *By salutary show of example.*
>
> . . .
>
> *But thou by friendly arrow pierced,*
> *In execution of decree by fate,*
> *Thou fell, O eagle of common kin,*
> *Upon the purifying fire!*
>
> *Believe the word of Russia's folk,*
> *Thy ashes live in sacred trust*
> *And phoenixlike, our freedom shared,*
> *Will rise from them reborn anew.*

These lofty beautiful words were essential to me. The music, the echo, the rhythm of a Tiutchev verse and his enchanting power were soothing. Everything was right. Tiutchev was for us. He had predicted precisely the way it would all be.

There is whim in the world: *I want to.* And there is duty: *I have to.*

To live according to duty is loftier and purer than living by whim. At this very time our favorite teacher, Vladimir Grib, was analyzing Racine's tragedies in his lectures. Racine's heroes suppressed their self-will and egotistical feelings according to the laws of classicism. They lived by the motto "I have to."

There was a great deal to pick up in Grib's lectures. This was what I learned above all. Grib allied himself with Tiutchev. Everything was right.

In 1939 we had strong and purified rear lines—purified by arrests (among the imprisoned there had been people who had at least asked questions), purified by terror, purified from thoughts, from doubts, from nobleness. And thus, there was little, very little opportunity for sympathy for the Poles, either intellectually or emotionally.

Who at that time would have written even secretly about a dismembered Poland? If someone did write about it, then no record of it remains.

Even in 1956, when I was in Poland and people told me about bitter Polish grievances, they invariably would mention Katyń, the uprising of 1944, and economic policies. But I heard nothing about the partition of 1939.

In newspapers and magazines, writers and journalists were praising our march into the western regions. Stepan Shchipachev, Viktor Shklovsky, and Aleksandr Tvardovsky set out for the west.

George Bernard Shaw was supporting the "peaceful policies of the USSR." Anna Louisa Strong refuted the "fables of the bourgeois press" to the effect that the Red Army "would destroy human values."

At the same time, Andrei Platonov was being criticized in the journal *Kommunist* for his article "Pushkin and Gorky" ("thoroughly confused and anti-Marxist"). The newspapers were lashing out at those critics who dared to find shortcomings in the songs of the nonpoet Vasilii Lebedev-Kumach. The novels of Wanda Wasilewska were printed. Then it was passed on by word of mouth how Wanda had heroically walked away on foot from the Germans. Wasilewska wrote novels, and Yelena Usievich praised these novels in her articles. A high-brow journal like *Literaturnyi kritic* printed these articles. And readers were convinced that everything was right. *That kind* of Poland did not deserve anything different.

The link between the facts of literary life and those of a military-chauvinistic intoxication is clear today, as is the roundabout link of falsehood: from the announcements of the government and the speeches by Molotov, to the speeches by writers. (I am talking about the objective falsehood. Some blindly believed, others pushed back their doubts into the depths of the subconscious, while still others lived cynically according to a double standard: they said one thing to themselves, and something completely different aloud.) And everyone was afraid. After all, the bloody nightmare of 1937 was still close at hand.

Of course, genuine literature continued to exist. The mortally ill Bulgakov finished *The Master and Margarita*, but only people close to him knew about that. Akhmatova wrote poems about warring Europe, filled with vivid pain and threatening premonitions. But these poems belonged to just a few.

A few days ago, during a really painful conversation about Czechoslovakia, someone said: "Don't say anything in front of the children. Why make them unhappy?"

During that earlier time I desperately wanted to be happy. And I was. And I lived with my eyes tightly closed.

In November 1939 our troops attacked Finland. If in the case of Poland I had read the novels of Henryk Sienkiewicz and the verses of Adam Mickiewicz in my childhood, Finland was an empty concept to me. If, God forbid, we had attacked France—in this case there was a great deal of affinity, from childhood and youth—then that would not have been so easily laid to rest. But in the concept of Finland there was nothing to be laid to rest.

This was a completely different war. It was nothing but a white frozen catastrophe. People were killed there.

If I thought about Finland, and that was very rarely, then it was about our own people. I knew that Sergei Narovchatov was there. The thought that Finns were dying there as they protected their soil did not penetrate in the least. (Is it possible for me to say today, in 1980, that the death of Afghans and the zinc-lined coffins of our own dead are of equal meaning? I don't know. I rather think not. But today there is the death of the Afghans, at least this is a poignantly sore point, whereas forty years ago it didn't exist.) Moreover, the Finns were called White Finns. This smallest of philological operations immediately simplified everything: a war of expansion was turned into something different. After all, we had been taught since school that *White* Finns had fought against us in the Civil War.

Once again our frontier was pushed back. The old border had

been close to Leningrad and I myself had seen it. Rumors reached us about our losses, about a blacked-out Leningrad. For these rumors I had a response that popped out automatically: "hostile."

One twelve-year-old girl who was celebrating the New Year of 1941 offered the toast: "To our defeat." She had been raised by her own powerful thoughts, her perceptive eyes, and the ability to ask questions.

The majority of people strive for prosperity, for happiness. But knowledge has never made people happy, least of all a knowledge, an understanding, of the real situation. I wanted my world—my beloved husband, faith in the revolution, my child, my friends, dreams of the future, poetry—I wanted that world to remain untouched. I didn't take into account that this world was constructed on the grief of the Russian peasant, the worker, the perceptive Russian intellectual, and on the tragedy of the *zeks*. And added to it now was the grief of the inhabitants of Lvov, Drogobych, the grief of Finns I knew nothing of.

As far as could be judged from the press, the war with Finland was neither hailed nor praised. Only brief bulletins were published.

This war was reflected indirectly in literary life, through yet more attacks on writers who seemed to be out of line. Evgenia Galperina, polemicizing with Georg Lukács, wrote in *Literaturnaya gazeta* (February 26, 1940): "There is an inherent logic in the fact that admirers of the reactionary movement 'to the roots' in Soviet literature have hoisted Andrei Platonov as their banner, a talented writer, but one who plays the fool-in-Christ, who epigonistically continues the line of petty Dostoyevskyism."

Viktor Pertsov accused Anna Akhmatova, affirming that reading her poetry was like walking between two walls of a narrow canyon. M. Charny exposed Konstantin Paustovsky for his "distortion of the image of Lieutenant Schmidt in the book *The Black Sea*." The article was called "A Serious Case."

In March 1940 our former maid came to see us. She told us about hunger in her village. I knew her well; she was an honest woman, one who was simply incapable of inventing anything. But how could there be hunger in the twenty-third year of Soviet power?

What ranks today as our national misfortune, pain, and shame is the people's support or, rather, their indifference, which is transformed into support for the occupation of Czechoslovakia—this stems from a long history.

Listening to many people today, I hear myself the way I was yesterday. The motives were different, the spiritual attunement was different, yet the objective result, which in newspaper jargon is called moral-political unity, is exactly the same.

In the summer of 1940 Latvia, Estonia, and Lithuania were annexed by the USSR. Pillaging was conducted on a wide scale in these three rich and flourishing countries. Everything was hauled away from there. Funny stories were related about how our ladies, the wives of officers, went off to a formal reception in nightgowns, which they thought were evening gowns.

A Hitler existed in 1939–1940. It was nothing at all like the present-day "imminent invasion of Czechoslovakia by the Federal Republic of Germany," which has been invented by our press. The actual existence of Hitler, which did not in the least alter the immorality of our aggression, prevented us from recognizing its true nature. That fact obscured everything and permitted us to say that, after all, it is either us or them.

I did not participate in those military campaigns. I did not enjoy any special benefits from the occupation. I did not speak out in the press (incidentally, no one asked me to). And still, I was part of the occupation. Because without such people, without those who gave their support at that time, without those who give their support today, no occupation is possible.

The roots of the old consciousness are rotting, but they still remain and it's painful to pull them out. These roots went down even more deeply because the great war came along and the preceding little wars dissolved in all our blood that was spilled, in our abundant grief.

November 1956. Hungary. This time I did not accept anything on faith, I did not approve, and I did not give my support. But I did coexist with the invasion relatively peacefully. I was working for the journal *Inostrannaya literatura*, which printed articles about the "counterrevolutionary overthrow." I read with interest and sympathy, but still without any clear realization, the speeches of Sartre and Vercors that condemned our invasion. Being in charge of the department for criticism, I myself prepared, together with the authors, articles that argued with the Polish "revisionists."

I heard about leaflets in our country, about student circles, and shortly after, a group of historians was arrested, the group around

Krasnopevtsev. There was a trial. But that did not concern me—it existed only on the periphery of my consciousness.

My life could go on calmly in the old fashion. That is, in the new fashion, in the hope of liberal reforms after the Twentieth Congress. One had to struggle for the kind of changes that would make another Hungary impossible.

Here we were, finally printing Hemingway's novel *For Whom the Bell Tolls* or settling accounts with a literary scoundrel. Now that was a victory.

At that time I could still continue to be a part of that system that had crushed the Hungarian workers and the intellectuals from the Petöfi Circle with tanks . . .

XXIV

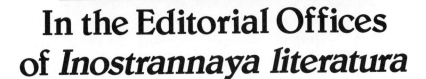

In the Editorial Offices
of *Inostrannaya literatura*

1961–1962

The decision to create a new journal was adopted at the Second Congress of Writers in December 1954. People tried to talk me out of working on the journal. Aleksandr Chakovsky, the editor in chief, was well known for his repugnant behavior during the time of the struggle with cosmopolitanism.

At first none of us knew what had to be done, and we searched for books, articles, and—first of all—people who knew how to do something, above all those people who at one time had worked on the journal *Internatsionalnaya literatura*. Nikolai Vilmont took charge of the section for literature from the capitalist countries. Some critics from the older generation came to us with articles, translations, and suggestions. The succession was partially preserved.

For the first issue we prepared Aleksandr Anikst's article on the novel *Heroes of the Empty View* by the British writer James Aldridge.

After reading Anikst's article on Aldridge's novel, I saw that it was possible to write about foreign books while expressing the same things that we were thinking and arguing about and that concerned us personally.

That article, as was subsequently the case with any talented article, book, or sketch, had a difficult time making it through. Chakovsky's appointed assistant, Savva Dangulov, spoke out sharply against the article. Anikst was developing the thought (far from new) about a novel of ideas and a novel of images. Nowadays it is difficult to belive that an article could be rejected on that basis, even within the boundaries of a quite conservative journal. But that was precisely the pretext at the time. Anikst's entire article was suffused with a new, innovative challenge. Both its opponents and supporters sensed that underlying current perfectly. Ehrenburg supported the article (he was a member of the editorial board for a few months but then left specifically over Anikst's article). Motyleva was frequently at Ehrenburg's on business concerning the journal. By way of reconciliation, she remarked: "Ilya Grigorievich [Ehrenburg], only a tiny little piece has been cut out of the article. It will be published after all."

"Tamara Lazarevna [Motyleva], you can cut a very tiny piece off a man and he will cease to be a man."

The stories of Erskine Caldwell were earmarked for the second issue of the journal. One of them concerned a twelve-year-old girl who was being sold by her mother because there was hunger in their house. It was a very frightening story and likewise provoked arguments. Since then, a multitude of similar stories, novels, and plays have been published. But that was the beginning. Every new name, every new thought, every fresh line, had a difficult and embattled time breaking through into print.

In defending Anikst's article or Caldwell's stories, I acted on instinct. Later I understood the connection between the rehabilitation of Hemingway or Steinbeck and the rehabilitation of unjustly condemned Soviet citizens: they were rehabilitated concurrently just as they had been concurrently condemned. If we were living in a besieged fortress, then all efforts had to be applied to the struggle with the enemy, both the one within and the one without. All the openings and holes had to be stuffed solid. But if we were a strong power which had won a victory in a cruel war, then might we not allow ourselves to raise the Iron Curtain somewhat, might we not allow ourselves expansiveness, openness, and might we not recall the universality that Dostoyevsky defended?

In publishing foreign writers we were partially opening up that world by whose light those dull-witted chauvinistic concepts of exclusiveness invariably had to fade. "Only in our country . . ." No, as it turns out, it's not only in our country. Then it began to appear that there was not even as much in our country as we had thought.

Every line of our journal, despite all forms of the harshest censorship, revealed that fine writers who wrote fine books that were akin to us and dealt with normal people who were also akin to us—that such writers were living abroad. The concept of a general decay and ruin in Western culture had been collapsing. Of course, the journal played merely a small part in that process, and besides, its special role was diminishing. Other journals and publishing houses had begun printing more and more foreign books.

On many occasions our editorial board refused to print "on ideological grounds" books that subsequently appeared in other journals and publishing houses, among them *The Little Prince* by Antoine de Saint-Exupéry, the first stories and novels of Heinrich Böll, and even an excerpt from John Reed's *Ten Days that Shook the World*. Nowadays it sounds quite unlikely, but the book by Reed was turned over to the readers of *Novy mir* (November 1956).

Foreign films were coming out; newspapers and journals from the East European countries were beginning to be sold; Soviet citizens were traveling abroad and foreign tourists were coming to visit us. More and more people were listening to foreign broadcasts. One tear after another appeared in the Iron Curtain. It split and started to slide apart. Truthful information gave birth to questions and led to answers.

As we began to realize that we were living as captives of a false inhuman ideology, that for a long time we had been deceived and had been deceiving others and ourselves, we convulsively sought a different ideology, a different set of beliefs that would include, without fail, moral principles, truthfulness, and humanity.

Society was undergoing a period in which there was a tumultuous reassessment of values—a reassessment and search. What, in fact, did people live by? Where is the truth? What do we believe in? People sought the answers along a variety of roads: in a Marxism that was purified of Stalinism, in a Marxism that was united with freedom and humanity, in books by Russian poets, prose writers, and thinkers that were formerly inaccessible. The stamp of their being White émigrés had deprived us for a long time of Bunin, Tsvetaeva, Berdiaev. In 1956 they started to become available once more. We went searching through their books. We were searching for an answer in religion. And in foreign literature.

Beginning in 1955–1956, in the Soviet Union the books of Remarque, Hemingway, Böll, and Salinger became our daily bread, our spiritual sustenance. The works of these and other writers began to fill the spiritual vacuum . . .

Many pages of our journal were adorned with boring novels and ruminative articles, principally from East European countries. Still, several important articles, such as Ehrenburg's "The Lessons of Stendhal," appeared. It was a model of anticensorship propaganda, of Aesopian language. Chakovsky had several comments. Nikolai Prozhogin, the head of the publicistic department, and I were sent to see Ehrenburg to get him to accept these comments.

Ehrenburg kept us for several hours, although the corrections were inserted within a few minutes. For example, he had written: "Stendhal did not care one wit about the critics, but the guardsmen were standing behind the critics." Chakovsky had placed a fat tick here. Ehrenburg produced an ironic grin and inserted "royal" in front of "guardsmen."

Ehrenburg would not let us go because he felt like talking, telling stories, refuting things, and explaining. We, of course, wanted to listen. Ehrenburg said approvingly: "I frequently want to stamp my feet too. It's impossible to argue anymore."

We asked whether Ehrenburg liked Sholokhov's "The Fate of a Man." "No, I did not. Sholokhov's tragedy is more terrible than that of Fadeyev. He is slowly dying before our eyes. Since the beginning of the war. He wasn't for us in those days because the cossacks weren't for us. And that tie is a blood tie for him, both from a human and a creative point of view. Then began the vodka and the anti-Semitism. And his milieu, a shameful clique. He and I met in 1943 and he said to me: 'You're fighting the war while Jews are bargaining away in Tashkent.' I flared up and shouted at him: 'I don't want to sit at the same table with an anti-Semite.'"

Ehrenburg continued. "Sholokhov is in torment because of our quarrel. He sends me letters and telegrams." We read one of the telegrams ourselves. It was for Ehrenburg's sixty-fifth birthday: "I embrace you, a great Russian writer."

"Sholokhov is a very honest artist," Ehrenburg went on. "He cannot lie, he cannot bear a double standard." Ehrenburg returned to this thought several times. "And an upstanding person, he never trampled anyone underfoot, he didn't make his way over the corpses of others. Everything bad in him is superficial, because of the milieu he's in. His behavior reminds one of Yesenin's behavior on the eve of his suicide. He used to say: 'I'm going out on the street right now and shout "The Jews have sold Russia!"' I held him back and said: 'No, you don't.' But those were different times, he could have been taken off to the police."

He then said: "I wrote the introduction to Tsvetaeva, Mandelstam, and Babel. There's a battle under way for Tsvetaeva."

Ehrenburg was alien to me both as a writer and, judging from the few and aloof encounters, as a person and as a public figure. But I was grateful for his memory. He himself had once written in his Spanish verses: "One thing I cherish: a simple memory."

It only seemed simple. To remember is a very difficult thing. In my own lifetime I had not experienced all that much that was truly terrible. But then there I was walking over the ashes of Maidanek at the end of 1944. I felt nauseous—from the horror, from the odor, from the questions of American correspondents: "How many pairs of children's shoes are in storage?" The Americans love preciseness. The Americans reacted skeptically to the stories of atrocities. At that time I could not imagine that we could ever have lied about anything.

There were the gas chambers. There was the collapse of faith in man. *Homo sapiens?*

But I have in fact forgotten about Maidanek. It is normal for a person to guard himself from terrible memories.

I myself saw Maidanek. Yet the sense of the tragedy—the planned destruction of people because they were Jews—penetrated my heart not through what I saw with my own eyes but rather through the writer's word, after I had read Vasilii Grossman's *The Hell of Treblinka* (1946).

I had a long road to travel before I could put myself in the place of a prisoner in a concentration camp, be it one of Hitler's or Stalin's. Until I reached the books of Solzhenitsyn . . .

I wandered away from the walls of the apartment on which hung original works by the best artists of the twentieth century. Works that were autographed. Ehrenburg was talking about Fadeyev: "He suffered a great tragedy. He had been living a double life for a long time. At meetings he used to revile Pasternak, but then he took me to a restaurant and asked: 'Do you want to hear some real poetry?' And then he read Pasternak for hours." Ehrenburg claimed that Fadeyev had a guilt complex over Grossman: he was always trying to justify himself. It concerned the criticism of Vasilii Grossman's novel *For the Right Cause* in 1952. The second part of the novel was suppressed in 1961. (The second part—*Life and Fate*—was published in 1980 in Russian by the publishers L'Age d'Homme in Lausanne.)

The writer Vsevolod Ivanov told us about a conversation with

Fadeyev in 1939. "Sasha [Fadeyev], why has Meyerhold* been arrested?" The reply: "Because he was a *provocateur* and a spy for three powers." "The only thing left to talk about with him," said Ivanov, "was hunting."

Ehrenburg aided in the publication of Hemingway's *The Old Man and the Sea.* If we could start the journal with Hemingway, it would mean that we were continuing a tradition and acquainting Russian readers with a new work that had become universally recognized. Chakovsky understood that there was nothing seditious in the text itself. He understood that it was the best beginning.

In March 1955 Molotov, who was then Minister of Foreign Affairs, discussed the plans of the journal with Chakovsky. Chakovsky returned in an angry mood, his mind made up. He called the small editorial group together: "I questioned Molotov about *The Old Man and the Sea.* He replied: 'I haven't read it myself, but I've been told that it's a stupid book. They keep trying to catch some fish or other.' I hope that it is clear to everyone that the question of publishing this book has been excluded from our consideration. I am requesting that there be no further conversations about Hemingway."

I was grieved. But I wasn't indignant.

In June 1955 Ehrenburg met Molotov in Vienna. He went up to him and asked: "Vyacheslav Mikhailovich, did you forbid *Inostrannaya literatura* to publish *The Old Man and the Sea?*" Molotov replied: "No, I haven't read the book. They can decide for themselves."

Ehrenburg returned and passed on the conversation. The novella was quickly included in the next issue, the third. Thus, in September 1955, the veil was finally removed. After a gap of sixteen years, the name of Hemingway had appeared in print once more.

Ivan Kashkin, who discovered Hemingway in the 1930s, wrote an article called "On Rereading Hemingway." It was a time when people were rereading a great deal. I too returned to Hemingway. By no means as a duty to my work. The thaw was filled with romantic illusions. And it was at that time that a romantic writer returned to us. "The Snows of Kilimanjaro" and *A Farewell to Arms* began to reveal themselves to me in a different way. I began, but just began,

* Vsevolod Emilievich Meyerhold (1874–1940), Russian theater director. An opponent of socialist realism, he experimented widely with new ideas. The circumstances of Meyerhold's death during the purges still remain unclear.

to see the world in its true colors. Not to flinch. "To endure"—Faulkner brought that later. But at that time it meant to resist without loss of dignity. Even though it was precisely at that time that life was overflowing with hope, at the same time a certain new code of behavior was crystallizing, a code of behavior that did not rest on external supports—as before—but rather on oneself. "Not the way we were, but the way we might have become and still can become"—that was how I might have defined (paraphrasing the title of his old story "A Way You'll Never Be") my attitude toward Hemingway at the end of the fifties. Hemingway helped me find myself. Pasternak and Akhmatova were able to help as well, but these, my great compatriots, I knew worse than the distant American . . .

It was long and difficult work for me and Kashkin. The critic strove to write about what he had seen of good and value in a beloved author. But the editorial board was trying to steer him into an enumeration and condemnation of shortcomings: "Hemingway didn't understand"; "Hemingway didn't reflect"; "Hemingway didn't know how to rise above . . ."

There were more defeats than victories, and with increasing frequency I asked myself the question: Did our work have any sense?

The following anecdote reached us from Poland at this time. A teacher of mathematics, a reactionary, stated that two times two was nine. After a stubborn battle the reactionary had to leave. He was replaced by a liberal, who declared that two times two was seven. And the boy who shyly tried to stutter that two times two seemed to be four was regarded as insane or a villain: "Do you really want two times two to be nine again?!"

For a long time I was among those who rejoiced at the possibility of saying that two times two was seven . . .

The events, the time, and even to a certain degree probably our own efforts had their effect, and the editorial board was forced to print talented works that liberated the mind and conscience.

First it was Louis Aragon that would help, then Vercors, then Halldór Laxness . . .

Among the intelligentsia today there are those who are reading, or say that they do, the novels of Faulkner. But how many times was it necessary to go on repeating like an incantation: Faulkner, Faulkner, Faulkner. And how difficult it was for me to make the breakthrough to Faulkner.

Endless battles took place for Hemingway's novel *For Whom the Bell Tolls.*

For the second time the manuscript of the translation (prepared back in 1940) found its way after 1956 into a nascent *samizdat.* About 200 people read our copy—it was one of the few manuscripts that was literally obliterated (the pages were torn, and it was by then impossible to make out the letters).

In 1954 the editorial head of the Foreign Literature Publishing House listed Hemingway's novel among the books intended for publication. The indignant letters of Spanish and French Communists came in an avalanche. The book was withdrawn from the plan. In 1959, after Mikoyan visited Hemingway in Cuba, the journal *Neva* announced that it would publish the novel. The newspaper *Sovetskaya Rossiya* printed the author's telegram: "Very pleased that you are printing the novel. Best wishes. Hemingway." The writer was premature in being pleased, just as the readers were. He never succeeded in seeing his novel in print in Russian during his lifetime.

But efforts did not cease. At the beginning of 1963 excerpts from the novel were being prepared for the newspaper *Nedelya* (Week). Evgenia Kalashnikova showed me the galley proofs. But publication was forbidden once more. However, in August 1963 an excerpt from Chapter 43, the concluding chapter, was published in *Literaturnaya gazeta.*

My article "On Revolution and Love, on Life and Death" was printed in the journal *Zvezda* (The Star; No. 1, 1964). I checked the quotations that I had made in the article from the *samizdat* edition with the clean pages in the State Publishing House (Goslit). But even this time the Russian edition did not appear, and the plates were destroyed: the Spanish Communists Dolores Ibarruri ("La Pasionaria") and Enrique Lister, together with their supporters, protested decisively against the book.

In 1968 *For Whom the Bell Tolls* finally appeared in Russian in the third volume of Hemingway's collected works. A twenty-eight-year-long controversy ended in victory. I believe that the events of 1968 played a telling part in this victory. When the novel was being prepared for publication, the hopes for "socialism with a human face" were being revitalized. After all, for thirty years before the Prague spring many idealistically attuned Communists and leftists (including Hemingway's character Robert Jordan) believed that they were fighting for a better world, for true brotherhood.

The novel was published in Russian with cuts (principally in Chapter 18—Jordan's recollections of the Hotel Gaylord, where the Russians were living).

Hemingway put his seal on the flight of revolutionary hopes and illusions (when they were on the decline throughout the entire world) and on their fall . . . In the mid-1950s, after the Twentieth Party Congress, I and my friends were struck above all by his picture of the bureaucratic degeneration of the revolution. At that time many Russian intellectuals read this book as the artistic embodiment of what practically all of us were talking and arguing about: about means and ends, about crimes and falsehood, about the tyrants and maniacs who had emerged out of yesterday's revolutionaries.

The depiction of André Marty coincided with Khrushchev's speech about Stalin at the closed session of the Twentieth Congress, even in the details. Khrushchev said that Stalin had poked at a globe of the world with a pencil, determining, often illiterately, the movement of divisions, armies, and fronts. That was precisely how Marty, the commissar of the International Brigade, had acted in the novel . . . And he had given orders to shoot people cruelly and senselessly—just as Stalin had done. And he loved to kill—just as Stalin had loved to do.

During a period of torturous crisis many of us discovered Hemingway's novel—perhaps the most Russian foreign novel of the twentieth century?

In those days we were still trying to accommodate Hemingway to ourselves rather than accommodating ourselves to him. In part, his romanticism facilitated at first an ecstatic, then a disillusioned but not a sober view of his work. Only later did I learn to accept him for what he was. If I did in fact learn how to.

In 1958 the novel *Death in Rome* by the West German writer Wolfgang Koeppen was translated. It was an antifascist novel with a very powerful portrait of an SS officer, written in that subjective fashion that just barely allowed it to squeeze through the narrow cracks of our publishing houses and journals.

A long, very complicated fight to publish this novel culminated in a meeting of our editorial offices with the propaganda department of the Party Central Committee. The chief, Dmitri Polikarpov, spoke at length.

"We are dealing with bourgeois literature from the period of imperialism. It contains things that are both acceptable and unacceptable to us. We do find ourselves in a state of war between two ideologies, not only politically speaking, but also in a moral-aesthetic sense. Regardless of how we want to proceed under other circumstances, it is impossible to do so at the expense of making concessions. In Koeppen's novel we lose more than we gain. At first it seemed to me that it was possible to change a few things by way of free translation.* But the second part excludes such an approach. In the second part we have pornography, a pathological tumult of the flesh and swine sucking.† [SS—swine sucking—this expression enriched our editorial jargon.] But the journal is being read by teenagers . . . There are some healthy bits as well, but they're in a cup of hogwash. Russian classical literature was a chaste literature. And we've inherited that. The appearance of such books as Remarque's *Arch of Triumph* and *A Borrowed Life* has provoked irritation in very broad circles of readers. [That was a lie.]

"We opened the floodgates with these books. I am not criticizing the author. He is truthful. That's the way bourgeois life is. Sex cannot occupy that kind of place in the life of the proletariat—the worker hasn't got time for that . . .

"How is the Jewish question presented in the book? After all, the Nazis destroyed not only Jews."

Further, he declared that the editorial board, of course, had a right to disagree with him. Chakovsky, naturally, hastened to assure Polikarpov that he agreed with him.

On November 1, 1965, I simultaneously pulled out of my mailbox a copy of *Pravda* with Polikarpov's obituary and issue No. 10 of *Inostrannaya literatura* containing Koeppen's *Death in Rome*. A mysterious coincidence.

From approximately 1957, major battles began to swirl around Remarque. During that whole period there was not a foreign writer who could have provoked public opinion to such a degree and so appeal to the youth. Particularly his novel *Three Comrades*.

I recall one speech at a conference in a small library in Zamoskvore-

---

* This means to distort the novel by cutting and even by adding.
† The Russian is literally *sobachya svadba*, or "dog's wedding."

chye. A proofreader, still quite young, said: "I can't manage without Remarque. After all, we did have Stalin. Everyone believed in him and I believed in him as though he were a god. I didn't even imagine that he went to the toilet. And suddenly it turns out that he did so many horrid things, he killed so many people. Pick up *Pravda* and you get nothing. That's why Remarque makes such an impression. We too have prostitution, so why doesn't anyone write about that. Our young people don't believe in the Komsomol, a lot of them don't believe in the Party. Remarque had a really strong effect on me. His heroes also experienced great disappointment. I never got such impressions from Sholokhov or Fedin." People applauded him loudly. Immediately an older person leapt up out of turn and shouted: "I totally disagree; only a spiritually defunct person can make those sort of speeches. People were attracted to Remarque because they found out about a life they weren't familiar with. How can one not believe in the Komsomol? Prostitution has been mentioned. But those are isolated facts. He's talking nonsense. How can you not recognize Sholokhov? Sholokhov is recognized worldwide. There is no one better than Sholokhov!"

At another readers' conference, a postgraduate student spoke out: "*Arch of Triumph* created a stunning impression . . . I felt sorry for our literature when I had finished. What makes Remarque powerful? How does he grip you? Different people read him, both the snob and the ordinary working fellow . . . A great deal that Remarque writes about we cannot find in our books, even in the best. After all, the main thing is contemplation, the movement of the human soul. What does a person live for? Whom does he love? Whom does he hate? Furthermore, the things that our critics avoid with shame: the problems of women, of love. Remarque is not afraid to write about our intimate life . . . For which woman will we go to the ends of the earth, and which deserves to be treated like an animal? What is the meaning of life? What is truth, honor, and villainy?"

Remarque was severely criticized in the press, but to no effect. Or rather there was an effect, but the opposite one from what was intended. In 1960, when a commission from the Central Committee carried out an anonymous survey at the philological faculty on "Who is your favorite author," Pasternak and Remarque shared first place.

At some point we even got fed up with Remarque. There had been so many questions about him, so much talk and argument. Naturally, his significance was exaggerated and he wasn't that great a writer. But at that moment he proved essential.

In 1961, when I understood that I could not simultaneously work, write a book, and somehow take care of household affairs, I left the journal.

Addendum (1980)

The journal has just completed a quarter of a century.

Our first issue was not the way it appears today but in a blue cover. There it was lying on the table, amid the bottles and plates of *hors d'oeuvres* in the Aragvi Restaurant, where we were celebrating its birth by drinking, eating, and having a good time. Chakovsky sat down at the piano, and we sang and danced. Some were young, while others had become young.

I am looking over the present list of members of the editorial committee: only Tamara Motyleva and Mikhail Sholokhov (the latter, of course, took no part in the actual work of the journal) are left from that first year.

Within a short time, foreign authors began to pay us visits. The meetings customarily took place in the editor's office and were chaired by him. But frequently they continued in our own rooms, on the streets, in the homes of our co-workers, and at our apartment. I never recorded any of our conversations.

During the years of work at the journal many writers visited us: C. P. Snow with Pamela Hansford Johnson, Jean-Paul Sartre and Simone de Beauvoir, John Uplike, John Steinbeck, William Saroyan, Erskine Caldwell (who vaguely recalled our first meeting before the war), Albert Maltz, Graham Greene, Friedrich Dürrenmatt, Max Frisch, Hans Magnus Enzensberger, Heinrich Böll, Anna Seghers, Erwin and Eva Strittmatter, Christa Wolf . . .

Some of them I only saw at the official receptions, while with others I had long talks afterward. Still others, like Böll, became close friends. Everything—in contrast to the VOKS years—was unofficial.

At all our ad hoc meetings and at all our editorial consultations I defended talented books and that part of a great, universal literature of which the Soviet readers had been robbed, and I always insisted that our duty was to bring back what had been concealed. I tried to protest against the mediocrity that flooded our journal as well as others.

But within a sufficiently short time I understood that, as before, very little depended upon me. And if earlier I had submissively reconciled myself to the fact that I was just a tiny cog, then now, on the editorial board, it became increasingly difficult for me in what was essentially a different time. I had begun to be conscious of myself as an individual. That was partially thanks to those very same books that in the performance of not only my professional duty but, as it turned out, my spiritual duty as well, I had to read first in the original, then obtain a translation of, then fight for their publication so that others could read them as well.

The feeling of responsibility deepened within me—the joy and pride for everything that was good, as well as the shame for any mediocre novella or any vile article. These inner changes were facilitated by the entire atmosphere at the end of the 1950s and the beginning of the 1960s. I was living among souls that had been awakened. People wanted passionately to mix with others, to share things with one another. We were involved in literary work, and the *word* itself, as Heinrich Böll said in one of his speeches, was a "refuge for freedom."

The feeling was firm in my heart: enough of double standards. I could no longer put up with them.

In May 1957, after the first meeting of the government with intellectuals, Chakovsky returned to the editorial offices, summoned me, and said: "The discussion that has gone on for almost a year is finished. The Party leaders have clearly supported the line of Sofronov, Kochetov, and Gribachev."

"I won't support that line."

"That means that you cannot head the section for literary criticism in our journal."

"Aleksandr Borisovich, find a replacement for me."

The search for a replacement (and perhaps the vacillations, for after all, the line kept changing all the time) took a year.

At the same time, I was afraid to leave, to leap into the unknown. From the age of eighteen I had had to go somewhere every morning—to work. And I never, almost never, felt work to be a burden. On the contrary.

Was it too late to learn it anew, was it too late to begin the morning at home?

The working morning. Now I love the morning more than the

evening, the spring more than the fall. The promise more than the fulfillment.

Even though there's the crowd, even though it's difficult to find a place on the subway, I love the feeling itself, of people going to work, of children going to school, and there I am in the crowd, and the peaceful day in which we all share is beginning.

I had grown accustomed to the people in *Inostrannaya literatura.* We frequently spent time together—we celebrated birthdays, house-warmings, and all the editorial office and general holidays were invariably accompanied by humorous evenings that were frequently very witty.

Even now, years later, when those assemblages seem to be such utterly peculiar combinations of people, even now I remember several men and women from the editorial offices with wistful tenderness. The ones I do remember will know whom I mean.

Nevertheless, in 1961 I handed in my resignation "to leave for creative work of my own volition."

Incidentally, I did not leave entirely. Remaining as a consultant on American literature, I would come once a week, read the American press, and compile monthly surveys. As before, I was invited to the receptions for American writers. Once a year my articles were published. I was made privy to editorial news, gossip, and the "back-room" goings-on. My place was taken by an old classmate from the Institute of Philosophy, Literature, and History, Naum Naumov. All of that prevented me from feeling like an outsider.

When I left my regular work, I lost nothing in doing so. And I was not completely aware of the change that had taken place. External life continued to overwhelm me. There were more requests for articles. There were far more lectures and lecture tours around the country. There was a contract for a book on American literature. I was a member of the Writers' Union and a member of the editorial advisory committees for two of the largest publishers. I was the executive secretary for the section on literary criticism of the Writers' Union. There was no sedition either in my articles or in my lectures. But I had ceased to be a tiny cog once and for all. For that reason it does not seem to me to be a coincidence that I began to write my testimonial in that same year, 1961.

XXV

Poland

I didn't know Polish and I hadn't studied Polish literature. However, in April 1956 the editorial offices sent me on a trip to Warsaw to select stories, novels, and articles for publication at home. During the little time remaining before my departure, I feverishly prepared myself by reading and asking questions.

At the end of March, at the session of the Polish Council on Culture, Jan Kott had given a report entitled "Mythology and Truth." In the Soviet Union his report was translated and circulated in *samizdat*. In the epigraph were the words of Marx: "Shame in itself is already revolution. Shame, this is a type of wrath that is turned inward. And if the entire people were actually seized with shame, they would be like a lion that is getting ready to spring."

Jan Kott stated: "We do not strive for knowledge of the truth, but rather for explanation and justification. At any price. Even at the price of truth.

"The thesis that has been instilled in us that supposedly every stage in the revolution and the construction of the socialist state is without fail a step forward could not help but lead to a situation where the qualities of 'divine infallibility' were attributed to the leadership and those who represent it . . . Stagnation began in the thirties. Literature and art ceased to speak the truth, they ceased to understand the historical process, they ceased to be the conscience and reason of the revolution . . .

"If one takes account of how life has seemed for the last three years, a life where 'nocturnal conversations among countrymen' have been going on, a life in which each of us is wrestling with his own conscience, a life which is seeking new ways and ceaselessly thinking about the same things, how is it possible to demand that this anxiety, this bitterness, this pain, not spill forth in poetry, that heroes of novellas and stories not speak and think about all these things, that they possess ready-made conclusions, a spiritual trust, a virginal naïveté, and a rosy optimism!"*

All this applied to us as well. We too carried on those endless nocturnal conversations. We too were taking account with our own conscience.

Before my departure, I made the acquaintance of Wiktor Woroszylski, who was a graduate student in literature at that time. He was defending his dissertation on Mayakovsky. Earlier he had been a passionate believer, a confirmed Stalinist. And his faith had been shaken, just as mine had been and that of thousands of others.

In October 1956 he left for Hungary as a correspondent for *Nowa Kultura* (New Culture). The Soviet tanks that opened fire on the Hungarian insurgents put the finishing touch to what had begun for him in 1953. His "Hungarian Diary" is a most sincere and passionate outcry of the soul. I am convinced that if I had been there, I would have seen people and events in a light similar to Woroszylski's.

On several occasions in Poland I heard judgments of the following kind: it was impossible to believe Woroszylski.

During the first years of the thaw one frequently had occasion to hear that everyone had lied. Those kinds of statements used to drive me into helpless fury. Nowadays I can, after a fashion, explain the nature of that fury to myself: I really had not lied. And I had thought, as it is typical for people to do, that all those who uttered my words aloud had not regarded them as devalued currency. Or, at the very least I had believed that my words had been endowed in any event with a reserve of sincerity if not with *realia*.

Finally, I set off for Poland. At the station I was welcomed by Ziemowit Fedecki, a translator of Russian poetry who had spent seven years in the Soviet Union. It immediately became clear that he knew more than I did about our affairs, both general and literary. He took me to the hotel.

He asked me whether I had read Tvardovsky's narrative poem

* Jan Kott is now living in England.

Tyorkin in Hell. VOKS had instilled in me for seven years that one must not talk with a foreigner about an unpublished work! But in Poland from the very first moment all that was sent head over heels. And of course it was not a question of crossing a state border but of the change within one's heart. Yes, I had read it.

"And Naum Korzhavin's poetry?"

"That's the first I've heard of him."

Now Korzhavin is being published both as a poet and a critic. I read his unpublished poems about three years after visiting Poland. Some lines stayed with me for a long time.

Fedecki said that the Society for Polish-Soviet Friendship had succeeded in creating a united anti-Soviet front. There they were, the fruits of VOKS' work. Photographs of luxurious six-room workers' apartments sent by us.

He said: "We are living through a very critical moment: there is a chance, not a very great one, and it must not be missed."

The first conversation was a kind of table of contents for everything that I subsequently saw and heard in Poland. The youth journal *Poprostu* (Simply), posed the question about the dissolution of the Komsomol because the Komsomol had been "transformed into an organization of slanderers and informers."

At the embassy I was greeted by the first secretary, Bryzgalov. I wrote in my diary: "Bryzgalov is one of 'them.'" I too was part of "them." The differences are in the nuances.

I went to the president of the Polish Writers' Union, Jerzy Putrament. The conversation began like this: "Let's get acquainted. I'm the Polish literary Beria. Do you want to go on with the conversation?"

"What else can I do?"

A handsome, powerful fellow, he struck poses and wanted to make a good impression with his sincerity and abruptness. And he succeeded in doing so. "You are getting in the way. I don't know who you are personally, I'm seeing you for the first time, but you are a representative and a part of the blame is falling on your shoulders. You are getting in our way. Party politics in cultural questions was wrong. We want to correct that. We turn our eyes to you from force of habit. But you are silent or even worse. The *Literaturnaya gazeta* is provoking general indignation. [Vsevolod Kochetov was the editor at that time.] Beginning in my youth, I became accustomed to evaluating phenomena by trying to imagine how they were being evaluated in the USSR. I had to wait too long for you to speak out. It's impossible to wait any longer . . . There's a difference: your thaw comes from above, with broad support from the bottom and the opposition of the middle levels. In our country everything proceeds in defiance of the Party leadership. Bierut* is not a bad or stupid person. During the most difficult years he wouldn't let the imprisoned Gomulka be killed. But when the situation changed, he started to apply the brakes.

"You were building the socialism of a beleaguered city. But now we have a completely different situation. We are experiencing a crisis, the most crucial crisis in a half century of the worldwide workers' movement."

I felt the difference between our situation and theirs. The representatives of the most orthodox, dogmatic thinking in Poland were viewed by us in the Soviet Union as people who were destroying the foundations. That was what had happened with Putrament himself. On October 20, 1956, a communiqué appeared in Pravda, "Anti-Soviet Statements on the Pages of the Polish Press." Putrament, "borrowing the political arsenal of the 'Voice of America,' is pleased to affirm that this system can work 'only within the conditions of police terrorism.' What is this revisionist proposing? . . . Four slogans: 'Openness of State Life,' 'Decentralization,' 'Democratization,' and 'Sovereignty' . . . The articles provoked legitimate displeasure from honest patriots."

I never saw any of the "honest patriots" in whom, according to the article, a "legitimate displeasure" was provoked. In fact, the article afforded Putrament extraordinary help, naturally contrary to the intentions of the correspondent. When we revile a person in the Soviet Union, this is taken as proof of his decency in Poland. But all the same, people did not believe Putrament in Poland, they did not like him; his previous behavior was not forgotten.

In 1960 Putrament paid yet another visit to the USSR and was a guest at a house where David Samoilov was reciting his poems. Putrament made some biting remark about revisionism. Samoilov flared up. The conversation generated a very tense atmosphere. Putrament passed on information about it to the proper people. Samoilov had problems at the publisher's. On his return to Poland, Putrament was rebuked for "squabbles abroad."

---

* Bierut was the Party secretary at the time.

That same year, 1960, he took Natasha, a former secretary in our editorial offices, back to Poland and made her Mrs. Putrament.

Natasha was a beautiful, kind, and foolish female. In December 1962 she arrived in Moscow, came to our editorial offices, and started to shout that Solzhenitsyn's novella *One Day in the Life of Ivan Denisovich* should not have been published, that it was harmful, and who needed us to go on and on opening our wounds when even so we were hated everywhere. Behind it lay a simple statement of the type: "I don't want it." She was the wife of a powerful Polish Party chief who was hated over there. And her one hope was a rock-solid Soviet Union. Rock-solid at any price, even at the price of falsehood.

But all of this lay ahead, whereas then, in the spring of 1956, before Hungary, before the Polish October, before the first workers' revolt in Poznań, even Putrament allowed himself to criticize the USSR.

I was at Jan Kott's house. He was pleased that many knew his report back in the USSR and that we too found him indispensable. We argued a little about the literature of the 1930s. He said: "We banished the feeling of tragedy, yet there is no great literature without it. The last revolutionary writer was Malraux." That Polish home gave me back my youthful infatuation with the books of Malraux: *Man's Fate* and *Days of Wrath*.

"People ask two questions at all of our Party meetings: the Katyń provocation and the Warsaw uprising."

Kott himself had been a part of that uprising. The city had flowed with blood, while a powerful Red Army stood on the other shore.

While I was sitting at Kott's, a telegram arrived. It was from an old friend. "Free. Returning to my homeland."

War, prison camps, poetry, books—everything was compressed in Poland within a small space, within a small time. It was as though I were speeding over a kind of accelerated course of instruction. The subject of "study" was not Poland at all, but rather my own path, my own homeland, and my own soul.

The following day I had a meeting with Stefan Żółkiewski. He was in charge of propaganda in the Polish Party Central Committee (later he became Minister of Higher Education). For a long time we hadn't been able to print a single one of his articles on Marxist aesthetics. He said to me: "Everything that you will write will be of use only if you'll finally start a criticism of Zhdanovism and all the old policies in the realm of culture."

In the editorial offices of the literary monthly *Tvurchost* (Creativity) there was an interesting conversation. The assistant editor, Roman Karst, a Germanist and author of a book on Thomas Mann, spoke out sharply. He accused me of the sins of *Literaturnaya gazeta*. Of course I joined in the criticism. But the feeling was ambiguous. I myself felt like criticizing *Literaturnaya gazeta* and all the rest of the Stalinists even more vehemently. But with those on the outside (and after all, the Poles were on the outside) I wanted to argue. There was no basis for argument, only outmoded emotions. Karst rejected all of Soviet literature, wholly and completely, with the exception of Viktor Nekrasov.

I was at the home of Adam Ważyk as well. During the Polish thaw he played approximately the same role as did Ehrenburg in the Soviet Union. He was a bilious, very clever, and self-confident monologist. "No creative alliances are necessary. Leadership, it's all harmful nonsense. Literature can develop only around journals. We won't tolerate any more administration. I myself was a dogmatist, but then I saw the light." Fedecki recalled the following pronouncement of Ważyk around 1950: "Better to have ten mediocre stories than a single controversial one."

Ważyk believed that the classification of literature (critical realism, romanticism, socialist realism) was all "demonology."

I read in a letter from Pasternak to D. P. Gordeyev (December 16, 1915): "Symbolist, futurist, acmeist? What appalling jargon! Clearly this is a science that classifies balloons according to a system of where and how the holes that prevent them from flying are located in them."

In this argument, as in many others, I was forced to defend Tvardovsky. For the Poles he was not a poet but a "harmonica." I cited Mayakovsky, Blok, and Verlaine. Ważyk praised me with condescension and a sort of surprise.

The main thing for me was my ever-growing understanding of the Polish tragedy, of the profound social and national roots for their animosity toward us. And the understanding of our own tragedy. A bitter and shameful feeling of guilt and compassion.

Arthur Sandauer, a translator and critic, belonged to those who never believed, who had never deluded themselves. Not only was he cool toward me, but very unpleasant as well. We immediately began to argue about Kazimierz Brandys's story "The Defense of Grenada." Before my departure for Warsaw, it had been decided, on the crest of the Twentieth Congress, to publish this story in our journal. Our editorial committee had been split in two over this story. I was faced with the prospect of explaining the points of view while in Poland.

This story remains unpublished in the Soviet Union. In it we find a Party functionary whose task is to convince fine, honorable young men that it would be harmful to stage Mayakovsky's play *The Bathhouse*, whereas in the interests of the revolution they should stage the mediocre Polish industrial play *The Shock Brigade*. The functionary is presented as a typical character, an outgrowth of the system.

I was proud of even our *intention* to publish "The Defense of Grenada," whereas for Poland it was a stage that had been left behind.

Brandys himself surprised me. At first glance he seemed to be a dandy, one of the habitués of Polish cafés. But no sooner did he open his mouth than all of that was forgotten. I questioned him about the criticism of "The Defense of Grenada." He replied: "I and several of my comrades have traveled a difficult road. For Sandauer I exist solely as the author of the first formalistic novel. Whereas for me that's in the distant past, to which I won't be returning. Above all, I was interested by the question, and even today it interests me more than anything else, namely, how it could have happened that my heroes, fine lads, not cynics, not madmen, how they could have believed in *The Shock Brigade*. Khrushchev's speech didn't give an answer to that."

Władysław Broniewski, one of the poets of the older generation, was totally drunk when he met me (even though I had come in the morning). He was bloated and sick. He wouldn't let me talk about business, and we traded verses with each other. Then he said bitterly: "I wrote 'The Song of Stalin.' What am I supposed to do about that now? For a month and a half I couldn't pull myself together." It seemed to me that Broniewski was somehow akin to Sholokhov. At the conclusion of the conversation he again returned to our past and asked: "Did Stalin really allow torture?" and he started to weep.

I had arrived in Poland with a letter addressed to our ambassador, Ponomarenko. I handed it over to the embassy secretary at our very first meeting. He expressed doubt as to whether the ambassador would be able to see me. Unexpectedly, Ponomarenko summoned me. I said that Polish writers had a good opinion of him. That was important to him. He started out by trying to prove with stories that he deserved the Poles' love. He told the story of how in Byelorussia in 1939–1940 he was secretary of the Central Committee. "I was also in charge of repatriation. In 1938 a decision came from the secretariat of the Executive Committee of the Comintern for the liquidation of three parties—the western Ukrainian, the western Byelorussian, and somewhat later, the Polish—as 'filthy spies.' And there was a secret addendum—to execute the leadership of those parties. The ones who were in the Soviet Union were shot. Those who were abroad had the same sentence waiting for them. Lumley, a member of the [Polish] leadership of the Communist Party and an old underground worker, crossed the border. He asked me: 'Will I be seeing you again?' I promised him that we would meet again. The Ministry of State Security demanded that I call up Stalin. I called. And I took responsibility for it. So the man remained alive.

"When I arrived in Poland—I was a young diplomat, you know—I was ordered to pay a visit to the dean of the diplomatic corps, as well as to the Italian, American, English, and French ambassadors. But I decided to make the rounds of all the ambassadors. I was advised to ask Moscow first before going off to the rest, but I wasn't about to ask. The Mexican ambassador greeted me in his sombrero and got drunk for joy."

He said that the Poles were living in poverty. "The Polish gentry wanted to create socialism before anyone else. But it didn't work out."

I never chatted with a person of such high rank either before or after that. He continued: "I can look people in the eye with a clear conscience. Nowadays many affect an innocent look. In 1937 I was told to sign an order for the arrest of a man in Byelorussia. I asked for proof. I was told there was a mountain of proof. 'Show it to me,' I said. The phone rang. Nikolai Yezhov, the Minister of State Security, was calling from Moscow. He shouted: 'You're doing it backwards!' I didn't sign the order. Why? Probably because of my youth. I went around as though I were in a cage. I was collecting material against them and they were doing the same with me. All the time they were trying to force women on me. I sent a coded message to Moscow asking to be heard out. State Security was in charge of counterrevolutionary activity. They tried to suppress the coded message. I sent my assistant to Moscow with a sealed envelope, and a blank piece of paper proved to be inside. The message had been stolen along the way. I arrived in Moscow. I made my report to Stalin (Yezhov had already been shot). Three hundred innocent people who had been arrested were set free."

Among the affairs of 1937–1938 he recalled the following one. Twenty-six of the best train engineers were arrested and charged with sabotage, and under torture they "confessed."

"I succeeded in summoning one of them and I said to him that I myself had been a train engineer and I knew that what had been written down in his case was impossible. Why had he brought slander on himself? He rushed at me with a cry: 'The torturers, the tormentors, they beat us for three months and now everything is supposed to be the other way around? What do you want from us?' "

And having related this story, Ponomarenko immediately said: "The Party, regardless of everything, was following the path of socialism." Perhaps both of the things he said were said in sincerity. That was the most amazing aspect of the whole mechanism. At that time I simply wrote it all down side by side in my diary without sensing the *absolute* disparity of one and the other.

Ponomarenko was convinced that Stalin did everything for the good of the country. "I knew him for twenty years. Now people dump anything they like on him. But for the sake of the revolution he would have joyfully gone to his death. He had no one close to him, not a single friend or a woman. If we now go ahead and paint anything superfluous on him, the succeeding generations will remove it like experienced restorers."

He called the Polish intelligentsia "rotten." "Here," he said, "you have real cosmopolitanism, the genuine thing. Cosmopolitans look only to the West, but we cannot fight against it because in the USSR this fight has been compromised by anti-Semitism."

Why was he so frank? Apparently he needed someone to express himself to. And for him I was somewhat like a fellow traveler in a semi-darkened railway car.

I visited the editorial offices of the student journal *Poprostu*. It was closed two years later. Side by side with these youthful enthusiasts I felt ever so old, yet none the wiser for my age. I was told that at higher institutes of learning the Komsomol was not supposed to be a mass organization, otherwise it would lose all sense. "We're carrying on the struggle for Party politics, but by other means," the editor said to me (in the Soviet Union, this kind of youth, at the very best, could only become the editor of a school newspaper). "In the realm of art we are defending the right to experiment."

I was also at an open Party meeting. There I recalled Sandauer's phrase: "Bravery has become devalued, whereas intelligence has gained in currency."

Austere, tall, and resembling Don Quixote, Jerzy Andrzejewski, the author of the novel *Ashes and Diamonds*, complained: "If you can't give a Marxist explanation to everything that's happened and is happening, then there's only magic left. Stalin was good and became bad. Yet you wouldn't explain National Socialism by the ugly character of Hitler."

The May Day celebration was short and cheerful. When the students marched past the podiums and the editorial workers of *Poprostu* marched past, they shouted: "Down with bureaucracy!" and "Leave science to the scholars!" From the podium broke out the response: "Hail to our courageous youth!"

The journalist Eva Fischer, the wife of the Dutch director Joris Ivens, said to me that the Polish people had demanded "bread and discussion." For the time being they were still not able to get bread.

Almost a quarter of a century has gone by and they still haven't managed to feed the Polish people. At that time they believed that they would shortly be fed. But now they don't believe it. And they won't put up with it. They're staging strikes (1980).

Natalya Modzalewska, a literary critic and translator, and widow of the former Minister of Foreign Affairs (we subsequently became friends and met many times in Moscow), took me to Maria Dąbrowska, the oldest Polish writer, a small, white-haired woman with very clear eyes and a clear mind. "I already see the other shore," she said. "I mustn't squander my energy. No one will write my books for me. Others will do the rest. Everything that is thought to be of value now will remain.

"There's one thing that I don't understand. Why is it that those same people who are crying the loudest about Stalinism are the very ones that caused so much bad? It's the same here as it is in your country."

In fact, it is difficult to understand. Namely, why it is Vladimir Yermilov writing about Solzhenitsyn's *Ivan Denisovich* in *Pravda* and

Aleksandr Dymshits writing in the journal *Literatura i zhizn* (Literature and Life). *Those* are the very same people.

During those two weeks I heard more than I had heard for entire years. Everything was mixed up in my head. I had to sort it out. And I did try to sort it out for a long time.

XXVI

Boris Rozenzweig

1964

"**I**t is with deep regret that the editorial board of *Inostrannaya literatura* announces the death of Boris Isaakovich Rozenzweig."

At the beginning of 1964 I learned that Boris Rozenzweig had cancer.

Who was he to me? I could not have included him even among my distant acquaintances, but as it turned out, there was an inner obligation to inquire every day for two months in a row: "How is Boris Isaakovich?" And to learn about his transfers from hospital to hospital, about his operation. And to go to the funeral.

The editorial offices, where so many of my days were spent, where there were so many discussions, so many meetings, and where I used to have so many arguments with Rozenzweig. Everything was draped in black. A flower-covered coffin on a large table. Colleagues from the editorial offices and translators. There were a great number of people for a hot day. The yellow transformed face and a portrait at his feet. A portrait of a man who was not young but was smiling, of a *living* person, with an intelligent expression.

The wake. After the funeral service, after the eulogies, we went from the editorial offices to the Vostryakovskoe Cemetery—the "new territory," a "new building project" burial ground. Not a single solitary tree or shrub, just nothing but graves, one practically on top of the next. Six feet of flat ground. A merciless sun. And those same Hamletian gravediggers: "In it goes," "toward you a little," "to the right a bit."

.   .   .

Boris Rozenzweig first made his appearance in our journal as the author of a short-tempered letter. In the spring of 1955, Savva Dangulov, the assistant editor, sent a chronicle of literary events in almost all the socialist countries, to be published at the end of each issue, to his old acquaintance from *Krasnaya zvezda* Rozenzweig. In the return letter, which was written in a very idiosyncratic handwriting, our awkwardness, lack of skill, and unprofessionalism were unmasked (and quite justifiably). Why were there no big names? Why were there no more important events? Why were we passing on information about inconsequential things? Those were the menacing inquiries made by this unknown person.

Soon after, he arrived at the journal and began to prepare the chronicle of events himself. At every meeting he used to ask others the very same questions, more often than not in an offensive form. Nominally, he was subordinate to Nikolai Prozhogin, who had only just finished graduate studies at the Institute for International Relations. Prozhogin was half Rozenzweig's age. True, the chronicle of events was an independent section, but still Prozhogin was the boss. A few more years passed and Rozenzweig was made director of the section for literature from capitalist countries, a member of the editorial board, and finally executive secretary. All of that shortly before his illness. He had made a career for himself in our editorial offices. Yet, right up to his very death there remained the feeling that he had not yet succeeded. (Dangulov even expressed that idea in his eulogy at the cemetery.) Indefatigable but frustrated ambition raged in him.

One of the first and most persistent impressions of him was as though something were eating away incessantly at him from within. And when that ambition had barely begun to be satisfied, he was devoured by a genuine and not a metaphoric tumor.

Perhaps his subordination to Prozhogin was enough to make one comprehend, not justify but comprehend, the reasons for the chip on his shoulder. He had struggled through to the top with great difficulty. He had not been spared and so he did not spare others. He had been ordered about and now he was doing the humiliating. How many times he must have asked himself the question: why exactly was Chakovsky running the journal and not Rozenzweig, despite the fact that he, Rozenzweig, was more educated, more industrious, and no worse a journalist?

Boris Isaakovich had been dismissed from *Literaturnaya gazeta* for an error: he had roundly criticized Bertrand Russell. He had been carrying out a directive from above, but, typically, he had been excessive in his *criticism* and *not* in his *praise.*

My animosity toward him possibly began with his predilection for big names. It was completely natural that the well-known writers would interest the reader the most. But with Rozenzweig this assumed dogmatic proportions. To this sense of the grand scale was added his bureaucratic servility. He somehow or other missed the process that had begun in 1956, missed the moment when Aksyonov or Yevtushenko became names that were more famous and more in demand by the reader than Fedin or Leonov, not to mention a number of really talented young critics.

He stubbornly believed that there was "too much equality" and "too much democracy" in the editorial offices themselves. The observance of rank was absolute for him.

When the journal came into being, *The Diary of Anne Frank* was all the rage throughout the world. Rozenzweig at first believed (or assured us that he believed) that the book was simply a falsification. It was he who did not allow even a mention of *The Diary* (which was not at all difficult). In 1958 the play *The Diary of Anne Frank*, written by two American playwrights, appeared, and this play, which had made the rounds of all the stages of the world, was also translated into Russian, published, and presented at the Moscow State University Theater. Boris Isaakovich expressed loud dismay at the "political nearsightedness" of the publishers. He told me that he was going to write a harshly critical article for *Literaturnaya gazeta* about the publication of the play. I replied: "Boris Isaakovich, if you do write it, then you'll be committing an act of villainy, whether you intend to or not. I don't want someone speaking out against *The Diary*. That would bring shame on all of us, and I don't want you to get involved in that dirty business." I am not certain whether I convinced him, but in any event I did frighten him. He did not write the article. However, he did not curtail the struggle against the book within the confines of our editorial offices.

In his argument Boris Isaakovich kept repeating that it was repulsive for him to see Jews only as humiliated victims who were waiting, waiting with the submissiveness of a rabbit, for the arrival of the SS. The argument was a serious one. I must admit that seeing the film *The Diary of Anne Frank* I felt something of the same. But that did not alter the essence of the matter. Rozenzweig had a panicky fear of everything connected with the Jewish issue, a fear and even a revulsion. God forbid, that people might think that he was supporting or resisting whatever book it might be simply because it concerned Jews. In objective terms this led to the most common and repulsive kind of anti-Semitism, which was our own kind. For me it was a long and agonizing process, often fraught with reversals, before I was able to break away from the very same thing. Relapses would still occur. And I wasn't the only one.

Shortly before his illness, Rozenzweig spoke out sharply against the publication of Rolf Hochhuth's play *The Deputy* in our journal. The young West German dramatist was accusing the Catholic Pope of collaboration with Hitler. He was accusing those who knew about the annihilation of the Jewish people by the Nazis and did not fight against it. The sincerely pious Jesuit, the Don Quixote of contemporary Catholicism, Riccardo Fontana, went into the ovens at Auschwitz together with the Jews who had been condemned to death because there was nothing else that he could do.

Rozenzweig disliked those who disrupted order with a kind of personal hatred. "We were all sitting in a burrow, so there was no need to pretend that it was possible to crawl out of that burrow"—that was what he seemed to want to say every time something exploded. And something was exploding all the time during those years. It would always perplex him, or worse, outrage him.

Viktor Nekrasov's sketches *First Acquaintance* were published in *Novy mir* in 1958. Boris Isaakovich and I chanced to meet at the subway exit—we often bumped into each other there—and walked together to the editorial offices, sharing our impressions. On that occasion he was not aggressive; rather, he was distracted. "I cannot understand the position of *Novy mir*," he said. "Is the entire company marching out of step and is only the lieutenant in step?!"

In 1970 Tvardovsky was removed as editor in chief of the journal, and there's nothing left of the old *Novy mir*. And there is no out-of-step lieutenant.

In the summer of 1961 a reception for Sartre and Simone de Beauvoir was held in the editorial offices. Chakovsky uttered some vile stupidity. Yelena Zonina, who was supposed to translate, remained silent.

"What's the matter, why aren't you translating, Yelena Aleksandrovna?"

"No, I won't translate that." She said it calmly, with a complete awareness of her own correctitude and dignity. I don't know why, but at that moment I just had to glance at Rozenzweig. There was a moment of perplexity, and then, real anger directed at Yelena.

Could one, as it transpired, treat the chiefs that way? No, no, one must not, otherwise the earth would collapse underfoot . . .

His attitude toward Ehrenburg was particularly bad, and he was delighted when Ehrenburg left the editorial board. Every new work by Ehrenburg, whether it was "The Lessons of Stendhal" or the essays on Chekhov, provoked a burst of hatred. There was nothing to be said about the memoirs *People, Years, Life*. Many people criticized Ehrenburg, and there was a great deal of justification in that criticism. But Rozenzweig constantly and stubbornly criticized him precisely for what he called "crawling out of the burrow." He criticized Ehrenburg from the position: "What's the point of it all when everything nevertheless remains the way it was." Or from the viewpoint: "Who do you think you are anyway?"

And he always closed ranks with the authorities, whether big or small. He really did close ranks (and in my opinion that is very important to underline). In other words, he did not simply repeat the orders from the authorities, but proceeded by his own path and arrived at the very same conclusions as Chakovsky.

Naturally, I have remarked upon what divided us because that was the main thing. But there were other things as well. There was his interest, his amazement, even approval, when he was told about our Party meeting in 1956 after the Twentieth Congress. It was also there in his shy, kind smile and in his secret love for children—he had never been a father.

He knew what was what in literature. He was the one who energetically promoted the books of Greene and Hemingway. He wasn't the first and he didn't throw himself into the line of fire, but nevertheless he did so when there was a multitude of obstacles in the path of these writers. Incidentally, one shouldn't write about this in the past tense. The obstacles are far from being removed and a crack barely opens up at times, only to close again.

The journal was his passionate love. At times it was an unintelligent love that blocked out the entire world. He was jealous, envious, and unjustly humiliated the Foreign Literature Publishing House in every conceivable fashion. He believed that in the bloody confrontation with Blinov, the executive director of this publishing house, all means were acceptable. He reacted morbidly to criticism and with foaming lips defended the honor of the uniform independently of the objective truth. He himself was capable of sharply and maliciously criticizing the journal (at closed meetings), whereas to others, particularly those who in his estimation lived the easy life of free-lance writers, he would refuse the right to criticize. In doing so he would frequently fall into stupid situations and would arouse unanimous hostility.

He reminded me of Olga Alekseevna Gilveg, the head accountant at VOKS, who used to lovingly pay out our salaries to us, who would do everything in her power in order to increase our salaries, and who despised the people who were paid honoraria because it was as though they were stealing her own personal money. She used to practically fling the money in their faces and would strive to do everything possible to "snatch" something away for the good of the state.

Rozenzweig considered all contributors to the journal, whether regular or occasional, to be eternally assigned to the editorial offices. Both in personal conversations and at meetings he would reprimand everyone who published articles anywhere else.

A toiler to the marrow of his bones, he was a selfless worker, a workaholic, a person of an ascetic cast. Although he had assimilated all the specific vices of our system, he did not suffer in the least from the disease of becoming bourgeois. He was modest in the extreme. For a long time he wore the same threadbare suit, and the purchase of a new one assumed an importance for the entire office. Unlike his co-workers, he used to spend every Saturday in the editorial offices. This was partially explained by the fact that he clearly did not enjoy going home (and subsequently there was the affair that arose within the same editorial offices). But that was not all. There was that same psychology of the cog subordinate to the machine, and the machine was always more important.

Once a year, and sometimes more frequently, a battle for discipline in work would be initiated in the editorial offices. It was immediately forgotten that the editorial offices were a creative organism where one day, if business demanded it, you could work right through until nighttime, whereas the following day you could play hooky. It was even necessary to play hooky so that you could spend some time thinking, reading, and finding out what was happening around you. Rozenzweig did not recognize any of that. And he was much more demanding than the editor in chief and his assistants. Rozenzweig spoke out at all of the meetings as the guardian of discipline and the ally of mediocrity. He was particularly agitated when, besides the editors, the workers from the subsidiary departments, such as, for example, the department of information, made claims to a free library day. Or when not only the editors but the proofreaders and the secretaries wanted to go to performances of the English theater. In this case, as in a great deal else, Rozenzweig was a true son of his times. He expressed and enforced the ideology of the times.

He was a twisted person. It was not only the concentration camps and prisons that mutilated people. He belonged to that not insignificant number of people who would constantly suppress their inner self. And he did have things to suppress. Perhaps it was in his malicious humor that there appeared foremost what was lurking in the depths, what might have developed—had he been free.

Not only could he not squeeze the slave out of himself, he even refused to recognize that slavery, or else he considered everyone else to be a slave too. People like him are the most important building matrial of our system by the very virtue of their asceticism, their unselfishness. In fact, why should a person who was being oppressed as he was also join in the humiliation of other people? Or join in anti-Semitism? Yet he did that.

Even as a journalist he suppressed his own personality. Yes, he was a capable journalist—he was inventive, he saw the journal as a whole. He understood the significance of headlines and the importance of typefaces and overall design. And what was called news: how to discover things, to attract attention. But his articles were the embodiment of yellow journalism. Free and easy, lightweight, and with no regard for the reader. And, most important, false. During the American Exhibition of 1959, he wrote about their "bluff," about how they, the Americans, actually lived badly. And everything that had been brought over was just window dressing. He convinced both himself and others of that, even though, of course, he had his own underground deep in his consciousness where no one was admitted.

He had suppressed himself in his own personal life. Only now, when we saw his wife at his funeral, was it possible, at least in part, to imagine his domestic existence. While still sitting at the bedside of the dying man she had declared: "I'm not going to bury him. Let the editorial offices take care of the funeral." I never heard of a widow saying beside an open grave: "Thank you for your attention on behalf of myself and on behalf of Boris Isaakovich." A provincial, failed actress. During the course of many years she had made a profession out of being ill.

Her every word was like a knife grating against glass, like the green sash in Chekhov's *Three Sisters*. She tore off the kerchief that her relatives had put on her as she entered the editorial offices and forebade anyone to cry: "It's harder for me than all of you, but I'm not crying."

Such a mean look, a contempt for people (this is what nourished him as well). It was as though she could not forgive the deceased for this final insult: he had left her, he had died first. Hands were offered in support, but she tore herself free and, turning to all of us, declared: "And who is going to support me tomorrow?"

"Goodbye, Boris, we'll be seeing each other soon."

And he had spent thirty years with her.

He sometimes liked to sit on the sofa, prattle on, crack witticisms, listen to others. But more frequently he would shut himself up in his tiny office and practically press his nose to a manuscript. More often than not he would be unfriendly and would repel many people and even repel them from the editorial offices. He always suspected ulterior motives in everyone, and he always assumed that the person he was talking to was a guilty party. He was a man from the era of alienation, when people were afraid of one another, when they shut themselves up within themselves. In this regard he was typical. He despised a great many people, particularly those who, with identical or lesser qualities than he, had achieved more than he had.

At the funeral it had been said that Rozenzweig was a genuine intellectual. He was not. Perhaps he had been one at some time, but he had since ceased to be. In his *Village Diary*, Yefim Dorosh writes: "The quality of being intellectual, so it seems to me, . . . begins at the point where a person has arrived at his own judgment, which he has worked out about everything, perhaps even achieved with suffering. Whereas the philistine, on the other hand, conducts himself according to the so-called generally accepted opinion, a divergent truth that bears neither the burden of reason nor conscience."* Boris Isaakovich, if he had actually worked out his own opinions, had managed to hide the fact assiduously. But gradually the ability became atrophied, and he was least of all prepared to arrive at them through

* *Novy mir*, No. 6, 1964.

suffering. And he did not believe that other people who found themselves in completely identical situations as he *could* go on searching for the truth.

When on November 22, 1963, an article appeared in *Izvestia* entitled "Encounters with Don Quixote," which told the story of Lev Kopelev and those who had defended him, Rozenzweig asked me with extreme ill will why the article had appeared. What kind of machinations were going on behind the scenes? He was certain that it could only be taking place on someone's orders or according to someone's directive. He had his own particular and personal estimation of the Don Quixotes and their tilting at windmills. They were destroying his conception about a humanity that was being driven. They were denying the wisdom whereby he had lived all those years: ears do not grow higher than one's forehead, and you can't chop wood with a penknife.

XXVII

Novella Matveyeva Sings

1965

For several nights in a row I rocked on the waves of her songs. I would doze off to those rhythms. Then I would wake up—rocking. Again and again, words, lines, and whole fragments of the songs would go on repeating themselves. There was none of the maniacally obsessive repetitiveness that is always connected with insomnia for me.

Bulat Okudzhava, Aleksandr Galich, and other poets who have recorded our life and emotions in songs live in a world where there are "clodhoppers with secretaries," where "a special messenger dashes off from the Central Committee of the CPSU," and where even the melancholy question will be heard: "Have you had any chance to think it over, executed father of mine?" There's none of that in the songs of Novella. She lives in another dimension. In her world the boundary between stone and tree, tree and horse, horse and person, is barely distinguishable. It's a world of bonfires, the gypsy encampment, of a dammed stream, a magician, and the Flying Dutchman.

Her poetry grows out of what is simple, everyday, out of everything surrounding us, and comes to that which is the most important. She barely starts up and "night sets in, warm like ashes," a laundry tub with its concrete mass rocks like a "bark in the sea," things come to life as in *The Bluebird*. And from the depths of youth my night rises up, "warm like ashes."

That was in 1936, after a carnival in the Park of Culture and Recreation. How I waited for the miracle all my youth, all my adult life, all my approaching old age! In those days, in place of the miracle, there were poor, homemade costumes and masks, the long lines for ice cream. There wasn't money for anything else. And there were dances. Your feet ached unbearably in those beautiful new shoes, red shoes with ribbons. Later, on the way home, I took off the shoes, and it felt better and I went home barefoot. Through the entire city. Lyonya carried my shoes, holding them out in a funny way in front of him. He was pronouncing some kind of tender words and we were laughing ourselves to tears the whole way. And I, ever so stupid, did not realize that this was happiness. Later, during the interminable nights of wartime, I would recall that carnival. It would come back to me with all of its colors and sounds in the songs of Novella Matveyeva.

The landscape of her songs is either the fairy-tale world or, more frequently, the everyday world of our surroundings, the landscape of barracks, dormitories, a modest, neatly poor landscape. Poverty as a vital choice. Because in poverty the scale of values is truer, easier, so that "black is black" and "white is white." There's something very melancholy and very Russian in that, even though there was the whole wide world of oceans in her songs as well.

On a gentle April day we gathered to listen to Matveyeva at the home of Vsevolod Ivanov. That room was the room with the fireplace in it, the middle room. The red brick fireplace afforded cosiness even when there were no logs crackling in it. On every shelf there were toys—a lot of strange little toy animals, dolls—and stones. And a great many books everywhere. That was true throughout the entire house. By means of those books alone it would have been possible to "read" the nature of their owner.

A television, a large table, and buffets. The room had become accustomed to guests, to long Russian tableside arguments; it had grown accustomed to the reading of new poems, of new stories. Probably all of that had settled within the walls, and were it all to be brought to life, the sounds would have thawed out, the voices of people would have started to resound, the voices of those who had departed along ago and not so long ago.

We sat there and waited for Novella. The guitar was already in the room. She came to the door and knocked. We had gathered to listen to her. She knew that, yet she couldn't enter someone else's room without knocking.

An angular young girl started to sing—a fairy princess. At first it was as though a piece of gauze had been carelessly tossed against the Peredelkino sky. Off-white in color and without shape. The contours grew clearer and more defined. A roundness. White. It could still be taken for a cloud of an unusually even form. Novella was singing, the moon was turning yellow. It was she who was summoning the moon with a touch of her guitar. It grew dark in the room. And it seemed that if the woman were to fall silent, the moon would disappear.

I was listening for the third time. I already knew many of the songs, and joyfully savored what was familiar. Someone was beside me. A stranger. The room was full of people. No, the stranger had not come for my family. Something light and soundless drew near, not at all resembling the repulsive gangrenous hyena, as death was depicted in Hemingway's "The Snows of Kilimanjaro." There was no smell. For the first time in my life I sensed death not in my mind but with my entire being . . .

A yellow, by now quite yellow, moon, the semigloom, the measured, muffled sounds, the blurry image of the face of Novella Matveyeva . . .

Death was standing near our friend and neighbor Frida Vigdorova. It had come for her.

Life, love, art, songs, friends—they all tried to resist death and do battle for Frida. She was overjoyed to listen to Novella Matveyeva, to win a few hours from death. She would go on giving herself over and over again to people. What she had already given others was indestructible and beyond death's grasp.

My daughter was listening. I couldn't see her, but as always, I could feel that she was near. She had a son. Perhaps, in spite of everything, we won't disappear without a trace, perhaps we will remain in someone else?

I need the kind and modest poetry of Novella Matveyeva. It helps me to bear the horror of disappearance.

XXVIII

Frida Vigdorova

1966

On March 16, 1965, the fiftieth birthday of Frida Vigdorova was celebrated at the dacha of Vsevolod Ivanov in Peredelkino. She had just returned from the hospital and was very weak. We, those who were close to her, already knew that she had cancer, we knew that very little time remained even though we kept hoping . . .

The telegrams came in a flood. Yelizar Maltsev and Timur Gaidar came from the Writers' House and, kneeling down, congratulated her in the ancient fashion. Frida herself reacted both with humor and seriousness to the greetings. It gave her pleasure to read the telegrams. She was surprised, she laughed and rejoiced. She didn't let on that it made no difference to her and accepted the innumerable signs of attention as something natural. She was herself.

On that evening everyone was not simply trying to be cheerful—we truly were rejoicing, making witticisms, cracking jokes, and proposing toasts. As before, there was a comic newspaper and musical parodies at Frida's celebrations. Even though there was a gnawing in your heart. No, no! Yet a heavy melancholy was pressing down.

In the fall of 1964 we decided to spend the winter in Peredelkino at the dacha of the Ivanovs. Frida heard about it and immediately asked whether a room could also be found there for her and her husband. A room was found. And then the doubts began: would we manage to get along together? We were all people who were entirely set in our ways. Frida Vigdorova and her husband, Aleksandr Borisovich Raskin. Lev and I. Four different characters. Four desks.

If it had only been a question of the four of us . . . But we had two large families, and each one had become overgrown with dozens of friends and acquaintances. There were many who tried to dissuade us from this joint undertaking because we were all looking for solitude. How were we to cope with the complexities of a daily life together without irritating even those who were closest to us.

All our apprehensions proved to be in vain. Not only the first weeks, before Frida took to her bed, but even the succeeding ones, after the operation, after the hospital—we lived through them all with amazing ease. A community quickly emerged, a community in which the peculiarities and eccentricities of each of its members were respected. This was facilitated by the comfortable dacha and by Natasha, the Ivanovs' maid, an exquisite woman, quiet, tactful, and who had long since known that sitting at a desk and scratching away with a pen meant work that was not to be disturbed with conversations or questions. Natasha read a great deal. She read Frida's books as well and became truly attached to her, just as she did to all of us.

We quickly estimated how much we could spend on food. A box stood on the windowsill and we kept putting money into the box, and anyone who went to town or to the store took money from it.

On Saturdays and Sundays, Vsevolod Ivanov's son, Koma, would come with his wife. In the spring Koma lived with us for almost a month.

An unreal idyll reigned in Peredelkino. I frequently said to my friends: "It never happens like this in life."

Guests came to visit us from near and far. We shared every guest. I saw Frida as the hostess who became accustomed to caring for others, to calculating, to saving, who became accustomed to bearing this burden with ease, a daily, tedious, and thankless burden. She succeeded in organizing things sensibly so that everything would be good for all of us.

The long Peredelkino evenings. Comfortable little Frida in an armchair with her feet tucked up, in her Estonian slipper-socks. Lidiya Korneevna Chukovskaya dropped in frequently. Kornei Ivanovich Chukovsky knocked on the door with his cane and kissed Frida on the top of the head (I never saw him act so tenderly toward anyone). Here Anna Akhmatova and Arsenii Tarkovsky read their verses to us, and Novella Matveyeva sang.

We read a great deal together during that winter. We all shared the manuscripts we had with one another: Solzhenitsyn's *The First Circle*, Varlam Shalamov's stories and essays, Valentin Katayev's *The*

Holy Fount (the galley proofs had been withheld at that time by the censor), Marina Tsvetaeva's article "The Two Goncharovas."

We read our own work to one another. Frida gave us all the written chapters of her last novella, *The Teacher*. She read the beginning of Lev's book on Brecht and went through it with a pencil. Her comments were intelligent and precise.

During the first half of the day everyone worked in his or her own room. But if the patter of the feet of the little Pasternaks (the grandchildren of Boris Pasternak, who lived in the neighboring dacha) echoed beneath the windows, Frida could not resist. It was a serious friendship—the Pasternak offspring sensed one of their own in her. It was very important for her as well whether a toy ship would sail on the large spring pond, or whether it was still possible to build a snowman or was the snow too soft by then. It was important to her not only to answer their hundreds of thousands of why's, but for her own part to ask over and over again of people, the trees, and the stream—to ask why indeed? A cheerful, mischievous little girl lived inside her right up until her death.

When she was not able to write, she dictated letters to me to the district executive committee as an elected deputy: to help yet another person, yet another family. She wrote and dictated with a childlike belief in justice.

We talked a great deal about children and never talked about love.

I had seen Frida for the first time in 1940 and had not liked her at all. A quarter century passed by. And in 1965 I was sitting at the table and looking at Frida with a feeling of such ecstasy, such intimacy, such gratitude for the fact that she was alive and had entered my life. At the same time I was looking with terror, with gloomy premonitions, with a hollow emptiness . . . How could I have failed to notice her charms at the very first meeting?

Even my conception of her physical appearance had altered. Earlier I had considered her unattractive and ill-favored. But now . . . Frida comes out so marvelously well in photographs that a person who has never seen her can judge for himself about her face. Her hair is cut short (here there's a monastic or schoolmarmish quality). Her eyes are bright, mercurial, and profound. At the same time there is something mischievous, perky, and urchinlike.

She had become twice as old, and to my eye, much more attractive.

. . .

In March 1949 Tamara Motyleva and other selected "cosmopolitans"
at the Institute of World Literature were dismissed from the Party.
I related the stories of the meetings at the Institute of World Literature approvingly to my friends, who in turn passed on my words to
Frida. She and I met by chance. She questioned me about Tamara
Motyleva and did so in a hostile tone. I gave her an even more
bellicose reply. Approximately the following kind of dialogue took
place:

I: I hardly know Motyleva. You know her better than I do, but,
after all, the entire collective is against her.

SHE: The collective isn't always right. When people are seized by
a mass psychosis, they can perpetrate only God knows what.

I: Well, I can't agree with you on that. Individual people can
be wrong, but the collective is always right.

In a letter by the Russian writer Vladimir Korolenko from 1893 I
read: ". . . one must serve this good and truth. If in doing so one can
proceed with the crowd (it sometimes happens), that's fine, but if one
is forced to remain alone, what's to be done? Conscience is the sole
master of your actions and there's no need of idols." What I read
coincides with my present-day thoughts. But at that earlier time I was
passionately worshiping idols and, above all, the idol whose name was
the collective.

Frida's eyes were already open, and in essence there was nothing
for her to talk to me about. I felt that immediately. And perhaps
unconsciously a defensive feeling began to assert itself in me: how do
you like that, she's a fine one! She carries her virtue around in front
of her like an icon. And she thinks that others ought to march after
her in blissful silence. But I don't want to march along after her.

Much later, during the Joseph Brodsky affair, similar pronouncements about Frida came to my ears and I remembered the way I had
once reacted.

I had read Frida's first books, *My Class* and *The Story of Zoya and
Shura.* She was among the first creators of books whom I saw up close.
But the literary persona and the everyday persona did not coincide in
my consciousness. It was as though these books had been written by
someone else. Incidentally, these two aspects did not coincide even

later for all the lyricism and autobiographical quality of her books. At first it seemed to me that the books were more significant than the person who wrote them. Later it seemed the contrary—namely, that Frida was immeasurably more important than the books she had created. The qualities of the person and the writer had barely begun to merge completely in her final, unfinished novella, *The Teacher*, but by then it was too late.

At the Moscow meeting of writers in March 1957, I applauded Vigdorova's speech. From the podium she spoke aloud about the things that I too had been thinking about, about what I myself had spoken about. She defended the author's right to criticism, to the struggle against willful falsehood, the right to truth.

In the summer of 1959 Frida and her family settled in the village of Zhukovka, where we had been longtime residents. Here Frida became friends with Lev. Somehow they immediately found each other and later called each other brother and sister. Lev told Frida that he had read her book *My Class* in prison, but the first pages were missing so at that time he didn't know who the author was. But in prison the book had proved to be indispensable, indispensable in its purity, honesty, and goodness.

In 1959 Frida began to share manuscripts and friends with us. She gave us the play *The Dragon* by Evgenii Shvarts. Fifteen years later, after the first performance (shortly thereafter prohibited), I and my family got to know this brilliant play. In all, seven years have passed since that time, but it's impossible for me to imagine that we could have existed without *The Dragon* at one time. Now, in a collection of reminiscences about Shvarts, I read that the play *The Naked King* lay in his desk for more than thirty years, until it was staged by the Sovremennik Theater. Everyone had lived without *The Naked King*.

Through Frida I experienced the first stinging sensation of Tsvetaeva's prose ("An Otherworldly Evening" and "Art in the Light of Conscience").

By her nature Frida could not read something important or significant and not share it with others. "Read it fast, there's a lineup behind you." She was a true enlightener: everything that was revealed to her she had to reveal to others, to those near and far.

. . .

In the summer of 1959 Frida began to work on the book *Family Happiness*. Practically every day she would go off into the woods on the other side of the railway tracks, and on a tree stump she would ponder and write. Once she said joyfully: "A big event has happened to me: the third person has come." Her previous books had been written in the first person.

She gave us her amazing "children's" diaries to read. She had recorded the first words, phrases, and actions of her daughters from birth itself. These diaries are among the best of her books. Selections from the diaries were prepared for publication by Lidiya Chukovskaya. The book never appeared.

It was that summer of 1959 that I heard Frida sing for the first time. In a pleasant deep voice she sang old and new songs, as well as off-color and prison-camp ones. Songs were her constant passion. Her girl friend Runya sang, as well as their daughters. The young poet from Leningrad Aleksandr Gorodnitsky sang at their place, and it was there on New Year's Eve 1964 that I first heard the songs of Aleksandr Galich on a tape recorder.

It was particularly pleasant to watch her give one of her friends something new, be it a poem or a song; she would peer anxiously to see whether they would like it as much as she did, she would rejoice twofold because she was not the only one who liked it . . .

On New Year's Eve in 1960, which we celebrated together, her daughters presented her with a typewriter with the first money they had earned and wrote: "The best typewriter in the world from the best daughters in the world."

"Why didn't you write: 'to the best mother in the world,'" Frida pretended to grumble.

In the fall of 1960 Frida introduced us to Lidiya Chukovskaya, about whom she had told us a great deal. It was approximately at this time that our "trial period" came to an end. It was possible not only to give to us, but ask of us as well. We were also able to start helping her, or rather to help those whom she was helping.

Lev and I read the book that Lidiya Chukovskaya had just published, *In the Editor's Laboratory* (given to us, naturally, by Frida), and we both took part in the discussion at the Writers' Union.

We also began to read Frida's articles and books in manuscript. We read *Family Happiness*. We discussed this manuscript with her in detail. But at that time I didn't tell her about my doubts regarding the very conception at the heart of the manuscript because I hadn't thought it out for myself.

Tolstoy, from whom Frida had bravely taken the title, for all the complexity and tormented quality of his attitudes to problems of sex, had written so that this basis for happiness, or unhappiness, in man and woman always came through. In Vigdorova's *Family Happiness* this foundation did not exist even in the deepest subtext. In the copy of the manuscript that we were reading, alongside the sentence "They were expecting a child" there was someone's note in the margin: "By what means? After all, they only went for a stroll in the rain."

She frequently and willingly traveled on official business. She would return home, overburdened with the fates of strangers, and read to us from her amazing notebooks.

In one of his letters, Vladimir Korolenko writes: "A week has already passed since this family turned to me and since the surname Lagunov has been transformed for me from a newspaper abstraction into the name of a living person surrounded by horror and pain." Frida possessed this ability: not only could she sense the living person with his living heartrending misfortune behind the "newspaper abstraction," but by the magical power of her account and through her personal involvement in the lives of others she could force us, the people who hadn't been where she had been and hadn't seen what she had seen, also to see, hear, and become involved.

Frida told us that a "benevolent society for good deeds" or "small miracles" existed whose "president" was Kornei Chukovsky, whereas she was the "executive secretary." At that time they (it seems that it was the final time that it was "they," because it became "we" afterward) were busy with the case of a group of Leningrad Jewish students who in the course of doing their practical work had clashed with a boorish superior who was the captain of a vessel and an anti-Semite. They had responded with sharp words to his rudeness and despite the fact that they were studying in their fourth year and had good grades, they were dismissed from their institute.

We began helping her, but I continued to be afraid of Frida, right up until the time we lived together in Peredelkino. The preceding years stood between us.

I didn't want to mimic her—as with other people who had come to understand before I did—and agree in everything, although inwardly I was agreeing with her more and more. The reasons for avoiding this were by now different from those in my youth: I didn't want to appear better than I was in actual fact.

Frida herself wasn't in the least born with the convictions, with the manner of acting, that she arrived at later. Like everyone else, she came to them; in other words, she had her own road to travel. In general, my road was similar to hers, just as it became the common way for dozens of people and then later for hundreds of thousands: from ignorance to knowledge, from faith to doubt, from naïveté to bitter sobriety. But for all the similarities there were individual differences that were much more substantial than the similarities.

She recalled a conversation with one of her friends, who had said to her immediately after the terror of 1937–1938: "If this had all been a haphazard chain, then they ought to at least tell us the truth now. But once the government doesn't speak the truth to its people, it means that it doesn't trust the people and despises them."

"For me," Frida recalled, "those were shockingly new ideas, but quickly I became convinced that my friend was right."

Nor did Frida escape the collections of various clichés, incantations, precepts, and myths that she had absorbed at school, at the institute she had attended, in Magnitogorsk (during her first teaching assignment), from her relatives, from friends, from the air.

Without that kind of background, the journalist who had begun her activity in *Pravda*, the writer Vigdorova, simply would not have been the same kind of person. And it was not simply a matter of asserting the sacramental formulas, or the article wouldn't be printed and the book wouldn't be published, but rather because the pen itself was writing and the hand itself was producing the customary words. It should be said, however, that in her writing these general clichés were considerably less frequent than in the works of others.

Precept number such and such declared: "Innocent people are not imprisoned in our country." Frida had not yet pondered the content of the precept, she had not yet placed it under doubt. But when her first and favorite teacher, Anna Ivanovna, was sent into exile, she went to see her there. The concept of "boldness" is somehow out of place here, although in those years a great deal of boldness was demanded for that kind of action. She simply could not act otherwise. When her close friend Runya Zernova was arrested together with her husband, then it was natural for their daughter, Nina, to live for a long time in the Raskins' home, and everything that could possibly be done—paying the lawyer, writing applications, protests, and letters —all of that was done.

We were walking along through the spring mud of Peredelkino and over and over again, for the umpteenth time, we were talking about 1937. Over and over again we asked each other: "Why did it happen? When did it all start? Why did many, including myself, believe? How was it possible to believe?"

Frida was wearing enormous felt boots, a black fur coat, and a black hat cocked at a rakish angle. Her eyes had become much larger and had a feverish gleam to them. Not for a moment did I think about the fact that I was walking with a dying person. I was walking with a living woman, who wanted to manage to do as much as she could. She had to, she just had to finish this novella that was such an important one, such a new one for her.

She recalled her own year of 1937 and the meetings in the pedagogical institute where she was studying. The principal orator, the principal prosecutor at those meetings, had been a female student toward whom Frida felt a revulsion. Frida, even though she didn't realize it at the time, believed in the witness borne by one's eyes, ears, and heart and not those dogmas that had been pounded into all of us and into her as well.

She reminisced about that woman (her name was Manefa). In her novella *The Teacher* she had to write a scene from one of those meetings. She was searching for a name for her character who was based on the woman at the institute. She was searching for the kind of Slavic name that would sound a bit old-fashioned nowadays.

We never will read about the meeting that she and I talked about at that time. A great deal has been written about 1937. A great deal more will be written. But what she and only she might have said, no one will ever be able to say *that* and say it *the way* she would have.

For Frida the road to truth was easy because it completely coincided with her nature and instinct, with an attitude toward human beings that was for her a norm. But this road was also a difficult one because the road to truth is always difficult and bitter for the additional reason that it unavoidably leads to many ruptures and much discord, to a resistance against one's milieu. And she herself was a harmonious person and was naturally attracted to harmony. She was conceived and created in order to be at peace with herself and with the world. Tolstoy "wrote" her, not Dostoyevsky.

Her soul consisted of innumerable rooms, corners, and niches. I visited only the ones closest to the entrance. There's hardly anyone who saw them all.

For all her extraordinary openness, during the final years of her life Frida became increasingly closed and fenced off, and she drew together the folds of her soul all the more firmly. By that I mean not only the fact that the phone was disconnected in their home, that more and more frequently she would leave Moscow and go off to work somewhere. I am talking about a "fencing off" of her inner self. She would be sitting in the midst of a noisy throng—and suddenly she would be "gone." She was physically present, but in reality she was somewhere far, far away. During the final months she would frequently be "gone," but by then it was already a different kind of departure . . .

One of the first cases that we shared arose in the spring of 1961. Frida told me that a letter had been received from Ira Yemelyanova, the daughter of Olga Ivinskaya, who was in a prison camp. Ira was writing about the monstrous conditions in which she found herself, in the power of female criminals, thieves, and lesbians.

The international press was involved in the case of the arrest of Ivinskaya—the beloved of Pasternak—at that time, and protests from foreign writers and from public figures were under way. Nehru and Bertrand Russell addressed Khrushchev. But everything was to no avail. No attention was paid to these appeals. And if those kind of people couldn't succeed, who would listen to us? How often such completely rational arguments have disarmed and continue to disarm people . . .

Frida would not be disarmed. Action was needed. We went to an acquaintance of ours, the president of the Collegium of Advocates. He knew the case well and he himself had defended Ira at the trial. An acquaintance of Frida's in the Writers' Union went at her request to the president: "Our international prestige is suffering." Mechanisms of which we knew nothing came into action, and Ivinskaya and her daughter were transferred to better conditions. Before the end of her term, Ira was freed, and then after the fall of Khrushchev, Ivinskaya was freed.

It meant that if you knocked at locked doors long enough, behold, one might even open up. The realization arose, still very timidly and slowly, that action was not useless. Therefore, it was essential to act.

In 1961 the anthology *Pages from Tarusa* was in preparation (the essay "Eyes Empty and Eyes Magical" by Vigdorova was one of her best). The compiler of the anthology wanted to publish the prose of Marina Tsvetaeva for the first time in the USSR. It was reminiscences of her childhood in Tarusa—completely harmless. Nowadays it's difficult for even us to understand what there was to object to in their publication. But two anthologies of verse by Tsvetaeva have appeared, and she is being printed in all the Soviet magazines. A significant portion of Tsvetaeva's prose has also been published in the USSR. But everything was difficult the first time.

Glavlit (the official censorship department) declared: "The anthology *Pages from Tarusa* can appear only if some important and famous writer will write a preface to the excerpt from Tsvetaeva." A big cover-up name was required. Frida passed on to us a request from the editorial board to ask Vsevolod Ivanov. This very modest commission was fulfilled and the preface was written. In the copy presented to us Frida inscribed: "Without you, you see, this book might not have come out." It was in this way that she always exaggerated the significance of the actions of others, even such insignificant ones as this. And belittled her own actions.

In August 1961 Frida and Runya Zernova settled in Zhukovka for two weeks. They were writing the play *Ring Twice*. Frida still had to correct the second part of *Family Happiness* (she had received comments from the editor of the journal *Moskva* (Moscow).

The comments that Frida had received made her annoyed and indignant. She was angered but she calmed herself, made the corrections, and redid it. We frequently recalled the lines of Boris Slutsky about how a poet writes his lines and hopes:

> *. . . I break their legs off,*
> *I chop their arms off,*
> *. . . Still something I manage to hide*
> *And a few things save aside.*
>
> *The best and the most gallant*
> *I surrender to no one.*
> *Still, without corrections,*
> *I'll have this book published.*

Few are the Soviet writers whose good fortune it has been to see their books printed in the USSR "without corrections" during their lifetime. Frida Vigdorova shared in the common fate; she fought, saved a few things, reinstated them in the galleys.

Our life in Zhukovka was very cheerful. We read to one another what we had written, we talked a lot, laughed, and sang. The farewell evening was particularly fine. Essentially there are no longer many of those kinds of light, carefree moments in life. One of the legends about Frida was destroyed at that time, namely, the legend about her "dryness," that she was a stern person and that it was awkward and out of place to have a good time in her company.

In the summer of 1962 she and I fell sick almost simultaneously with a vascular attack. The same doctor was treating both of us. And, lo, Frida sent me a mischievous little note that the doctor had come. "He told me about you. And he was practically swearing bloody murder, both at you and me. He predicted a lot of bad things if we didn't come to our senses. What do you think, should we do it? Let's come to our senses.

"We'll give up drinking. We'll retire all our lovers. We'll stop making the rounds of the restaurants. It'll be hard, of course. But let's strengthen our will."

In a hospital letter Frida informed me with pleasure: "Yesterday my mother and brother brought me two potatoes in their skins—I ate them with salt." And in another letter: "I woke up today with the thought . . . Galya brought some sour cream . . ." Here are some more lines from her hospital letters: "And, in general, if you give it some thought, I have more than a little to be happy about. After all, it does happen that terrible pains are part of this illness [she thought she had kidney stones]. Yelena Sergeevna suffered a great deal, and the old woman in the next ward wails and moans. But *for the time being* my stones are mute. That is a gift. And the snow on the other side of the window is a gift. And the nurses, they are all so truly good-looking."

This inexhaustible ability to rejoice at life came from her childhood and from her inner being. Typical of Frida was also her constant ability to bestow cheer on other people, to share what was good with them. It was as though she were saying to us, the healthy ones: "It's all right, my dears, don't get downhearted, everything will turn out for the best with me."

In her final winter Frida began to visit our friends for their musical Thursdays. She was drawn above all by the beautiful music that resounded in that house every week. But, laughing, she also talked about how she now drank vodka regularly on Thursdays. It seems to me that love for simple earthly blessings came into her life along with maturity. In her youth she was more ascetic.

One Thursday Frida put on a new, gray silk dress that had been specially made. After that there was no need to sew anymore. When she returned home, the relentless vomiting started. That was how the illness began.

She and I were chatting about the film *Yevdokiya*, based on the novella by Vera Panova. "It's a very bad film," Frida said abruptly. "It's not really a matter at all of the fact that the kind woman Yevdokiya adopts the children of others. The whole delight in Panova's novella rests on the fact that Yevdokiya has a special kind of love affair with each child. But that's absent in the film."

Frida herself had her own "love affair" with each of the people who were close to her—with her daughters, with her granddaughter, with her friends. She never mixed up these affairs; she loved, valued, and knew how to build a separate relationship with each person.

She was endowed with an amazing gift for friendship. As a friend, she was direct, tender, caring, faithful, stern, and demanding. She harshly condemned Lev when he gave Lidiya Chukovskaya's manuscript to a friend to read without obtaining permission first. As we found out later, she wanted to "deprive" him of manuscripts. And her anger did not give way to favor at once.

A collection of translations was published in which Pasternak's own translations were removed after the scandal over *Doctor Zhivago*. Yefim Etkind, an excellent translator and a noble person, was asked to contribute his translations in place of the ones that had been removed. Etkind knew that in any case Pasternak would not be published and that if he refused, they would simply get translations from someone else. And so he sent in his translations.

He was Frida's close friend, but she sternly condemned his action even though then, in 1958, most decent people would have acted as he did. Even today you could still count the examples on your fingers where writers would refuse to publish their works, saying "I don't want to do so in place of a person who is being persecuted, I won't give in to the villain who is at the head of the journal" and so forth.

In 1964 Iraklii Andronikov was still threatening to remove his name from the editorial board overseeing the collected works of Lermontov if the name of Yulian Oksman was not rehabilitated. The threat worked. (But today, in 1980, I am quite incapable of citing similar examples.)

Frida supported the appearances in print of one of her favorite students, Natalya Dolinina, and mournfully shook her head: why had she found it fitting to quote Khrushchev for no apparent reason whatsoever?

She had enough strength to bestow on strangers as well.

In 1964, after reading Evgenia Ginzburg's remarkable manuscript *Journey into the Whirlwind*, we were expressing our delight only to ourselves (like the majority of readers of the manuscript), whereas Frida immediately sent a telegram to the author in Lvov. When Evgenia Ginzburg arrived in Moscow, they got acquainted and Frida "presented" her to us.

I had to tell a lie to Evgenia Ginzburg, as to a great many others in January and February of 1965. "No, Evgenia Semyonovna, the tumor isn't malignant; no, really, it isn't malignant," I kept repeating obtusely, carrying out the promise I had made to Frida's daughters: not to tell a single person. So that, God forbid, Frida wouldn't find out.

An ever greater number of people were drawn to her out of love and hunger. A greater number than it was physically possible for her to "assimilate." Her firmness began to manifest itself at that time. "It's unavoidable that you betray someone," she said, replying on the telephone that she was going out of the house while in fact she was waiting for someone else. "It's impossible to please everyone. If you try, then you end up pleasing no one. After all, if I hadn't just told a lie this moment, I wouldn't, in fact, have seen either A or B. You have to make a choice."

She seemed to me to be a remarkable mother; that is, a mother who was seeking, making mistakes, and suffering. She was an enlightener in everything, including her relationship with her daughters. She was convinced of the fact that the milieu, the circumstances and surroundings, played the dominant role in the formation of a person. But by some extraordinarily intelligent and sensitive instinct she began to surmise early on the disposition and character that were embedded in the tiniest infant, to surmise genes and heredity.

One theme passes incessantly throughout her diaries, throughout all her letters and books: what kind of material do we get and how do we raise it? Where, when, and how are we mistaken? That same theme permeated her life as well. During the period of her serious illness I saw her devoted daughters, daughters who were nurses, daughters who were friends at her bedside, daughters who were stern, frequently jealous and protective of their mother.

"I'm all involved in my new book and therefore I say firmly: no more business of others. The one thing that I still want to be involved in is a registration card and a room for Nadezhda Mandelstam. I am decisively abandoning all the rest." Frida said that to me in November 1963. Then on November 29 a lampoon entitled "A Pseudoliterary Drone" was published in the newspaper *Vechernii Leningrad* (Evening Leningrad). That was how the case of Joseph Brodsky began, which became Frida Vigdorova's final and practically most important case.

The first we heard of the poet Brodsky was from Anna Akhmatova. "What, you don't know our premier?" she asked tenderly and in amazement.

The year was 1964. Brodsky was reading his poetry at the home of some friends. I arrived after everyone had already gathered. The room was divided by a bookcase. There was a buzzing sound, as though a wind instrument was being tuned. The sound, the buzzing, and the drone preceded the verses, accompanied them, and echoed on after the final line had fallen silent.

The year was 1972. He was granted permission to emigrate and came to say farewell to us. He read "Candlemas," one of my favorite poems because I can still hear his voice.

On becoming acquainted, he also read verses at our house and we talked for a long time. It turned out that he knew English and American poetry marvelously well. Behind the exterior, a shy, very mournful boy was revealed, a boy who was carrying sorrow within himself. A momentary glimmer, and then the invisible switch clicked and the person became impenetrable for me.

Frida became involved in the Brodsky affair from the very first days, immediately after the appearance of the lampoon. At that time she was in Leningrad and had made several efforts from the very outset to curtail the persecution. All her appeals to people went unanswered. On February 18, 1964, the trial took place. For apparently the first time Frida was unable to get a journalistic assignment from a single newspaper. And so she went to the trial as a private person.

After the second trial was over, she wrote to Chakovsky, the editor of *Literaturnaya gazeta*: "Dear Aleksandr Borisovich, I am asking you to read my letter carefully.

"In the middle of February I requested an official assignment to Leningrad from *Literaturnaya gazeta*. My request was granted, but I was specifically warned not to interfere in the case of the young Leningrad poet-translator. I asked whether I might use the name of *Literaturnaya gazeta* to gain entry to the trial should it be a closed one. I received the reply no. Probably I should have immediately turned down the assignment; after all, I had in essence received an expression of the most insulting distrust.

"Unfortunately, it was at the trial that I understood this with particular poignancy when the judge, in the rudest fashion, forebade me to take any notes, and in response I could not produce the credentials of the newspaper to which I have been a contributor for many years and which I never once failed. Is it really possible to deprive a journalist of his natural right to see, record, and penetrate the meaning of what is taking place?

"Therefore, I am returning my assignment unwritten, and, naturally, I shall return the money to the accounting department."

In the letters that Frida wrote and in her approach to people, this is what is striking: even then she remained the teacher, the enlightener, she never considered that what was clear to her was clear to others. She incessantly searched for the arguments in order to convince. This was not simply a device, this was the essence of her nature manifesting itself—a belief in rationality, a belief in the human ability to assimilate arguments, to comprehend, to change.

At the end of the first trial, Brodsky was sent for a compulsory psychiatric examination. We telephoned Frida from Moscow. She couldn't utter a single word, she was sobbing. We found out later what happened during the trial. Frida's tears were uncustomary, strange, and even terrifying.

Naturally, she had encountered injustice earlier as well. She was a seasoned journalist of twenty-five years' experience and a deputy representative of the district soviet. She made the rounds of all our godforsaken spots. (She had resettled a hundred people out of basements!) She had seen a great deal that was evil, bitter, monstrous, and dishonest without evaluating or enumerating it. But earlier she had always been protected. For all her extraordinary ability to listen to and absorb the grief of others, she was still beyond grief herself.

At that point, though, the judge, in concert with the darkest forces, had judged her as well, just as every Soviet intellectual was being judged.

Witnesses for the prosecution stated one after the other: "I don't know Brodsky, but if they wrote about him in the newspapers, then it must be true." That was applicable to any one of us. For that reason it was impossible to read the transcript of the trial without horror.

Echoing through Frida's uncustomary sobbing was the horror of what she had seen and become conscious of for the first time *in that fashion.*

Frida returned from Leningrad after the first trial, and Lev met her at the railway station and took her to Lidiya Chukovskaya's. She had already gathered her wits to some degree, and Frida's typical business conversation proceeded: how to help the boy? Whom could they turn to? We decided to send a telegram to the secretary of the Leningrad district committee. That telegram, like the others, went unanswered.

A great number of people and writers took part in the Brodsky case. The list was headed by the names of the elders: Akhmatova, Chukovsky, Paustovsky, Marshak, Shostakovich. And later on, the witnesses for the defense in the trial: Natalya Grudinina, Vladimir Adoni, Yefim Etkind. And those who wrote letters, spoke out at meetings, tried to convince acquaintances in power, wrote character references for Brodsky, made the rounds of the departments, gathered commentaries from the foreign press, and, finally, went to the trial: Lidiya Chukovskaya, Evgenii Gnedin, Natalya Dolinina, Iosif Metter, Tatyana Khmelnitskaya, Yuna Morits, E. Linetskaya, Sergei Narov-chatov, Lev Kopelev, Daniil Granin, Yelena Zonina, Vyacheslav Ivanov, Irina Ogorodnikova, Nikolai Otten, Yelena Golishcheva, Aleksei Surkov, Nikolai Bazhan, Yevgeny Yevtushenko, Andrei Voznesensky, Bella Akhmadulina, Rasul Gamzatov, Yakov Kozlovsky, Zoya Bogu-slavskaya—those are the people that I knew. But there were many others as well, younger writers in Leningrad, like Andrei Bitov, Rid Grachev, Igor Yefimov, and B. Vakhtin. It's strange and bitter to reread this list. The subsequent paths of these people went in different directions. But the very fact that a group of people had temporarily joined together bore witness to the creation of a public opinion that emerged at that moment and then was once more suppressed.

However, it was Frida Vigdorova who did more than all the rest. Her record of the trial, irrefutable as a document and talented as a work of art, put a weapon into the hands of all the defenders. The word was precise. The capacious word once more demonstrated its power. The word of an uncompromised conscience.

In the spring of 1964 *samizdat* circulated the record in innumerable copies and later the record of the trial was printed abroad.

Frida had taken account of the consequences of her actions. She was prepared to bear the responsibility. (It is essential to remember that it was still 1964, before the Sinyavsky-Daniel affair. Everything was just dawning, just beginning. She was a part of a beginning. And nowadays more than a hundred writers who are living *here*, in the Soviet Union, are being printed *there*, abroad.

She was a public figure, one of the first public figures of a new type. She wasn't simply doing good in a microworld. In the most terrible and the bloodiest years good people shared money, bread, knowledge, and shelter. But Frida went further. What she was doing exceeded the boundaries of the smaller world of relatives, friends, acquaintances, and assumed a social significance.

In 1964 the reputation of Vigdorova as a fighter for justice had already become so widespread that even such well-known writers as Ehrenburg and Paustovsky would pass on to her from time to time letters that they had received—cries for help.

Frida was properly indignant: "Well, is it really possible to compare our names, connections, and opportunities?" But she would take the business up. She would not ignore someone else's misfortune, and, as it turned out, it was possible to make a comparison between herself and those well-known people.

In the summer of 1964 she was living in Tarusa. We received a note from her: "I'd very much like to see you. I have a disgustingly nasty temperature, I have no strength, and my outlook on life is gloomy. Two deaths in a row, Samuil Yakovlevich [Marshak] and Georgii Ivanovich, have completely knocked me off my feet. What's more, Lidiya Chukovskaya is ill and so miserable. Then we were expecting you, and Lev fell ill. And my work is not progressing."

The Brodsky affair was at a standstill. We got ourselves out to

Tarusa for two days, and our meeting with Frida was very gloomy. Three years in all had passed since the cheerful times in Zhukovka, yet it was as though we were all different people.

Lev went swimming in a small stream, while Frida and I sat on the bank. It was as though the river and the woods were not beautiful and the Tarusa attractions gave no joy this time. "I don't feel like thinking about how much grief lies before us. After all, our loved ones are getting older: Kornei Ivanovich Chukovsky, Anna Andreevna Akhmatova, Konstantin Georgievich Paustovsky. How cleverly it's all been arranged that a person doesn't know when he will die." She had named those who were over seventy. Yet she herself was the first to depart.

In the fall of 1964 the directors of the Moscow Writers' Union began to prepare the Vigdorova "case." They tried to find accusers among people with a good reputation so that the accusations would sound more convincing.

Perhaps if it hadn't been for the removal of Khrushchev in 1964 at the October Plenum of the Central Committee—the government had been concerned with an internal struggle—the Vigdorova case might have gotten under way.

In May 1965, when she was being pumped full of chemicals in the second hospital, she said to me: "A completely different kind of medicine is required. Now if only they brought the boy [that is, Brodsky] back, then I would get better immediately." In one of the first letters from the hospital she wrote: "Everything that tormented and upset me still torments and upsets me, but everything has *regressed*. Is it true that Joseph won't be released before the New Year? Lord!" She wasn't talking just about the personal fate of a single person, even though for Frida a *single* human fate meant immeasurably much. She had to decide whether she would be able to live in her former world.

Finally, the moment arrived when it was impossible for her to go on living in her former way. That was what the Brodsky affair meant to her. Not because at that time she had found out something fundamentally new about our reality. But a road, and no insignificant one, still must be traversed from *knowledge* to *behavior*.

Before the Brodsky affair, Frida Vigdorova coexisted relatively peacefully with the state. She would go to the editor of *Izvestia*, Aleksei Adzhubei (Khrushchev's son-in-law), to the Minister for the

Protection of Public Order and the offices of his ministry. She would use all her journalistic connections. She did it in order to help someone. In doing so, naturally, she had to smile and conform and resort to the inevitable everyday compromises.

She was a direct person, at times even simplistic and lacking in cynicism, lacking even in the possibility of mustering different forms of behavior—one for the outside world and one for herself.

Owing to the absence of journalistic credentials at the Brodsky trial, she sensed both weakness and strength. A weakness that derived from isolation and defenselessness. And a new strength, the strength of a public figure, of a person who was acting on her own fear and at her own risk. She sensed a liberation from the dogmas, from the precepts, from everything that had intimidated her nature. Lacking an official assignment, she felt all the more fully her unofficial one.

And, lo, a multitude of new moral problems arose before her, ones that were, to a significant degree, unsolvable. After all, this was not a young person just setting out on her path. This was a life that was tied and tangled up in a multitude of indissoluble obligations. Any single step of hers would, inevitably, involve other people as well, people who were close to her. I'll list the possibilities.

Could she have, would she have wanted to emigrate? I don't think so.

Could she have joined some kind of "underground," even a purely literary one? Hardly.

Perhaps she might have written merely "for posterity," retreated within herself, and left the newspapers and her legal public activity (several signs of that kind of withdrawal were noted during her final months). One thing is clear: she could no longer smile at Adzhubei, she could not have entered into any "councils of the profane." One of the foundations of enlightenment had been shaken—she understood that the authorities had no need of rational and good counsel.

How many times during that year and a half did we imagine to ourselves Brodsky being freed. Everything happened in a very mundane fashion. At the beginning of September 1965, a month after the death of Frida, a friend telephoned and said that a decision had been made. Lidiya Chukovskaya and I kissed each other and were mournfully silent: Frida had not lived to see this day. Later in Sukhumi, where Lev and I went on vacation, we received a letter:

the business had dragged on for another three weeks because the decision was dispatched, whether intentionally or by error, to Astrakhan Oblast (instead of Arkhangelsk Oblast), and they were searching in vain there for the "parasite Brodsky." Finally, Brodsky returned: "I wasn't the one who was supposed to open the door to him, I wasn't the one who was supposed to cook him an omelette," Lidiya Chukovskaya wrote to us. She was thinking, of course, of Frida.

Each time I visited Frida in July 1965 could have been the last time. I said good-bye to her on July 20, even though afterward I dropped in for two or three minutes, held her hand, and tried to be somehow useful to her family, for example, by answering the telephone. In the middle of the night I suddenly understood whence came the fear: it was because her skull was stretched tight. Her head had become square. Its roundness had disappeared. And her mouth was swollen. The words reached me from far away as though over many thousands and thousands of kilometers. The distance from life to dying.

Her pain communicated itself—you could feel the physical tension. And I remembered how in the hospital I had fed my seriously ill eight-month-old daughter Masha: I myself was biting my lips and swallowing. It seemed to me that if I did so, it would be easier for her to swallow, and after all, whether she lived or not could have depended on every swallow she made.

I was chatting with Frida. By then I had none of those humorous stories that I usually gathered beforehand by way of preparation for going to see her. I was telling her about my grandson: Lyonya was already beginning to recite children's verses. I told her that Yevtushenko, after he returned from Italy, wrote about the harm that the Brodsky affair had caused us. Earlier she would have been happy. But now she was silent.

I brought her David Samoilov's new poem "Pestel, the Poet and Anna," lines we lived with all that summer and have been living with ever since. I timidly asked her whether I should read them.

"Yes."

In the midst of the reading she squeezed my hand and moaned.

"Are you tired?" I asked.

"Don't stop."—She said it sharply and energetically, like the Frida of old.—"What a poet! His verses keep getting better and better. Amazing."

We talked about Andrei Bitov's prose, and again she said as she used to: "I gasped when I was reading 'Penelope.' "*

She asked me sternly whether I had sent Novella Matveyeva what I had written about her.

I remembered Lidiya Chukovskaya's manuscript of *Sofia Petrovna.* "If I have need of it . . . if in general I have need of anything . . ." Her only hint. And for the final time she said: "Now, if I eat a piece of black bread with salt and can keep it down, then I'll be lucky . . ."

After death had struck, I stood for a long time alone at the coffin. And everything that I had ever heard about resurrection, about death-like comas, kept creeping again and again into my head. It was still quite impossible to reconcile oneself with the thought that she was gone.

Seven months before, we had received a postcard from her in the hospital:

13/1/65. Raya and Lev, thank you, my dears. Raphael's Madonna was just what I needed! I was overjoyed with her. Kisses from me. Look after Shura.† He doesn't know that the operation is tomorrow, that is, the 14th. If only you could really drag him off to Peredelkino.

Kisses, love, and warm embraces: Till the morning . . . F.

On the day after, January 14, Professor Vinogradov declared a sentence with no appeal: "Inoperable cancer of the pancreas." A terrible evening. Lidiya Chukovskaya and I walked around Peredelkino and were silent for the most part. To believe, to grasp at chemistry, at medicine, to hope for a miracle—all that came later, especially after Frida returned from the hospital and seemed to be getting better. But then—the impenetrable darkness. Lidiya Chukovskaya said: "That's the second time the main support has collapsed in my life" (in 1960 Tamara Grigorievna Gabbe had died of cancer; for Lidiya Chukovskaya she had been a lifelong friend).

I couldn't have said that. I had been blessed with the friendship of Frida for too short a time. I cannot say that she effected a decisive turnabout in my views. No, we met and became close to each other

---

* One of Bitov's first short stories.
† Frida's husband.

in a real fashion only after that turnabout had occurred. But during these last years it was she who had become the kind of person by whom everything was measured: your actions, your attitudes to people, what was written and thought, the past and the present.

XXIX

Aleksandr Yashin

(A Sketch)

1969–1971

Aleksandr Yashin was not one of my friends. However, whenever I walk past the black door that is next to ours, the door of his final earthly home, I experience a mournful feeling.

When I learned that Yashin had died, I did not recall those words of John Donne so familiar to me: ". . . any man's death diminishes me, because I am involved in Mankinde; And therefore never send to know for whom the bell tolls; It tolls for thee." I had repeated those words many times at lectures on Hemingway and in my articles. But in actual fact I did not at all feel literally every death as a disappearance of a part of myself. I would simply skip over with my eyes the majority of death notices, even those of people whom I knew. When I'm listening to the radio and I hear about executions and hangings, I die for a moment from terror. Is it Prague? No, I have a shameful sense of relief. It's not Prague, it's Baghdad.

The same thing with people who died in their beds. But the death of Aleksandr Yashin affected me deeply.

I heard him for the first time at the Second Congress of Writers, in December 1954. Sitting high up, in the gallery of the Hall of Columns, I couldn't see him, I could only hear him. He was speaking about his narrative poem *Alyona Fomina*—he had whitewashed the extreme poverty of his village. That poem brought him the Stalin Prize, an apartment on Lavrushinsky Lane, a dacha in Peredelkino, a car—all the tokens of a front-rank Soviet writer. When, after writing the poem, he visited his native village again, he became horribly ashamed of his false verses. And he talked about this sense of shame from the lofty stage in that hall.

Poems like Yashin's were published by many writers during the Stalin years. Some of those writers also had a feeling of guilt. But very few found the courage in themselves to talk about it aloud.

The thaw had only just begun, and the gates of the concentration camps had not yet opened. Perhaps it was precisely at that time when I was listening to Yashin that I felt the need to take account of my complicity and one of the first impulses arose for my book.

In the fall of 1956 Yashin's story "Levers" appeared in *Literaturnaya Moskva* (Literary Moscow; No. 2).

Scene One: an everyday conversation among five members of a kolkhoz, an honest talk about the woes of agriculture in the fifties. The same kind of discussions were going on at that time all over the country. Scene Two: a Party meeting. The characters are the same five kolkhoz workers. But each of them ceases to be himself. People have disappeared—they have turned into the levers of a machine that is crippling those very same people and others as well. They all feel awkward; after all, they were themselves only a moment before, but suddenly it is as though they've become buttoned up, they've changed their dress, their words, and their souls.

The metaphor has embedded itself in our language. "Levers" is an artistic investigation, a social study. A generalization emerges from a truthful picture, a picture that is faithful in all its details of country life. It was about all of us. Thirteen years have elapsed since then, and what years they've been! Yet that story hasn't lost its contemporary resonance.

In 1960 I saw Yashin up close. It was as though I were seeing him with a kind of double vision: through my own eyes and through those of the woman who was in love with him. We were coming down from the Karadag mountain and they were just going up. There in front of us was a Jack London–type of hero: strong, tall, and handsome.

We became acquainted in April 1962 in Yalta. It was a crazy kind of evening (Lev had just turned fifty), but we were feeling quite young. Yashin and his girl friend came to visit us—for her these were the "hundred hours of happiness" she wrote about in her poetry. We talked randomly about everything in the world and we felt that all four of us were close to one another. Our conceptions of the world coincided, we coincided in the people we loved and the people we hated. We ran down to the store for wine; we couldn't find any—it was already too late—but that evening is still seen through a haze of intoxication.

Yashin read poems and stories. Now they've all been published, but at that time there was the added feeling of sweetly forbidden fruit.

There was a story about a bear hunt. Naturally, that kind of man should go out hunting for bear with just a spear. How wonderful it is that such men still exist. The cave people needed strength and valor, and we need them too in the twentieth century.

And again, it wasn't just I who was gazing at him, listening and feeling ecstatic. Even with my back turned I couldn't help but feel her loving eyes. "Here's the kind of wonderful man that I fell in love with," her gaze was crying out. "Everyone likes him and both of you like him, and that's the way it should be because there's no better in the world than he." She was not embarrassed to give expression to something (so it seemed to me and still seems) that ought to be hidden from everyone, even from the person to whom it is directed.

While still in Yalta I heard that Yashin's new story "The Vologda Wedding" had appealed to Paustovsky. For the first time in contemporary literature the word "self-immolator" appears in this story. Yashin was talking about his fellow villagers, about the Vologda peasants. At that time he still could not have even imagined the Czech Jan Palach burning himself to death in January 1969 in Prague on Red Army Square as a sign of protest against the Soviet occupation of Czechoslovakia. And the self-immolator in Riga and the self-immolators in Kaunas, something that was already on our own soil.

Within Yashin himself were combined a striving for truth (the retribution for that striving could have been the loss of everything gained) and a fear of martyrdom together with the desire for a normal sheltered life, a life that was being sheltered for the sake of literature, for the creation of books.

Yashin frequently repeated: "I want to be a director." He wanted to be in charge and it didn't matter of what. He wanted to sit on the presidium. He wanted power. After the vicious criticism of "Vologda Wedding" in the press, Sofronov met him and asked: "Well, what have you got from *your* Jews? As for us, we're feeding *ours*."

It constantly seemed to Yashin that he was being left behind, that he had been forgotten, that not enough was being written about him.

At his fiftieth birthday, words were even spoken in the toasts about prizes that had not been awarded and about medals. It was done with irony, in jest, but not only with irony.

In the spring of 1964 Yashin received a letter from the émigré

Russian journal *Grani*, published in Frankfurt am Main. At that time many of our dissident writers—or those who were considered by foreigners to be dissident—were receiving similar letters. He came to our place, and sat for two days putting together a reply. The man who went bear hunting, the author of "Levers" and "The Vologda Wedding," had disappeared. We had a frightened person who considered that he should give them a rebuff. Not because he felt the inner necessity for it. He believed that he should demonstrate to the bureaucrats from the Writers' Union that he didn't need any defenders from the West.

In 1965 Yashin came with his wife, Zlata Konstantinovna, and his son to visit us in Peredelkino. When they left in the evening, I felt a sense of physical relief. Yashin vented his spleen, cursing one and all, both Soviet power and its enemies, both the old and the young writers, both the "liberals" and the "conservatives." He was feeling miserable. And he wanted to prove to himself and to others, perhaps above all to himself, that it was not he who was guilty but rather the structure of the universe, that everything that appeared to be good was only hypocrisy.

His son was sitting at the table, looking very much like his father. He wasn't simply listening, he was taking it all in.

The following day I sent Yashin a letter, saying something like the following: you are a talented person, but you are creating a "scorched" earth around yourself and that has never been a fruitful soil either for life or for art.

I sent the letter off, but then I began to doubt. Not where the heart of the matter was concerned, but because he and I really did not have the sort of relationship where you could and should say everything as to someone close who would at least listen to you. However, in this case, my doubts were unfounded. He even thanked me for the letter.

Terrible misfortunes began to pile up on him. In the summer of 1965 his girl friend, Veronika, died of cancer. Half a year later his son shot himself, that same boy with the clear eyes who listened so lovingly to his father. The boy had had an unhappy love affair.

In the winter of 1967 Yashin moved to a one-room apartment on Aeroportovskaya Street. That was how we became neighbors.

Except for that deceptively relaxed April evening in Yalta, I found it difficult to get along with him. I never managed to address him familiarly, as Lev came to do shortly afterward. And after all his misfortunes, communication, naturally, became even more difficult. Now and then we exchanged manuscripts and cups of sugar.

In March 1968, when Lev was in the hospital, Yashin had just returned from Novosibirsk. At our place he read Lev's letters in defense of the arrested Aleksandr Ginzburg and Yuri Galanskov, he read the article in the Austrian communist journal *Tagebuch* against Stalinism. He asked the very same questions—how many people had already asked it—why? What good is it? Can one really hope to change anything? But he asked in a kind of uncertain way, both with love for Lev and with anxiety on Lev's behalf.

At that time it seemed to me that the entire world revolved around what I was consumed by: the trial of Ginzburg and Galanskov, around the memorial evening for Andrei Platonov,* after which those who spoke openly about Platonov's fate and the general problems were punished. We were being dragged into a new Stalinism. That very same mechanism that Yashin had depicted in the story "Levers" was working successfully. The active Party membership in the Institute of the History of Art, which had just brilliantly defended its "petition signers," had unanimously voted, on a directive from above, for a resolution in which both the "hostile group of Ginzburg-Galanskov" and "their defenders" were condemned.

And besides, life and death were hanging over everything.

In March 1968 I was not listening to Yashin. Two months later he was put into the cancer ward. Lev and I visited him at the institution in Kashirka. Earlier we had already been back and forth to that accursed cancer hospital of our own accord. My anxieties and Lev's had proved to be false. But in Yashin's case it proved to be rampant cancer—three operations, metastases everywhere.

In the corridor was his wife, hunched up, compressed like a spring. "What day did Veronika die?" she asked us immediately and almost calmly. "Sasha is expecting death on that same day: he believes in the magic of numbers." (Veronika died on the seventh, and he died on the eleventh.)

It was difficult to recognize him, even though I had seen him only four months before. He looked like the nineteenth-century poet Nikolai Nekrasov before his death, as depicted in Perov's portrait. Nothing but sharp angles: knees, elbows, and chin.

---

* One of the best Russian writers of the twentieth century. Some of his best books, such as *The Pit* and *Chevengur*, were published abroad after his death (1951). He was severely criticized several times, once, in 1931, even by Stalin himself.

His wife was living in the hospital beside him. "Sing me to sleep, Mother, he asks me, and I sing him to sleep. He remembers how I used to sing the children to sleep while he was writing his first books."

Yashin spoke with difficulty. He frequently lapsed into unconsciousness.

His request that Aleksandr Solzhenitsyn come to visit him in the hospital was passed on to us. ("Why?" Solzhenitsyn asked. "We aren't even acquainted." Lev replied: "You know how people who are dying like to confess. That's why he's calling for you." "Well, if that's the way it is, I'll have to come.")

"Aleksandr Isaevich telephoned. He's coming to visit you as soon as he gets to Moscow."

"The telephones are bugged. Better not talk on the telephone," the dying man said.

Now the literary authorities wanted to quickly "give him his due": books, editions, honoraria, fame. He was being printed in all the newspapers, in all the journals. How he had needed all of that not so long ago. Now he no longer needed it.

On the way to the hospital, sinner that I was, I kept thinking that perhaps Yashin would sign some letter or other in defense of those who had been sentenced; after all, he had nothing more to fear now.

When I found out that General Pyotr Grigorenko kept visiting his friend, the dying writer Aleksei Kosterin, suggesting that he keep signing new letters (one of them was addressed to the Budapest meeting of Communist parties), I had an unpleasant feeling. It was possible that Kosterin was so perturbed that it hastened his death. Moreover, the transformation of Kosterin's funeral into a political meeting had been unpleasant for me, regardless of the intentions. After all, it is the same: "The end justifies the means"; "The common cause is above the personal"; and so forth.

But I too was going to the dying Yashin with "selfish" intentions. I was thinking in those categories, wherein people think among the living. Meanwhile, the process of dying was under way.

"Lev, Raya, come again, you live so close by." His conceptions of space were getting mixed up. The living cells in his brain remembered that the polyclinic had been next to our house.

Zlata, his wife, was raising a container of beer to his lips.

It was impossible to say that he was breathing his last. It wasn't a peaceful or a natural death. It was still early for that. He hadn't reached fifty-five yet.

Zlata said in the corridor: "He passionately wants to live. He needs everything: the sky, nature, hunting, hiking, poetry, wine, women. We're all mortally tired, dissipated, but he still needs everything." I couldn't sense that. There was almost nothing of his body. Zlata wiped each of his fingers separately, like a child's.

I had sat beside him for the last time at a Party meeting in the winter. We were indignant together when Vladimir Soloukhin was denounced on the podium for wearing a ring with a depiction of Nicholas II. Even then Yashin was quite thin; even by then the sharp angles were protruding. It was just that neither I nor other people closer to him had noticed that yet. Even if we had noticed it, could we really have done anything? Could we have staved it off?

He radiated poetry. I don't mean the writing of poems (as a prose writer he was much stronger), but the poetic quality of his nature and its inherent artistry. I mean his healthy, tender soul. I mean his talent for beautiful, daring, and chivalrous actions.

Yet, at the same time, something contrary would manifest itself in Yashin. He was an ill-bred person. In Nikolai Berdiaev's *The World View of Dostoyevsky*, the following is written: "Russian nihilism is a perverted Russian sense of the apocalyptic. This kind of spiritual attitude is a great hindrance to the historical work of the people, to the creation of cultural values. It does not favor a lofty spiritual discipline. This is what Konstantin Leontyev* had in mind when he said that a Russian can be holy but he cannot be decent. Decency is a moral medium, a bourgeois virtue, it holds no interest for apocalyptists and nihilists. And that quality has proven to be fateful for the Russian people, because only a few chosen people can be holy and the majority are destined for dishonesty."

These thoughts seem important to me for an understanding of maximalist individuals like Yashin.

In Yashin the forcibly accelerated development of our land was compressed: from the remote Vologda village to contemporary times, from illiteracy to the heights of poetry. There was nothing natural, no uninterrupted continuity of the species, slow and flowing.

There was a breadth of soul together with its generosity and riches. There was nothing of the English garden, which has been cultivated for 600 years. No, everything in a single short human life, all the

---

* Konstantin Nikolaevich Leontyev (1831–1891), Russian writer and literary critic, best known as author of articles on politics, culture, and history.

upheavals, all the grimacing, all the zigzags of our long-suffering history. From the remotest antiquity to our contemporary pitfalls.

This explains in part the outbursts of hysteria, the hardness, at times a severity, that is directed against those closest to you. And a sadistic severity with respect to oneself.

An unkempt garden. And even after a half-century there aren't any glimmerings, there hasn't been either peace or freedom.

After death he is being turned into an idol. This is expressed not only in the memorial erected in Vologda, not only in the innumerable iconlike memoirs.

Writers like Vasilii Belov, Fedor Abramov, Viktor Astafiev (whose move from Siberia to Vologda came as no coincidence), and Valentin Rasputin are all searching for their forefather and original source in Yashin as part of their literary heritage. But there are people as well who are deeply alien to him—the new chauvinists.

He died at a moment of ideological confusion, before the tanks in Prague, at a time when whimsical ties sometimes seemed like friendship.

Still it seems to me that the poetry might have gained the upper hand and not the desire to be a director. For me, as for many of his friends and simply readers, what we need is not a statue but the living person, who abides in our memory and in his best books as the one who was torn by contradictions and who was passionately striving toward good and truth through the debris of evil and falsehood.

Solzhenitsyn visited Yashin. The dying man had already lost consciousness.

Aleksandr Isaevich was finishing writing a letter in the hospital corridor when Zlata Konstantinovna came out of the ward. "It's over. It's too late."

In the evening of that very same day Zlata Konstantinovna showed us the letter. I am recalling it from memory.

Dear Aleksandr Yakovlevich!

You are at the bottom of a deep well. It's very hard for you. I know, I myself was in that kind of well. But even from there you can look out at a piece of the sky.

From the hospital in which you are lying you can see the church that is dear to the heart of every Russian.*

---

* Voznesenie Church in Kolomenskoe.

I am praying for you.

The author of "Levers" will remain forever in Russian literature. They've turned a few things, these levers.

Dressed in black, Zlata Konstantinovna said to us: "Hurry and do good deeds."

XXX

Someone Distant
and Near

1975–1977

A tragic face and a hand with a cigarette are cast into relief
against the dark background. There is an inscription on the photograph: "To my dearest Raya and Lev. Do you remember how I was
when I was young? Here I am remarkably old, but I still love you
both. Aleksandr Galich, January 29, 1974."

No, he wasn't old yet. But you couldn't recognize immediately from
the person in the photograph the young boy that I met in the spring of
1935 at a performance of Artistes Variétés. Then he was dressed in
a short jacket of blue velvet. I heard the word "velvet" later; only
many, many years afterward did I see this fabric in a store.

When I first visited Sasha Ginzburg* in his cramped room on
Bronnaya Street, I was struck by the walls: they were bottle green
with stripes.

"Lincrusta," the host remarked carelessly as he followed my gaze.
"Lincrusta" popped up in my vocabulary even later than "velvet."

We went to a musical show, the first in my life. The rhythms were
enchanting and Sasha Galich could repeat them perfectly:

> *There was a war*
> *Seven years in a row*
> *And no single hope of peace in the world.*

An age would pass before I found out that it was Brecht.

During those months of 1935 I had the feeling that I was being

---

* Ginzburg adopted the name Galich later.

unfaithful to my ideals: the world revolution, "proletarians of all countries, unite," cities liberated from capitalism. And what was I busying myself with? I was singing songs, kissing boys, and drinking wine. Sasha was an inseparable part of that "betrayal," part of our "sweet life" of the 1935 variety.

Sasha joined the literary circle of young poets. He was initiated into that marvelous order of those who were writing.

Lyonya and Sasha read their poems to each other, and we would argue for hours on end. Together we would plunge into romantic poetry and the mysterious names of Liss and Zurbagan were forever connected with our tiny room, where we would go on fantasizing about the unknown future.

> *We dreamt about seas and oceans*
> *And prepared to head straight for Hawaii.*

That is how it was with us.

We greeted 1937 with humorous poetry, wine, a fir tree, merry-making, and the profound conviction that we were living in the most beautiful of all worlds. The new year was personified in the most miniature of our girls, Khanka Ganetskaya. Sasha carried her in on his arms, wrapped up in a blanket, to the festive table.

We cast some kind of horoscopes, but who could have foreseen that Khanka would face the prospect of living through the death of her husband, that her father and brother would be shot, that her mother would be imprisoned, and that a year later she herself would be sent off to the camps.

A different road was predestined for Sasha, a more devious one, but in the end, Khanka's fate and the fates of her innumerable comrades in misfortune would converge into that road:

> *I'm frozen forever in the sleigh track,*
> *Like a horseshoe in the ice.*

That would all come later, decades later. For the time being we had no inkling about that icy track.

We spent an excessive amount of time with one another. We would meet at the theaters, at evenings where Yakhontov performed, at the conservatory.

Later came 1941 and the play *The City at Dawn*. Sasha played the director of construction in Komsomolsk who is later unmasked as a Trotskyite. Like the other participants in this play, he wrote his own role, directed, composed songs, and designed sets. The studio directors pooled all their efforts: Aleksei Arbuzov edited the entire text, and Valentin Pluchek did the directing. The play and the performance were the fruit of collective creativity, in the original sense of the word—yet another nuance of the times.

The years passed. We lost touch with each other for no particular reason. It was as though our childhood friendship had simply melted away.

And so sixteen years passed.

In the summer of 1957 Lev and I were taken to Galich's to hear the play *Seaman's Silence*. The second process of acquaintance, like the first, began with a visual impression: the apartment on Aeroportovskaya Street was furnished in mahogany and Karelian birch; there were a lot of books, albums, and pictures. Rare china. The things were crowding out the people. I only glanced around before the reading began. Afterward I no longer saw anything.

Seaman's Silence merged into the general stream of impressions from those years.

A Jewish boy from a small provincial town had become enchanted by the name of the Moscow street Seaman's Silence. His life was difficult; he came to Moscow, became a musician, and then was killed in the war.

We had opened our eyes. Our eyes had been opened. We had passed through a terrible period, innocent people had been imprisoned and shot. That would never be repeated again. The truth had been pronounced from the lofty podium.

I reread the play. Except for the intentionally optimistic final act, it was the best thing that Galich had done as a playwright.

The first songs that I ever heard of his were "The Horse Had a Heart Condition," "Lenochka," "Tonechka," and "The Red Triangle." The songs stunned me.

He had found himself in songs. Escaping from a bitter dissatisfaction with himself as a playwright and a scriptwriter, he had found a lifesaver, a prop. He had found a "calm and joyful consciousness of the fact that for the first time in my long and mixed-up life I am doing what I was intended to do on this earth" (*Dress Rehearsal*).

He had discovered it late, and thus with an even greater effort he strove to make up for lost time. But perhaps it isn't correct to say "late." His time had arrived. Earlier his soul had not matured, his shoulders hadn't yet squared out.

Galich's songs were born out of the social movement of the 1960s. To the extent that the birth of art is determined by social causes. The birth of his songs was mysterious, unconditioned by anything, like the birth of true art.

What was given to him to perfect went far beyond the boundaries of the "bardic phenomenon" or "muckraking," even though it was connected with both.

The new Galich and the new period of our relationship with him had begun. Most frequently he would come by, read his new verses and stanzas, and even single lines before they became songs. Thus he read for us, without guitar accompaniment, "Night Patrol," "Ave Maria," "Karaganda," "Petersburg Romance," a song about Pasternak, "The Ballad of Awareness" ("Arise, Yegor Petrovich"), "About the Devil," "The Ballad of Korchak," and many others.

I began to memorize them after the songs appeared. Every one of them intruded on me and inflicted a wound on me for a long time. Each one would drag something out of my soul and not let me be. At times I resisted, but to no avail. Thus, for a long time I couldn't admit the following lines into my heart:

> *And just as in the good old days*
> *He reviews the parade of the freaks!**

For more than twenty years I had marched in those columns at the demonstrations. And to feel myself or be called a "freak" was not an easy thing.

In the winter of 1965–1966, after the arrest of Daniel and Sinyavsky, I repeated the words:

> *Just keep mum—and it's rich you'll become!*
> *Just keep mum, keep mum, keep mum.†*

The song spoke as a direct challenge. Life began to unfold according to Galich and to be named according to Galich.

* Translation by Gene Sosin.
† Translation by Gene Sosin.

. . .

December 1966. We were together at the Writers' House in Peredelkino. Sasha was writing a song about Pasternak. He sang a great deal,
at different dachas and in our room on the second floor.

It was a pleasure for me "to present" him, our Galich. I loved to
watch the way people listened to him for the first time, to witness
that moment of stupefaction. I had already seen Sasha singing so
many times that I could allow myself the pleasure of keeping my eyes
fixed on Kornei Chukovsky.

Galich possessed a contemporary, arch-contemporary language.
Right up to the minute. Chukovsky was in his ninth decade on this
earth. How our vocabulary, phonetics, and intonation had changed!
It would seem that everything ought to have been foreign. And irritating to a certain degree. Even the details were foreign. One could
vouch for the fact that Kornei Ivanovich had never seen the way a
bottle would be split among three people. In life he would not have
tolerated this kind of behavior; he'd have sent away a Galich that
arrived drunk. But in art . . .

Chukovsky grasped immediately, instantaneously, the polyphony
of Galich's songs and all the nuances of meaning. He delighted in
the flavor of Galich's speech. He relished it and savored it, he per-
ceived it sensually, not only with his head, his soul, and his heart but
even with his fingers. With his amazingly long fingers it was as
though he were feeling his way, passing over the protuberances, along
the twistings and turnings, through all the multivalency of speech . . .
He would leap to his feet. Cry out. Laugh. Grow somber. Chukovsky
presented Galich with a book inscribed: "You, Mozart, are a god and
know it not . . ."*

The songs well up in me over and over again.

At that time, in Peredelkino, Sasha read some chapters from Lev
Kopelev's *To Be Preserved Forever*. He began to write a song. Not
about the "abstract humanist" who was attempting to protest the rape
and pillage perpetrated by the soldiers and officers of the Red Army,
but about the marauder ("Ballad of Eternal Fire" is dedicated to
Kopelev).

Galich was constantly drawn to complete transformation, to the
foundation of the pyramid.

Then, at Chukovsky's, he put aside the guitar—he was tired—

---

* From Pushkin's "Mozart and Salieri."

and switched to cognac and food. A rich repast. We heard about the chauffeur who got rid of the *kisel** for his sister's boy—he himself ate the "hospital shit." Miserable Russia.

Later Galich would write in one of his most terrifying songs:

> *I am serving up to your tables*
> *Great civil passions and sufferings.*

He was telling us about how *Seaman's Silence* was once again in rehearsal. "I won't be able to bear the veto."

Artists were tearing away the bark from falsehood: one with the truth about agriculture, the other (most often female) with the truth about everyday life and the family, the third with the truth about those who were governing us, and all of them with the truth about the human soul.

This is probably why the new falsehood, of the type "A Romance About Lovers," is so unbearable. It was especially painful to strip away the previous falsehoods, the way decorative wallpaper is torn off the walls, leaving them pitiful, naked, and pasted over with old newspapers.

In 1966, on a Peredelkino street, I asked Galich what was the most important question for me: "What about us? You have only executioners and victims. Is it really possible to understand that era without us, without those who were deluded, who sincerely believed? Nowadays there are so many people who affirm that they always understood everything, but in actual fact we know that it was not so."

"We" is not correct. Sasha and I had lived in different worlds until our second meeting. Our delusions had been different.

He replied with an abruptness that was uncharacteristic of him: "In all of my songs I am running away from us, from myself. Moreover, the time hasn't come to talk about us, about how we were deceived, how we deceived ourselves. Too little is said about the terror, about the moral decay, about how deeply the evil has become embedded and how deeply it has spread."

Speaking with me was an artist who rightly felt that he had to escape from himself.

In his songs of everyday life, on behalf of, in the image of, in the skin of the Hero of Socialist Labor, of the worker who was splitting

---

* A kind of gelatinous dessert that can have various flavors.

a bottle three ways, of the unhappy female cashier, the flirt and the *zek* in the same hospital ward, in all of these changing aspects, in each and every one of them is a revelation. The song is a drama, the song is a short story, the song is a pamphlet. Details that are precise, uniquely precise. Words that are precise, uniquely precise. The songs have lasted and they are being sung by a new generation because time has become imprinted in the ageless word.

A security officer has to inform the prisoners about the Party congress and the order to blow up the monument to Stalin:

> *Our "godfather" swallowed his pickle*
> *And muttered in anguish:*
> *"Our Father has turned out*
> *To be no father, but a son of a bitch."*

"Father" came into usage and assumed the meaning of a common linguistic cliché. Figurative clichés from "officialese" were often used:

> *And so I say that my moral image shows*
> *signs of rotten Western influence.*

Most frequently the word creates a discrepancy and everything depends upon the context. Thereby is born the unexpected, a new weight and a fresh meaning.

Galich introduced widely the language of the street and various forms of slang into poetry. He introduced it without exaggeration— something that rarely succeeds with masters of jargon.

In his songs not only the theme and hero are from the people, not only the vocabulary is from the people and in common usage in workers' quarters, but the grammar and the pronunciation as well.

We were told the story of how at one of Galich's concerts in Switzerland, an old émigré lady turned to her neighbor and asked: "What language is he singing in?"

This is a serious question. He sings in the Soviet language.

When there is no transformation, when the author appears in the foreground, the songs pale and precise words surrender to approximate ones as the unconditionality of art begins to waver.

In Galich's apartment there were many mirrors, and he frequently gazed at himself. But reflecting himself in the literal sense of the word—he rarely succeeded in that.

Galich, of course, carries on the tradition of the satirist Mikhail Zoshchenko and the *skaz*.* His song "On the Hills of Manchuria" is dedicated to Zoshchenko. The principal hero here, though, turns out to be not a writer tormented by calumny but the waitress Tomka; her lover is an uncouth lout, an organ-grinder with a monkey. Whereas the strange intellectual who asks for a bottle of mineral water and kisses Tomka's hand is only in a corner of the song as he sits at a corner table.

Among the songs not dealing with everyday life, some remarkable ones cropped up: "We Are Buried Somewhere Near Narva"; "The Ducks Are Flying."

Galich created a world that was terrible for me to behold after all the exposés and self-revelations. The grand ball in that world was not being directed by Satan, not by Woland, but by hundreds of thousands of petty demons.

I heard practically every song of Galich's in his own rendition a number of times. I was fortunate: the very perception of this phenomenon that was Galich presupposed both hearing and seeing. He was not merely a poet. He was not merely a bard. He was both together: an amalgam.

When I read the songs later, some things grew lifeless and dissipated. But a great deal was reinforced because I was perceiving it now on the basis of what I had heard. It was as though the word had become invested in sound.

All of us, those who deceived and were deceived, became people according to the extent to which we changed, rejected the falsehood, and freed ourselves from the past that was linked with the falsehood. Aleksandr Galich also traversed that path. In part he talks about it in his book *Dress Rehearsal*, which appeared abroad.

Like the majority of us, he too had things he had to free himself from. Around 1960 Frida Vigdorova, who was seeing Lidiya Korneevna Chukovskaya off to Moscow from Peredelkino, put her in a taxi with the Galiches. The following day Lidiya Korneevna gave her stern opinion: "Fridochka, how could you have sent me off with such people? The whole way they kept babbling on about some kind of Finnish furniture and dinner service. It's been a long time since I've had to swallow so much vulgarity."

* A type of first-person narrative in a fiction work in which a character's status and speech differ from the author's style and point of view.

Several years passed. Lidiya Chukovskaya heard Galich's first songs and said to Frida: "It's justice that such parents raised that kind of remarkable son. Serves them right."

One and the same person created songs and spoke about Finnish furniture, the same person who had been abroad many times and had participated in film productions in cooperation with France.

When a song burst forth, he would sigh with relief.

A complicated, slow, internal process was under way. He said to me in 1966: "I don't want to make money anymore. Let them do what they want. The songs are begging to surface. I'm fed up with being afraid."

Who were "they"? Certainly not his wife, Angelina Nikolaevna. He was the one who wanted to earn money, or rather, he had become accustomed to and wanted to have a lot of money in the house. That continued for a long time, while he was *simultaneously* the author of these very same songs and still the author, co-author, and ghost-writer of hackneyed scenarios that brought in money.

He couldn't conceive of existence without comfort, and it was with all the greater fury that he judged, condemned, and reviled those who somehow had established themselves in a world where there were Butyrkis, where there were Auschwitzes, Hiroshimas, who had established themselves after "raising the blinds and mopping the floors."

He drank. Every day. At first a glass would make him feel better, cheer him up. Later it got worse and worse. He would run to the bar in the station. And where, if not in those drop-in spots, did he see the inner and outer sketch of his characters, overhear the stories, expressions, and words.

We were sitting at the same table in the Writers' House in 1966. For a whole month I saw the kind of daily drunkenness that had propelled me into the worst decade of my life during my second marriage.

At times he would be seized by despair, a black hopeless despair. There are few people who spend their lives without hours, days, or even months of despair. In the case of Galich it was the despair of not being able to express himself—the despair of the writer, the creator.

The despair of a person who could not live the way he believed he had to and ought to.

The despair of breaking with the past. However it might have been, it had still been a normal life. But what lay ahead? A leap into the abyss . . .

The despair of a sick man: there it was, death, right beside him, drawing closer, bearing down on him.

And the most frightening despair—the one without cause.

Gazing at him in the midst of crowds and in rooms where he was the center, the magnet, the source of joy, it was difficult to imagine that abyss.

His verse is rich. Contradiction is embodied in its language. Not hypocrisy, which is provoked by the social structure, but a reinforced ambivalence, a double meaning, a bilingualism. A system of phrases that is directly opposed to real life and to the real meaning of the words.

When writers, including Aleksandr Galich, moved into the first cooperative house on Chernyakhovskaya Street, they furnished their apartments lovingly and (whoever could) luxuriously. At that time we heard of a conversation in which someone said: "But what if a revolution comes and they take all of this away?"

Sasha knew about that conversation. Perhaps it was then that the first kernel was formed of the future "Ballad of Surplus Value," in which the revolution has come true and provokes terror in its wake. It has long been known that our ruling class, our government, is one of the most conservative in the world. In the "Ballad of Surplus Value" this commonplace fact becomes an artistic revelation, acquiring a grotesque concreteness in the individual instance.

Sasha read masses of books in three languages. He knew what was good and what was bad in art. A friend remembered how together in Paris they saw Charlie Chaplin's *Limelight*: "The lights were turned on and there beside me was Sasha's face, as happy as can be and ruddy in the glow."

In March 1968 a festival of bards was organized on the university campus in Novosibirsk. "Two and a half thousand people stood listening to my song about Pasternak." A moment of silence. An ovation.

He understated what happened. Our friends from the campus told the story of how those who were present heard the truth not secretly, not just together with selected people of like mind, but in a large hall, in a crowd. To share that joy with others and to hear the truth expressed in precise speech—that was an exhilarating experience.

God, how he needed that success! After all, he was still an actor. Mere rooms were not enough for him regardless of how many people could be packed into them. He needed overflowing halls of crowds of strangers who nevertheless knew and loved his songs. Nowadays in Paris, London, and Zürich there are such overflowing halls.

Once again I am listening to the old tape recordings. Almost every song is accompanied by a tumult. A unique kind of choir. No, of course they aren't adding a choral accompaniment for him. That tumult (either before or after the song, rarely during) is an ecstatic one. Those who have gathered know, love, and are savoring the songs in anticipation. I recognize familiar voices.

I am listening to foreign recordings and records. A dead silence. A concert. And he himself is singing differently, perhaps with more affectation. The line "our train is leaving for Auschwitz" is accompanied by the noise of a real train. It's painfully out of place. As though people wouldn't believe, as though the song itself is insufficient without the sound of a train.

It's difficult for a Russian poet, more so for one who is so much from the soil, to exist without Russia. I didn't err when I said "from the soil." In recent years this was combined with the ever-waxing awareness of his Jewishness.

He needed those full halls in Moscow and Leningrad. And then all of a sudden Novosibirsk came as a gift. That was the height and the finale to an open life here.

After the Galanskov-Ginzburg trial in 1968 and after the petition compaign, the freezes began. Harsh articles directed against Galich appeared in the newspapers of Novosibirsk.

Eight songs were printed in the émigré journal *Grani*. That issue was slipped into his mailbox. He immediately sent the journal off to the executive secretary of the Writers' Union. He said that he did not want any unsolicited Western defenders or unsolicited publications.

The process of external and internal changes proceeded slowly, not directly, and often retraced its own steps.

For the director Mark Donskoi he wrote a filmscript about Chaliapin. He was still a member of artistic unions. He was still entirely a part of the old system, both the general one and his own personal. But he was outside it as well—in his artistic thrust.

Galich was exposing Stalinism. That, on the superficial level, was one of the initial impulses and in part explains the unusual dissemination of his tapes. It joined in the mainstream of the thaw during the 1960s.

But he also spoke out against the professional milieu in which he had been formed, against the fellow travelers, the prose writers and poets whose books were being published, against the artists whose pictures were being exhibited at official exhibitions, against himself as the author of many previous plays.

It was immeasurably easier to condemn the leader, the godfather, Stalin, than it was one's comrade from yesterday.

In the song "We Are No Worse than Horace" Galich speaks about the new literature—"without Gutenberg":

> *The "Erika" makes four copies;*
> *That is all, but it will do.*

About songs without the radio, without concerts, without television:

> *There is no orchestra, no loge or tier,*
> *No claque with its hullabaloo,*
> *A "Yausa" tape recorder's here,*
> *That is all, but it will do.**

The song "We Are No Worse than Horace" tells about the birth of the second culture. We argued about this song. Galich (and others) decided that this is the *only* culture.

But the majority of people in this enormous country cannot spiritually nourish themselves on underground and overseas publications. That's why every published book (naturally, if it belongs to genuine culture) is uncommonly important.

There are honest and talented writers whose books are published, honest and talented directors whose movies and plays are staged.

I believe that Russian culture and Russian literature are one. A single entity. Naturally, the division by a boundary, be it a state or an internal one, means that old and new differences arise. But the unity is deeper and more important than these differences.

Our literature is developing both here in Russia and abroad. There are few good books (which is normal) either here or there. Émigré and underground literature not only stands in opposition to the so-called official literature but is tied up with it as well. There is a flow in both directions. There are as well a multitude of borderline phenomena.

* Translation by Gene Sosin.

. . .

The meaning of a verse from another one of his songs has only been fully revealed to me now:

> *Just go ahead and drop by drop*
> *Squeeze the slave out.*
> —*"I Am Choosing Freedom"*

In my opinion, since Chekhov ("to squeeze the slave out" of yourself "drop by drop") few words have been spoken that are more precise and more important. Since then, spiritual slavery has increased a hundredfold in strength and it is all the more essential to squeeze it out.

Yes, gradually. Yes, drop by drop. You might not succeed, you might die before your soul has become utterly free. But any artificial acceleration leads only to a great deal of bloodshed and new "petty demons" (Dostoevsky). (Need it be stipulated that remaining in slavery is still worse?)

Galich provoked the ire of his former colleagues and fellow drinkers, who continued their old way of life.

"He's one of us, one of our people. As for Litvinov, Bukovsky, or even Sakharov and Solzhenitsyn, they're from another world. We never even saw them. But Sasha?! Why, I know him like the palm of my hand. Him a denouncer? Him a fighter for truth?! That's a good one!"

How these miserable folk rejoiced at his every misdemeanor!

But how much strength, how much noble faithfulness to oneself, how much gnawing conscience he would have required in order to break away. To break away from the everyday, easy, and cushioned concept of "let's live like all the rest." Drink, deceive, and go to premières at the House of Film. He had broken out of that decrepit and debilitating milieu, he had broken out as an artist.

In the summer of 1968 Sasha invited us to come join his wife and him. They were living in Dubna—an international center of physicists on the Volga—in a hotel. We went to Dubna and spent August 1968 there.

The preceding half year, the Prague spring, the Prague summer, filled his songs with fresh nuances that were even more bitter. I can see the faces of the young scholars. They were listening for the first time to the songs and there were tears in their eyes.

In distinction to his nonintellectual characters, Galich was an intellectual artist; he required not only applause but also professional discussion. We used to sit in our hotel room and talk about overstrained sounds, about the "plaint," about sentimentality. All the while, young physicists were walking along the embankment with guitars and singing his songs.

On the morning of August 21, 1968, Lev was pounding furiously on the door of the bathroom. "Come out right now! Tanks are in Prague."

Together with Sasha, the three of us went off into the woods. What was going to happen in Prague and in Moscow? What would happen to us now? At that moment there were almost no doubts, only mass terror. What way, by what means, could they be stopped from swallowing up Prague?

To ourselves we seemed to be omniscient and clear-sighted, but how much there was that we didn't know as yet about the internal mechanisms of our society, about the basic mentality of the people, about ourselves.

All during August, Galich worked on "Petersburg Romance" and read portions of it to us:

> *And standing in formation*
> *Are the regiments on alert*
> *From the Synod to the Senate*
> *Like four lines—*

It was during those days, immediately after the intervention, that the following refrain was completed:

> *Do you want to enter the square*
> *Can you go and enter the square*
> *Do you dare to enter the square*
> *At the appointed time and hour?*

On August 24, before our departure for Moscow, he gave that song as a present to us and signed it. In the evening our daughter Maya came with her husband, Pavel Litvinov, to our home. Lev read the song to them, just as he always read immediately anything new, be it from Galich or any other poet. On the following day, August

25, a protest demonstration against the intervention in Czechoslovakia took place at noon in Red Square.

Galich liked it very much when before any performance of "Petersburg Romance" I would give this information: the song was completed *before* the demonstration. That information was recorded on a great number of tapes. The poet had not simply described but had anticipated!

Life didn't end with Czechoslovakia, neither life in general nor our own. Our pessimistic prognoses at that time, fortunately, were not justified.

In Galich's song about how to "split a bottle three ways," a worker, after drinking, falls asleep: "He sleeps while his ambassadors cook up war and peace"—instead of him, in place of him, but partly in his name and partly expressing his thoughts and feelings.

If democracy and freedom of expression were suddenly to appear in our country through the magic wave of someone's wand, how would the working class react? How would they react to the "Israeli warmongering," to the intervention in Czechoslovakia, to the suppression of the intelligentsia? I don't know. In Portugal there was a totalitarian dictatorship for half a century as well, yet, lo and behold, the Portuguese had voted for democracy. But I know nothing about that small country, either about the nature of its dictatorship, or its present or past.

In his songs, with their precise contemporary details of content and language, there is also a universality, a worldwide generality of problems.

> And all Judaea was in an uproar,
> Not wanting to remember the dead.

Two thousand years have passed since those times. People want to live, if not in a joyful world, then at least in a comfortable one. Often enough their wrath turns not against those who create evil and grief but against those who do not want to forget about evil and grief.

Galich won't let us forget.

He was dismissed from the Writers' Union at the very end of 1971. I went to visit him. He was half-lying down. His wife, Angelina, was holding a syringe. He listed the literary people who had immediately telephoned him or come by: Vladimir Maksimov, Yurii Dombrovsky, Bella Akhmadulina, Yevgeny Yevtushenko, Lev Kopelev, Yelena Zonina, Vera Shitova, Inna Solovyova, Aleksandr Sharov, Boris Nosik. (Downstairs in the Central Writers' House, Yelena Bonner-Sakharova, Sara Babenysheva, and a young friend were waiting for him.) It was important to him.

In the summer of 1972 we saw each other especially frequently. He was living on the same small street in the village of Zhukovka where Sakharov, Solzhenitsyn, and Rostropovich had lived.

We walked in the woods, and he sang on my birthday. We roasted shashlik.

His greatest resentment from that summer was that Solzhenitsyn refused to meet with him. Any person, any writer, would have resented it if another writer whom everyone esteemed, a world-famous writer who lived nearby, refused to speak with him. Particularly at that moment when Galich had been driven out of the Writers' Union, as two years later Solzhenitsyn himself would be. I feel ashamed now that at that time I did not sense his resentment poignantly enough and did not share it.

Galich doubted himself. Not only was approbation important to him, but *understanding* was important as well. Just a comment. I know that Kornei Chukovsky's inscription "You, Mozart, are a god and know it not . . ." was among his most genuine treasures.

Now I think that the songs of Galich are at the source of an entire stratum of contemporary satirical prose to which belong *Moscow-Cockerels* by Venyamin Yerofeyev and *The Yawning Heights* by Aleksandr Zinoviev. In the songs of Aleksandr Galich our time has been imprinted more profoundly, more precisely, and with greater talent than in many of the *samizdat* novels or in many of the collections of documents.

In the summer of 1972 Galich and the Sakharovs established a fast friendship (Galich had known Yelena Bonner back in their youthful days.) He signed two protest letters composed by Sakharov: one against capital punishment, and the other, a call for political amnesty.

When our daughter Maya and her husband, Pavel, returned from exile, Galich sang at the celebration for their return. On the way home he said to me: "A year ago I wrote 'The Song of Exodus' and I sincerely believed that I would stay. But now I have decided to go . . . There aren't any more prospects here. I won't be able to bear any new summonses to the prosecutor's office. Life isn't finished yet. I want to see the world. I want to hold my own book in my hands."

For my part (of course, this was to myself), I recalled his old song:

> *The "Erika" makes four copies;*
> *That is all, but it will do.*

No, he was trying to convince himself in vain. It wouldn't do.

It's given to few people to know beforehand what they are prepared and not prepared for. Another year and a half of painful attempts to leave. He emigrated by the general route: a call from Israel. True, he also had an invitation from the Scandinavian society for newly converted Christians. He lived the first year in Norway, where he gave lectures at the University of Oslo on the history of the Russian theater. He moved to Munich and from there to Paris.

In the first foreign edition of Galich's songs, it was stated in the introduction that he had served time in a concentration camp and had been in the war (the author was being identified with his lyrical heroes).

In the presidium of the Writers' Union he was particularly hurt by the speech of his former friend Aleksei Arbuzov, who became indignant over that invented biography. Arbuzov's speech, mean-spirited in that particular situation, hurt Galich moreover for the reason that he knew himself that his own actions, his life, his deeds, and his words, be it in a film script, a play, or a song, frequently were in great disparity. Just as was the case with a great number of writers.

An ever less tractable conscience dictated new words. And it was still difficult for a person to conduct himself in accord with the new words.

The process itself of composing a different biography for a lyrical hero became one of the sources of creativity.

He understood how painful it was—the plank beds, the transport of prisoners, the common labor—how hungry one could be, how weighed down, and how his rosy body would have altered and become covered with scabs and withered away. He didn't want that.

Galich had no wish for an evil fate for himself; he wasn't prepared for suffering. It was all the more courageous of him that he did not stifle his own songs. Not only daring was required but also a firmness and a loyalty to oneself.

After all, when he was beginning, when his songs were already flying in every direction through Moscow, through the country, and even over the border, there was as yet no mention of any emigration, of the French P.E.N. Club, of the possibility of another choice.

Had he been of a different personality, closer to the image, closer to the icon, his extraordinary songs would not have existed.

The gulf between "seeming" and "being" is a vile one. That's how it is according to the generally accepted morality, according to the verdict of conscience. But the laws of another verdict, the verdict of the word, are different. It seems to me that it is precisely out of this gulf that Galich's songs are born. They are born not only in spite of the gulf but because of it as well.

In June 1974 we came to say farewell to Sasha. They were leaving by plane the next morning. Sasha was terribly tired. He had been delivering his luggage to customs.

The apartment was already completely stripped.

He was in his customary pose: reclining on the couch. It was hot and he was stripped to the waist, and there was a large cross around his neck. Lying there he was being served a fried cutlet, along with fried potatoes, cucumbers, juice, and tea with lemon.

I never saw him again.

I made a rough draft of these recollections after his departure, and in the summer of 1975 I returned to my manuscript. I was living in the Writers' House in Peredelkino. On several occasions we made trips to Moscow (a film festival was on). The doors to our rooms weren't locked. In September a manuscript entitled "What Galich Sings About," written on tissue paper and signed R. Orlova, was tossed into the mailboxes of L. Chukovskaya and several other people.

The beginning was mine. But further on, painstaking "editorial–co-authorial" work had been carried out on the manuscript: everything good that had been said about the person and the poet was deleted and all that was left behind (and augmented) was what was said about his shortcomings. And there were simply distortions. For example, in the original I had written "Arbuzov's speech, mean-spirited in that particular situation"; this became in the new version "Arbuzov's speech, *just and tactful*," and so forth.

There could be no doubt. The manuscript had been stolen out of my desk, and a copy had been made and "reworked." The calculation was a simple one: to vilify Galich and to do so not at the hands of his enemies but of his longtime friend.

I immediately wrote to Galich about it.

That was how the KGB (though I do not exclude "public volunteers") interfered in my unfinished work.

Instead of a Requiem

On December 15, 1977, we learned that Aleksandr Galich had come to an untimely end. I could neither comprehend it, nor accept it, nor even have a good cry. I frequently repeated, both about others and about myself: "Leaving the country is the same as death." "The airport is like a crematorium" is a line from a poem by Lidiya Chukovskaya entitled "Russia Departs from Russia."

But, departure is one thing and death another. It turns out that when people leave, somewhere at the very bottom of our hearts we still hope for a meeting.

For long sleepless nights I can clearly see our apartment, down to the tiniest detail. Not the one where we're living now (we moved into it after Galich was already abroad). Nor the one Galich frequented, where he read the verses that had not yet become songs, sang innumerable times, told stories, listened, complained, rejoiced, and drank vodka.

No, I see the apartment of my childhood on Gorky Street, where the handsome Sasha Ginzburg still not knowing what he would do—write verses or paint pictures, compose music or act on the stage—where that Sasha, seized with the premonition of fame, was sitting at our brokendown piano, singing the hit songs of the thirties, and we were joining in . . .

Not all those who have departed have disappeared. Several live on in love and antagonism, in friendship and enmity, in harmony and disharmony. But after his departure Galich disappeared. It was as though Galich had never existed in our lives.

But he had existed. Otherwise that deadly Parisian electric current would not have been such a blow to us. The pain required an immediate release: words, tears, solemn silence. Ritual.

We cannot bury him.

Where is the room large enough to accommodate all those who loved him, for whom it was as painful as it was for me, who wouldn't say rationally: "It's better for him that way, a quick death."

On December 17 funeral rites were held in the church on Bryusov-sky Lane. My church . . .

Thirty-five years had passed. Again I entered the church. I stood through the service for the departed, a lengthy list of people who were unknown to me. Then there was the sermon by Bishop Pitirim, a brilliant orator, about Saint Barbara the Martyr and John of Damascus.

Finally, a separate requiem for God's servant Aleksandr. In a chapel to the side, seven of us were huddled in a group . . .

The young priest spoke rapidly and swung the censer sharply. The six others crossed themselves furiously . . .

When I am alone in church, I sometimes cross myself as well, as I did in my childhood. But in the company of others, I cannot and must not do so.

Here too I was an outsider.

"You came to the church too, Raya?"

"No, I came because of Sasha."

I was never with Sasha in this or any other church. I drank wine with him and exchanged kisses on Bryusovsky Lane . . .

If each of those who were standing beside me in the church truly believed that they would meet up with Sasha in heaven, what fortunate people they were! How I envied them! But I am beginning, just beginning, to realize that he has died. That means that a part of me has died as well, a greater part than it had seemed.

He was never a friend in the true sense of the word. But there was something irreplaceable about him. There is now a black hole in that corner of my soul.

Sasha. Whom I shall never see again in Moscow, in Peredelkino, in Dubna, in Paris, or in the Kingdom of Heaven. Not anywhere.

"Forgive him his sins, voluntary and involuntary . . ."

Right now I cannot think either about his, or about mine, or about anybody's sins. I cannot think about the songs even though there won't be any new ones. Just about him.

Right now I am only remembering good things about him, his extraordinary giftedness and the carefree youth we shared, for which we had to pay so dearly. Right now I agonizingly miss that terrible day, which I, who have been left behind, ought to spend with the departed one: to go up to the coffin, to be horrified at the face that has altered, to lay down the flowers, and kiss his forehead. Afterward, icy from the cold and grief at the cemetery or the crematorium, to warm oneself at the wake (with vodka, food, and the touch of an elbow), those of us who loved him, all of us together . . .

The four of us, including my sister Lyusya and her husband, Misha, reminisced about Sasha and listened to his songs . . . But I still haven't buried him. I need everything together: that big apartment and that big table from my visions and those who love him. I need the songs to go on pouring forth, a great number of them, many more than space would be found for. I need people to come, both friends and strangers, both distant and near.

After all, for me he was both someone distant and someone near.

XXXI

Before the Rising Star
(Pages from a Diary)

August 24, 1968   1972–1974

We are leaving Dubna. A month has flown past. No, it flew at
first, but then August came to a halt—a collapse—and slowly the
treads of tanks crept forward.

For three days we didn't move from the radio. Memories of the
first war years returned. Then we heard: "After stubborn and protracted battles, our troops abandoned . . ." At that earlier time I hated
the "black plate" (that is, the radio loudspeaker), which brought
grief and shame. But could one really compare the shame now, a
quarter of a century later? And I hate the modern polished box with
the long steel needle that brings the shame.

As I ride the commuter train from Dubna to Moscow, Galich
verses ring out and the question gnaws at my heart:

> *Do you want to enter the square*
> *Can you go and enter the square*
> *Do you dare to enter the square*
> *At the appointed time and hour?*

A warm August evening. The railway station is jammed. We stood
in a long line for a taxi, got fed up, and dragged our things to the
subway. I peer out—but no, there are no traces of Czechoslovakia
visible. Moscow wasn't affected; it was a relaxed Moscow weekend,
festive, sated, and a bit tipsy.

Our daughter Maya and Pavel Litvinov dropped in on us. They
were worried and upset and were dashing off somewhere.

Maya and I were in our bathroom. (Apparently that was the first and last time that I held a conversation in the bathroom. Later that type of conspiracy began to seem ridiculous.)

"Don't involve Papa. I'm afraid for him."

"Why?"

"Prison!"

"But really, people are completely defenseless and still they aren't afraid."

"I can't help but be afraid. Prison for him again at this moment would mean the end."

A sense of alienation arose between us. Their friends came to get them. All of them were under continuous KGB surveillance. I was in another room and I could only hear their voices. For a second it entered not my brain but somewhere lower: "Why are they coming here? Why are they bringing those accursed black cars?"

Unpacked trunks, the move from Dubna to Moscow. And the unbearable pain that could not be swallowed up by anything: tanks in Prague.

August 25, 1968

Before leaving for Dubna we had received a letter from Solzhenitsyn with an invitation to visit him at his dacha in Borzovka. This was partially why we had hurried back to Moscow. The invitation was kind and businesslike, completely in keeping with his character: a railway timetable, which car to sit in, where they would be waiting for us with an automobile, "just so it'll be possible to show you our places with a wave." That's the way he had been before becoming famous and thus he remained now. We were met, and at first he took us to see Dmitri Mikhailovich Panin. His property—he had built the house himself—turned out to be about 12 kilometers from Solzhenitsyn's, and Panin ran that distance everyday. It was the first time that I saw his wife, Evgenia Mikhailovna Panina, sweet, peaceful, and very Russian. They were completely different people. They greeted us like "exalted guests."

On the way, Solzhenitsyn said: "The kind of day like today when I'm not writing is a rarity for me."

At Panin's, Lev very inappropriately began to read the verses of Mao Tse-tung. That interminable argument immediately boiled up.

(Just as though they were still in the *sharaskha*. When had it begun? In 1902? Lev broke off dispiritedly.)

It turned out that a letter had come from Ryazan: the chief of the propaganda department of the party regional committee would like to talk with Solzhenitsyn.

"Are you going?" Lev asked.

"What for?"

A magical forest all around.

Next to the Panins' shanty the modest two-story house of the Solzhenitsyns seemed a real palace. We made the rounds of the orchard and the flower garden. Among other things we were shown the unsophisticated signaling system for friends: depending on how the bucket was set, it meant "everything is in order" or "don't enter" or "a search is on."

Lev: "Russian literature has returned to the country houses."

Along the way Natalya Alekseevna Solzhenitsyna took photos of the three of them, the heroes of the novel *The First Circle*: Nerzhin, Rubin, and Sologdin twenty-five years later.

With pride our hosts showed us their possessions. From time to time we discussed Czechoslovakia. They had everything recorded on a tape recorder, everything during those *four* days, *just four* days, four days by now. We listened. We told them about meeting scientists in Dubna, and Solzhenitsyn interrupted us angrily—he was completely disillusioned with academics.

We talked about Czechoslovakia while the tape recorder was on. But it shortly turned out that something had not been turned on properly and we had "simply" chattered away for forty minutes. Solzhenitsyn became quite childishly angry. For a long time he couldn't forget about Natalya's blunder.

The principal theme was the shame of our complicity, the shame of our servility.

"A new Herzen has to appear who would say loudly: 'Today I am ashamed of being Soviet.' "*

Lev and Solzhenitsyn began to argue heatedly. For a long time I had not sensed so graphically their ties, so distant and deeply rooted. Thank God that after their argument a peace had been restored.

---

* Herzen wrote in 1863, at the time of the Polish uprising, "I am ashamed of being a Russian."

Something had to be done.

That phrase hung in the air. I said to Solzhenitsyn when we were alone for a moment: "You have no right, you have a different duty. Lev won't survive prison again."

He interrupted me sternly. "Now it is impossible to think about that, about the consequences. I am constantly thinking about what's to be done. One thing is clear: you won't help by writing letters to the government."

In Dubna we had imagined that the occupation of Czechoslovakia was like the burning of the Reichstag, and the brown columns were bound to continue doing their horrible business along the leveled road. We were wrong. After all, here we were in the house where one of the first bombs ought to have fallen. But it was calm there. This tiny house and the stream and the birch grove, they were all living their undisturbed life. Only the radio bore the pain of Prague, and it echoed inside us.

What to do? Over dinner we discussed in detail Andrei Sakharov's memorandum. We read a chapter from the new (and first) version* of *The First Circle* (where Clara is walking with Innokenty near Nara—that was where we were then). Then the author read the chapters about Stalin. Like an actor he spoke Stalin's lines with a Georgian accent. I could hear the personal hatred. And the artist's satisfaction.

I didn't take to these chapters the first time, but the author's voice possessed a magnetic force.

He read the foreword.

On the way back in the car Solzhenitsyn said: "I'm going to go on being a troublemaker. For another year or year and a half."

We returned home late.

August 26, 1968

Around noon Maya burst in on us. "Yesterday on Red Square there was a protest demonstration against the intervention in Czechoslovakia. Everyone was picked up."

"How many took part?"

"Seven."

---

* The "96-chapter" version.

"No!!!"

This is what I screamed, but she also shouted at me: "Don't!" But I was already weeping and the rest of the story I heard through tears.

"Five minutes. Perhaps ten. They were sitting at the Lobnoye Mesto.* They had unfolded the placards. Everyone was seized and shoved into cars. Me as well, even though I wasn't sitting with them. They beat us. Some volunteers from the public helped them. They took us away to the militia. After the interrogation the KGB officials came to our place in Medvedkovo and there was a long search. They took a lot of things away."

"Eat."

"What do you mean, Papa? I'm in a hurry. I have to go to Lara's parents. And Natashka Gorbanevskaya came to the square with a baby carriage."

"She must be crazy!"

"Papa, you don't understand. They're all marvelous people. Pyotr Yakir didn't make it to the square, he was hauled off to the militia."

"Strange . . ."

"Papa, don't you dare talk like that! Those villains at the militia—well, I really gave it to them! I told them everything I thought of them. They even tried to talk us out of it: 'What's the use, fellows, you won't really change anything . . .' "

Seven. With the exception of Pavel I didn't know anyone. I had only seen Larisa Daniel in passing.

The seven. The Decembrists† had brought out the troops.

> Do you want to enter the square
> Can you go and enter the square
> Do you dare to enter the square
> At the appointed time and hour?

Those seven had dared. On behalf of all those who wanted to, who were in anguish, but who didn't dare. They went out. A large square. They were alone. They were defenseless. There, on the Kremlin towers were the ruby stars. But they had been extinguished. Pavel

---

* In Old Russia a place of public executions.

† Dissatisfied with despotism and the backwardness of Russia, a group of young aristocrats staged an uprising on December 14, 1825, against the tsar. They subsequently came to be called Decembrists.

and his comrades were between the extinguished stars and those that had not yet risen. Would they ever rise? When?

Pavel was in jail under lock and key. So that was what Maya had in mind during our conversation of the day before. The day before, but already beyond the pale.

I was trying to find the time to say to her: "Now you have a choice before you: like the wife of Sinyavsky or the wife of Daniel. If you want to help your husband, to make the journey with him and do things so that he will have support from the rear, then you are obliged to be healthy, to withstand everything, and to work. And, in addition, to be careful. Or if you yourself wish, then he can remain without your help. I know neither of those two wives, but I would have acted like Marya Sinyavskaya."

Why was I talking like this? I reproached Lev for his exhortations, while I myself . . . Moreover, Maya didn't sleep all night.

We left the house together. Life was going on as before. I had to pick up 50 rubles at *Izvestia*—we didn't have a kopek. At the cashier's I bumped into Pyotr.

"Raisa Davydovna, has something happened to you?"

"It seems to me that something has happened to all of us, Petya."

"Ah! But I like it when everything is made clear."

I turned around and left. What's there to rejoice over? What clarification?

Seven people. A hostile square. Everyone was hurrying to the Lenin Mausoleum or the stores. What did they care about Czechoslovakia? What did they care about Dubček?

We had to help Maya. Pavel now was our affair as well, whether we wished it or not.

In Dubna I was writing about Martin Luther King. For a long time I couldn't fall asleep: Red Square, crucifixion, the murder of King, the lines from Nikolai Nekrasov that were inside me since childhood suddenly sounded different:

> *Say not: "He put aside caution!"*
> *He will bear his own guilt for his fate . . .*
> *No worse than us he saw the impossibility*
> *Of serving good without sacrificing himself.*

Is this the epigraph or the end? Seven of them in jail and I dare to think about an epigraph.

October 11, 1968

"In the name of the Russian Soviet Federated Socialist Republic . . . The defendants Bogoraz-Bruchman, Litvinov, Babitsky, Delone, and Dremlyuga, being in disagreement with the policies of the Soviet government, decided to organize a gathering on Red Square with the purpose of propagandizing their defamatory prefabrications. In order to confer widespread publicity on their designs, they prepared placards beforehand with the following texts: 'Down with the Invaders!' 'Hands Off the Czechoslovakian Soviet Socialist Republic!' 'Freedom to Dubček!' 'For Our Freedom and Yours!' and other patently false prefabrications defaming the Soviet state and social system . . .

"Litvinov, Pavel Mikhailovich, according to article No. 190/1 of the Criminal Code of the RSFSR . . . is sentenced to banishment for a period of five years . . .'"

May 20, 1970

The airport in Chita. A heavy bag of food had been assembled for me in Novosibirsk. My mind was still there. I was giving a special course of lectures devoted to American literature. I was in my element. I was happy in my work.

I was flying to Usugli, where Pavel and Maya were in exile. A friend was supposed to visit them, but he emigrated unexpectedly to Israel. So I had to take our eldest grandson, Dima, to Moscow for the summer.

The plane resembled the Singer sewing machine out of my childhood. I crawled out, and the bag was tossed out behind me. There was no airport, just a reddish-colored field. Someone was waving his arms and running toward me. It was Pavel, and we embraced. Then we were on his motorcycle, I in the back, and 7 kilometers later we were at their house. Maya had a child in her arms.

Forty-eight intoxicated hours later I was making notes. Dima asked: "What are you writing?"

What was I writing? Was it really possible to note down the spring knolls, was it really in my power to do so? The blossoming rhododendrons, the freedom that one felt a ten-minute walk away from their house?

It was not the Pavel Litvinov who occupied such a leading and high-level position in the democratic movement and whose portrait I had seen in a hundred foreign newspapers and journals who proved to be the one closest to my own heart, but rather the lad before me, with close-cut hair, his good looks almost lost, and wearing a tattered padded coat.

Maya was happy. I was seeing our Maya happy, so what else was needed? Pavel was at peace with his conscience. He had done what he thought necessary. Thereupon followed arrest, jail, trial, and deportation. But here he was in exile and not in a prison camp. He was working as a machinist-electrician at the mines. People treated him well. A woman he loved was with him. And a baby—how he would bend tenderly over that little bundle and get me to repeat incessantly: "Yes, Larka is beautiful."

I ironed the beautiful baby's diapers. We ate something or other. We talked endlessly; I told stories and asked questions. We got on amazingly well. All three of us together, and the following day just the two of us, after Pavel had left for work and Maya and I were left alone.

I hadn't felt that good in my heart for a long while. Soviet exile is the best in the world!

For forty-eight hours not a hitch, not a moment of discomfort or awkwardness. "Why do they need me?" The feeling that I had flown to them with was utterly gone. They need me, I thought, because of the special situation, because of the estrangement from Moscow. Frankly speaking, they had not needed me in such measure in ordinary life and I thought they probably wouldn't now. But perhaps the most important thing was that I was needed, just the way I was. Not a heroine, not a self-immolator. Perhaps they had made me up in their minds as I had them in mine.

In the middle of the cluttered hut was an English-style baby's bathtub. How clever that there was an oilskin undercloth fastened in it on which the baby could lie, and thus the mother had both hands free and could bathe it without help. And how infinitely difficult everything was: the firewood, the stove, the well, the outdoor toilet. Maya didn't whine, good girl that she was. She had completely different cares and woes.

Time to leave. Pavel had driven Maya off to feed Larka. We were waiting for the plane and chatting with two local women. They were flying to Chita and cursing Moscow a great deal: "Last year we went on vacation. Everywhere it was full of people: you couldn't get a room in a hotel, you couldn't eat in a restaurant, and at the exhibition there was nothing but pushing and shoving." When they found out that I was from Moscow, one of them said out of sympathy for me: "Now, now, Lyuda, one can live anywhere, even in Moscow . . ."

Pavel made it back for the flight departure and seated me with Dima in the cabin, and suddenly I realized: I could fly to Moscow but he couldn't. He would have been able to reconcile himself to the crush of people. No freedom. Captivity. Even though it was better than one could expect, nevertheless it was captivity.

They tried to convince me to stay longer, but the twenty-third was my mother's eightieth birthday.

Their house was smaller than it had seemed in the photos. Dima was better than expected. Once again we had sacks with us: Dima's things.

Where did those forty-eight hours disappear to? Did they just flow like water into one another? Meanwhile, I must bear them back to Moscow and Lev without losing a single one of them.

October 8, 1972

Again the airport in Chita. Again the flight to Usugli, but this time with Lev. We were flying from Vladivostok, where we both had been lecturing. For the past two and a half years: Maya's illness, her arrival with Larka in Moscow; and we kept drifting apart, the kilometers between us becoming not 6,000 but 60,000, 600,000 . . . And once again the question: why were we flying there? We didn't receive a reply to the telegram we sent from Vladivostok. On the field stood a motorcycle, but someone else's. No one was there to meet us. Lev telephoned the post office. They replied: "Pavel Mikhailovich was here yesterday and received your telegram only in the evening. He's expecting you. Don't be annoyed; after all, these are the backwoods here."

They came riding up on the motorcycle; we embraced and fussed over one another. Once again our time was restricted.

Soon, everything developed according to the laws of a fairy tale! Maya was defending some date or other in the history of Russia, the end of the Tatar yoke.

"The fifteenth century."

"No, Papa, the fourteenth."

"No, the fifteenth."

Pavel said sternly: "Maya, don't you dare contradict my father-in-law."

Laughter and conciliatory silence. We were basking in the joy of togetherness. We would become engrossed, shake ourselves in surprise and plunge in once more. For a second I would suddenly have a premonition: Moscow, everyday life, disagreements, quarrels—and then I would dismiss it all.

In their house the disposition of the closetlike rooms was different after being repaired. We were allotted the only sofa. True, they did not let us go to sleep, even though it was late.

We brought them a new book of verses by David Samoilov.

Both of them looked bad, pinched, pale.

We talked about what the meaning of "sacrifice" was and about the new emigration, about their friends and ours, and about relatives. Most of all we talked about Russia.

The winters there were without snow; the weather was intensely cold, and the winds would blow away all the snow. It turned out that the bitterest day for them during their entire exile was when they woke up once and saw that Usugli lay under snow. For a whole day and night the snow piled up. They became inconsolable. They had the physical sensation of how badly they needed Russian snow.

We even went to the housewarming party of one of their friends there. We drank homebrew, sang, and danced, with Maya holding Larka in her arms. I saw that they were respected and that they were their own people there. They weren't condescending to the local people, they didn't preach, they were living there and had done so for four years and a bit. And perhaps, who knows, they might not have been the worst years of their lives.

Maya and Pavel frequently uttered the same words, as though they had already celebrated their silver anniversary. Considering what they had been through, they *had* celebrated it.

They talked about the future as well, about the reunion in Moscow; but they did so distantly, superstitiously, avoiding the topic.

Me: "Now we'll tell you something solemn: there was a Czech at our house, he saw Pavel's photograph, he had tears in his eyes and he said: 'Thanks only to these young people, *all* Czechs do not hate *all* Russians.'"

There had been only seven of them. I had cried over that four years ago. But there had been a demonstration on Red Square, and that was a joy and a tiny ray of hope—for us, for the Czechs, and for everyone.

Maya and Pavel had to consider how to live from then on, both in the elevated sense of being (how not to come down from this height), as well as in the sense of everyday life, work, apartment, registration card, Larka . . .

Pavel's boss, who had been drinking, came to them and told them how before they moved into this house, he himself had installed the bugging equipment, but he had put it on the wrong frequency and it hadn't worked for four months. That was typically Russian: the bad implementation of bad laws.

Maya asked him: "And did they pay you?"

He replied: "Of course. They gave me twenty-five rubles, but it was filthy money. I didn't take it back to my family, we drank it up instead."

December 2, 1972

The large Litvinov apartment on the Frunzenskaya Esplanade had trouble accommodating that many people, forty, or so it seemed. The celebration, the ritual, the confirmed joy. A crowd of people, a full table, tasty food, a lot of drink and music.

The return of a hero. The return of heroes.

By chance they sat down on the sofa at the set table exactly the way they had sat at Lobnoye Mesto: Natalya Gorbanevskaya, Konstantin Babitsky, Vadim Delone, Pavel Litvinov. Three were absent for respectable reasons: Larisa (she was now married to Marchenko) was in the hospital, Fainberg was in a psychiatric prison, and Vladimir Dremlyuga was spending a second term in a prison camp.

Four of them here. They were reunited and they embraced. They had done it. They had survived the punishment. Now they were free, and they were still young.

Alik Ginzburg and Pavel had last seen each other on January 21, 1967, when Alik was arrested. And Pavel Litvinov's public life had begun. He spoke openly about the summonses to the Lubyanka, and during the Ginzburg-Galanskov* trial Pavel and Larisa had given

---

* Aleksandr Ginzburg had compiled a "white book" of statements and petitions, both Soviet and foreign, about the Siniavsky-Daniel trial. Yuri Galanskov had compiled a *samizdat* magazine.

foreign correspondents a statement to world intellectuals, and in August there had been Red Square.

Pavel and Alik were touching one another as though they were testing to see whether in fact they were merely dreaming it, just as they had dreamt all of this for those long years. No, it was actual fact. In his white shirt, Pavel looked very good again.

Galich sang to them. He sang to them and about them.

They remembered Galanskov, who had just died in the camp. Pavel ran into the bathroom and wept. Alik tried to console him, and they were both weeping.

The joy of meeting, the grief of meeting, the wine, the songs— everything together.

Dina Kaminskaya came in. She had been Pavel's defense counsel at that particular trial (as at many others). She cried: "They're sitting exactly the same as they were then!" Someone said: "How beautiful they are." Dina replied passionately: "If you could have seen what beautiful people they were at the trial!"

They drank to those who were in prison. They drank, without clinking their glasses, to the dead. Gorbanevskaya offered a toast to Fainberg. She herself had been in the Kazan insane asylum.

Pavel's mother, Flora, grown younger and even more attractive: "Let us drink to our friends, to those without whom it would have been difficult to bear these years." We drank, ate, and listened to Galich.

The songs filled the room. An image from a poem by Natalya Gorbanevskaya was still echoing inside me:

> But the Cathedral of the Holy Veil
> Unfolds its wings over my back.

I knew that each of these people—Gorbanevskaya, Babitsky, Delone, Litvinov, and Ginzburg—each had his or her own life, and in each life, as in every life, everything was intertwined, the lofty with the base. There were things that seemed confused, petty, infinitely alien, and simply mundane to me.

Even on that solemn day I caught snatches of ordinary conversations from a Moscow apartment of the 1970s:

"Nadya has a poncho."

"When is Arina expecting?"

"Lara has something wrong with her kidneys."

"Girls, where can I get some slacks?"

But on that day I was seeing all of them in a different dimension. At the trial Delone had said: "I was free for three minutes on Red Square. For those three minutes I was prepared to be in jail for three years." In that handsome boy that day I saw those culminating three minutes.

The spirit of emigration is a type of attitude that is created within a small group that is surrounded by an alien or even hostile world. When natural ties have been broken, what is of secondary importance unwittingly replaces what is primary.

Among them there was more of what is called the spirit of emigration than in other societies and fraternities. It was understandable: they were few in number, they were embattled, and an inner decay had set in. Like all of us, they already knew that their imprisoned friend Pyotr* had begun to name names, to betray his comrades . . . All that could not help but provoke disagreements, quarrels, disharmony, and schisms. There would be more of that to come rather than less.

Even earlier I had asked myself: what can save me from this spirit of emigration?

If there were no recourse to mighty examples—it was impossible to demand of ordinary people that they be like Nabokov or like Berdiaev, who had broken away from what was devouring and what had devoured the life of their comrades in emigration. They had broken away and had embodied their experience in word and thought.

But what would save the ordinary people?

They would be saved by that inner lucidity, by that clarity of the soul that was capable of resisting whatever circumstances. No, that's not so. The fact is that one should not resist anything, but in a natural fashion, like breathing, go on living one's life, without any dependence on external circumstances. That's how it is with good people, that's how it was with Frida Vigdorova and some other friends. Complete absorption in whatever job can save you. But the majority of young people who had gathered here either hadn't found time to find work or they had been dismissed. You can be saved by a preoccupation, one

* Pyotr Yakir (1932–1982), son of a Soviet general who was shot in 1937. Pyotr himself, as a "son of an enemy of the people," spent years in prisons and camps. At the time of the early thaw, he was very active in the human rights movement. After his arrest in 1972, he repented and spoke on television.

that is total, in your microworld, by the concern over children, over a loved one, over grandchildren, friends, and parents. You can be saved by an unceasing activity that simply doesn't leave time for self-absorption.

All the same, the main thing is your inner spiritual state, the kingdom of heaven within you. Otherwise they will be lost. You will be lost. We will be lost.

We were talking with Evgenii Aleksandrovich Gnedin. A clear, wrinkle-free face and clever, kind eyes. Seventy years old. The Ministry of Foreign Affairs under Maksim Litvinov. He was arrested in 1939. He was beaten in Beria's office. The most terrible jail, Sukhanovka. Prison camp.*

I said to him uncertainly: "If humanity doesn't perish, then in the textbooks of Russian history of the twentieth century they'll write first of all about Red Square."

Gnedin supported me: "In my life, which has not been bereft of events, there has never been a more solemn day, and you are right, a more historical one."

> But the Cathedral of the Holy Veil
> Unfolds its wings over my back.

The drawn-out vowels. A drawn-out tragic history. Barma, Postnik.† Blinding. The *streltsy*. The Lobnoye Mesto. Minin and Pozharsky.‡ Lenin's funeral.

We are rarely conscious of the fact that we are living in history. We are immersed in the stream of everyday.

These seven were no exception. I don't know in which of these the deed was equal to his or her character and soul, or proportionate to the person as a whole. No, I was not seeing angels there. They were people. Ordinary sinners. And why are we talking about the young people? What about us?

Both then and now many ask why they went. Would it really change anything? And what were the ideas they had gone with? What

---

* Gnedin gave an account of his life in the book *Catastrophe and Second Birth* (Amsterdam: Herzen Foundation, 1977) and *Coming Out of the Labyrinth* (published in Russian, New York: Chalidze Publications, 1982).

† Barma and Postnik—the builders of Saint Basil's Cathedral on Red Square. According to legend, they were blinded by the order of Ivan the Terrible.

‡ Minin and Pozharsky headed the Russian resistance to Polish invaders in the sixteenth century.

did they want, what were they opposing, what were the slogans? What if suddenly people had joined them?

In order to justify their own inactivity, and for many other reasons, people said a lot of bad things about Pavel and his comrades. Youthful sins were enumerated against them: one drank, the other played the horses, the third was unscrupulous in his love affairs . . .

When they set out, I was writing about Martin Luther King. Now, four years later, I am writing about John Brown. In 1859 twenty-two men (seventeen whites and five blacks) penetrated into the heart of the slaveholding South, seized the arsenal at Harpers Ferry, and held it for almost forty-eight hours. Six of them, with John Brown at their head, were hanged. And many asked: why did they go? Did they really hope to change something?

A year and a half after Harpers Ferry, the Civil War began in the United States and the soldiers of the Northern armies sang:

> *John Brown's body lies a-mouldering in the grave,*
> *His soul goes marching on.*

After the demonstration in Red Square, an entire era had passed. In Czechoslovakia there was the "normalization," although the Prague spring is not forgotten. A generation of boys and girls has grown up who don't know that seven people went forth in Moscow and made a peaceful demonstration on behalf of them, the Czechs, themselves, and Russia.

Yes, in practical terms they achieved nothing other than punishment for themselves, a punishment that endures.

Anatolii Yakobson, their friend and adherent, quoted the words of Leo Tolstoy in his open letter in connection with the demonstration: "The arguments about what might generally be the result for the world from one action or another of ours cannot serve as guidance for our actions and our activity. Man has been given a different and unquestionable guide: the guidance of his conscience, following which he unquestionably knows that he is doing what must be done."

Besides the purpose, before the purpose, there is the meaning. Predestination. They heard a voice, they fulfilled what had been inscribed for them at birth. And that is not often given to people.

These seven ordinary, sinful people committed a great act.

Those seven were not about to wait for the stars. And they weren't about to ask: "What are the gifts of freedom for the crowd? What is freedom for those who hurried on their way shopping, who hooted, who joined the chastisers?"

They went forth. And sowed the seeds. We won't live to see the harvest. I don't know whether they will. But the seeds are sown.

Perhaps at some date a monument will be erected on Red Square to those who rose up against dishonor.

XXXII

"After I'm Dead..."

The fall of 1965. Abram Aleksandrovich Belkin was sitting in our room and reading my recollections of Frida Vigdorova. He raised his head. "Are you going to write about me?"

I was silent. He took in the silence. "I understand. After I'm dead, right?"

I came for the first time to Belkin's place on New Year's Eve, 1957. There were a lot of guests. We were having a good time in the one room, but we felt awkward about going into the adjacent room. It was like a museum. Almost six years had passed since the death of his wife, but all of her things still lay there as though she were still alive. Her photographs were on the walls and the desk.

You enter into friendship with some people in a leap. Then there are those with whom friendship has to be learned, just as it is necessary to learn how to read unfamiliar books. Abram Aleksandrovich, for all his voracious interest in people, for all his affability, was an extremely selective person. It was with difficulty that he admitted people into his soul, and one had to learn friendship with him, overcoming resistance. Both his and my own.

In a relatively short time he became Boba to me and not Abram Aleksandrovich. Boba Belkin. It seemed strange to call a grown man Boba. The name had a childish and somewhat ridiculous ring to it.

He was small in stature, not handsome, but that was forgotten in the first minutes of acquaintance: he radiated such charm with his sharp mind, talent, and inherent goodness.

At the special memorial evening at the Moscow Art Theater, the actor Monukov described Belkin's kindness as "furious" and his intellect as "an assembler of thoughts and feelings, that lived not only in him and for him, but also inspired others as well."

He was given to intricate old-fashioned rituals. Once we were on the way to his place on an ordinary day. Lev stopped by a flower vendor.

"Flowers for a man?" I asked in amazement. I learned how to do that, to bring flowers to a man without any pretext. He loved beautiful things and presents a great deal.

He found it increasingly difficult to put up with large gatherings of people and he almost ceased, for all his tender love toward Lev, to visit our noisy home, but asked us to come to him.

At home, he arranged his guests the way the Japanese arrange bouquets. There ought not to be any incidental people present. It was also important that the people gathered there should suit one another, should "rhyme" as he would express it.

Every time he invited someone, he would ask: "Are you acquainted?" Or "What are your relations with Oksman? With Belinkov? With Zamansky? With Shitova? With Sinyavsky?"

"Why is it that you write me with increasing tenderness and affection," Belkin wrote, "yet we see each other with increasing rarity, chance, and insignificance. We ought to discuss it." (September 9, 1965.)

Even then, I realized that we saw people whom we needed much less and who needed us much less than he did. We saw them simply because they were more demanding; they would come without calling because they lived close by or would insist on inviting us to their places. And without any reasons as well.

Belkin's passionate love was nineteenth-century Russian literature. At the evening already mentioned, V. Zamansky said: "He considered himself to be among relatives in Russian literature."

He told his small circle of friends about his new researches: he read on his own "The House with the Attic" and "The Student" by Chekhov, Pushkin's "Mozart and Salieri," "The Legend of the Grand Inquisitor" from *The Brothers Karamazov*. Such readings were a special ritual. Long beforehand, he invited the participants to arrive at an exact time. To be late was a mortal sin. No chatter, no idle talk. We immediately came to the main topic; all made notes. After his readings, a discussion, sometimes a heated one.

Each time the reading of his work was presented with increasing pomp. At first I inwardly opposed it, until I understood that there was not the least vanity in it. It was simply that he had a very serious, almost religious regard for what he was involved in: Pushkin, Chekhov, Dostoyevsky, Tiutchev. His attitude was serious toward our work as well, the work of the researcher, critic, and interpreter.

During the time of the campaign against cosmopolitanism in 1949, Belkin had turned out to be a victim: he had been defamed at a meeting and then driven from the university. The students had taken a hand in it as well.

There was a pride, long scorned, in his passion for pompous reading. They had tried to trample the man underfoot, but he had not let them succeed, he hadn't allowed himself to be humiliated. He had kept his soul. And here he was now, standing erect, liberated, or rather freeing himself before our very eyes in this same room.

He needed not only again and again to prove his own understanding of the classics, he needed not only the moral victory over dark forces but the solution of an intellectual problem.

It was essential for Belkin to get to the heart of the matter, to understand why the talented young student Y., subsequently the author of fine books, had acted in such a fashion at that time. It was essential not simply for the reason that he had become a victim himself, but because within him dwelled a constant need to be aware of the paradoxical entanglements of good and evil in the depths of the human soul. His attraction to Dostoyevsky was by no means accidental.

Dismissed from the university, Belkin was fortunately hired shortly afterward to work at the encyclopedia and at the Moscow Art Theater school. There he remained until his death.

I was listening to his lecture at the Moscow Art Theater school (September 1965). He was beginning to quote Dostoyevsky's famous words about the difference between honesty (a truthfulness to one's convictions) and morality (the truthfulness of the convictions themselves): "Thirty years ago I was convinced that Stalin would lead us to harmony. And I acted in accordance. Was I being moral?"

He turned to the audience and asked them to vote. The audience voted "Yes, you were."

"No, because my convictions were wrong and I did not verify them."

Belkin did not hide himself behind the circumstances. He demanded responsibility first of all from himself.

The thirteen years of my friendship with him, from 1957 to 1970, represented an important time for Belkin; they were the years of an abrupt inner break. The process was a painful experience for him as it was for many of us.

It was difficult for him to part ways with his earlier beliefs. He was afraid of being left in the wilderness. He didn't want to cross out the life he had lived. But his characteristic intellectual honesty and his striving for the truth did not leave any room for turning back. He could not forget, he could not and did not want to pretend, even privately and just for himself, that everything remained as before.

The profound spiritual shock that he had experienced was evident in every lecture he gave, in every line he wrote. For him, as for many other writers and nonwriters, that shock was personified in Aleksandr Solzhenitsyn and his work. Belkin thought about him a great deal and asked questions. It turned out that Solzhenitsyn himself recalled how he had been tested before the war by Belkin on nineteenth-century Russian literature.

It wasn't with simple politeness but rather with affection that Solzhenitsyn responded to the letter that was passed on to him from Abram Aleksandrovich. Solzhenitsyn was particularly interested in Belkin's study of Tolstoy's folk tales. Solzhenitsyn was thinking about "how to extricate prose from all literary conventions, to make it accessible to a person who was not overly literate, and to put it into the simplest sentences, almost without adjectives, indirect objects, enumerations, and interpolated phrases (something like Tolstoy's 'A Prisoner of the Caucasus') and to present a great deal within a small scope. That is, a prose that, crudely speaking, is anti–late-Bunin."

Belkin wrote to us from Shchelykovo (July 7, 1963): "Here I am reading Leskov. I haven't read him just *for myself* for a long time, and generally I never did read a great deal of him. The devil only knows how much I haven't read that is beautiful.

"Take for instance the story 'The Immortal Golovan.' After Solzhenitsyn now I keep bumping into the theme of devoutness everywhere. Perhaps Aleksandr Isaevich doesn't suspect that the topic of devoutness is possibly the most important, albeit the vaguest, in the world, both in his story and generally in literature and particularly in our time."

In Leskov the author and his grandmother are chatting about the amazing fellow Golovan and the woman he loves.

"But after all because of him they deprived themselves of all happiness!"

"Yes, but then what does happiness presuppose: there is a devout happiness and there is a sinful happiness. A devout happiness doesn't transgress against anyone, whereas the sinful transgresses against everything. It was the former one that they loved rather than the latter . . ."

"Grandmother," I exclaimed. "But those are amazing people!"

"Devout people, my friend," the old woman replied.

Belkin was constantly surrounded by students and took responsibility for the fate of each of them. He could not allow himself to abandon them in a wasteland of skepticism.

He could not play the hypocrite. By the very makeup of his life he was obliged to discover truth, not simply in the depths of his soul and not simply for himself. He sought those truths that he could share with his students. He sought them and found them in the books of the great Russian writers.

He knew how to fall in love with people. Arkadii Belinkov naturally appeared among his impetuous passions as well. Belkin was generous in his delight over Belinkov's talent and for a short time he was close to him, although more frequently they argued furiously. His attitude to writers was diametrically opposed to that of Belinkov. For Belkin the Russian classics never became a means for allegory, a means for achieving extraliterary ends.

It was with relative indifference that I read what Belkin wrote for publication; but I invariably felt myself being enriched when I listened to him.

No omniscience, no absolute truths. The constant intonation of a question: shall we try this, perhaps we have the most fruitful road here? He always gave reference to his precursors. He would introduce proofs against himself, against a mounting conception. Frequently he would provoke and perplex his audience, he would try to antagonize them, even to bewilder them and lead them along a false trail.

His games were not always harmless. At times he would gain pleasure from the mistakes of others! "Aha, I've got you!" And that included the mistakes of friends. Perhaps that was the mentality of the encyclopedia, where he had worked for almost twenty years, but that mentality did coincide with his own specific character.

His examinations were terrible—one of the graduates remembered

—"not only your knowledge was tested. There was another test: to prove what you were worth."

Sometimes he was stern and captious at examinations, even at times to a fault and unjustly. Once a young girl came to an examination at the studio of the Moscow Art Theater wearing a plunging neckline, and Belkin, a Victorian, became angry. Even though she was well prepared, he drove her into a corner and only gave her a fair grade, on purpose.

The unique quality of his pedagogical and lecturer's charm was based on immediate rejoinder, on instantaneous response. At the intersection of his own conjectures and discoveries, and the reaction of his audience, a unique and new understanding of a classic was born. Dialogue entered into the very substance of his method of research.

He discovered new things in those books that seemed to have been well known for a long time. In works that everyone knew from childhood, like "The House with the Attic," "The Student," and "Mozart and Salieri," he uncovered things that were unknown and unexpected.

All of these journeys became possible because he was cleansing his soul and freeing himself from the burden of the past.

Belkin knew how to appreciate Pushkin and Chekhov better than anyone. But he himself was also standing there alongside. Moreover, in every analysis one could find evidence of Abram Belkin's personality that reflected his difficult path, his experience, and a personal fate that resembled the fates of others and yet at the same time was unique. That was not manifested in autobiographical digressions (there are practically none of those) but rather in his very approach to old books. It might have been at the surface because he, like all of us, had been obliged over and over again to resolve the eternal question of the correspondence between means and ends, and that is why his analysis of "The Legend of the Grand Inquisitor" had such a powerful ring to it.

A profound lyrical quality often existed in his analysis as well, namely, in his incomplete work on Tiutchev, which, unfortunately, was not recorded on tape. In this work he practically avoids social problems and speaks about life and death, tragedy and the absurd.

> Take courage, friends, be diligent in struggle,
> Though the battle be unequal, the fight hopeless.

I was not one of his students. But Belkin's analyses were instructive in the most elementary and practical sense of the word. In criticism it had been the word, the very flesh of prose, that had specifically attracted me for a long time. But I had no experience whatsoever, and it seemed impossible to begin learning so late. Yet listening to him I understood that it was possible.

For what little that I did during those years in my analyses of American literature, I am indebted also to Abram Aleksandrovich.

Belkin read chapters out of the autobiographical books that both Lev and I began writing at that time. He criticized them sternly. To me he said: "What you're writing is brave. Brave in our social sense. But somewhat simplistic. You are afraid to peer beyond the final, beyond the main boundary. And it is truly very frightening to peer there, into chaos." These same motifs were echoes in his work on Tiutchev.

He was reading every one of our publications and most often was the first one to ring us up. Insincere compliments were alien to him. He would be malicious and angry in poking fun at banalities. Naturally, we made presents of our books to him, and they are all marked up with notations. This was the fruit of reading by a creative person who loved his friends with a demanding love: he wanted them to strive for perfection even though it was unobtainable.

He was jealous, at times childishly and ridiculously so. He loved Lev with a furious love and spoke out as a witness for the defense at Lev's trial in 1947.* At that time this kind of act demanded enormous courage, for every witness for the defense could find himself transferred to the defendants' bench at any moment. I don't know which of his young students he cultivated so constantly and yet so inconclusively as his old friend, that balding, graying, and bearded man.

Boba wrote threatening and reproachful letters and notes. Here is one of them.

Levushka!

I understand that you will subsequently be distressed because of my criticism and will even accept it in part. I beg you, do be distressed and accept it in part.

Understand, there are situations wherein people of a *historical* cast, like yourself, experience in a specific fashion the following: *talent* is dis-

---

* Lev had been tried for "compassion for the enemy"—he was against robbing and raping. See *To Be Preserved Forever* (Philadelphia: Lippincott, 1977).

torted by *frivolousness,* while *syntheticism* and diversity are distorted by *dispersal.*

That is what I do not want in you.

For I love you a great deal and am envious when people can think ill of you.

Boba

P.S. I wish to have genuine criticism of myself from you as well.

February 10, 1968, was Boba's birthday. That day was observed with a new work, "Dostoyevsky and Einstein."

The trial of Ginzburg and Galanskov had finished. Lev had written a letter of protest, and read his letter during the celebration at Boba's. Boba was profoundly excited. "I fear ever more for you than usual. And I am proud of the fact that I am your friend. But to act as you are doing, that I cannot do."

Belkin did not want to address the government with any petitions whatsoever, be they collective or personal ones. His world view was gloomier and more skeptical. Naturally, he was also afraid.

Hope rang in Lev's letters and in all of Lev's activities. But Belkin had no hopes.

He did not wish for upsets in his life. That would contradict a nature that was profoundly conservative and hungrily longing for stability.

He was approaching his seventh decade. There had been the school of the Moscow Art Theater, and the theater for him was not simply a spectacle, it was not simply one of the arts—the theater was a constant desire of the soul.

There were the students. There was the work at the encyclopedia. The encyclopedia had been one of the possibilities for realizing himself, however small that might have been. And there was the possibility—in a peculiar way—of preserving a great culture. To pass on a baton. I would like some Slavist to compare the section on the Russian classics in the first and second editions of the *Great Soviet Encyclopedia.* Real progress was made, thanks to time, but also because of Abram Belkin.

There had been the lectures in museums, consultations for performances in theaters. The feeling had grown: "You are needed."

There had been the familiar "security" (it's not by chance that there is no precise Russian equivalent for this English word of many meanings, and thus is expressed the deep differences between countries). Who of us can consider himself "secure," even for a short while? However, Belkin did not want to lose his relative security.

Various people are still striving by various paths to save Humanity. At least to save Russia. But Belkin, like many of his contemporaries, believed that it was possible only to save one's own island: "Doesn't it really seem to you there that all we have left are nature, love for our dear ones, and the theory of petty deeds?" He wrote that to us while we were staying in Yalta (October 13, 1967).

Many of us lived and continue to live on islands without realizing it at times. Zhukovka (this is where I am writing)—a table made of planks, the greenery scorched from the unbearable heat of the summer of 1972—is also an island. The city brings the noise of waves each time; that hour is nigh when the waves will drown my island.

He never concealed in the least that he wanted other people to always like him. He knew how to be attentive himself and he was painfully hurt by lack of attention, both in serious and frivolous matters.

There was nothing of old age in him. "You have to be friends with young people so that your heart won't grow weary," he once said. And it was not egotism that made him say it. He died, but youth has remained in his home. And we, his friends, together with his wife, decided that it must continue—once a month there would be Belkin readings. His friends would speak about what they were now working on.

I sat down in the large armchair with the carved back (earlier only the host used to sit in it). The honor of beginning these readings had fallen to me, and I was supposed to talk about Salinger's *The Catcher in the Rye*. But before doing so, a word of gratitude to the Teacher. Homage to ritual? No. A profound inner necessity.

His former students and their friends and friends of the friends, as well as strangers, gather here by the "fire."

I believe in the spirit of the house. His spirit lives on in these two small rooms. His radiance continues.

But time marches on. Another person is sitting in his place at the encyclopedia. A different teacher is lecturing on Russian literature in the school of the Moscow Art Theater. In his close friends the wounds of loss have begun to heal. But the feeling of his irreplaceability cannot disappear.

Abram Belkin had not been a mutineer, had not been a dissident, had not been a devout person. He had been an honest Russian intellectual. Thanks to people like him, Russian culture has been, is, and will be . . .

XXXIII

A Precursor

1972–1973

In April 1961 we made the acquaintance of Arkadii Belinkov—we were together at the Writers' House in Maleyevka, near Moscow.

The face was one of those that one encounters not on the streets of Moscow but rather in the rooms of Leningrad's Hermitage Museum in the paintings of the old Italian or Spanish masters. His pallor contrasted sharply with the darkness of the room. Later I understood—it was the pallor of illness. He could have been either sixty or forty years old.

He was in a semireclining position (I don't recall any rocking chairs in Maleyevka; it was neither a chair nor a bed, but rather something that was curiously sloping). He was covered with a checkered rug. He was almost immobile; only his narrow dark eyes would flare up, grow dim, and cast lightning bolts. His hands moved from time to time, hands with long fingers, the cultivated hands of a gentleman. It was difficult to imagine that these hands had held a spade, a pick, and a tin basin. In general, I couldn't imagine Arkadii in a prison camp, in a prison transport, or on plank beds. On the other hand, it seemed to me that he would have fit nicely into social drawing rooms, artistic cafés, and special clubs.

He held forth slowly and languidly without allowing himself to be interrupted. Alongside him, in his presence, I had a gnawing feeling of our plebeianism. By some signal or other, he made it known that he was exhausted and that the audience was concluded. His wife, Natasha, translated the signals into ordinary language.

The lordliness of Arkadii's behavior might have seemed ridiculous. But much more powerful was the fact that the man had been in prison for twelve years! And he was the author of a talented book on Yuri Tynyanov, one of the founders of Russian formalism and a gifted novelist.

My impression from that first meeting was not simply that of the magnetism of talent, but the radiation of a powerful personality as well. Herzen called it a "demonic magnetism." From the beginning I was attracted to Arkadii.

Belinkov did for criticism what Solzhenitsyn had done for all of spiritual life: he set it free. He showed that it was possible to work differently. We read his book on Tynyanov while it was still in manuscript form and thought: this is how one must try to write about literature.

During the brief thaw of the 1960s, Belinkov enjoyed a resounding success: the publication and republication of his book on Tynyanov, a triumphant reception into the Writers' Union, ecstatic reviews in the press. Viktor Shklovsky's review of Belinkov's book on Tynyanov in *Literaturnaya gazeta* was entitled "Talented!"

When candidates from among the literary critics were being proposed for Lenin Prizes in 1962 I suggested Belinkov's book: "We are all of like mind that the prize should be awarded to the work of the grand old man of our profession, Kornei Ivanovich Chukovsky, for his work *The Mastery of Nekrasov*, the result of long years of work. But why not use the prize to anticipate a literary biography when the beginning has been so brilliant?"

Now, less than ten years later, it all sounds wild: the *Lenin* Prize to Belinkov?—just as, incidentally, a Lenin Prize for Solzhenitsyn's *One Day in the Life of Ivan Denisovich* sounds wild. But that was the thaw, the beginning of liberation, thousands of people had just exited from behind the gates of prison camps and jails, hundreds of thousands had shattered the jails in their souls. And an unimaginable confusion of the most elementary concepts.

By Soviet standards, Belinkov prospered: he received an apartment from the Writers' Union. A third edition of his book *Tynyanov* was being prepared—an almost unprecedented occurrence in our literary criticism. He was allowed to go abroad twice.

Evgenia Knipovich, an official critic closely tied with the literary authorities, was also the editor of the book on Tynyanov and called Arkadii and Natasha "my children."

We never became real friends with Arkadii although the inscriptions on two of his books that he presented to us were quite enthusiastic. We met only a few times.

But we did publicize his book on Tynyanov, emphasizing our enthusiasm for it. We tried to convince and did convince our friends in the Art Publishing House to draw up a contract for his second book, on Yuri Olesha, one of the brilliant writers of the twenties and the author of the novel *Envy*. When the assistant editor at the publishing house had read a hundred pages, he recoiled—the book could not pass the censorship. I set about noting the necessary cuts and obtaining Belinkov's permission. Lev managed to persuade them to pay sixty percent in advance to the author. The momentum of the thaw was still operating. There were many who still wanted to support, by whatever means, a person who had come back from the prison camps, particularly if the intercessor was also an ex-convict.

Whenever I was near Arkadii, I kept experiencing the radiation of his talent. The strength of his resentment was overwhelming. But it became increasingly difficult for me to endure that saturated solution of hatred.

Such literary figures as Tvardovsky and Vsevolod Kochetov, one the editor of *Novy mir*, and the other the editor of *Oktiabr* (October) and a Stalinist, meant something quite different to me. Belinkov said he would hang both of them from the same tree.

We began to argue. Then for the first time I felt the abyss that separated us. That feeling persisted until the end.

At first I was amazed when I found out that those close to Yuri Tynyanov (in particular his wife and Venyamin Kaverin) did not accept a great deal in Belinkov's book. I understood them when I read the manuscript of the work on Olesha. In that work it became manifestly apparent that the woeful, and in many respects tragic, life of Olesha had served as a means, as the building material, for a denunciation of the Soviet intelligentsia, which Belinkov was accusing of betrayal.

As a rule, Belinkov did not make up his facts. Olesha, like the majority of his contemporaries, strove to conform to law and order. It is very important to remember this and underline it today, when over and over again (and by far not only the supporters of authority, but its irreconcilable opponents as well) people are trying for the umpteenth time to willfully rewrite our history.

In his best novel, *Envy*, Olesha recorded the inferiority complex that was so characteristic of the Soviet intellectual in the 1920s and that had been so successfully implanted from above. He recorded it in the character of Kavalerov, who provoked contempt in some and a compassionate perplexity in others.

Now having reread *Envy*, neither Mandelstam nor Bulgakov appear to me as real prototypes for Kavalerov, but those kinds of association did occur to Olesha's contemporaries.

Olesha wanted to be in step with everyone after he himself experienced the prosecution, harassment, and doubts over his talent. In 1936 he wrote: "I read in the newspaper *Pravda* that Shostakovich's opera is 'a muddle instead of music.' *Pravda* said that. What am I supposed to do about my attitude toward Shostakovich? In the life and activity of our state there are no policies that emerge and operate independently . . . If I do not agree with this policy in some particular aspect or other, then the entire complicated design of life that I think and write about will collapse personally for me: I must cease to like what I find so charming. For example, the fact that a young worker* in a single night revolutionized the operation of extracting coal and became world famous . . . or the fact that Stalin's replies to the American journalist Roy Howard are being quoted with enthusiastic respect by the newspapers of the entire world . . . And for that reason I agree and say that in this particular phase of art, the Party, as in everything, is right . . . [These words are read today by young people. They laugh. They scorn Olesha. Now I think: could someone justify nowadays the exile of Sakharov with similar proofs? I think not.] From these positions I begin to think about the music of Shostakovich. I continue to like it as before. But I remember: in certain places the music always seemed to be condescending . . . This condescension toward the 'unwashed' gives birth to several peculiarities in the music of Shostakovich: moments of unclarity and capriciousness, which only he finds necessary and which disparage us. It is these caprices that are born of condescension that in *Pravda* are called a 'muddle' and an 'affectation.' The melody is the best that an artist can extract from the world. I beg for melody from Shostakovich; he breaks it for whatever unknown reasons, and that is disparaging toward me . . . Comrades, reading the article in *Pravda*, I had the thought that Leo Tolstoy would have signed his name under such an article." (*Literaturnaya gazeta*, March 20, 1936.)

* Stakhanov. See p. 70.

Margarita Aliger, a poet of the next generation, recalled this speech by Olesha at a discussion on formalism. She had just been admitted to the Writers' Union. There before her stood the author of *Envy*. According to her recollections (indeed, from the tone of what was printed), Olesha was conducting an argument with himself. He set the questions and refuted his first responses.

Reading Belinkov and remembering his book, I keep trying to defend Olesha before Belinkov. But why do I feel less sorry for those many readers—among them the intellectuals of subsequent generations, as well as myself—whom the sensitive, talented, and sophisticated Olesha forced to believe, if only partially, in what neither the Party writers nor the authorities of the past, even Gorky, could force us to believe in?

After reading Boris Yampolsky's essay in the émigré journal *Kontinent*, published in Paris, I understood more clearly what was lacking in Belinkov: the tragedy of Olesha was presented by Yampolsky as a genuine tragedy.

In these recollections there is no direct argument with Belinkov about Olesha. What Yampolsky has written compares with what Belinkov has written the way a tragic portrait with the many layers that are essentially inherent in a large painting compares with a one-dimensional grotesque representation.

But then criticism is literature, too, only not about people but about books. It means that in criticism there can also be both satire and the grotesque. The simple truth is that Swift and Shchedrin are alien to me. I do not reread these writers, and that is my blind spot, my waywardness. It is a fact of my human biography as a reader. For that reason also, Belinkov is alien to me.

When he began to write as a critic, there was still no contemporary Russian prose that was adequate for his critical method. I try imagining to myself how he might have written about *The Yawning Heights* and how essential that book would have proved to him, along with the entire work of Aleksandr Zinoviev. And probably Vladimir Voinovich's *Chonkin*. And *Moscow-Cockerels* by Venyamin Yerofeyev.

Arkadii started a book about Akhmatova. More than a hundred pages had been written. But it didn't work for him. The critical epos and the critical ode were not his genres. He did not know how to express rapture. Overthrowing something was his particular strength.

His book on Solzhenitsyn was unfinished as well.

Early on, perhaps earlier than all the dissidents, he sensed that one not only had to write books, one had to create what in the West they call an "image" as well. In this regard he anticipated his own time.

During the trial of Daniel and Sinyavsky, rumors were circulating that Belinkov had written a most biting letter of protest. That was the way it was supposed to be—according to how he imagined himself and the way he wanted others to view him.

But no one saw the letter.

He sat at the discussions on Solzhenitsyn's novel *Cancer Ward* (November 1966) with a prepared written speech. But he did not send a request to the presidium to be heard. He did not take part in the discussion (his speech was later appended to the record that appeared abroad).

In his undelivered speech there was the sentence: "Solzhenitsyn presumed to write his books." At that time I was very much struck by the word "presumed." Belinkov himself had also presumed, but he was out of step with the times for several years. He was somewhat premature.

In the Writers' House at that time, Belinkov became acquainted with Solzhenitsyn. Earlier Belinkov had sent him his book on Tynyanov, signing it: "To the great Russian writer, Aleksandr Solzhenitsyn." In reply he received an unusually warm letter. Aleksandr Isaevich wanted to ask Belinkov about the peculiarities of the method of Dos Passos. He was preoccupied with that at the time. The "folios" of *August 1914* were either being conceived or written.

On several occasions we became convinced of the fact that Arkadii was not speaking the truth. The story about how his interrogator telephoned Yermilov (he was the "KGB expert in literary matters") right in the midst of the interrogation was related by Belinkov three times in our presence and each time in a new version.

He told the story about his years of confinement—first on death row, and when his death sentence (he had been charged with "terror") was commuted to twenty-five years, then all the time he spent at common labor.

In 1977 by chance I met an elderly woman who had been a fellow convict of his. I recorded her recollections at that time.

We learned that among the newcomers was a student from the Moscow Literary Institute. How we waited for him! After all, our contingent was from 1937 and what a long while it had been without any news from the world of books.

We surrounded him—and he was handsome, clever, and voluble. He knew all the writers by their first names and patronymics. He had even been at the houses of well-known writers.

Every evening after work there were stories. We made great efforts, and he was left with us as a medical assistant in the sick bay. He read poetry; he remembered entire chunks of prose by heart. What talent! Here you are thinking of him as a talent, but just imagine what he signified to us there behind the barbed wire! To me and my friends he brought back an entire piece of a life that had been taken away. We loved him like a son. We began to look forward to our parcels so that we could feed him.

A rift occurred between us when he treated a girl badly, a fellow convict and medical assistant. If we, the older ones, had fallen in love with him, then clearly she had done so at first glance . . .

New girls made their appearance and everything was just the same: at first he would be all sweetness, and then he would rudely reject the girl. There was nothing out of the ordinary in that even in normal life, and don't we encounter that sort of thing on the outside every step of the way? But in him they saw an extraordinary person.

His eyes and his voice are preserved in my memory. Later it didn't matter what book I opened, I would always hear Arkadii's voice.

I myself observed several of his "affairs," naturally of a different nature than in the prison camp, but the scheme remained the same: a stormy beginning, a cooling off, and then the break. And torrents of abuse and insults, and at times a quarrel over the person who had just been the object of affection.

Obviously, in any "affair" with him one could not go beyond a certain boundary. He did not forgive any deviation or what he took to be deviation. That wasn't a unique individual characteristic. How many people did Nadezhda Yakovlevna Mandelstam "excommunicate," at times over trifles.

In February 1967 we moved into a new apartment. Just before the move, Arkadii gave us his 1,000-page-long manuscript on Olesha.

It was impossible not to take it simply for the reason that we wanted to read it and, furthermore, because we couldn't hurt him by refusing. He never put himself in the day-to-day circumstances of others.

But it was impossible to read at the rate he figured. Trying to cope with this tempo was also unbelievably difficult, what with packing, moving, and setting up an apartment in the winter. Yet I was obliged to abandon the workers in the new building and amid complete havoc dash to his place in order to deliver chapter after chapter and give my opinion on what I had read.

He could also be tender, affectionate, and attentive. He was interested in other people, their manuscripts, their misfortunes, and their illnesses. Invariably he knew about health matters and was able to give extensive medical advice. He usually telephoned us when our publications appeared. But just as invariably he made me understand how great the abyss was between *his* affairs and the *insignificant* affairs of myself and the people around me. That included even those who were closest to him.

The Belinkovs celebrated New Year's in 1963 in Peredelkino at the home of friends. Natasha forgot Arkadii's manuscript on Olesha on the hall stand at the Writers' House, where they were then living. She remembered all of a sudden, ran off, and fetched it.

They sat down at the table to celebrate. Arkadii pushed a dish of olives over to his wife and said: "Eat them!" She ate them. All of them. Later it came out that she couldn't stand olives. It had been a punishment for her crime: she had dared to forget the manuscript.

I told him that Stalin's daughter, Svetlana Alliluyeva, had defected. The languidness and deliberateness of his movements disappeared instantaneously. Arkadii was seized with excitement—he shouted, rejoiced, and asked for a drink. He asked me to repeat it several times, and then he himself repeated it to everyone who came in.

At that time I thought that this vindictive joy meant: there's retribution for you from your own seed. I thought that for him Svetlana's flight was a harbinger, the beginning of the predicted and passionately awaited collapse of the system. But, in addition to that, probably at that same time, the thought was born that it was possible. It was possible for him, Arkadii Belinkov, to do the same. And his resolute will triumphed in doing so.

Two chapters from the book on Olesha, *The Poet and the Fat Man*, managed to slip into the journal *Baikal* in the spring of 1968 (these chapters even now are being copied by typewriter from the journal, as well as photocopied).

In May 1968 Arkadii Belinkov requested political asylum in the Federal Republic of Germany.

And yet, when Belinkov was gone (here I mean when he left, before he died), I felt his absence.

The emotional foundation of his talent was his hatred of Bolshevism. It was more than the foundation, it was the very material, the substance, of that talent. His books were refutations. Whether you agreed, disagreed, or partially agreed (incidentally, there was no room for "partially" with him), all the same you were refuted. It wasn't easy not to submit to the flow. He regarded himself as a messiah (he demanded that every writer be a prophet), and he cherished himself like a precious vessel. People around him were either accepted or rejected, and even his malice was unveiled in direct proportion to whether they served him, Arkadii Belinkov, and his mission on earth.

He was convinced of the fact that now thousands, hundreds of thousands, and then millions as well, would follow him, the prophet. They would follow his truth and the power of his word. In his native land he at first had been left to rot in a prison camp and they had practically killed him, and then later they had gagged him. But now in the free West everything would change. However, he was met with indifference, or rather what he took to be indifference. The people he encountered proved to have their own concerns, their own enemies, and their own goals.

Long before Solzhenitzyn, Belinkov had denounced the Western liberals for the fact that they were preparing a new Munich.

Without understanding what was happening in the West, and without trying to understand (he didn't know any foreign languages and didn't study any), Belinkov pronounced a malediction against the Western intelligentsia for their cooperation with the Soviets. He suggested that Lillian Hellman and Jean-Paul Sartre (who had never been a member) be excluded from the P.E.N. Club, as well as William Styron, and that Yuri Galanskov and Aleksandr Ginzburg, who had both served prison terms, should be admitted. And, naturally, Solzhenitsyn.

This open letter to the P.E.N. Club made the rounds in *samizdat*. It enjoyed and still enjoys a great deal of success among many of our intellectuals.

In the letter were listed the foreign writers who had been in our country and had not called for a boycott of the USSR. Foremost were Hellman and Styron, who had condemned Anatolii Kuznetsov.* In my view they had both clearly and correctly written that they were

---

* A rather gifted writer, known at the time of the thaw. Defected to England in 1969 and later said that he was a stool pigeon. Died in 1979.

condemning Kuznetsov for the price that he had paid in giving up his Soviet citizenship, that is, for making a denunciation. But Belinkov had seen something else in their letters: the statement that the bravest people wage war with evil inside their own country. In Hellman's letter, published in the New York *Times*, these people were listed: Solzhenitsyn, Grigorenko, Litvinov, Larisa Bogoraz . . . And it turned out that he, Arkadii Belinkov, was not among them.

Arkadii could not bear that. He responded with an attack: "You, following the example of Camus, believe that one shouldn't depart from a plague-infested city, so then it's even worse to pay visits to a plague-infested city." This problem, whether the well-known writers should visit the USSR or boycott it, was discussed many times by dissidents.

I never believed, for example, that the visits of Heinrich Böll to our country were a blemish on him. I have said many times and I repeat it once more: if you have relatives or friends in prison camps, you want to send them food, medicine, or simply take them to your bosom and make them feel that they are not alone. In order to get into the prison camp you have to make contact with the director of the camp, write him an application or a request. How is an honorable person to act? Preserve one's robes unstained or try and lighten the lot of others? For me the answer is one and the same. For Belinkov it was one and the same as well, but directly the opposite.

After the death of Arkadii his widow, Natalya Belinkova, put out a collection entitled *The New Bell*. (The best article in my view was Raisa Lert's "On the Charms of the Knout," directed against the praise of the reign of Nicholas I in the journal *Molodaya gvardiya* [Young Guard]. There was a feature story as well by Belinkov, unpublished during his lifetime, about how they had fled from their homeland.)

Their emigration is sometimes called a flight. So, then, it couldn't be the same for him as it was for everyone else. And if he meant flight, then it should have been flight in the etymological sense of the word—not the journey, approved by the Writers' Union, on a personal invitation to Hungary, from there to Yugoslavia, West Germany, and a request for political asylum and an airplane flight to the United States.

Belinkov believed that before 1945 two kinds of fascism existed in the world. After the defeat of Nazism one still remained. And all people of good will on the earth were obliged to join forces in their struggle against it. Those who did not do so were villains. Those who allowed themselves to become occupied with other things (protesting against the war in Vietnam, against racism in South Africa, against the killings in Pakistan), those who were dissatisfied with their own governments (American, English, German, or French), were fools or good-for-nothings. More likely scoundrels.

In the United States Belinkov became a professor at Yale University, spent time in Europe, gave lectures and interviews. But what he had expected and what he had hoped for he did not receive in the West.

Several people in his audience were disenchanted with his lectures on Soviet literature. "We came to hear about the literature of the 1920s, but the lecturer was denouncing the Soviet state." The listeners themselves either knew about the vices of the Soviet state or had no interest in them whatsoever.

At times an insufficient knowledge of the subject came to light: he could not give a correct answer to the simplest bibliographical questions.

Was his talent a superficial one? I don't believe so. His book on Tynyanov had been read by many. People hadn't simply read it—they had experienced its effect. And it wasn't difficult to discover Belinkov's "imprint" in critics who were highly talented.

His shortcomings were immediately apparent, and it was easy to uncover them. There he is, a sensitive person, understanding one of the late Pushkin poems in a very trivial fashion: "When is a 'secret freedom' attractive? When there is no open one, as this poem clearly demonstrates."

The richness of Pushkin's orchestration, his multivalency, the real necessity for Pushkin of precisely that inner freedom and those rights that he was writing about—all of that remains beyond the bounds of Belinkov's definition because it did not enter into his political conception.

It turned out that there were many factual errors in the book on Tynyanov. But for Belinkov if it didn't fit his conclusion, then "so much the worse for the facts."

Lidiya Chukovskaya supposed that Belinkov had no ear for art and that generally he should not have even concerned himself with artistic literature but only with political pamphleteering. I don't think so.

> *Thump-thump go the horses' hooves in a police state,*
> *Tut-tut says the censor to the gentlemen poets.*

The word of a critic functions like a poetic word. Not only in its thought but in its form, rhythm, and phonetics. "Thump-thump" and "tut-tut" are hard and pounding sounds. You can't miss it, you can't leaf through it obliquely.

He created the image of Tynyanov the writer. He created the collective image of the people of the 1820s, after the Decembrist Uprising, people who had been broken in two.

Belinkov's books force you to read quickly: the avalanche is descending and it's impossible to stop. But slowly the words stick and demand that you return; you want to go over them again and you absorb them like quotations.

If you were to tell him that he was the heir to the traditions of Russian revolutionary criticism under nineteenth-century censorship—to Vissarion Belinsky and Dmitri Pisarev—he would be dismayed. But in fact, it is partly so. Imprisoned passions were essential to his particular genius.

He was a precursor of what as yet, fortunately, does not exist in our life: "If I were able, I would blow up bridges." That kind of passion nourished his books. He insisted that he was ready to press the button that would make "everything explode." "Everything" here meant the Soviet system. But "everything" also meant hundreds of thousands of innocent bystanders.

The terrorist Ivan Kalyayev didn't throw a bomb into the grand duke's carriage because the duke's wife and children were in it. True, Kalyayev never lived through the GULag.

The socioliterary activity of Belinkov was totally compressed into less than a decade: the 1960s. But he was the precursor of the 1970s. Perhaps even the 1980s.

"He Belonged to Russia," this was how one of the obituaries was entitled in one of the émigré publications. He belongs to our present time, a time that is, in part, past and, in part, still here. But he was also the precursor of other times.

It turned out that he was a prophet right in his own fatherland, even in his own profession.

In order to completely understand Belinkov's books, a person from the outside would need to have something like an interlinear translation or glossary. One has to know who Olesha's "best friends" were. One has to know how to decipher his Aesopian language, the thousands of allusions that inform not only our greater or lesser history, but our domestic history as well, our literary daily life, our behind-the-scenes life. One even has to know the gossip.

But one thing is clear to everyone from the very first lines, because it is as though it were written in the large letters of a poster. Whether attention was focused on Tynyanov or Olesha (Belinkov was in the midst of writing a book about Shklovsky as well), in actual fact the theme, the idea, the cry was the same: *"Delenda est Carthago"* ("Carthage must be destroyed"). The Soviet government was condemned and was declining beneath the weight of its crimes.

Everything was dedicated to this single fiery passion: life, literature, books written and unwritten, personal relationships.

I have heard the following judgment as well: when Belinkov was able to say everything he was thinking in the West, it turned out he had nothing to say. I do not agree with that. He had something to say, and he spoke his mind in two books.

He didn't know how to listen to others. Later in the West people didn't listen to him.

In the summer of 1973 Victor Erlich was a guest of ours. He was the author of a book on Russian formalism and the head of the Slavic department at Yale University, where Belinkov had been a professor. We asked him why until then not a single book of Arkadii's had been published in the United States.

"Because it wouldn't sell; there aren't any readers. Even our university presses are commercial."

It was very bitter to hear that. In the realm of Slavic studies a multitude of books are published in the United States that are average or below average.

In an obituary, Erlich wrote that Belinkov found that "The adjustment to the new environment was not easy. Virtual isolation from the mainstream of the university life—due to the language barrier—was hard on the articulate and forceful man who only a few months earlier had been at the center of his native country's intellectual ferment. To a victim and impassioned foe of Soviet totalitarianism, determined to tell the West about the wave of political repression in Russia, the lukewarm responses of some of his colleagues or students, preoccupied with painful American dilemmas, smacked of indifference, if not hostility, to his message—hence the abrasiveness which seems to have alienated some of the potential beneficiaries of Arkadii's vast experience . . ."

Belinkov's books did not enter the intellectual life of Western intelligentsia. In 1975 his book on Olesha was finally issued in Russian in Barcelona in an edition of 500 copies. Where else, I have no idea. I haven't heard of it being translated into any foreign languages. In our country this book is read by many, and it has more than a few passionate disciples.

Though protesting furiously against the erroneous ways of Western civilization, Herzen never once believed that there was but a single woe in the world, namely, Russian serfdom. Simply, it was his own personal woe. For Herzen, the blood of the Paris workers, which was spilled in June 1848, was not blood of secondary importance. For Arkadii Belinkov and his admirers, however, the blood of the Vietnamese, and correspondingly the Americans' crimes, did not exist.

There is a single grief in the world: "my own." There is one woe: "my own." One injustice, which has been perpetrated against "me." The selectivity of grief, affliction, and injustice. Whoever does not comprehend that becomes a transgressor himself.

Belinkov's brief and tragic confrontation with the West cannot be attributed either to his individual peculiarities as a writer and a person or to the peculiarities of the intelligentsia in the West. It is no one's fault and everyone's loss. The people who might have understood both of those worlds are rarely found.

The confrontation of Belinkov with the West is yet another chapter in the history of that love-hate relationship, of that attraction and repulsion, of the "love affair," that has been going on for two centuries. Nowadays, when the "third emigration" has become quite an influential force, Belinkov's fate stands out all the more clearly as a kind of symbol.

First, you conjure up in your imagination, while sitting in a Russian torture chamber, a dream of a West that is free and wholly preoccupied with our terrible afflictions, a West that will follow after you without fail, will believe in your burning words. And afterward you seek revenge on the real West because it turned out differently.

There was a natural pain in this love affair that he and others shared. The pain of not being understood, the pain caused by the impossibility of not having one's cries heard.

Yet, perhaps Belinkov, like his great predecessors and followers, was more clairvoyant than others. Back in 1972, when I began this chapter, who would have envisaged Afghanistan? Every year that we live through confirms what our ever-expanding empire can bring to the world.

Arkadii Belinkov was a person of rare spiritual force. He survived everything: solitary confinement, the death sentence, incarceration, the burning of his novels, prison-camp outbreaks, the ebb and flow of our thaws and freezes. But he wasn't able to survive his disappointment in the West.

True, he did have a sick, a very sick heart. But in May 1968 in Budapest, on his way to Yugoslavia, Arkadii, filled with joyous hopes, ran around the city in such a fashion that two young sturdy Hungarians could barely keep up with him . . .

Arkadii Belinkov belongs to that number of people in whose presence an era arrived that was new for me and for my country: the era that began in the years 1953–1956.

The first sensation that I experienced (long before meeting him) was a sensation of guilt: he had been *there* and I hadn't. Even worse was the fact that I didn't know that he was there where millions of my compatriots still were. He wasn't the first or only person in connection with whom I experienced this feeling of guilt. But in the case of Belinkov I found it easier to define and isolate this feeling, because it was unaccompanied by any love.

The new era emerged among people who knew everything or almost everything much earlier than I did. Belinkov was one of these. And that elevated them in my eyes. In them and in their experience I sought and found moral support, up to a certain moment. I studied from them. I hope that I managed to learn something.

My views were changing but I myself remained my former self. My earlier typical cult mentality and my striving to glorify others remained. Only the "objects" were changed.

At the beginning of the thaw, both the general one and my own, I repeated many times the words of Solzhenitsyn from his letter to Tvardovsky to the effect that he belongs more to Russian penal servitude than to Russian literature.

It is good fortune and a miracle that he broke free, that he succeeded in shouting out the suffering of millions of convicts to the entire world, that people heard him. However, Russian penal servitude, like every other kind, not only strengthened but also maimed. It also doused the mighty light of Russian literature.

Over and over again I make the assertion that the traces of penal servitude itself in human souls are incommensurate with those moral mutilations that those people suffered (and suffer) who voluntarily or involuntarily cooperated with the jailors.

But by attempting to ignore the presence of this other form of spiritual affliction, or by recognizing it without trying to rid oneself of it, people, even those with the greatest stature, even the most talented, even the most courageous involuntarily have become and are becoming the advocates of dogmas that are externally the contrary of those of their enemies, yet as far as the moral foundations and outlook on life are concerned, are identical.

One of the new extremists has declared that literature has survived only in the GULag Archipelago, and morality only in the church . . . Another wrote a letter to Andrei Sakharov from a prison camp with an appeal to deprive one of the convicts of his designation as a political prisoner, just as in the outside world dissidents were deprived of their academic positions on instructions from the Party. These are symptoms of a general disease.

Of the people I knew, Arkadii Belinkov was the first to have suffered through that disease, to have fallen victim to it. But I remind myself: those who go to extremes (or end up in an extreme position) deprive many of a calm existence. The books of Belinkov, of Nadezhda Mandelstam, and even more so the books of Solzhenitsyn jar us when we read them, and it is more difficult to reconcile ourselves with what surrounds us and with things that we have reconciled ourselves to even though they are evil.

Again and again I sternly ask myself: is it because I have seen certain shortcomings in the people in whom only yesterday I found the embodiment of truth that these shortcomings seem to justify a reconciliation with what is impossible to overcome? I am not sacrificing my life. Moreover, I deeply regret that for reasons beyond my control I am no longer allowed to publish or to teach. And I continue to respect deeply and love tenderly those of my friends (and not only my friends) who live and work within the system.

In the old hymn we have the words:

> . . . *all the world of constraint shall we level*
> *to the ground,*
> *And then . . .*

To "level to the ground," that, perhaps, is the most terrible thing that awaits Russia. May I not live to see it.

A worldwide conflagration is alien to me. It is alien to my nature. And I am both unable and unwilling to alter that nature today. Political upheavals that invariably bring blood and tears are also alien. The conflagration of words is just as alien.

For that reason, Arkadii Belinkov is even more alien to me today than ten years ago.

The terrible thing that has arisen and been constructed in our country is collapsing in an equally monstrous fashion. That is probably inevitable. The people who are taking a hand in its more rapid collapse (I am speaking only about people of the word) probably could not be other than they are. They are first and foremost revolutionaries. They are made of iron. Invariably they would not hesitate over a single teardrop.

The mighty edifice of Solzhenitsyn's *The Gulag Archipelago* could not remind one of Greek temples carved of white marble; it has no place for any gods imbued with a calm grandeur. Probably perversions of a different sort are inherent in similar unparalleled edifices. That historically essential grinning maw of hatred, the very one that repulses me so much today, is internally embedded in those edifices.

Arkadii Belinkov is a historical character, a character of a transitional period who did not coincide with the time.

"The devil makes his appearance in the foam on the lips of the angel who embarks on the struggle for goodness, truth, and justice, and thus it goes, step after step to fiery Gehenna and Kolyma . . . terrible is the spirit of hatred in the battle for the right cause," writes Grigorii Pomerants ("A Dream of Just Retribution"). Devils are terrifying to me in whatever guise. In the guise of warriors for what today as well is the most righteous cause.

"I was put in prison for a cause," Belinkov said frequently. "I always hated the Soviet government."

Arkadii Belinkov is a precursor. In my opinion, Bolshevik party spirit, fanaticism, and a disregard for the individual person were embodied in him earlier and more fully than in many others. Everything was embodied—only with the reverse features.

He did not know how to listen to other people. He was unable to hear the voices of the other world.

XXXIV

The Emanation
That Is Sakharov

1982

In 1964 the regular elections to the Academy of Sciences of the USSR were under way. Among the candidates for membership in the academy was Nuzhdin, one of the minions of Trofim Lysenko, who at that time was still all-powerful.

A young man ascended the podium of the general assembly and calmly proved that this candidate was a pseudoscholar, that he, like Lysenko, bore the responsibility for the destruction of genetics in the USSR and for the persecution of scholars. He called upon his colleagues to vote against his admission into the academy.

The director of the department at the Central Committee, Leonid Ilyichev, asked Mstislav Keldysh, the president of the academy at that time, in a furious whisper: "Who is this brat?"

"The creator of the hydrogen bomb," Keldysh replied loudly.

The participants at the assembly told the story of this episode. That was how I first heard about Academician Andrei Sakharov.

I saw him for the first time in 1971 at an evening devoted to poetry at the Writers' House. In the ensuing years I never once stood with him at the doors of those innumerable courtrooms, I never signed the letters that he composed, I was never his comrade-in-arms. We were family friends, met rather frequently, read verses, went to the cinema, and spent holidays together.

The Sakharovs lived in a cramped Moscow apartment. He did not have a separate study, he did not even have a separate desk. But he lived in a world that was immensely vast. He pondered the fates of countries, of the world, the planets, the construction of our galaxy, the infinity of the universe, and the laws of the microworld.

Once he asked his wife: "Do you know what I love most of all in life?" (Yelena Georgievna Bonner later remarked: "I expected that he would say something about a poem or a sonata, or even about me.")

"The thing I love the most is radio background emanation."

Later he explained to us that this was the barely discernible reflection of unknown cosmic processes that had ended billions of years ago.

Although constantly assailed by anxieties over war and peace, by problems of the energy crisis, and above all by the misfortunes of friends, acquaintances, and utter strangers, he himself radiated tranquillity and calm. We too were lucky to experience that restorative tranquillity of his.

But in later years the authorities increased their assault on him, the persecutions increased, and it became more and more difficult for him to preserve his tranquillity.

Tuesday is open house at the Sakharovs'. Both rooms, the kitchen, and the corridor are full of people. In one small group a recent arrival from the camps is being questioned: he had been a participant in a strike at a large port in the south and had spent five years in prison. In another corner the wife of an exile is telling the story of her and her husband's life in a faraway Siberian village. In the kitchen, people are being served food and tea.

Ruth Grigorievna (the mother of Yelena Bonner) and two of her lady friends from the days of imprisonment in the Stalinist camps are making comparisons with the way it was in their time. Several people are arguing about the building of atomic power plants. Some creator of yet another project for the reconstruction of Russia is insisting that Sakharov hear him out immediately.

A young couple has arrived to convey their thanks and say good-bye: they have received permission to go abroad. Sakharov made mention of them several times, by way of trying to prove the right to emigrate.

The doorbell produces a jarring ring over and over again. Americans arrive, Germans, the French, correspondents, former camp inmates, scientists, and scholars.

In the bedroom one of the guests is tapping out another appeal from the Helsinki group on the typewriter. In the kitchen there is an outburst of laughter: someone has seen for the first time the way the host warms up a piece of cheese and a tomato—he eats everything warm.

At the refrigerator Yelena Georgievna is pulling out the academic ration they have received, packing canned goods, sausage, and oranges into bags. Friends are collecting parcels for the exiles. Someone is amazed: why chewing gum? People explain to him that in the camps gum is currency, something like vodka. For gum one can extend the time of a reunion, get a ticket for a train or a plane, have medicine passed on.

The telephone rings over and over again: from Moscow, from Siberia, from Georgia, from Paris, from London. Yet another statement of Sakharov's is transmitted over the telephone to the press.

On several occasions I was obliged to be his interpreter. He reads and speaks both German and English fluently, yet the precision of each word is so important to him that he requests assistance for serious conversations.

It was on January 22, 1980, that I was obliged for the final time to act as interpreter in his apartment. The Sakharovs had been taken away to the city of Gorky. The correspondents were questioning his mother-in-law and his daughter-in-law, Liza Alekseeva, and they were telling the story of how it all had happened.

Sakharov conversed with academicians and schoolchildren alike, with American senators and yesterday's prison-camp slaves, with well-known Moscow writers, and with shy Baptists from the "backwoods." He conversed with them simply, as with equals. His democratic ways were not really restricted to his view of the world. That was his nature, his custom. He simply could not do otherwise. He is a democrat, an enlightener.

His father, the physicist Dmitri Sakharov, published a book in 1925 about electricity entitled *In the Struggle for Light*. Andrei Sakharov is struggling for a different light, a moral light. He believes that the light of truth can overcome the darkness of falsehood, that it is possible and necessary to knock at the locked doors of the courtrooms, the jails, the government institutions, in the hope of being heard.

His belief is rooted in his family traditions. His great-grandfather was an enlightener, an educated priest from Arzamas (there is almost a mystical irony of fate here: the exiled Sakharov was settled in the city of Gorky on Gagarin Prospect, which had earlier been called Arzamas Avenue). His grandfather, a lawyer, had been an enlightener who had fought against the death penalty. And his father had been an enlightener. Sakharov's belief is rooted as well in the traditions of Russian history when he calls on the Soviet government to exercise wisdom, humanity, and to observe its own laws.

Andrei Sakharov is an heir to Aleksandr Herzen, who as an émigré sent appeals to Tsar Alexander II, trying to achieve the abolition of serfdom. He is an heir to Leo Tolstoy, who sent appeals to three Russian emperors, demanding mercy for the condemned, demanding the abolition of the death penalty. He is an heir to Vladimir Korolenko, who petitioned not only the tsarist government but the Soviet government as well, appealing to the Poltava Cheka on behalf of those arrested in the years after the Revolution.

Sakharov is an enlightener who still believes that it is possible to find something human in practically every heart.

In 1965 Sakharov for the first time signed a collective letter against the restoration of the cult of Stalin addressed to the Twenty-third Congress of the CPSU. This letter was signed by the ballerina Maya Plisetskaya, the writers Ilya Ehrenburg and Kornei Chukovsky, and the academicians Pyotr Kapitsa, Mikhail Leontovich, and others, as well as by Sakharov. Thereafter, he wrote countless statements, appeals, and letters to the government, to Brezhnev, to the Ministers of Public Order and State Security, to the prosecutors. He spoke about economics, disarmament, international politics, culture, ecology, and, above all, the miserable fates of individual people. He continues to address letters from his exile.

In 1978 Sakharov, together with his wife and son, went to Potma to request a meeting with the imprisoned Eduard Kuznetsov. They stayed in the visitors' building, which was where the heads of the guard detachments who took the prisoners out to work also lived. In the evenings they watched television together. The "neighbors" told the academician their stories.

"Why would you even talk with people like that?" asked his indignant son.

"You have to talk with everyone."

Sakharov listened to the camp jailers as well. And to those who would burst into his apartment with a shout, with curses, with threats, calling themselves Palestinian terrorists or relatives of those who had died in an explosion in the subway. And he listened. He asked questions. He gave answers. The visitors would gradually calm down. He spoke without haste. He probably spoke the same way in seminars on theoretical physics at the academy's Institute of Physics.

At times, in the midst of friendly disputes in his home, there would be a few who tried to outshout the others. Sakharov never tried to outshout anyone. But even when he was silent and listening, he exerted an influence on those around him.

Once he was asked: "If aliens were to land on earth, would you find a common language with them?"

"Naturally. I would draw the Pythagorean theorem. The triangle is universal."

He believes in the existence of universal values and concepts that unite people regardless of frontiers, barriers, and walls. He possesses a very rare art, namely, that of understanding other people and those who are completely unlike himself.

When he learned that he had been awarded the Nobel Peace Prize, he said: "I hope this will make it easier for political prisoners."

In response to the question of a correspondent as to whether he felt any fear, he replied: "For the members of my family and for my friends. I try not to think about myself."

And he succeeds marvelously in not thinking of himself.

I see Andrei Sakharov at Chkalovskaya, in a dacha at Zhukovka with his grandchildren, in our home. I see him as a guest at a costume party at friends' where he is a Roman senator, dressed in a toga made out of a bedsheet. I see him at Sukhumi on the beach. I see the way he looks lovingly at his wife everywhere.

But all of that is erased by what I have not seen: Sakharov in exile in the city of Gorky, with a militiaman at the door, a special militia unit across from the house so as to prevent anyone from getting through to him.

He does not proclaim absolute truths. His words and actions, which affect so many, are seemingly addressed to a single person. His radiation is free of flashes, of external effects. It is measured but profound.

I was dismissed from the Party and the Writers' Union for signing a letter protesting the exile of Sakharov. That circumstance was essentially fortuitous: I could have been dismissed earlier for something different. He has played a salient role in my life, but that role is more or less independent of external facts. Nor did that role manifest itself immediately and completely.

I was fortunate to have spent time in his home. He and his wife were frequently in our home. We conversed at length. That joy of simple communication probably prevented me from comprehending, from discerning in full measure, who he was, the kind of person he was.

The exile to Gorky and then our departure abroad automatically drew a line.

During the years we have been separated, he has continued to be a part of my life—more than an increasing anxiety, more than a yearning for his presence, more than the innumerable and inconclusive attempts to help, or the despair of impotence.

He has remained an example, or rather the unparalleled example, of how a person can behave under current Soviet conditions. He represents the path that has led him from the height of prosperity to the depths of suffering, a path that nevertheless signifies a genuine ascent to the truth.

I believe that I shall go on feeling, to the very end, that inimitable, irreplaceable emanation that is Sakharov.

In Lieu of an Epilogue

1961–1981
Moscow, Peredelkino, Zhukovka
Komarovo, Cologne

I have lived through several eras.

My childhood was a rosy one. Loving parents, a nanny, a room of my own, and the reflected glow from red banners. Mother's smile, which she turned on us, her children, and anyone else who entered our home, blended with the verses of Pushkin, the novels of Dickens, my childhood God, and the world revolution. Then the vague but most important concept arose, namely, the concept of Good.

I loved everyone and everyone loved me—or so it seemed to me.

My childhood lingered on for a long while. The feeling of being in harmony with the world, of having faith in it, was carried over from those days and has lasted a very long time. My youth, with its happy first love, was permeated with it.

The following words are carved into the pedestal of the Pushkin monument that I used to play around in my childhood: "And I appealed for mercy for the fallen." In the new era that my country was entering at that time these words became an anachronism. My homeland was turning into a mighty power. I was not aware of a threshold even though my awareness of the world was being suppressed practically at every turn. I wanted to be like the others. In my youth I never considered myself as a separate "I," because "I" for me was a hostile force or an echo of "decrepit intellectuality." It was a time of accommodating oneself to the external world and suppressing the inner world.

The old slogans did not suit the new era: "The human race will arise with the Internationale"; "All workers are brothers!" Other incantations came into force: "Whoever is not for us is against us"; "If the enemy does not submit he will be annihilated."

That second era was cut in half by the war. Millions of "I's" dissolved into "we": "*We* are the Soviet Union," "*We* are Russia," "*Our* troops have retained," "*Our* troops have liberated." I am not ashamed of this unity.

The eight years following the war were the most shameful ones in my life. I was still trying to go on believing, accepting, adapting myself to what was happening in society at that time. To go on living in conformity, keeping in step.

The country began to awaken after the death of Stalin. It was at this point that the divide between eras, a worldwide and historical divide, coincided exactly with my personal division. I was conscious of this. Everything that happened afterward in my life, right up to this very day, represented the most direct or indirect consequences of the mute explosions from the years 1953–1956.

The feeling of the limitlessness of human possibilities, which had almost been lost, reappeared once more. The 1960s were years of hope, of *rapprochement*, of interchange. I was by no means living among those who were dissenting, but rather among those of like minds. We—those of my generation, my friends, acquaintances, and colleagues—were trying to extricate ourselves from Stalinism, we were trying to break free. Some succeeded sooner, others later. Some were more consistent, others less so. The break was painful and acute, yet the memories remain of amicable harmony and cooperative response.

I was an inseparable part of the concept of "we." *We* discussed Dudintsev's novel *Not by Bread Alone*. *We* buried Boris Pasternak. *We* were astounded by Solzhenitsyn's *One Day in the Life of Ivan Denisovich*. *We* asked for Daniel and Sinyavsky to be bound over to us on bail . . .

At the time when the concept of "we" was in the ascendancy (not in the state or even secular sense, let alone, of course, the underground sense), my "I" awoke. It was then that I started to write this book.

This era has come to an end as well. The process of its aging and dying also represents my personal aging and the dying of a part of my soul. I have preserved a gratitude for and a fidelity to this era that are no longer in fashion today.

The latest era resembles the second period in our history, not so much with the portraits of Stalin that have reappeared once again, as it does in the threatening, heavy tread of the state.

And it is at this point that I have parted ways with my time once and for all.

Our circle began to diminish after 1968. Those 2,000 who filled the Peredelkino field between Pasternak's home and the cemetery on June 1, 1960, or the 2,000 who came to the Moscow Writers' House on May 30, 1967, to celebrate Paustovsky's seventy-fifth birthday—where are they now? In which countries? Some are no longer alive. Others are beyond recall. Those who not so long ago were of like mind have since followed separate paths and at times their views are now even further apart than the distance from Russia to America.

Are human hearts accessible, are eras accessible? Can one era understand another? Is it true that if the door is tightly shut then the story about the past will not reach our children and our grandchildren? They won't hear or they'll hear differently?

If I thought that it were so, then I couldn't have written a single word. But to this very day I have preserved the belief that the dreams and delusions and vain hopes of the parents are accessible to the children. The grandchildren can share in the joys, the sorrows, and the passions of their grandparents.

On November 12, 1980, the hermetically sealed doors of the airplane slammed shut behind me. Later I was deprived of my right to return to my homeland. But life did not come to an end. I read over and corrected this manuscript for the last time in Germany.

Brecht once described a garden on a hillside that was crumbling away. For all these years I have been trying not to let my garden become overgrown, not to let my memory become neglected.

I won't live to see the harvest. Perhaps my children, and even my grandchildren, will not live that long. Perhaps no one will.

But as long as my mind is still clear and as long as my hand can hold the pen, I am trying to tell the story—of how we lived.

About the Author

RAISA ORLOVA was born in Moscow and was educated at the Institute of Philosophy, Literature, and History, from which she graduated in 1940. She worked at VOKS, the Soviet bureau for international cultural relations, and traveled as a Russian cultural representative to other countries inside the Iron Curtain. She later served as an editor of the Russian magazine *Innostranaya literatura* (Foreign Literature). She is the author of several critical books in Russian on American literature.

Orlova and her third husband, Lev Kopelev, helped to see that Solzhenitsyn's revolutionary book *One Day in the Life of Ivan Denisovich* was published in the USSR in the 1960s, and were instrumental in fostering dialogue between dissident Soviet intellectuals and the West.

Orlova resigned from the Communist Party in 1980. She and her husband were subsequently deprived of their Soviet citizenship and are now citizens of the Federal Republic of Germany.

About the Translator

SAMUEL CIORAN is Professor of Russian at McMaster University (Hamilton, Ontario, Canada). Among his other translations are Fyodor Sologub's novel-trilogy *The Created Legend* and *The Petty Demon*, as well as Saltykov-Shchedrin's *The Golovlyov Family*. He has written a number of critical works on the Silver Age of Russian Culture at the beginning of the twentieth century which include *The Apocalyptic Symbolism of Andrej Belyj* (The Hague, 1973) and *Vladimir Solov'ev and the Knighthood of the Divine Sophia* (Waterloo, Ontario, 1977).